THE RURAL MIDWEST SINCE WORLD WAR II

T0323761

THE RURAL MIDWEST SINCE WORLD WAR II

Edited by J.L. Anderson

FOREWORD BY R. DOUGLAS HURT

NIU PRESS / DeKalb, IL

© 2014 by Northern Illinois University Press

Published by the Northern Illinois University Press, DeKalb, Illinois 60115

All Rights Reserved

Design by Shaun Allshouse

Library of Congress Cataloging-in-Publication Data

The rural Midwest since World War II / edited by J.L. Anderson ; foreword by R. Douglas Hurt.

  p cm

Includes index.

ISBN 978-0-87580-694-5 (pbk : alk. paper) — ISBN 978-1-60909-090-6 (e-book)

1. Middle West—Rural conditions. 2. Middle West—Economic conditions. 3. Middle West—Social conditions—20th century. 4. Agriculture—Middle West—History—20th century. 5. Sociology, Rural—Middle West. I. Anderson, J. L. (Joseph Leslie), 1966-, editor.

HN79.A14R87 2013

  306.0977—dc23

2013017744

IN MEMORY OF

Evelyn L. and Ronald G. Anderson

and

Violet E. and Leslie L. Robison

CONTENTS

FOREWORD

R. Douglas Hurt

The Midwest is an amorphous region. Neither scholars nor the public, including those who live in the region, agree on its boundaries or what is included. In some respects it is an imagined and sentimentally idealized region where rural people on farms, in small towns, and in the countryside have created an exceptional, culturally defining region that is morally and ethically superior to all other sections of the nation. Here, rural midwesterners enjoyed and defended independent, egalitarian, and democratic lives far removed from the cities, which they considered corrupt, violent, and poverty-stricken.

This concept of the Midwest as a moral and ethical ideal remained a common belief into the twenty-first century. It can best be visualized in the paintings of Grant Wood, John Steuart Curry, and Thomas Hart Benton, who comprised the Regionalist School in American art during the 1930s but whose paintings remain as mental images for many people because these artists concerned themselves with the symbols of midwestern rural life. They used farms and the rural landscape to convey their idea that life in the rural Midwest exemplified American culture. By depicting the rural ideal in midwestern life, they painted a benevolent nature in which rural midwesterners lived peaceful, secure, well-ordered lives and provided the foundation for a strong nation. The Regionalist painters reinforced the idea that the rural Midwest was a region of agrarian and small-town family values, commitment to hard work, and cooperative efforts among rural people. Above all, the Regionalists' Midwest was a place of social stability. Change and the social, economic, and political threats that accompanied it occurred elsewhere.

Midwestern Regionalist painters and agrarian philosophers such as Wendell Berry helped transfer the philosophical assumptions of Crèvecouer, Jefferson, Emerson, and Thoreau into the twentieth-first century. Indeed, the paintings of the Regionalists created images that Americans took for reality, that is, the history of the region. In the Midwest, rural life provided a strong economic, political, and social foundation and made the region exceptional among all nations. By the twenty-first century, the image and idea of the Midwest as the rural ideal remained fixed in the public mind.

Ecologist and Wisconsin native Aldo Leopold took the rural midwestern ideal a bit farther when he wrote *Sand County Almanac*. Leopold advocated a "land ethic" that invoked the term "community" in the sense of biological interdependence in nature, or the concept that environmentalists now call an ecosystem. He also stressed the cultural connotations of "community." For Leopold the land yielded a "cultural harvest" that would help inform men and women about their association with nature, the land, and the values that could be learned from and applied to rural life in the Midwest. He recognized that the Midwest had the most productive farmland in the world, but he also believed that midwesterners needed to practice good stewardship of the land to prevent its abuse. The land in the Midwest had meaning and value, and the people who lived in the countryside and who made their living from the land could lead productive, ethical lives that had meaning and purpose. Leopold understood, however, that people could never achieve "absolute harmony with the land" any more than they could achieve "absolute justice and liberty."

During the twentieth century radio, television, and the movies perpetuated the ideal of the rural Midwest as a place where optimism, personal responsibility, and hard work ensured a moral, ethical, and meaningful life. Although the *Wizard of Oz* reached the movie theaters in 1939, more people have probably watched it on television as network offerings and via DVD rentals. The essential optimism and perseverance of Dorothy, the main character and midwesterner, was center stage for every viewer to see and believe. During the 1970s and 1980s the popular television shows *M.A.S.H.* and *Little House on the Prairie*, which continued as reruns well into the twenty-first century, also conveyed the innocence, ability, and achievement of their midwestern characters who had a persistent and unequivocal belief in right and wrong. Although choosing between the latter two usually caused moral angst, they typically resolved their problems by doing the right thing.

No one more than Garrison Keillor, however, has reaffirmed a host of commonly held mental images of others about midwesterners via his radio show *A Prairie Home Companion.* Keillor's characters, who live in the small rural community of Lake Wobegon, are decent, helpful, and kind, as well as conscientious and friendly. They are often nostalgic and sentimental, and they know that God will punish them for excessive pride, self-satisfaction, and happiness. Keillor also reaffirms the belief that small-town midwesterners give their communities strength and continuity, that is, stability and order across generations. Keillor's rural midwesterners, as the millions of his radio listeners through the years well know, are a people who do the best they can with what they have, and they know that no one should give any less. If they do that, everything will turn out all right in the end. For Keillor and those who listen to him, radio reinforces the myth, stereotype, or belief, call it what you will, that the Midwest is a place of conformity and convention, both of which can be stifling and liberating. For Keillor, rural life in the

Midwest can never be escaped, at least not philosophically, even by those who have never lived there.

Although agrarian ideals continue to define the ways that people view the rural Midwest, and while economic realities have failed to keep people on the farms and in the small towns, many people continue to maintain sentimental attachments to the region and nostalgic views about rural life in the Midwest. Ideas about hard work, thrift, and honesty as well as neighborliness remain essential associations about the region. At the turn of the twenty-first century, urbanites rather than rural midwesterners were among the most devout believers who willingly accepted the myths about the Midwest. That these views were stereotypes mattered not at all to most Americans.

There is, however, a different reality about the Midwest, particularly since World War II. It is a region that has undergone rapid demographic shifts, ecological change, and transformations in agriculture and manufacturing. The rural Midwest became a region dependent on the federal government for the subsidization of agriculture and rural life through a host of rural development, conservation, and farm commodity programs, not to mention social service programs such as Social Security and Medicare. It also remained a region where racism colored relationships between whites, Latinos, and African Americans. Differences were often more the matter of culture and education than skin color, but racial distinctions still created distrust and social fractures.

This sweeping collection of essays about the rural Midwest since World War II should provide a counterbalance to the stereotypes that many people hold about the region, particularly as a bucolic farming region where white protestant families pursue their lives in their own distinctive although often idiosyncratic ways, peacefully isolated from the world around them. Indeed, the contributors to this collection show the great diversity of the region from its landscapes, shaped by dynamic agricultural and demographic change, to the movement of light manufacturing into the countryside, often drawing on farm and nonfarm men and women who needed jobs and who were willing to labor for less than union wages. It is possible to see how communities attempted to redefine themselves to meet economic changes and to preserve living standards. Here, readers can gain an understanding of the importance and purpose of federal, state, and local agricultural policy, with all of its tensions created by interest groups sparring over ecosystems, food supply, subsidies, and the proper role of government in the countryside.

The story of the rural Midwest since World War II has been shaped by the contributions of women and the changing nature of childhood, education, and the movement of the young from rural areas to the cities. This collection of essays will help us learn about the lives, contributions, and difficulties, born of racism, of African Americans living in the countryside and Latino farmworkers. And it will help us understand a region where the Amish often are viewed as the bedrock of a better, simpler time, but who, we now learn, are caught in the countervailing forces of rapid social and economic change. These essays about the rural Midwest since World War II also show that the hallowed sense of community has been seriously challenged, primarily because so few midwesterners now live in the countryside and even fewer on the farms. The Midwest, as David Danbom cogently reasons, is now a region that is less distinctive than most people believe, being homogenously more American rather than exuding a distinctive regional, rural identity.

This collection of essays helps us understand the complexity of social, economic, political, and cultural life of the region and the nation. The historical footprints of the region's past can be seen in the built landscape, small towns, and consolidated schools. It also can be seen in the large-scale, one- or two-crop, consolidated agricultural enterprises that are far different from the diversified small-scale farms that existed before the war. The footprints of change can also been seen in the small towns where empty storefronts, vacant houses, and closed schools mark life in a different age. They can be seen every morning as rural and farm women commute to work in the near-by towns and cities instead of gathering eggs or canning garden produce. Above all, this collection of essays provides the reader with an intellectually provocative, astute, and important introduction to the developments that have shaped the rural Midwest since World War II.

ACKNOWLEDGMENTS

It is a welcome opportunity to thank the many people who provided assistance over the course of this project. First, my thanks go to the contributors for their efforts. Their prompt attention and good humor lightened the work. The professionals at Northern Illinois University Press, including Susan Bean, Shaun Allshouse, and Gary Von Euer, provided valuable assistance and guidance. Two anonymous readers offered numerous suggestions that improved the manuscript. Greg Anderson prepared the map used in the Introduction and Logan Bruce prepared the map for Chapter 8.

Lisa McNeel of Schernikau Detasseling and Steve Guttormson of PioneerCare cheerfully provided permission for the use of photographs. Mary Mitchell graciously allowed the use of a photograph of her late brother, Dale Rommes. My sincere thanks go to her and her siblings for permission. Jason Allen, Anne Effland, and Bobbi Weaver provided assistance with Chapter 5. Margot Calvert of the Mount Royal University Library worked tirelessly to secure interlibrary loans on my behalf.

I am especially grateful for my parents. Their support over the years has been critical to whatever success I have enjoyed. My wife, Emma, continues to make everything better after all these years.

This book is dedicated to the memory of my grandparents, who taught me so much about the rural Midwest.

THE RURAL MIDWEST SINCE WORLD WAR II

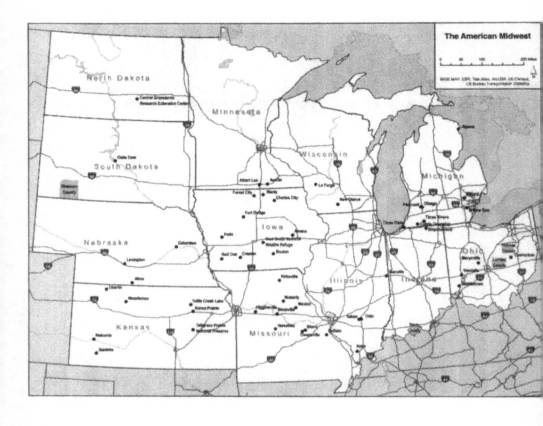

The American Midwest

INTRODUCTION

J.L. Anderson

"**T**he American middle west produces more benefits for humanity today than any region on earth," boasted Eugene Griffin of the *Chicago Tribune* in 1947. While Griffin made his claim on behalf of both urban and rural midwesterners, it was no exaggeration that the region's rural contributions to humanity were significant. During World War II, the Midwest was "the most productive and most important region in the world," as it "poured forth beef, pork, dairy products, corn, wheat, soybeans, eggs," and scores of manufactured products that sustained the American and Allied war effort. Midwestern farmers claimed one-half of the nation's total farm property values and produced half of the nation's dairy supply, four-fifths of the total corn crop, and almost three-quarters of the country's hogs. Production alone, however, was not what made the Midwest "the most national area of the United States," according to Griffin. Dr. Stanley Pargellis of Chicago's Newberry Library highlighted the fact that more students graduated from high school in the Midwest than in any other region, the region led the nation in the number of colleges and students enrolled in college, midwestern voter turnout in the 1944 elections was the highest in the country, and the percentage of the region's population who owned their own home was second only to "the thinly populated mountain states." The rural Midwest was and remains an important place for the world, nation, and the larger region, although few observers today would be tempted to make the kind of claims that Griffin and Pargellis advanced in 1947.[1]

The dominant narrative of the postwar and contemporary rural Midwest, however, is one of decline rather than leadership, essentialness, and vitality. Journalist Richard C. Longworth tellingly depicted midwesterners and their industries, institutions, and governments as slow to recognize and respond to the rise of globalization. Longworth's book, *Caught in the Middle: America's Heartland in the Age of Globalism* (2008, 2009), focused on the Midwest (minus the Dakotas and most of Kansas and Nebraska), emphasized that the region lost the first round of the globalization fight when many manufacturers closed shop and agricultural consolidation left fewer farmers on the land. Fellow journalist Richard E. Wood chronicled the ways in which residents of small towns in Kansas struggled to adjust to these developments. In *Survival of Rural America: Small Victories and Bitter Harvests* (2010), Wood described the strategies and hopes of rural Kansans but concluded that survival for most rural towns is a difficult if not impossible task. Osha Gray Davidson described a "Broken Heartland" in 1990, claiming that rural America (not just the Midwest) did not simply need economic development. Instead, Davidson argued, the only way to prevent the ghettoization of rural areas was to address national issues such as antitrust laws, labor laws, tax code reform, and electoral reform. In 1992 historian Mark Friedberger detailed the declining fortunes of midwestern farming, small-town life, and rural industry while calling attention to the mixed blessings of suburbanization and rural tourism and recreation. For farmers and small-town residents, the period up to the mid-1980s was one of "trauma and decline."[2]

The challenges of globalization notwithstanding, the postwar rural Midwest has also been a place of social and economic fault lines that are sometimes papered over with "Minnesota nice." Stephen Bloom documented the conflict between small-town Iowans and members of the Jewish Lubavitch sect who purchased a meatpacking plant in *Postville: Clash of Cultures in the American Heartland* (2001). When the orthodox outsiders made little attempt to assimilate, locals became frustrated and angry, simultaneously exposing, creating, and feeding anti-Semitism. The portrait of Denison, Iowa, drawn by the Pulitzer Prize–winning team of author Dale Maharidge and photographer Michael Williamson was one of conflict and, to a limited extent, accommodation over the recent Hispanic immigrants. Their book, *Denison, Iowa: Searching for the Soul of America through the Secrets of a Midwest Town* (2005), revealed the ways in which demographic trends not only divided newcomer and native but exacerbated conflict among natives. In *Debt and Dispossession: Farm Loss in America's Heartland* (2000), anthropologist Kathryn Marie Dudley examined the ways in which the farm crisis of the 1980s exposed such divisions in a rural Minnesota community. Families with deep community roots who borrowed from private lenders looked down upon those who utilized the lender of last resort, the U.S. government agency Farmers Home Administration (FmHA). When families lost their farms, the old guard perceived the loss as a moral failing on the part of the less skilled and less worthy FmHA borrowers. By contrast, those who lost farms accused bankers of rushing to lend and rushing to foreclose when property values crashed and debt-to-asset ratios skyrocketed. The wounds lingered, reflecting the fact that farmers are ultimately in competition against each other. Dudley related a story of one of her informants, a farmer who prophesied the coming of "the last farmer." One day, the story goes, there will only be one farmer who farms the land east of the Mississippi River and a counterpart west of the river. After a land drainage project on one side of the river forces the other farmer out of business, the last farmer will confront the inevitable tractor breakdown, but there will be no one to help with repairs. The rural society that the farmer sustained, which in turn sustained the farmer, will end.

The race for the last farmer is on in the Midwest. While the number of farmers with small acreages has held steady, the proportion of total farm production raised and grown by the largest farmers has increased dramatically. This has been accompanied by a demographic shift from country to city that has been the most important fact that undergirds stories of rural decline. In 1964 sociologist Calvin L. Beale observed that the shrinking farm population was already old news, but, he noted, "the decline has become so prolonged, so deep, and so common that it has been widely noted and accepted as a fact of life." Government policy, costly new technology, high land values, and changing aspirations among young people made farm and rural living unnecessary for many people and undesirable for others.[3]

The depopulation of the countryside in the Midwest has occurred in what may be described as the most American manner. Changes in the Midwest's rural population most closely mirrored the changes in the rural population of the United States. In 1940, 43.5 percent of the U.S. population was rural and 41.6 percent of the Midwest was rural. Up to 1990, each U.S. census revealed similar proportions of rural population in the United States and the Midwest. Change came to the postwar South much faster. Rural people comprised 63.3 percent of the southern population in 1940, but thereafter the percentage dropped precipitously. In 1990 the South was still more rural than the Midwest, but its rural population had fallen from 63.3 percent to 31.4 percent. The rural West experienced a similar dramatic shift in population from 41.5 percent rural in 1940 to 13.7 percent rural in 1990. The Northeast has been the outlier from the trend of decline, maintaining roughly the same urban-rural ratio throughout the postwar period. In terms of raw numbers of people, the rural Midwest has been remarkably stable since 1940. Approximately 16.7 million midwesterners lived in rural areas in 1940 while almost 16.9 million did in 1990. The twelve midwestern states have been second only to the South in the total number of rural people. The Midwest has been home to between two and three times the number of rural westerners and for much of the postwar period has had almost twice the rural population of the Northeast.[4]

Percentages and total numbers, however, do not tell the entire story. Since 1990, the most rural areas in the region, those counties not adjacent to metropolitan areas, have experienced true population loss, while a handful of rural counties continued to grow. Rural counties in all twelve states reported negative growth from 2000 to 2009, ranging from relatively slight losses in Wisconsin and Indiana of 0.2 and 0.3 percent respectively, to major losses of 11.1 percent in Nebraska and 11.7 percent in Kansas. The new rural dwellers, as David Danbom notes in this volume, are those who live in the counties that border urban counties and have chosen to live in the country and work in the city. There is little about their lifestyle that is different from that of urbanites, and they often have little or no connection to the rural places they call home. This stands in contrast to what historians have documented about a distinctive rural culture of the pre–World War II Midwest. What happened in and to this place to transform it so significantly? This is the foremost question that contributors to this volume seek to answer.[5]

For all the high-quality scholarship historians have produced on the rural Midwest, little of it has focused on the postwar period. By contrast, the rural South and rural West during the postwar period have been studied in depth and from multiple perspectives. R. Douglas Hurt noted the enduring historical fascination with both subjects and the fact that the South has been one of the most written-about regions in the United States in his edited collections titled *The Rural West since World War II* and *The Rural South since World War II*. Members of the public and the academy tend to see both of these regions as coherent. Southerners are not just southerners; they are "Southern by the Grace of God," although the extent to which this has been a creation of the postwar media is open to debate. In the years since 1945, western men have often identified themselves with distinctive boots, hats, bolo ties, and a political culture that staged a "Sagebrush Rebellion." Defining the Midwest proved to be a more elusive problem, even for midwesterners. Residents of Kansas, Nebraska, and the Dakotas sometimes view Ohio and Michigan as eastern while Ohioans and Michiganders tend to identify Kansas, Nebraska, and the Dakotas as western. Non-midwesterners frequently conflate Iowa and Ohio (and even Idaho).

This lack of attention to the rural Midwest has been due to the fact that the region is the standard by which other regions' distinctiveness has been measured. Midwestern farms and rural areas have been viewed as typical rural American landscapes. Cultural geographer James Shortridge and historian Mark Friedberger have shown that many Americans associated the rural Midwest with pastoral images. The region's farm families and rural communities have been relatively prosperous and have lacked much of the dramatic social, racial, and economic conflict of the South or the West. While the Midwest was the site of Farm Labor Organizing Committee (FLOC) activism, the actions of the United Farm Workers, César Chávez, and the *huelga* in the rural West overshadowed events in the Midwest. The National Farmers Organization (NFO) challenged America's economic system by staging holding actions, but there was no Haight-Ashbury or Stonewall Riots. Rural midwesterners lived with economic, ethnic, and racial hierarchies, but these paled in comparison with southern sharecropping, wage labor, and the racial politics of Freedom Summer. Stories of postwar changes in the rural Midwest appear mild even in comparison with those of the urban Midwest, which experienced wrenching and violent economic, political, racial, and social conflict. Postwar urban riots in Chicago, Detroit, and Kansas City as well as the environmental crisis in Gary, Indiana, and a legendary fire on a stretch of the Cuyahoga River in Cleveland attracted attention from outside the region. This does not mean that rural midwesterners did not experience drama; the NFO milk dumping of the 1960s and the farm crisis of the 1980s focused national attention on the region. These flashpoints, however, were anomalous during an age in which native midwesterners Lawrence Welk and Walt Disney ruled weekend television and defined cultural norms for working and middle-class Americans.[6]

It does not follow that the people, events, and trends of the region were less important because they were quieter compared to what occurred in the rest of the nation. Nitrogen fertilizer deposited on cropland across the region still finds its way to the Gulf of Mexico, contributing to an ever-growing hypoxic zone. Thousands of farmsteads were abandoned and destroyed yet thousands of other farmsteads in the rural Midwest remained and were rebuilt to adapt to ever-larger machines and crop yields. The amount of cropland in the region since 1945 has been remarkably constant, even though there are far fewer people to operate the farms. Many small towns have experienced what historian Richard Davies labeled "Main Street Blues" as the population that supported local businesses left for larger places. Transformations—economic, environmental, political, social, and technological—created a very different place in the early twenty-first century than that of the mid-twentieth century, but those transformations were often hidden in plain sight.[7]

For all the reality and perception of the decline of the rural Midwest, it is not the whole truth. Sociologist T. Lynn Smith visited twelve rural communities in 1970 to assess how much had changed in those communities since he conducted his doctoral research in 1930. Smith's initial study was an examination of changes from 1900 to 1930. While there had been a significant depopulation of the countryside since 1930, many rural towns were growing. From the vantage point of 1970, the decline of Main Street was still in the future. Smith concluded that popular assessments of rural decline were mistaken. Furthermore, many of the changes of the intervening years were positive, including greater cultural heterogeneity, which, Smith noted, made the rural Midwest more like urban America.[8]

More recently, sociologist Robert Wuthnow challenged the declension narrative in his *Remaking the Heartland: Middle America since the 1950s* (2011). Wuthnow suggested that nostalgia is an important ingredient in perceptions of decline. The rural Midwest of Garrison Keillor's Lake Wobegone and the family farm that appeared "natural" to people who grew up in the region was, in fact, created quite recently. This landscape of Main Street and 160-acre farms only looks natural when viewed through the lens of our lifetimes. What we think of as the rural Midwest has changed many times, and the people who lived there have changed and adapted many times, too.

Like journalist Richard Wood, the authors in this collection, find "small victories" and many other stories to tell. Like Robert Wuthnow, they see midwesterners as dynamic people who shaped the physical and social landscapes of the expansive midsection of the nation. One of the most remarkable changes is in the land itself. While much of the rural Midwest was cleared, drained, and brought under the plow in the years before 1920, there have been significant landscape changes since 1945. James Pritchard contends that a more homogeneous and "simplified" landscape has prevailed in the postwar period and that the many species that inhabit the rural Midwest are in flux, adapting to monoculture, suburbanization, and landscape restoration efforts. Both agriculture and industry played a significant role in this landscape transformation, as Kendra Smith-Howard and Bill Warren show. Smith-Howard focuses on the "dynamism and diversity" in the region's agriculture, demonstrating the rapid pace at which midwestern farmers industrialized their techniques and responded to market conditions. Farmers, long associated with conservatism, possessed a tremendous capacity for change, utilizing new technology and farm organization to reshape the landscape. Warren's essay on rural industrialization challenges the prevailing notion of postwar decline. Rural industry thrived into the 1970s. Low labor costs, rural development initiatives, and demographic shifts made rural settings popular industrial sites. Rural manufacturing, however, was not immune to the changes that the manufacturing sector endured after 1970. Warren, like Cornelia Flora and Jan Flora in their essay on small towns and rural communities, demonstrates how small-town residents and leaders, rather than simply sitting on or wringing their hands, worked hard to stave off decline by searching for alternative industries or businesses. Rural industry survived in the region, most notably in the biofuel boom as farmers attempted to claim a greater share of the market basket for agricultural commodities. Small communities struggled with change, much of it beyond their control. The Floras show how leaders confronted dilemmas such as chasing manufacturing firms or cultivating their own capital. The extent to which communities have been able to develop their own resources has been a significant factor in community survival. My own essay on rural and farm policy reveals the ways in which midwesterners were conflicted about the role of government in their lives and communities, even as government involvement was necessary in sustaining communities and maintaining the quality of life for people in the countryside.

The people of the rural Midwest found much of the change in the postwar period wrenching, but they were not destroyed by it. Farm women reconstructed social networks while much of their world fell apart because kin and neighbors left the farm. Jenny Barker Devine depicts how rural women embraced new social and economic roles on and off the farm and how they asserted themselves in farm operations and management. Many rural women turned to activism in an attempt to secure the economic position of the family farm. Pamela Riney-Kehrberg describes how rapidly the rural world began to resemble the urban world for farm youth. High school attendance at consolidated schools meant that children had less time for farmwork. Consolidated schools were seldom the first choice for rural parents or school officials, but those consolidated schools unified changing communities, just as one-room schools were unifying institutions in earlier communities. Midwestern rural children remain over-represented among the nation's poor, highlighting the ways in which pastoral images cannot be reconciled with rural reality. For Hispanics, the rural Midwest was a place of opportunity, not decline. Jim Norris traces the trends in Hispanic migration to the region and the ways in which newcomers searched for economic security. Newcomers also negotiated the challenges of assimilation and maintaining ethnic identity. Debra Reid shows how landownership, long considered the cornerstone of the American dream, especially resonated with African Americans in the rural and urban Midwest. The reality of rural African Americans in the Midwest is even more obscure than that of Hispanics, due to the relatively small number of blacks who settled in rural areas. Despite their small numbers, African Americans persevered on the land by embracing modern techniques or through hobby farming. Perhaps the most striking example of social adaptation is the way in which the Amish have retained distinctive cultural practices while incorporating limited change on their own terms. Steven Reschly places the midwestern Amish in a North American context, showing the steady process of colonization and settlement that occurred in the region and the distinctive ways the Amish have adapted to cultural and economic changes. The example of the Amish highlights the ways in which change rather than decline is the big story of the rural Midwest, a conclusion that will not surprise historians but one that complicates and sometimes refutes received wisdom.

David Danbom concludes this volume with a reflective essay on rural midwestern cultural distinctiveness in the postwar period. One of the key problems in making claims for any kind of regional distinctiveness is that those who settled the region came from so many different places. Rather than a cultural monolith, the rural Midwest contained many cultures. The common element was a commitment to modernity and progress. Danbom contends that this is what made the Midwest in general and the rural Midwest in particular the most American region in the nation.

The claims by Griffin and Pargellis cited at the beginning of this introduction resounded with the pride of native sons, and in large measure, those who have cared most about the region have been native daughters and sons. While the contributors to the present volume are mostly midwesterners by birth or residence, they are not required to sing the praises of rural midwesterners or, by contrast, to assume the position of midwestern modesty and self-deprecation. These authors seek to better understand a particular piece of rural America, a place too often caricatured or ignored.

This book is an overview of the major stories of the rural Midwest since 1945. Each author synthesized current scholarship and, where there has been little or no published work, conducted original exploratory research for others to follow. The editor charged authors with keeping the stories in the foreground and moving the scholars to the background in hopes of reaching the broadest possible audience. The only departure from this format is the concluding essay by David Danbom, who directly engages other scholars in his effort to trace the historical presence of midwestern cultural identity. In Danbom's essay, the scholarship is the evidence. These essays invariably have some overlap in coverage, but the authors each deal with those subjects in their own ways. Scholarly readers will no doubt recognize the work of their peers and students will locate entry points into the existing scholarship to discover topics for future research. General readers and specialists alike will find interesting stories about people and places, some familiar and some obscure, during tumultuous times.

Notes

1. Eugene Griffin, "Benefits Flow to All Mankind from Midwest," *Chicago Daily Tribune*, April 21, 1947, 1, 6. Griffin and Pargellis focused on eight of the twelve states that currently comprise the U.S. Census Bureau's classification of the North Central region, which includes Illinois, Indiana, Iowa, Kansas, Michigan, Minnesota, Missouri, Nebraska, North Dakota, Ohio, South Dakota, and Wisconsin.

2. Osha Gray Davidson, *Broken Heartland: The Rise of America's Rural Ghetto* (New York: Free Press, 1990), 169–70; Mark Friedberger, "The Transformation of the Rural Midwest, 1945–1985," *Old Northwest* 16 (1) (1992): 32.

3. Calvin L. Beale, "Rural Depopulation in the United States: Some Demographic Consequences of Agricultural Adjustments," *Demography* 1 (1) (1964): 264.

4. "Urban and Rural Population, 1900–1990," U.S. Census Bureau, <www.census.gov/population/www/censusdata/files/urpop0090.txt> (accessed August 30, 2010).

5. Paul Lasley and Margaret Hanson, "The Changing Population of the Midwest: A Reflection on Opportunities," in *The American Midwest: Managing Change in Rural Transition*, ed. Norman Walzer (Armonk, NY, and London: M.E. Sharpe, 2003), 16–37; Liesl Eathington, "2000–2009 Population Growth in the Midwest: Urban and Rural Dimensions," *Iowa Population Reports* (Ames, IA: Regional Economics and Community Analysis Program, April 2010), 9–11.

6. Friedberger, "Transformation of the Rural Midwest," 13.

7. Richard O. Davies, *Main Street Blues: The Decline of Small-Town America* (Columbus: Ohio State University Press, 1998).

8. T. Lynn Smith, "Sociocultural Changes in Twelve Midwestern Communities, 1930–1970," *Social Science* 49 (4) (Autumn 1974): 195–207.

ONE — A LANDSCAPE TRANSFORMED

Ecosystems and Natural Resources in the Midwest

James A. Pritchard

The Midwest comprises one of the most productive yet highly modified landscapes on Earth. The Mississippi River drains over a million square miles, approaching 40 percent of the land area of the continental United States. This basin lies at the heart of the Midwest, noted for blazing hot summers and bitterly cold winters. It is a land flown over and overlooked, yet the region produces a substantial percentage of the U.S. agricultural product and boasts industrial and urban areas as well. Historic landscape transformations in the Midwest have profoundly shaped its ecosystems and how they function. One of the most significant changes has been a simplification and homogenization of the landscape. Since World War II, land use has intensified, and developments in natural resource conservation are a mix of successes and seemingly intractable problems. This essay discusses fundamental transformations in the midwestern landscape, associated natural resources including wildlife, policy trends, and efforts to restore ecosystems and make agriculture more sustainable. Its focus is mainly on the extensive grassland and prairie habitats of the Midwest, discussing what we have lost and what we are trying to put back.

Four fundamental characteristics stand out regarding midwestern ecosystems and natural resources: varied habitats, water issues, working landscapes, and a scarcity of public lands. Varied habitats are the product of a distinctly temperate and humid environment driven by weather systems originating from the meeting of three air masses from the Gulf of Mexico, the Pacific, and the Arctic. The moist air from the Gulf of Mexico provides the humidity and precipitation potential, while a central location in the continent produces wide annual temperature variations and relatively quick short-term swings in temperature. Much of the Midwest's regional identity comes from the native habitat types found in the region, including the large low-lying riverine systems, diverse forests, prairies, and wetland prairies. Issues relating to water resources, ranging from aridity to flooding, comprise a common thread for the region, whether on the shores of Lake Erie or at the 100th meridian in South Dakota. The majority of the Midwest consists of a working agricultural landscape. For the most part, the land is intensively farmed, although the Midwest also has major urban centers such as Chicago. Finally, another distinguishing characteristic of the Midwest is the relative paucity of federal lands, especially compared to the American West. The U.S. Forest Service, the Bureau of Land Management, and the National Park Service do not have as large a presence as in the West. The vast majority of the midwestern landscape remains in private hands, and thus significant advances in natural resource conservation will occur only with the cooperation of private landholders. Scientists are seeking to enhance biodiversity within the context of a working agricultural landscape.[1]

Agriculture and Natural Resources

In the years after World War II an industrial model of agriculture based on the substitution of capital for labor, specialization, and reliance on expertise gained general acceptance in the Midwest. While farmers were urged to adopt an industrial model as early as the 1920s, the widespread adoption of industrial techniques did not occur until after the crises of the Great Depression and the Second World War had passed. By the early 1970s, the use of pesticides and artificial fertilizers, feed additives in raising livestock, ever-grander machinery working larger fields, and mechanized dairy parlors, feedlots, and confinement buildings became the new standards for the automation of growing food. Significantly, the use of technology replaced human labor as it expanded production.[2]

In contrast to the industrial ethos, reformers have offered alternative ways of knowing and living in the Midwest. Agricultural reformers raised the issue of sustainability as early as 1868, when University of Illinois agronomist Cyril G. Hopkins discussed the idea of permanent agriculture. From the 1930s onward, agricultural reformers linked a maturing science of ecology to ethics, farming techniques, and the maintainance of rural communities.[3] Many important leaders of conservation came from the Midwest, including Aldo Leopold, who suggested the idea of "biotic farming," which "would include wild plants and animals with tame ones as expressions of fertility."[4] Recent contributors to rethinking agriculture include Wes Jackson, of the Land Institute in Salina, Kansas. Jackson explores the potential for agricultural systems utilizing perennial polycultures (a variety of species), in marked contrast to today's common practice of planting single species of annuals in vast fields.[5]

Our common understandings of biological systems have changed enormously since 1945. Particularly since the late 1960s and early 1970s, new views from scientists working in a variety of fields including landscape ecology and sustainable agriculture have informed opinion, practice, and public policy. The old view of stasis, equilibrium, and continuity in natural systems has yielded to an understanding of change and perturbation as the normal state of affairs in nature. The shift is reflected in changing metaphors, from a vision of the balance of nature to an interpretation centering on flux.[6] Today, ecologists discuss equilibrium in terms of resistance to change and in terms of resiliency (the capacity of the system to recover from disturbance).[7]

The unpredictability that ecologists embrace is the antithesis of the goals of an agricultural economy, in which most actors prefer steady and predictable conditions. The larger question for society is how humans can create productive agricultural systems that coexist alongside or within the inherent variability of natural systems. In the view of Laura Jackson and Dana Jackson, the postwar trend toward industrialized agriculture "is an unacceptable, unaffordable sacrifice" that is unnecessary to feed the world or to keep farmers in business.[8] Agricultural land, they argue, does not have to be a sacrifice zone where nature is shoved aside to make room for a land dedicated solely to producing the maximum possible product. Nature needs to be restored within the working agricultural landscape. "Sustainable agriculture" is the rubric used by many academics and practitioners looking to link environmental concerns and agriculture.

Continuing to practice the prevailing model of industrial agriculture may have unpredicted and substantial costs. Ecologist Sandra Steingraber contracted cancer and then investigated the link between cancer and environmental risks, which she described in her book *Living Downstream*. Steingraber explained how DDT applied more than 25 years ago on her family farm in central Illinois can still be measured in the soil, reminding us of the ubiquitous presence of chemicals within our own habitat and the long-term consequences of technological choices. Questions remain about the toxicity and long-term human health effects of chemicals that are widely dispersed across the Midwest and North America.[9]

The people of the nineteenth century who plowed midwestern prairies, felled midwestern forests, and drained wetlands followed their vision of a land of great promise, a rich landscape put to productive use. During the twentieth century, industrial agriculture and cityscapes as well expanded across most of the readily available nooks and crannies (biologists would call these edges and margins). Recently, ecologists and reformers have articulated a goal of a restored landscape to complement the traditional image of economic bounty in the land. This new vision of restored landscape functions, sustainable agriculture, and a healthy land and economy is no less hopeful than the outlook Euro-Americans brought to the region in the nineteenth century.[10]

The Simplified Landscape

While the rural Midwest appears to remain agrarian and pastoral, a heavy human imprint is ubiquitous.[11] Conversion to agricultural use is one of the predominant historical human influences in the Midwest. That transformation changed the fundamental ways the landscape works. Scientists describe ecosystems in terms of composition, structure, and function. Composition refers to the various elements of a system. Structure can be thought of in physical terms, such as layers of tree canopies and the height of grasses and shrubs. Modification of composition and structure leads to changes in function, or how wildlife, water, nutrients, and energy move through the landscape.

Extensive anthropogenic (human-caused) changes in midwestern landscapes occurred prior to and continued after World War II. From North Dakota's Prairie Pothole Region to Wisconsin's cutover lands, from Nebraska to the Ohio Valley, human activities have changed vegetation types and wildlife assemblages. The systematic pattern of one-mile-square farm roads so visibly present on the landscape, writes historian Curt Meine, came directly from the Land Ordinance of 1785 and a Jeffersonian rationality. A regular network of drainage tiles underlies vast areas of farmland. This grid of human development physically pervades the midwestern landscape, shaping ecosystems, hydrology, and wildlife populations.[12] Scientists examining the history of land use in northwestern Wisconsin's lower St. Croix River valley note two distinct periods of rapid change. The first occurred from 1850 to 1880, when trappers, loggers, and farmers each prospered under a successive economic boom, modifying the landscape in the course of their economic pursuits. The second period of rapid change in the St. Croix came after 1940 as urban and suburban development altered the landscape.[13] Significantly, maintaining those landscape modifications in their re-formed condition required a constant input of time and resources. The working agricultural and rural landscape of the Midwest is, in a fundamental sense, continually rebuilt.[14]

A simplification of the landscape is the most telling trend of the rural Midwest since World War II. The intensification of agricultural practices, including the introduction of synthetic fertilizers and pesticides, everlarger equipment and debt loads, biotech crops, and re-engineered irrigation and drainage systems shaped environmental outcomes and a landscape legacy.[15] Whether or not the end was consciously in mind, farmers intensified production agriculture and created a more simplified and homogeneous landscape.

Before 1945, the typical midwestern farm grew six to eight crops to feed several kinds of livestock and to maintain soil fertility and manage pests. After the war, with widespread use of fertilizers and a growing reliance on two main commodities (corn and soybeans), hay and pasture acreage declined. In Iowa, sod crops (small grains and hay) declined from about 10 million acres in 1950 to around 3 million acres by 1999, while row crops such as corn and soybeans expanded from about 10 million acres in 1940 to about 23 million acres in 1999. In Bremer County, Iowa, land area in prairie hay and tame hay in 1940 comprised 11.5 percent of land area, while pasture amounted to almost 31 percent. By 1997, prairie hay amounted to 0.0 percent, tame hay 4.3 percent, and pasture 5.3 percent, while conservation reserve and cover crops comprised 3.5 percent of total farmed land.[16]

Beginning in the 1950s, the industrialized approach to raising crops and animals meant a rapid increase in corn and soybean production. Soybeans were initially considered an alternative to hay or oats in a crop rotation, but by the 1980s the total number of midwestern acres in soybeans was second only to corn. Today, the dominant vegetation over millions of acres consists of two plants, corn and soybeans, with much of the grain destined to feed livestock. The portion of the total corn crop sold for ethanol (biofuel) production has increased substantially, in 2012 comprising around 40 percent, adding an economic incentive for planting these two crops.[17]

The very appearance of the landscape has changed since World War II. One noticeable difference is that a growing percentage of farm animals are now indoors, raised in concentrated animal feeding operations (CAFOs). In an effort to find greater efficiencies and to intensify meat production on ever-smaller parcels of land, hogs and cattle are concentrated in single-purpose barns or on feedlots. This means the manure from a growing number of animals is physically gathered into a smaller number of places, which makes for more efficient management of manure but, in practice, also creates the conditions for spectacular accidents. Manure spills occur when holding ponds known as lagoons rupture or overflow, most often during periods of severe rainfall. In streams and rivers downstream during a pollution episode, bacteria busily digesting the manure consume oxygen in the water, resulting in the death of large numbers of fish. As of 1999, animal manure was the prime culprit in 60 percent of the water bodies' being listed as "impaired" in the United States. Of possibly greater concern is the regular leaching of manure into surface and groundwater.[18]

The simplification and homogenization of the midwestern landscape had important implications for each major midwestern habitat type (rivers, forests, prairies, and wetlands), which in turn carried implications for wildlife and for large-scale ecosystem functions. This simplification of the landscape also was accompanied by an exodus of many people from the countryside. Frederick Kirschenmann, an organic farmer from North Dakota and former director of Iowa State University's Leopold Center for Sustainable Agriculture, argues that, "If the health of our economy, ecology, and community are to be achieved in concert, then our public policies must be redesigned to achieve that larger, integrated goal.... In the face of declining fossil-fuel resources, ecological restoration must be a centerpiece of the new policies." Kirschenmann echoes Aldo Leopold and business innovator Paul Hawken in contending that such policies should promote "smaller enterprises and creativity rather than consolidation and regulation. Sound ecological management can be carried out only by people living in local ecologies long enough and intimately enough to learn how to manage them well."[19]

Rivers, Forests, Prairies, and Wetlands

Although the midwestern agricultural landscape has been simplified in significant ways, rivers, forests, and remaining fragments of prairies and wetlands add critical patches of variation within that larger setting. These interspersed habitats are important in ecosystem functioning and for wildlife. Beginning in the 1930s, large-scale federal dam projects modified larger riverine systems including the Missouri and Mississippi Rivers. The Pick-Sloan Plan, passed by Congress in 1944, funded an extensive system of dams and the creation of an all-season navigation channel on the Missouri River. Riverine wildlife habitats have changed dramatically since then. Meandering oxbows, for example, have started to dry up. Biologists suggest that one-third of the river now is impounded, and another third is essentially channel-ized. Only 1 percent of the river, by one estimate, enjoys entirely natural flows.[20] Since World War II, dams were constructed on many smaller rivers, including low-head check dams. Many of these small dams were intended to ensure municipal water supplies by delaying a river's flow, facilitating the percolation of water down into the aquifer. Approximately 3,800 dams are spread across the state of Iowa.[21]

Part of the price paid for the modification of rivers has been damage to the habitats of riverine wildlife, starting with benthic (living at the bottom) invertebrates and mussels right on up the food web to sport and commercial fisheries. Even before the U.S. Army Corps of Engineers started to build large-scale dams on the Mississippi River, fishermen and scientists who studied mussel populations in the Midwest recognized that commercial fisheries would be compromised by segmentation of the river. Productive commercial fisheries in mussels and fish declined with the completion of the lock and dam system on the Mississippi River.[22]

Rivers disperse contaminants far beyond their sources. Manure spills from livestock facilities occur frequently enough that these events now are barely newsworthy. Nitrogen and phosphorus fertilizers that wash away during major rain events add surplus nutrients to the Mississippi River. Excessive nutrient loading of the Mississippi River contributes to a large hypoxic zone in the Gulf of Mexico, a shifting area devoid of most marine life.[23] According to the U.S. Geological Survey, 66 percent of the nitrogen delivered to the Gulf of Mexico comes from corn, soybean, and other crop fields, while 80 percent of the phosphorus loading comes from all agricul-tural sources (crops, pasture, and range). Enthusiastic lawn groomers in city and suburb add their share to nutrient loading. More than half of the ni-trogen delivered to the Gulf comes from Iowa, Illinois, Indiana, Ohio, and southern Minnesota.[24]

Not all rural contaminants are from the farm. In July 2010, as residents on the Gulf of Mexico struggled with cleanup after the Deepwater Horizon oil disaster, another spill occurred in the Midwest. Approximately one mil-lion gallons of crude oil flowed into Michigan's Talmadge Creek and then into the Kalamazoo River when an oil pipeline owned by Enbridge Energy burst near Kalamazoo, Michigan. Local officials declared a state of emer-gency and began attempts to mop up the oil, yet they faced immediate dif-ficulties with inclement weather. The Environmental Protection Agency as-sisted with cleanup efforts, while Enbridge Energy offered to buy properties adversely affected by the spill.[25] Thus pollutants we usually associate with urban environments can enter watersheds from rural places.

Midwestern forests, notably those in Minnesota and Wisconsin, historically represented a substantial resource for the region. The postwar boom in
recreation, along with a movement of the regional economy from extractive
enterprises (forestry) and agriculture toward a "recreation-based service
economy," meant an increase in forest cover over large areas of these two
states.[26] The pattern of abandonment of agricultural lands and the accompanying reforestation of millions of acres characterizing the southern and
eastern states during the twentieth century was not followed in other parts
of the Midwest, where farmland has generally retained or gained economic
value, or where there is simply not enough moisture.

Oak savannah formed a prevalent ecosystem type from pre-settlement
times in the prairie peninsula region of Illinois and Iowa. These stands were
characterized by a predominantly grass and forb understory with a canopy
of widely spaced oaks. During the twentieth century there were fewer prairie fires, since fire was equated with waste, and woody plants grew up under-
neath the canopy, eventually displacing the oaks. Disturbed habitats (such
as by intensive grazing or removal of prairie) invited many other nonnative
species to grow, including Siberian elm, white poplar, white mulberry, black
locust, species of willows, and exotic honeysuckle and buckthorn shrubs.
Fast-growing and opportunistic bottomland tree species (elms, box elder,
green ash, hackberry, and cottonwood) have thrived in disturbed areas.[27]
The net result is that midwestern forests are different in character and species assemblage from what was found in 1870 or even 1940.

Prairies comprise one of the most modified habitat types in North America. There is a tremendous diversity of prairies over the Midwest, depending
mainly on moisture regimes, from tallgrass in the east to a band of mixed
grass in central portions of the plains states, to shortgrass in the west. On the
dryer Great Plains, two-thirds of the prairie remained unplowed and was
used for pasture. In the Corn Belt, by contrast, more than 80 percent of the
landscape was converted to cropped fields.[28] Less than 1 percent of original
prairie remains in Illinois, Indiana, and Iowa.[29] The fertility of the prairie
soil, built up over millennia by the life and death of perennial forbs and
grasses, proved exceedingly productive for crops, and economic pressure to
plow the prairie won out.

Many prairie remnants exist on areas that were too hilly, too wet, or too
rocky to plow. Larger prairie remnants can be found in places such as the
Loess Hills of western Iowa and in the Flint Hills of Kansas. Small fragments
of land containing a good number of native species can be found in places
along railroad rights of way and in pioneer cemeteries if they have not been
tidied up too much. Honoring both human history and the region's natural

heritage represents a largely unrealized opportunity in pioneer cemeteries across the Midwest.[30] Small prairie remnants are still being lost to the plow. Economists claim that scarcity leads to an increase of value, but generally, market mechanisms do not seem to work in favor of rare native plants, insects, and wildlife that depend on these remaining prairie fragments.[31]

Today there is a widening appreciation for the aesthetic and ecological benefits of prairies, sometimes invoking a mythic or iconic representation of the Midwest during presettlement times. Many advocates actively participate in prairie management to control woody growth (trees and shrubs) that invade and edge in on grasses and forbs. In Iowa prairies the "proliferation of opportunistic woody growth," notes ecologist Cornelia Mutel, has served as "a force tending to homogenize the state's landscape."[32]

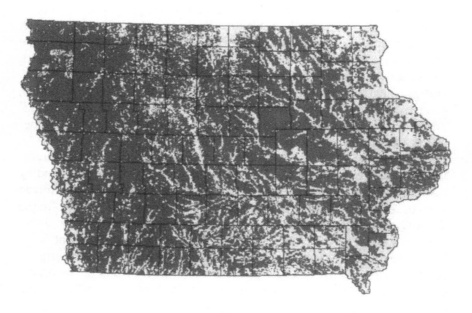

Figure 1.1: Extent of Prairie in Iowa, c. 1820. Shaded area represents prairie. Map created by Rob Fletcher, Robin McNeely, and the Iowa Gap Analysis Program at the Department of Animal Ecology and the GIS Support and Research Facility, Iowa State University, Ames, Iowa. Data sources included the Iowa Department of Natural Resources, Iowa Gap Analysis Program, The Nature Conservancy, and the Iowa Natural Heritage Foundation.

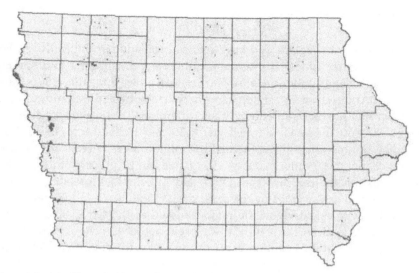

Figure 1.2: A landscape fundamentally transformed. Remaining native prairie fragments in Iowa, 1990s, not including restoration projects. In similar ways, the extent of wetland prairie types became greatly reduced in area. Map created by Rob Fletcher, Robin McNeely, and the Iowa Gap Analysis Program at the Department of Animal Ecology and the GIS Support and Research Facility, Iowa State University, Ames, Iowa. Data sources included the Iowa Department of Natural Resources, Iowa Gap Analysis Program, The Nature Conservancy, and the Iowa Natural Heritage Foundation.

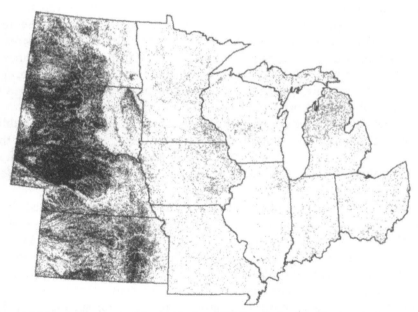

Figure 1.3: Map of midwestern existing grasslands, c. 2010. Grasslands still predominate in the western edge of the Midwest, on lands unsuited to row cropping. Grasslands for agricultural purposes have become scattered in former prairie areas, particularly in Iowa, Illinois, Missouri, and southern Minnesota and Wisconsin. Map created by Todd Hanson, Geographic Information System Lab, Department of Natural Resource Ecology & Management, Iowa State University.

The forces of progress also have reduced wetlands in the Midwest. For Americans of the nineteenth century, eliminating the miasmic swamps and bringing wetlands under the plow were critical endeavors. The 1850 Swamp Land Act transferred 15 million acres of federally owned wetlands to midwestern states, which subsequently sold or granted those lands for development. By 1860, Indiana had transferred 1,257,588 wetland acres into private hands.[33] Illinois originally contained 8.3 million acres of wetlands (almost 25 percent of its landmass), but by 1994 it had lost 85 percent of its marshes and prairie potholes. Michigan, Ohio, and Indiana had lost 80 percent of their elm and ash swamps by the same date.[34] Ohio lost a full 90 percent of its wetlands, particularly in the region known as the Great Black Swamp bordering Lake Erie. The state of Iowa lost about 89 percent of its wetlands, from approximately 4 million acres in the 1780s to around 421,900 acres during the 1980s.[35] Changing classification of varying types of wetlands, however, makes direct comparisons between time periods difficult.

Wetland conversions have added significant portions of croplands in the United States, much of this drainage activity aided by federal, state, and local governments.[36] A representative county (Story County, Iowa) increased the percentage of land in crops from 40 to 70 percent as a result of drainage activity. From 1850 into the 1930s, drainage districts were formed in the Midwest, indicating that drainage was a highly collaborative enterprise.[37] For example, in many places water was collected in downstream ditches that were communally maintained. By 1920, the majority of prairie wet soils had been consolidated into drainage enterprises. It is important to note that organizing formalized drainage districts meant that, while the rhetoric of free enterprise emphasized the individual, it was a collective effort that created some critical components of early natural resource public policy. Drainage also represented a long-term economic investment in the farm.[38] Culture entered the picture as well: an absence of standing water, like straight corn rows in the field, was considered an indicator of good farm management.

The physical extent of lands drained by tile systems has expanded since 1945. In four southern Minnesota counties almost as many acres were drained during the period from 1950 to 1979 as were drained from 1900 to 1929, the time of quickest development.[39] From 1954 to 1974, 87 percent of all wetland conversions were made for agricultural purposes. Loss of wetlands for agricultural purposes slowed to 54 percent of total conversions over the next decade, showing the growing role of suburban and other development. By 1985 concern was widespread regarding the continual losses of wetlands and the resulting impact on wildlife.[40]

Agricultural drainage is necessarily an ongoing enterprise, and thus humans are continually shaping the landscape. Drainage systems clog, fracture, and break, with time and shifting soils, and need to be cleaned out or reestablished. Historically, drainage pipes were made of ceramic tile (hence the term "tiling"), but today large trenching machines and huge coils of black plastic pipe parked in the middle of a farm field indicate the modern way to tile. The drainage industry is still big business in the Midwest, with machinery replacing hand labor. Directing the outflow of field drainage into larger systems of ditches has been remarkably effective in moving water downstream yet changed the way water moves through the landscape.

The benefits of drainage made sense on the scale of individual decisions—tiling a wet area on the farm meant more productive acres. On a landscape scale, however, certain ecosystem services are lost in the process. One of these functions is the ability of the land to hold or retain water for some period before the water moves downstream. During the early 1800s, wet prairie areas served as a great sponge, soaking up and holding vast amounts of liquid, allowing much of that moisture to return to the atmosphere by evapotranspiration (plants move water outward through pores), to move into streams as base flow, and to infiltrate down into groundwater aquifers.[41]

Stream development, normally a very slow geological process, was accelerated by agricultural intensification. An unexpected outcome of modern period drainage, channelization of streams, and extensive row-cropping has been the appearance of additional small occasional streams across the landscape. In some Iowa watersheds, the total length of stream channels has increased by three times over what the General Land Office originally surveyed in the early 1800s. This phenomenon demonstrates a shift in hydrological function of the landscape, whereby the land absorbs and stores less water than in former times, with a greater portion of rainwater essentially running off the surface of the land more quickly.[42]

The continual loss of organic matter and farm soil macroporosity (the space between particles of soil) since 1945 accelerated the loss of water storage capacity in the landscape. This gradual loss of organic matter and soil porosity can be measured in the millions of tons in relatively small watersheds. In the Squaw Creek watershed in Iowa (about two hundred square miles), organic matter in the top horizon has dropped from about 10 percent presettlement to about 5 percent today. The soil porosity in the top foot of soil has dropped from about 50 percent of open space in the soil structure down to about 45 percent. The ability to store water declined by 2,178 square feet per acre, or about 2 billion gallons of lost pore volume over the watershed.[43] Loss of water retention capability means vast amounts of water will flow somewhere else downstream.

Suburbanization became increasingly significant in the Midwest since World War II and has compounded flooding tendencies, mainly because of the extent of paving and other hard surfaces, which causes water to run off quickly instead of soaking into groundwater on site. In 1950, the U.S. census categorized just 5.9 percent of the American landscape as urban or suburban, but by 1970 the densely developed share of the land rose to 10.9 percent.[44] From 1982 to 1992, the nation developed about 1.4 million acres per year. During the mid-1990s, the rate accelerated again to reach 3.2 million acres of lost open space per year. From 1986 to 1997 a net total of 314,719 acres of Iowa agricultural lands shifted to other purposes, including residential, industrial, and commercial use.[45] Suburban and exurban development can also mean that developers and landowners are reducing stream sinuosity in the process of land development, augmenting annual flood events.[46]

Extensive flooding in 1993 provided a dramatic demonstration of the scale of the effects of rural, suburban, and urban modifications on the land. In the upper Mississippi River valley, the federal government declared that 523 counties qualified as disaster areas.[47] From 1993 to 2010, major floods occurred repeatedly in the Midwest. With each major episode, journalists repeated the word "historic" in their headlines. Many scientists agree that terms such as "100-year flood" are losing their meaning, since this magnitude of flooding occurs often. In fact, the defined level of a 100-year flood is revised with new data after each period of major flooding. Statistics on floods have been gathered only for about a hundred years, so our ideas about 100- or 500-year events will continue to change. While assigning causation for the increasing frequency of major flood events is not a straightforward task, it is clear that conversion to agricultural use, the loss of water storage capacity in soils, and the continued development of hard surfaces shedding water in urban areas all play a significant role, while global climate change may add to the intensity of rain events in local areas.[48]

Wildlife

The numbers and varieties of many wildlife species in the Midwest have changed significantly since World War II. While some species historically declined because of hunting, eradication campaigns, and the long-term reshaping of the vegetative cover of the entire region, other species thrived during the postwar era. Invasive, nonnative species have also entered the region, complicating the story of displacement, decline, and recovery.

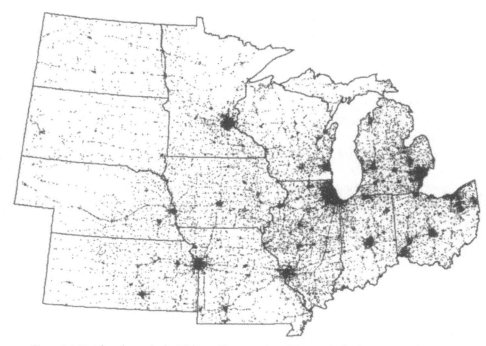

Figure 1.4: Developed areas in the Midwest. The expansion of cities and suburbs since 1945 has result-ed in shrinking rural and agricultural landscapes. Map created by Todd Hanson, Geographic Infor-mation System Lab, Department of Natural Resource Ecology & Management, Iowa State University.

Deer are one of the most visible examples of the shifts in wildlife popula-tions over the past 50 years. Overhunting reduced the numbers of white-tailed deer *(Odocoileus virginianus)* in Iowa so dramatically that they were essentially gone by 1898. Deer, however, are a generalist species that adapted well to the modified landscape, and gradually individuals dispersed into Iowa from surrounding states. The population had recovered enough by 1953 that the Iowa legislature authorized the first modern hunting season. Today there is a bountiful harvest annually (165,000 in 2007), as deer thrive on available forage in warmer months and crop stubble in the winter. Deer numbers have increased so much across much of the Midwest that they are often considered a nuisance, blamed for excessive defoliation of forest understory in both rural and urban environments. Other managed species have recovered and done well, including wild turkey and the now ubiquitous Canada goose.

One of the major reasons for species decline is the loss of critical habitat. Conservationists in southern Minnesota expressed concern for waterfowl brood marshes during the late nineteenth century, but despite these misgivings many acres of wetlands were lost during the first half of the twentieth century. In 1937, duck hunters and conservationists formed Ducks Unlimited (DU) with a keen interest in purchasing and protecting nesting habitat, particularly in Canada. In the early 1950s the Minnesota Bureau of Wildlife Development began to purchase wetland acres to prevent additional drainage for agriculture and launched a campaign to raise awareness of the importance of wetlands. By 1964, Minnesota designated an additional 112,000 acres of wetlands for wildlife management purposes. Ducks Unlimited has preserved over six million acres in Canada, over four million acres along flyways in the United States, and well over one million acres in Mexico, providing summer feeding and winter nesting grounds for birds that migrate through the Midwest.[49]

Grasslands, too, have lost critical habitat. In 2007, the Audubon Society suggested that over 30 percent of grassland bird species were in statistically significant decline. Greater prairie-chicken (*Tympanucous cupido*) numbers were affected by landscape transformations, but another immediate threat to the species has proved to be the ring-necked pheasant, imported from China in 1900. With competition from the aggressive pheasants, and disrupted in their display grounds during mating season, the native prairie-chickens did not fare well. They are most abundant in eastern Kansas, while only remnant populations can be found in Illinois, Wisconsin, Minnesota, and North Dakota.[50] Several attempts were made to restock prairie-chickens in Iowa during the 1980s with birds from Kansas, which promptly left their reintroduction sites in the Loess Hills and Ringgold County. State wildlife officials are reinitiating these efforts with hopes that improved habitat will allow for a more successful reintroduction.[51]

Two other examples demonstrate the tremendous impact invasive wildlife species can have on natural resources and human interests in the Midwest. During the 1940s and 1950s, sea lampreys (*Petromyzon marinus*, a predatory eel with a sucker-like mouth) invaded the Great Lakes, decimating the commercial fishery in lake trout. From 1940 to 1961, the commercial catch of lake trout dropped from 4,545 metric tons to 152 metric tons, or a reduction of 97 percent. In 1955, the United States and Canada formed the Great Lakes Fishery Commission to address the problem, and by the early 1960s an effective chemical lampricide reduced fishery losses.[52] It is interesting to note that this is a continuing issue, requiring monitoring and occasional use of the lampricide to keep the population in check.

Zebra mussels (*Dreissena polymorpha*), originally brought into the Great Lakes in ships' ballast water taken on in foreign ports and discharged when

Figure 1.5: Invasive species such as the ring-necked pheasant have successfully carved out an ecological niche and are a commonly hunted game bird. Pheasants, however, crowded out native species such as the prairie chicken. Source: Photo courtesy of USDA Natural Resources Conservation Service. Used with permission.

loading cargo, quickly proliferated in midwestern lakes. Zebra mussels are relatively small, attaching themselves to anything under the water, including city water intakes. Fishermen and other boaters unintentionally spread Zebra mussels from lake to lake. All the midwestern states have undertaken vigorous information campaigns designed to encourage boaters to empty all bait and fish tanks and to hose off boat hulls and trailers. Zebra mussels have spread widely, particularly up and down the Mississippi River, and in some places they are displacing native mussel populations. Zebras attach themselves to native mussels in such density that the native species cannot carry out necessary life functions.

Native mussels are one of the most threatened taxonomic groups of animals in North America, which has more native freshwater mussel species than any other continent. The Midwest was historically rich in the number of different species. The U.S. Fish and Wildlife Service reports that in Ohio, Indiana, Illinois, Wisconsin, Minnesota, Iowa, and Missouri more than half of the 78 known native species are listed as threatened, endangered, or of special concern by federal or state authorities.[53] Since World War II, the major forces working against mussels include habitat alteration, sedimentation, pollution, and exotic species. A representative native species is *Quadrula fragosa*, the Winged Mapleleaf, once found from Ohio to Illinois and from Missouri to Minnesota. Originally described in 1835, this species is now federally endangered, and a small remnant population is found only in Wisconsin. Mussels are an important food source for muskrats, minks, and otters, as well as some fish. Middens (piles) of empty shells on riverbanks are clues to the biological diversity of a productive system.[54] The declining status of native freshwater mussels signifies the enormity of habitat degradation in the Midwest.

Concerns about wildlife have provided a point of entry for Americans to learn about habitats, ecosystems, and the positive aspects of government action. In 1937, the federal Pittman-Robertson Act initiated a tax on hunting firearms and ammunition with revenue designated for wildlife habitat acquisition. Many midwestern wildlife refuges were purchased with these funds, and it is no coincidence that they are placed along the Central Flyway, where millions of ducks and geese migrate north and south with the seasons. The National Wildlife Refuge system preserves some of the best wildlife habitat in the Midwest. In Illinois, Indiana, Iowa, Michigan, Minnesota, Missouri, Ohio, and Wisconsin, the U.S. Fish and Wildlife Service administers 54 National Wildlife Refuges and 12 Wetland Management Districts, totaling 1.3 million acres of habitat. In 1965, Congress created the Land and Water Conservation Fund, maintained with a portion of receipts from offshore oil and gas leases, to purchase seven million acres of land for state and local parks and to conduct thousands of conservation projects in existing parks. The federal acquisition portion of the fund allowed the preservation of important pieces of wildlife habitat. The majority of the midwestern landscape, however, is privately owned. Habitat management on private lands will prove vital for future wildlife conservation.[55]

The Midwest has been home to important thinkers and doers who shaped the course of conservation in the postwar period. Aldo Leopold linked agriculture and wildlife conservation and is most widely remembered for his suggestion that modern society needed an improved "land ethic." In the 1950s, fellow wildlife ecologist and South Dakota native Paul Errington wrote thoughtful essays advocating for a wider recognition of the wildlife and human values found in wetland and marsh environments of the Midwest. The ideas of Leopold and Errington remain relevant to contemporary discussions of conservation and rural policy.[56]

The Critical Role of the Farm Bill

While contributions from wildlife advocates have been invaluable in mid-western conservation, shifts in national agricultural policy set the underlying stage for conservation in the Midwest. Federal legislation shapes the actions of most farmers in the region and therefore the landscape. Commodity payments, for example, shape agricultural systems and thereby the amount of nitrogen loading in rivers.[57] The nonprofit Soil and Water Conservation Society contends that the Farm Bill is one of the most important policy avenues toward maintaining a healthy Great Lakes ecosystem.[58] The federal government linked conservation on individual farms to farm policy during the 1930s. But in spite of periods of progress in reducing the rate of soil erosion, there have been times during which erosion rates have again increased. One primary culprit is the economic pressure of high commodity prices, which encourages farmers to not only plant "fencerow to fencerow," but to entirely remove existing fencerows. Larger fields of annual crops that accommodate larger machinery expose land to greater surface runoff, which erodes soil.

Rates of soil erosion vary due to landscape features, climate, soil, and farming practices. From 1982 to 2007, soil erosion rates fell from 7.3 to 4.8 tons per acre per year in the Corn Belt. Today, soil erosion statistics are compiled in conjunction with agricultural statistics by the Natural Resources Conservation Service of the U.S. Department of Agriculture and published in their Natural Resources Inventory. From 1982 to 2007, for example, soil erosion rates fell nationally from 3.06 to 1.73 billion tons. Of the latter figure, 0.96 billion tons was waterborne and 0.76 billion tons was carried off by wind.[59] These figures demonstrate that while erosion is a constant force, considerable reductions in soil loss still can be accomplished with continued diligence and targeted public policies.

The Food Security Act of 1985 was the most significant shift in postwar farm policy relating to conservation. This periodic revision to the Farm Bill responded to a variety of concerns that grew during the 1970s and early 1980s, including public perceptions that insecticide-contaminated groundwater comprised a threat to human health. Previous price and income supports had provided an incentive for farmers to convert marginal lands (both prairie and wetland) to cultivated acres.[60] Water quality legislation during the 1970s addressed non-point source pollution, and the 1985 Farm Bill incorporated similar elements and a conservation title (section).[61]

Congress assigned major parts of the federal conservation effort to the Soil Conservation Service (renamed the Natural Resources Conservation Service or NRCS in 1994). Program provisions have encouraged buffer strips and tillage techniques to minimize soil loss and nutrient runoff. The NRCS regularly assesses the benefits of the Farm Bill's conservation title to wildlife, and recent versions of the legislation have begun to address concerns about pollinators.[62] Critics suggest that NRCS offices only recently began shifting training from engineering-oriented solutions toward more environmentally sensitive recommendations.[63] A knowledgeable NRCS consultant, however, can make a tremendous difference in familiarizing landowners with the environmental benefits of the various programs.

Farm policy of the 1980s also ended federal subsidies for drainage projects intended to convert wetlands to agricultural production.[64] The "swampbuster" section in the wetlands conservation portion of the 1985 Farm Bill provided that any new farm wetland drainage project would mean the loss of other Farm Bill benefits (such as commodity payments) for the entire farm. This measure chilled further wetland development for agriculture. Wetland conversions for other purposes with associated regulatory opportunities for mitigation mean that some loss of wetlands still occurs in the Midwest today. Provisions for mitigation meant that permits for wetland development (under Section 404 of the Clean Water Act) usually required a similar wetland to be constructed, reconstructed, or preserved elsewhere. Although wetlands can be re-created, biologists note that fulfilling all of the functions of the original wetlands is very difficult to achieve.[65] A group of environmental lawyers recently argued that wetland mitigation programs would benefit by linking them to state and regional initiatives such as state wildlife action plans, which provide funding for conservation of rare midwestern species and their habitat.[66] Other federal efforts such as species recovery plans might also provide a framework for informing decisions regarding the mitigation of wetland loss.

The effectiveness of swampbuster at the local level is debatable. In North Dakota local Agricultural Stabilization and Conservation (ASC) committees allowed liberal exemptions. During the late 1980s, drainage rates increased to a decade high in Minnesota and North Dakota. During 1988, only two farmers in the nation were denied subsidies despite U.S. Fish and Wildlife Service reports to midwestern ASC committees of hundreds of drainage violations. In 1982, the National Wildlife Federation started public education programs in North Dakota, while Ducks Unlimited approached farmers directly, offering assistance with enhancing wildlife habitat. Historian Ann Vileisis suggests that the "decentralized structure of the agricultural agencies, which had made them so successful during the 1930s, undermined the USDA's ability to implement federal laws."[67]

For water quality and for wildlife, the Conservation Reserve Program (CRP) comprised a leading element in the conservation title of the 1985

Farm Bill. Land subject to a high risk of erosion could be enrolled for ten-year periods, with cost sharing for grass mixture plantings and enhanced by payments made to the farmer. CRP acreage typically comprises the largest block of idled farmland. Although not a panacea, CRP lands generally enhanced habitat for many grassland birds, helping to stabilize populations impacted by grassland conversions. Numbers of breeding birds in the Midwest, including Henslow's Sparrow, Sedge Wren, and Eastern Meadowlark, for example, have increased thanks to CRP and other set-aside programs.[68]

In the mid-1990s, CRP administrators introduced a continuous enrollment process (applications accepted year-round) that has been used for a variety of conservation practices, including buffer strips, grass waterways, windbreaks, and living fences such as hedges. The CRP began as a program planting highly erodible acres to grass, but changes to the Farm Bill since 1990 have helped fund buffer strips in the Midwest. Buffer strips slow down the transport of water, catch soil eroding off crop fields, and filter out nitrogen and phosphorus (thus improving water quality).[69] Minimum standards for buffer strips are 30 feet, but some midwestern landowners interested in wildlife habitat install buffers at least twice that width. A few enthusiastic farmers maintain buffer strips up to six hundred feet wide around wetlands. In some states, federal subsidies can be complemented with state subsidies to enhance the buffer width.[70]

Conservation gains through CRP remain tenuous, however. Many ten-year contracts were due to expire after the year 2000, and reduced congressional appropriations translated directly into fewer renewed contracts. In the Dakotas, programmatic changes contributed to declining renewals, while in states like Iowa, upward trends in grain prices tempted farmers to take lands out of CRP. In some midwestern counties from 2008 to 2012, 60 percent of CRP contracts came up for renewal. During the 43rd signup period (2012), in Missouri there was a net loss to the CRP program of 38 percent of the acres up for renewal at that time (145,000 acres, after figuring in new enrollments). In Minnesota, 65 percent of expiring acres were not renewed (190,000 acres), while North Dakota lost 77 percent (645,000 acres) of renewable acres for that one period.[71] While millions of acres remain in CRP, taking marginal land out of grasses and going back to planting row crops represents a setback to progress in reducing soil erosion and providing long-term wildlife cover. Shifting CRP enrollments present a good example of how farm economics and changing agriculture policy continually reshape wildlife conservation in the Midwest.

The 1990 reauthorization of the Farm Bill added the Wetlands Reserve Program (WRP). Permanent and 30-year easements are employed to restore former and degraded wetlands and to enhance wildlife values, particularly

Figure 1.6: Native grasses and trees in a conservation buffer along Bear Creek in Story County, Iowa. Since 1990 federal farm legislation has encouraged farmers to plant buffer strips to reduce soil erosion and the runoff of farm chemicals. Source: Photo by Lynn Betts, USDA Natural Resources Conservation Service. Used with permission.

for migratory birds. By 2000, over 277,000 acres had been enrolled in the Midwest.[72] After the extensive 1993 floods in the Midwest, this approach to reserving more wetland acres expanded to other areas of federal policy; traditional flood disaster relief began to be supplemented by a policy of buyouts of properties at high risk of repeated flooding.[73]

Conservation at a Landscape Scale

Government action has been essential to maintaining the large scale of effort needed to meet conservation goals. In 1986, the United States and Canada signed the North American Waterfowl Management Plan (NAWMP), the "largest-scale landscape planning process in the world."[74] This plan was characteristic of Reagan-era environmental policy, in that it had ambitious goals but modest funding. A central goal was to restore wildfowl numbers to their 1970s abundance, a breeding population of 62 million birds with a fall flight of 100 million. The plan identified habitat modification as a primary problem, and in a time when anti-government sentiment ran high, the strategy called for joint ventures instead of regulation. The program relied on cooperators who lived along the flyway to act in concert to protect and restore habitat. State and local governments, conservation and sportsmen's groups, businesses and individuals became involved and experienced success in working with private landowners, who held 74 percent of wetlands in the lower 48 states. Private foundations, The Nature Conservancy, and Ducks Unlimited purchased the most acres for protection. Out of eight joint venture areas, five of them met their goals within five years.[75]

Thinking on large scales, beyond the state level, is important to conservation because wildlife species do not respect political boundaries. A dramatic example of this interregional connectivity is the spectacular annual migration of snow geese and Canada geese through the Central Flyway. Nesting in the Prairie Pothole Region of Canada and North Dakota and traveling south for the winter months, they sustain an important seasonal tourist economy in central Nebraska. Disasters for wildlife in far-flung places can have delayed impacts on wildlife elsewhere. Approximately half of the 15,000 loons of northern Wisconsin and Minnesota migrate all the way to the Gulf of Mexico, where they rely on habitats affected in 2010 by the Deepwater Horizon oil well blowout. Other birds spending part of their life cycle in the Midwest migrate even further south to Mexico and Central America. Large-scale habitat changes in any of the habitats used by migrating birds will affect their survival rates. Since 2002, grants provided under the Neotropical Migratory Bird Conservation Act encouraged building international partnerships through habitat protection projects.

Similar to wetlands, grasslands historically received little attention from conservationists, whose preservation efforts of the late nineteenth and early twentieth centuries focused on rugged and remote mountainous areas, not the productive agricultural prairies. Not surprisingly, grasslands are the American biome least represented in the national park system. In the 1930s, University of Illinois ecologist Victor Shelford suggested to the National Park Service that a tallgrass prairie be preserved, either in the Osage Hills of Oklahoma or in the Flint Hills of Kansas. From the early 1960s, the National Park Service met opposition in its efforts to create a grassland park in the Flint Hills. In 1996, the 44-square-kilometer Tallgrass Prairie National Preserve was established. Environmental historian James Sherow, however, argues that The Nature Conservancy (TNC) has been more effective in protecting grasslands from development than the federal government.

In 1980, TNC bought the 60,000-acre Niobrara Valley Preserve in northern Nebraska, where bison and fire are used in management practices. The Nature Conservancy was also instrumental in creating the Konza Prairie, a prairie remnant comprising almost 35 square kilometers in central Kansas. Since 1955, the biology department at Kansas State University had wanted to establish a tallgrass prairie research site, and in 1975 TNC negotiated a land purchase. Under a long-term lease with the university, Professor Lloyd Hulbert organized a nationally recognized research program that secured one of the first Long-Term Ecological Research sites established in North America.[76] Located near the Kansas Flint Hills, a region not cropped extensively because of shallow soils, this prairie has provided a site for trials in prairie management, notably the use of fire, imitating naturally caused fires and native-set blazes that were once common occurrences.

An innovative proposal during the late 1980s to take large areas of short grass prairie and turn them into a "Buffalo Commons" created keen interest as well as controversy. Professors at Rutgers, Frank Popper (regional planning) and Deborah Epstein Popper (geography), examined rural economic trends in the drier northwestern parts of the Midwest, particularly North and South Dakota, Nebraska, and Kansas. They suggested that since cattle ranching communities on the short grass prairie were declining consistently, ending typical ranching activities and moving toward raising bison on a broad scale would offer significant benefits. They proposed federal buyouts of failing ranches, modeled after previous periods of public investment, with an associated managing bureau. Local critics vigorously opposed federal buyouts. Some of the resulting controversy was created by journalists painting the Poppers as advocates, but their work was actually very analytical in nature. A part of the vision of a buffalo commons is coming to fruition, as Native American tribes and other private bison producers aggressively market bison to a growing audience.[77]

The discussion resulting from the idea of a buffalo commons prompted people to think and talk about the ecological roles of grazers and humans on the plains. Biologists are interested not only in reestablishing good quality prairie on reserves but also in learning how to maintain economies and communities on working landscapes while preserving biodiversity. For example, a recent study examining patch-burn grazing systems suggests that cattle can play an important ecological role as grazers of grasslands if they are managed carefully and not overstocked.[78] Conservation biologists argue that nature reserves need to become "an integral part of the landscapes in which they occur" and that the contrast between nature reserves and the background matrix of private lands could become less distinct.[79]

Rural Biodiversity and Restoration Ecology

For all the conservation efforts of the postwar period, there is a relative paucity of biodiversity (variety of species) on the agricultural landscape compared to that during the early nineteenth century. Large herbivores and carnivores, including elk and black bear, were almost completely eradicated from the Midwest, with the notable exception of northern Minnesota, where robust wolf and black bear populations exist. But there is more to biodiversity than mega-fauna. Farmers manage biodiversity (or the lack of it) in the process of managing their agricultural systems. And because agricultural activities occupy most of the landscape, any strategy for encouraging enhanced biodiversity must work in the context of agriculture to achieve its ends. Scientists and farmers are increasingly concerned about "the myriad of soil organisms, pollinators, and natural enemies of pests and diseases that provide essential regulating services" in support of agricultural production.[80]

Many agronomists as well as those interested in wildlife today argue that increasing biodiversity in modern agricultural systems is a desirable and necessary step to enhance sustainability. Only very recently "has the global community acknowledged the significance of the full range of agricultural biodiversity in the functioning of agricultural ecosystems."[81] In his study of ecology and community in the rural landscape, Paul W. Brown suggests that "fostering the diversification rather than the further homogenization of agricultural landscapes" will be more likely to further "the common goal of enhancing rural vitality."[82]

Major issues for midwestern biodiversity include the loss of habitat and questions about how natural systems operate over landscape scales. The common historical pattern in midwestern landscapes has been the fragmentation of original habitat into small and widely separated parcels. The smaller a piece of remaining habitat and the farther it is from other patches, the fewer the number of original species that fragment can sustain.[83]

Restoration ecology has been and will be critical for sustaining and increasing biodiversity. Restoration ecologists attribute the beginnings of their field to Aldo Leopold. At their family retreat known as "the shack" near Baraboo, Wisconsin, the Leopold family planted pine trees and encouraged the wildlife species Leopold enjoyed hunting. In 1927, Leopold argued, "we need plants and birds and trees restored to ten thousand farms, not merely to a few paltry reservations."[84] In the fall of 1935, Civilian Conservation Corps workers assisted with restoring tallgrass prairie at the University of Wisconsin–Madison's Arboretum. This restoration met greater success in the 1940s after fire was introduced to the ecosystem in a classic series of experiments. With these two projects, the science and practice of restoration ecology began.[85]

Wetland restoration efforts in the Midwest are ongoing. From 1955 to 1975, the simple act of building new farm ponds created small-perimeter wetlands that totaled almost 2 million acres over the Midwest. From 1975 to 1985, these pond-associated wetlands increased by another 800,000 acres.[86] From 1987 to 1990, Farm Bill conservation title programs contributed to the addition of 90,000 acres to the national wetland inventory.[87] Some scientists, however, have pointed to the limited extent of restoration efforts. Between 1987 and 1991, in the southern Prairie Pothole Region (southeastern South Dakota, southern Minnesota, and Iowa), the acreage for all wetland restorations was about the same as a single 36-square-mile township.[88]

Prairie restoration has galvanized support among members of the general public as well as scientists and policy makers. Prairie advocates offer economic, aesthetic, and environmental reasons to keep and restore pieces of prairie. Preservation groups received a boost in 1989 when the North American Prairie Conference met for the first time. In 1990, the Iowa Prairie Network was formed with an educational and protectionist mission. Daryl Smith, a biologist at the University of Northern Iowa, created the Native Roadside Vegetation Center in 1998 (renamed the Tallgrass Prairie Center in 2006). Today the center publicizes the benefits of prairie and consults on roadside plantings. The center also provides information on native ecotype seed selection, which is an important issue as landowners consider installing prairie plantings. The Iowa Department of Transportation has adopted prairie plantings for wide use, providing wildflower beauty and wildlife corridors.

The Neal Smith National Wildlife Refuge in Iowa is a good example of a large-scale prairie restoration. Congressman Neal Smith embraced the idea of providing a place where bison could again roam on a piece of tallgrass prairie. When Iowa Power and Light decided to abandon a nuclear plant option on Walnut Creek near Prairie City, a path to federal ownership opened. In 1992, U.S. Fish and Wildlife Service employees and prairie enthusiasts participated in seeding the first sections of a potential 8,600 acres.[89] Biologist Pauline Drobney provided a good portion of the passion and technical expertise to launch this re-creation of a biodiverse prairie. Since then, bison have been introduced to the prairie, while host plants were planted specially for *Speyeria idalia*, a rare native butterfly.[90]

The Past and the Future

The conditions for the future of the midwestern landscape have their roots—quite literally—in thousands of years of vegetative growth in the wet-

Figure 1.7: Restored wetlands like this one in Iowa provide valuable cover for wildlife such as muskrat and migratory waterfowl. Source: Photo by Lynn Betts, USDA Natural Resources Conservation Service. Used with permission.

lands, grasslands, and forests, not to mention the rivers, of the Midwest. Human enterprises have transformed these native habitats in significant ways. Much of that transformation has been toward simplification and vegetative monocultures. A shrinking number of farmers raise crops and livestock, but on increased scales aided by fossil fuels, pesticides, and other farm chemicals. Habitat loss and the decline of some species have been dramatic in the postwar period. But the history of humans and nature in the Midwest is not simply a story of decline and loss. People and institutions have recognized that ecosystem services function at landscape scales and, consequently, have modified some actions and policies in the long-term interest of the rural Midwest.

The stories historians tell could inform the way midwesterners interact with nature in the future. Historian Geoff Cunfer observed that people "negotiate a compromise with nature, but one that shifts through time...."

Midwesterners will continue to negotiate with nature, hopefully with an enhanced sensitivity to nature's limits. Cunfer emphasized how people and ecosystems have demonstrated "resilience and sustainability rather than vulnerability and failure."[91]

Great challenges await the next generation, specifically improving water quality, protecting and enhancing biodiversity, and ensuring a sustainable use of the landscape for agriculture. Fortunately, many scientists, landowners, farmers, and ordinary citizens are deeply interested in our common natural resource heritage. We have abruptly bumped into many of nature's limits, and now the task is to find better ways to respect those thresholds, to develop a long-term way of living within the constraints of nature. The condition of natural resources in the rural Midwest is a source of concern, but the midwestern landscape itself and people's affection for the beauty of this land provide sources of hope and inspiration for positive action.

Notes

1. James R. Miller, Lois Wright Morton, David M. Engle, Diane M. Debinski, and Ryan N. Harr, "Nature Reserves as Catalysts for Landscape Change," *Frontiers in Ecology and the Environment* 10 (3) (2012): 144–52.

2. J.L. Anderson, *Industrializing the Corn Belt: Agriculture, Technology, and Environment, 1945–1972* (DeKalb: Northern Illinois University Press, 2009), 5, 12.

3. Randal S. Beeman and James A. Pritchard, *A Green and Permanent Land: Ecology and Agriculture in the Twentieth Century* (Lawrence: University Press of Kansas, 2000), 29, passim.

4. Curt Meine and Richard L. Knight, eds., *The Essential Aldo Leopold: Quotations and Commentaries* (Madison: University of Wisconsin Press, 1999), 94.

5. Wendell Berry, *The Unsettling of America: Culture and Agriculture* (San Francisco: Sierra Club Books, 1977).

6. S.T.A. Pickett and Richard S. Ostfeld, "The Shifting Paradigm in Ecology," in *A New Century for Natural Resources Management*, ed. Richard L. Knight and Sarah F. Bates (Washington, DC: Island Press, 1995), 261–78.

7. Frank Benjamin Golley, *A History of the Ecosystem Concept in Ecology: More Than the Sum of the Parts* (New Haven, CT: Yale University Press, 1993), 196, 75.

8. Dana L. Jackson and Laura L. Jackson, eds., *The Farm as Natural Habitat: Reconnecting Food Systems with Ecosystems* (Washington, DC: Island Press, 2002), 4.

9. Sandra Steingraber, *Living Downstream: An Ecologist Looks at Cancer and the Environment* (Reading, MA: Addison-Wesley, 1997); see also Michael Pollan, *The Omnivore's Dilemma: The Secrets behind What You Eat* (New York: Dial Books, 2009); Nancy Langston, "The Retreat from Precaution," *Environmental History* 13 (1) (2008): 41–65.

10. See also Joan Iverson Nassauer, "Landscape Ecology and Conservation Biology: Systems Thinking Revisited," *Conservation Biology* 20 (3) (June 2006): 677–78.

11. Jeffrey A. Cardille and Marie Lambois, "From the Redwood Forest to the Gulf Stream Waters: Human Signature Nearly Ubiquitous in Representative US Landscapes,"

Frontiers in Ecology and the Environment 8 (April 2010): 130–34.

12. Curt Meine, "Inherit the Grid," in Joan Iverson Nassauer, *Placing Nature: Culture and Landscape Ecology* (Washington, DC: Island Press, 1997), 65–84.

13. Osh (Barbara) Andersen, Thomas R. Crow, Sue M. Lietz, and Forest Stearns, "Transformation of a Landscape in the Upper Mid-west, USA: The History of the Lower St. Croix River Valley, 1830 to Present," *Landscape Urban Planning* 35 (1996): 247–67.

14. Useful statistics on land use in agricultural landscapes are produced by the USDA's Economic Research Service, particularly under "Agricultural Resources and Environmental Indicators," <www.ers.usda.gov/publications/AREI/>.

15. J.L. Anderson, *Industrializing the Corn Belt*, passim; see also Dennis S. Nordin and Roy V. Scott, *From Prairie Farmer to Entrepreneur: The Transformation of Midwestern Agriculture* (Bloomington: Indiana University Press, 2005).

16. Laura L. Jackson, "Restoring Prairie Processes to Farmlands," in Jackson and Jackson, *The Farm as Natural Habitat*, 140–41.

17. Laura L. Jackson, "The Farm, the Nature Preserve, and the Conservation Biologist," in Jackson and Jackson, *The Farm as Natural Habitat*, 39–52; Anderson, *Industrializing the Corn Belt*, 165; see also James J. Dinsmore, *A Country So Full of Game*, 186–88; on ethanol, see Bryan Walsh, "When the Rains Stop," *Time*, August 6, 2012, 34–37.

18. Jackson and Jackson, *The Farm as Natural Habitat*, 30; see also A.G. Wright, "A Foul Mess: EPA Takes Aim at Factory Farms, the No. 1 Water Polluter in the U.S.," *Engineering News-Record* 243 (1999): 14–26.

19. Frederick L. Kirschenmann, *Cultivating an Ecological Conscience: Essays from a Farmer Philosopher*, ed. Constance L. Falk (Lexington: University Press of Kentucky, 2010), 186–87; Paul Hawken, *The Ecology of Commerce: A Declaration of Sustainability* (New York: HarperCollins, 1993).

20. John E. Thorson, *River of Promise, River of Peril: The Politics of Managing the Missouri River* (Lawrence: University Press of Kansas, 1994), 83–85; on interspersed habitats, see Jackson, "The Farm, the Nature Preserve, and the Conservation Biologist," 43.

21. "DNR: 31 Dams in Iowa Have Structural Issues" *The Tribune* (Ames), August 3, 2010, A4.

22. Philip V. Scarpino, *Great River: An Environmental History of the Upper Mississippi, 1890–1950* (Columbia: University of Missouri Press, 1985). See also James A. Pritchard, "An Historical Analysis of Mussel Propagation and Culture: Research Performed at the Fairport Biological Station," U.S. Army Corps of Engineers, DACW-25-01-m-0312, <www.fws.gov/midwest/mussel/documents/an_historical_analysis_of_mussel_propagation_and_culture.pdf> (accessed July 28, 2013).

23. William H. Renwick, Michael J. Vanni, Qianyi Zhang, and Jon Patton, "Water Quality Trends and Changing Agricultural Practices in a Midwest US Watershed, 1994–2006," *Journal of Environmental Quality* 37 (5) (September/October 2008): 1862–74; EPA Science Advisory Board, "Hypoxia in the Northern Gulf of Mexico: An Update," Washington, DC: Environmental Protection Agency, December 2007, EPA-SAB-08-004.

24. Brian A. DeVore, "Nature's Backlash," in Jackson and Jackson, *The Farm as Natural Habitat*, 32.

25. Rex Hall Jr., "Oil Spill Update: State of Emergency Declared as 800,000 Gallons of Leaked Oil Begins Flowing through Kalamazoo County," *Kalamazoo Gazette*, July 27, 2010.

26. D.G. Brown, "Land Use and Forest Cover on Private Parcels in the Upper Midwest, USA 1970 to 1990," *Landscape Ecology* 18 (2003): 777. See also Thomas R. Huffman,

Protectors of the Land and Water: Environmentalism in Wisconsin, 1961–1968 (Chapel Hill: University of North Carolina Press, 1994).

27. Cornelia F. Mutel, *The Emerald Horizon: The History of Nature in Iowa* (Iowa City: University of Iowa Press, 2007), 179–83, quote and tree species on 180.

28. Geoff Cunfer, *On the Great Plains: Agriculture and Environment* (College Station: Texas A&M University Press, 2005), 237.

29. Ernest M. Steinauer and Scott L. Collins, "Prairie Ecology: The Tallgrass Prairie," in *Prairie Conservation: Preserving North America's Most Endangered Ecosystem*, ed. Fred B. Samson and Fritz L. Knopf (Washington, DC: Island Press, 1996), 41.

30. James Pritchard, "Prairie Cemeteries: Memories and Biological Heritage," *The Iowan* 54 (4) (March /April 2006): 14–16.

31. Richard Manning, *Grassland: The History, Biology, Politics and Promise of the American Prairie* (New York: Penguin, 1997).

32. Mutel, *The Emerald Horizon*, 180, 182.

33. Ann Vileisis, *Discovering the Unknown Landscape: A History of America's Wetlands* (Washington, DC: Island Press, 1997), 82–84.

34. Andersen et al., "Transformation of a Landscape," 247–67, esp. 263.

35. Iowa Department of Agriculture and Land Stewardship (IDALS), "Iowa Wetlands and Riparian Areas Conservation Plan," Division of Soil Conservation, Des Moines, 1999, 13. See also Katherine L. Andersen, "Historical Alterations of Surface Hydrology in Iowa's Small Agricultural Watersheds" (Master's thesis, Iowa State University, 2000), 26; R.A. Bishop, "Iowa Wetlands," *Proceedings of the Iowa Academy of Science* 88 (1) (1981): 11–16.

36. Hugh Prince, *Wetlands of the American Midwest: A Historical Geography of Changing Attitudes*, University of Chicago Geography Research Paper No. 241 (Chicago: University of Chicago Press, 1997); U.S. Department of the Interior, "The Impact of Federal Programs on Wetlands," Vol. II, A Report to Congress by the Secretary of the Interior, Washington, DC, March 1994, 2. For statistics on wetlands, see U.S. Fish and Wildlife Service, Wetlands Status and Trends, Wetlands Inventory, <www.fws.gov/wetlands/Status-and-Trends/index.html> (accessed July 28, 2013).

37. Mary R. McCorvie and Christopher L. Lant, "Drainage District Formation and the Loss of Midwestern Wetlands, 1850–1930," *Agricultural History* 67 (1993), 32–34. On wetland history, see Thomas E. Dahl, "Wetlands Losses in the United States 1780s to 1980s," U.S. Department of the Interior, Fish and Wildlife Service, Washington, DC, Jamestown, ND: Northern Prairie Wildlife Research Center, <www.npwrc.usgs.gov/resource/wetlands/wetloss/index.htm> (accessed July 28, 2013).

38. Prince, *Wetlands of the American Midwest*, 311.

39. Prince, *Wetlands of the American Midwest*, 306.

40. L. Pete Heard et al., *A Comprehensive Review of Farm Bill Contributions to Wildlife Conservation, 1985–2000*, Technical Report USDA/NRCS/WHMI-2000, December 2000.

41. Mutel, *The Emerald Horizon*, 62.

42. Andersen, "Iowa's Small Agricultural Watersheds."

43. Lee Burras, Iowa State University Dept. of Agronomy, personal communication, August 16, 2010.

44. Adam Rome, *The Bulldozer in the Countryside: Suburban Sprawl and the Rise of American Environmentalism* (Cambridge, UK: Cambridge University Press, 2001), 120.

45. Paul F. Anderson and Stuart Huntington (Iowa State University Extension Institute for Design Research and Outreach), "Land Use in Iowa: 1983–1998," for the Iowa Commission on Urban Planning, Growth Management, and Protection of Farmland, <www.public.iastate.edu/~fridolph/landuse2.html> (accessed July 28, 2013).

46. Andrew P. Rayburn and Lisa A. Schulte, "Landscape Change in an Agricultural Watershed in the U.S. Midwest," *Landscape and Urban Planning* 93 (2) (2009): 132–41.

47. Prince, *Wetlands of the American Midwest*, 320.

48. Cornelia F. Mutel, ed., *A Watershed Year: Anatomy of the Iowa Floods of 2008* (Iowa City: University of Iowa Press, 2010).

49. Prince, *Wetlands of the American Midwest*, 292; see also Eric Bolen, "Waterfowl Management: Yesterday and Tomorrow," *Journal of Wildlife Management* 64 (April 2000): 323–35.

50. See Audubon Society's State of the Birds Reports, <www.stateofthebirds.org>; see also James J. Dinsmore, *A Country So Full of Game: The Story of Wildlife in Iowa* (Iowa City: University of Iowa Press, 1994), 102, 113.

51. Dinsmore, *A Country So Full of Game*, 114.

52. Great Lakes Fishery Commission, <www.glfc.org> (accessed July 28, 2013); see also Daniel D. Chiras and John P. Reganold, *Natural Resource Conservation: Management for a Sustainable Future* (10th edition) (San Francisco: Pearson, 2010), 320–22.

53. U.S. Fish and Wildlife Service, Endangered Species Program, <www.fws.gov/midwest/endangered/clams/mussels.html> (accessed August 26, 2010).

54. Kevin S. Cummings and Christine A. Mayer, *Field Guide to Freshwater Mussels of the Midwest* (Champaign: Illinois Natural History Survey, 1992), 4.

55. James R. Miller and Richard J. Hobbs, "Conservation Where People Live and Work," *Conservation Biology* 16 (2) (April 2002): 330–37.

56. James A. Pritchard, Diane M. Debinski, Brian Olechnowski, and Ron Vannimwegen, "The Landscape of Paul Errington's Work," *Wildlife Society Bulletin* 34 (5) (2006): 1411–16.

57. Whitney P. Broussard III, R. Eugene Turner, and John V. Westra, "Do Federal Farm Policies Influence Surface Water Quality?" *Agriculture Ecosystems and Environment* 158 (2012): 103–9. See also R. Eugene Turner and Nancy N. Rabalais, "Linking Landscape and Water Quality in the Mississippi River Basin for 200 Years," *Bioscience* 53 (6) (June 2003): 563–72.

58. Soil and Water Conservation Society, "Great Lakes Clean Water: Realizing the Promise of USDA Conservation Programs" (Ankeny, IA: Soil and Water Conservation Society, 2007).

59. Natural Resource Conservation Service, Natural Resources Inventory (1997, 2007), <www.nrcs.usda.gov/technical/NRI> (accessed July 28, 2013).

60. U.S. Department of the Interior, "The Impact of Federal Programs on Wetlands," Vol. II, A Report to Congress by the Secretary of the Interior, Washington, DC, March 1994, 53.

61. Basil Gomez, "Assessing the Impact of the 1985 Farm Bill on Sediment-Related Nonpoint Source Pollution," *Journal of Soil and Water Conservation* 50 (4) (July/August 1995): 374–77.

62. Natural Resource Conservation Service, "Fish and Wildlife Benefits of Farm Bill Conservation Programs 2000–2005," <www.nrcs.usda.gov/wps/portal/nrcs/detail/national/technical/nra/ceap/blr/?&cid=nrcs143_014152> (accessed July 28, 2013).

63. Jackson, "The Farm, the Nature Preserve, and the Conservation Biologist," 46.

64. Prince, *Wetlands of the American Midwest*, 314–15.

65. S.M. Galatowitsch and A.G. van der Valk, *Restoring Prairie Wetlands: An Ecological Approach* (Ames: Iowa State University Press, 1994).

66. Jessica B. Wilkinson, James M. McElfish Jr., Rebecca Kihslinger, Robert Bendick, and Bruce A. McKenney, "The Next Generation of Mitigation: Linking Current and Future Mitigation Programs with State Wildlife Action Plans and Other State and Regional Plans," Environmental Law Institute and The Nature Conservancy, August 4, 2009.

67. Vileisis, *Discovering the Unknown Landscape*, 302–3.

68. James R. Herkert, "Response of Bird Populations to Farmland Set-Aside Programs," *Conservation Biology* 23 (4) (August 2009): 1036–40. See also Douglas Johnson, "Grassland Bird Use of Conservation Reserve Program Fields in the Great Plains," in *Fish and Wildlife Benefits of Farm Bill Conservation Programs: 2000–2005 Update*, ed. J.B. Haufler, The Wildlife Society Technical Review 05-2 (2005), 17–32; Steven Dinsmore (avian ecologist), Iowa State University, personal communication, August 2, 2012; the Breeding Bird Survey, <www.pwrc.usgs.gov/bbs/> (accessed August 2, 2012).

69. R.C. Schultz, T.M. Isenhart, W.W. Simpkins, and J.P. Colletti, "Riparian Forest Buffers in Agroecosystems—Lessons Learned from the Bear Creek Watershed, Central Iowa, USA," *Agroforestry Systems* 61 (2004): 35–50.

70. See also information from Natural Resource Conservation Service (NRCS) regarding buffers online, <www.nrcs.usda.gov/feature/buffers/> (accessed June 8, 2011).

71. Natural Resource Conservation Service, CRP Sign-up 43 Summary, 2012.

72. Charlie Rewa, "Biological Responses to Wetland Restoration," in *A Comprehensive Review of Farm Bill Contributions*, 95–116.

73. Prince, *Wetlands of the American Midwest*, 324.

74. Vileisis, *Discovering the Unknown Landscape*, 288.

75. Vileisis, *Discovering the Unknown Landscape*, 289–90.

76. James E. Sherow, *The Grasslands of the United States: An Environmental History* (Santa Barbara, CA: ABC-CLIO, 2007), 126–30.

77. Deborah E. Popper and Frank J. Popper, "The Buffalo Commons, Then and Now," *Focus* (43) (Winter 1993): 17–20. See also Anne Matthews, *Where the Buffalo Roam: The Storm over the Revolutionary Plan to Restore America's Great Plains* (New York: Grove Press, 1992).

78. S.D. Fuhlendorf and D.M. Engle, "Application of the Fire-Grazing Interaction to Restore a Shifting Mosaic on Tallgrass Prairie," *J. Appl Ecol* 41 (2004): 604–14.

79. Miller et al., "Nature Reserves as Catalysts," 144n1. See also Miller and Hobbs, "Conservation Where People Live and Work," passim.

80. D.I. Jarvis, C. Padoch, and H.D. Cooper, "Biodiversity, Agriculture, and Ecosystem Services," in *Managing Biodiversity in Agricultural Ecosystems*, ed. D.I. Jarvis, C. Padoch, and H.D. Cooper (New York: Columbia University Press, 2006), 1.

81. Jarvis et al., *Managing Biodiversity*, 1.

82. Paul William Brown, "Using the Past to Create a Sustainable Future for Agriculture: Environmental and Social Landscape Change in Iowa" (PhD diss., Iowa State University, Ames, IA, 2008).

83. Jackson, "The Farm, the Nature Preserve, and the Conservation Biologist," 40.

84. Aldo Leopold, "Game Cropping in Southern Wisconsin," in *The Essential Aldo Leopold: Quotations and Commentaries*, ed. Curt Meine and Richard L. Knight (Madison: University of Wisconsin Press, 1999), 121.

85. William R. Jordan III, Michael E. Gilpin, and John D. Aber, eds., *Restoration Ecology: A Synthetic Approach to Ecological Research* (Cambridge, UK: Cambridge University Press, 1987), 4–8.

86. Prince, *Wetlands of the American Midwest*, 329.

87. U.S. Department of the Interior, "The Impact of Federal Programs on Wetlands," Vol. II, A Report to Congress by the Secretary of the Interior (Washington, DC: March 1994), 2.

88. Iowa Department of Agriculture and Land Stewardship (IDALS), 13–14.

89. John Madson, *Where the Sky Began: Land of the Tallgrass Prairie* (Ames: Iowa State University Press, 1995), 291–92.

90. D.M. Debinski and P. Drobney, "Regal Fritillary and Its Host Plant Studied at Neal Smith National Wildlife Refuge (Iowa)," *Ecological Restoration* 18 (4) (2000): 254–55.

91. Cunfer, *On the Great Plains*, 234.

TWO — ECOLOGY, ECONOMY, LABOR
The Midwestern Farm Landscape since 1945

Kendra Smith-Howard

Ask most Americans to identify the nation's agricultural heartland, the home to iconic white farmhouses and red barns, and they will likely point to the center of the map. License plate mottos, university mascots, official state imagery, and pop culture references underscore the region's agricultural traditions. Wisconsin bills itself as "America's Dairyland." Nebraska, officially home to the Cornhuskers, also claims the moniker "beef state." The state seals of Kansas, Iowa, South Dakota, North Dakota, and Minnesota all prominently feature a plow. In the film *Field of Dreams*, set in Iowa, baseball players emerge from, of all places, a cornfield. Agriculture was and remains central to the midwestern economy, so much so that the region's leaders have often guided the nation's farm policy.[1] Visions of the Midwest as a repository of rural, pastoral values have only intensified in the twentieth century.[2]

Pastoral imagery about the rural heartland, however, fails to capture the dynamism and diversity of agriculture as practiced in the region. Since 1945 farm production practices and the character of the agricultural economy in the rural Midwest have been radically transformed. A close look at the midwestern agricultural landscape offers important clues about how industrialization and modernization revolutionized the region and shows how images and lore about the region obscure more about the region than they explain.

The Midwest, like other regions of the country, experienced a rapid decline in the number of farms and people engaged in agriculture after World War II. In some states, the decline was quick and dramatic; Missouri, for instance, lost 55 percent of its farms between 1945 and 1969. Overall, about 30 percent of the region's farms ceased to operate during this period.[3] As the number of people engaged in farming dwindled, fewer towns boasted businesses tied to the agricultural economy.[4] The Midwest became a place not just with a smaller number of farmers but fewer butter makers, cheese makers, and canning workers. Former farm families from the rural Midwest began to call home cities that were as close in proximity as Indianapolis and Chicago and as far away as the coasts.

By the 1970s, families who remained in agriculture shifted from general farming to specialized production. To be sure, geographic factors like climate, aridity, soil type, and proximity to markets had long encouraged farmers to focus their endeavors. In the upper Midwest, where hay thrived in the cool climate and hilly terrain made corn cultivation challenging, farm families concentrated primarily on dairy farming. Crops adapted to more arid climates, like wheat and sorghum, succeeded in Nebraska and the western Dakotas. The flat and rolling prairies of Indiana, Illinois, Iowa, and Missouri fostered corn growing, hog production, and fattening of steers. Despite these geographic patterns of specialization within the Midwest, though, most farm families maintained diversified operations in the early twentieth century. In western Wisconsin, where large barns and tall silos sustained dairy cows during the winter months, 60 percent of farms boasted at least one hog house, and 89 percent had poultry houses. In the western wheat-growing region, over half of the farms surveyed had hog yards. Nearly every Corn Belt farm family kept poultry.[5] After World War II, midwestern farmers narrowed the scope of production to boost efficiency and minimize human labor. They operated agribusinesses of greater size, scale, and specialization than ever before.

While agriculturalists across the country were touched by these developments, the Midwest played a particularly central role in the trend away from generalized farming. It was in the Midwest that new crops such as soybeans and novel techniques such as artificial insemination first became standard practice. Midwestern agriculture was also touched profoundly by the internationalized political economy. The increase in sugar beet and wheat production resulting from Cold War initiatives had its greatest impact on the physical geography of midwestern states. Documenting changes in midwestern agriculture and the farm landscape since 1945 provides a fuller picture of how farm families more broadly navigated the "second agricultural revolution" in American agriculture.[6]

The Corn Belt Landscape

The Second World War created new markets for commodities, reduced the farm labor supply, and stimulated technological innovations that re-ordered the rural midwestern landscape. Some changes were direct and immediate. The war cut off access to agricultural imports, prompting farmers to cultivate new crops such as soybeans. Soybean oil replaced Pacific-derived palm and coconut oils for the manufacture of soaps, margarine, and munitions. While soy flour was once promoted as a soil-conserving crop and used for animal fodder, in the 1940s the United States shipped it as part of its lend-lease support for Great Britain and incorporated it into the K-ration of its soldiers. On the home front, rationing policies favored the sale of margarine (made from soybean oil) over butter. Price supports encouraged farmers to plant soybeans.[7]

In no place did soybean cultivation expand more dramatically than the states of Ohio, Indiana, Illinois, Iowa, and Missouri, which together produced over 85 percent of the nation's soybean crop between 1940 and 1950.[8] Many observers predicted that once wartime markets declined, soybean cultivation would dwindle, but soybean production remained high in the 1950s. By the 1970s, the number of acres devoted to soybeans in the Corn Belt doubled, partly because of the use of soybean meal and oil in livestock feed.[9] Since the early 1970s, farm families across the region have embraced the crop; in 2006, North Dakota farmers planted seven hundred times as many soybeans as in 1986.[10]

To grow and harvest soybeans, Corn Belt farmers purchased new farm equipment. Combines, in particular, became essential. Until the 1940s, most midwestern farmers harvested small grains like oats, wheat, or soybeans in a multistep process. They cut grain with binders drawn by tractors or horses, raked it by hand into shocks, and after drying, hauled cut bundles to a threshing machine. At threshing time, farm people relied on neighbors or hired crews to operate a steam- or tractor-powered machine, scoop grain into storage bins, and stack straw for year-long use. In the 1940s, however, farm families began turning to combines to cut and thresh grain crops. Though the machines were initially expensive, farm families who purchased them traded away the expense of the upkeep of a binder, fuel costs, and the labor bill incurred at threshing time.[11] Midwestern farmers were more likely to adopt combines to harvest soybeans than any other kind of small grain.[12]

A rural labor shortage coincided with the expansion of soybean cultivation and cemented soybean growers' reliance on machinery. The departure of young men and women for the armed forces and defense industries left fewer able bodies for seasonal threshing crews. In southeastern Missouri, where landowners depended on sharecroppers, farm owners reduced cotton acreages in the 1940s because a single operator with a combine could bring in the soybean crop.[13] Wartime expansion of soybean acreage precipitated a reliance on harvesting machinery that intensified with the introduction of self-propelled combines in the 1950s and 1960s.

The soybean's rise came at the expense of crops once deemed important in the crop rotation, such as clover hay, barley, oats, and wheat.[14] Well into the 1940s, most Corn Belt farmers planted corn in rotation with small grains and hay. Leguminous hay crops replaced nitrogen in the soil, while oats and hay played a key role in feeding livestock, particularly horses and cows. The manure of these animals also contributed to soil fertility. But as farmers turned to chemical fertilizers rather than legumes and manure to provide nitrogen and depended on gas-powered machinery rather than oat-powered horses to perform farmwork, their devotion to the corn-oat-hay crop rotation waned.[15]

The turn to synthetic fertilizers and continuous corn, like expanding acreage of soybeans, had origins in World War II, during which the industrial capacity to manufacture synthetic nitrogen doubled.[16] As hay, barley, oat, and wheat fields disappeared from the midwestern landscape, farm chemicals and the equipment utilized to distribute them appeared in machinery sheds. By 1965, farmers in the Corn Belt states of Iowa, Missouri, Illinois, Indiana, and Ohio were more likely to have chemical spraying equipment than in any other region of the country.[17]

Farm people utilized newly affordable fertilizers to maximize yields. Hybrid corn—the mainstay in the Corn Belt by the 1940s—demanded greater soil nutrient loads than its open-pollinated predecessors.[18] Midwestern farm families that utilized hybrids readily adopted the new fertilizers. For corn cultivation, the leading fertilizer was anhydrous ammonia. Between 1950 and 1958, anhydrous ammonia applied in midwestern states increased from 1,809 to 161,121 tons.[19] Older farmers and those with smaller acreages adopted synthetic fertilizers less quickly, preferring instead to use manure and crop rotation to balance soil nutrients.[20] By the early 1970s, though, farmers utilized fertilizer on nearly all of the corn grown in the Midwest.[21] Treating corn with anhydrous ammonia enabled farmers to plant corn repeatedly in the same ground, a practice known as continuous corn.[22]

Like the growing reliance on chemical fertilizers, the use of insecticides encouraged farm families to abandon corn-oat-hay crop rotations. Prior to the postwar era, planting different crops on the same soil was an important way to control the spread of soil pathogens, insects, and weeds. But the pest control conferred by crop rotation seemed meager compared to the quick

Figure 2.1: Soybeans became an economically significant crop in the Midwest after World War II, displacing small grains, forage crops, and pastures in many parts of the region. Source: Photo by Scott Bauer, USDA Agricultural Research Service. Used with permission.

results of spraying chemicals to control insects. Having played a key role in overcoming insect-borne diseases such as malaria, DDT became familiar to farm families as a pest control agent.[23]

A final way that farm chemicals revolutionized corn growing was through weed control. Farmers wanted soils enriched with commercial fertilizer to nourish the crops, not weedy growth. Herbicides such as 2, 4-D presented a new alternative to clearing weeds with a tractor mower or cultivator, or slicing through Canada thistle along fencerows with a scythe.[24] Unlike chemicals previously used for weed control, like copper sulfate, many of the new chemicals targeted particular species but left others unscathed. 2, 4-D, for instance, was effective against broad-leafed weeds but not grassy weed species.[25] So farmers applied a combination of herbicides to get broad-spectrum results. Some farmers even stopped cultivating weeds mechanically and began to rely solely on chemical methods.[26]

If the use of farm chemicals encouraged farmers to abandon oats, wheat, and hay to grow corn, their adoption also prompted a dramatic postwar shift in crop storage: from harvesting and storing corn-ear corn in the corncrib to shelling corn in the field and storing it in bins.[27] In the 1940s, most farm families cut ears of corn with mechanical corn harvesters and stored the crop on the cob in wood-slatted corncribs. As farm families adopted chemical fertilizers, herbicides, and insecticides, corn yields increased rapidly, leaving many farmers short on grain storage space. Some farm families accommodated the record yields by constructing new corncribs or improvising temporary ones. When farm families purchased picker-shellers and combines to bring in their corn crops, though, the machines harvested just the corn kernels and left the cob behind in the field. By 1964, about 45 percent of Illinois farmers were harvesting shelled corn in the field.[28] Building plans for corn storage designed and distributed by the Midwest Plan Service illustrate this shift. In 1949, the plans described the capacity of corncribs and grain bins by how many bushels of *ear* corn they could accommodate. By 1969, recommendations focused exclusively on storing shelled corn.[29]

Shelled corn required only half as much storage space as ear corn, but the higher moisture content of shelled corn presented a new challenge: without proper drying, shelled corn could easily rot. If farmers were to store it, they needed drying equipment to ensure the corn did not mold or spoil.[30] Some farmers stopped storing corn on the premises, paying farm elevators to dry and store their corn.[31] Others constructed steel grain bins, designed specifically to store and dry shelled corn with artificial drying equipment. Such bins became the symbol of modern industrial corn production and slowly displaced older storage systems. As grain bins took over the role of storage

Figure 2.2: Corn continued to be one of the dominant crop species raised in the Midwest. During the postwar period, farmers ceased harvesting ear corn and instead harvested shelled corn. This harvest scene was photographed near Columbia, Missouri. Source: Photo by Bruce Fritz, USDA Agricultural Research Service. Used with permission.

that corncribs once played, the remaining wood corncribs were converted into storage buildings or fell into disuse.[32]

The final important shift in postwar era corn production concerned the grain's ultimate use. In 1950, at least half of the corn harvested in corn-producing states was destined for hog feed.[33] Corn Belt farm families used hogs to help balance the volatility of corn prices. In years when prices were low, farmers could convert corn into pork. Swine efficiently "hogged down" standing crops at harvest time, reducing labor demands while leaving their manure on the fields. Known for their role in balancing farm budget sheets as well as soil fertility, brood sows were commonly called "mortgage-lifters."[34]

By the late 1950s, labor shortages, combined with the advent of new technologies, began to split apart the once close connections between hog raising and corn growing. For some, the economic cushion that hogs provided was not enough to offset the energy spent raising them, including castrating, vaccinating, docking tails, and clipping eye teeth, but particularly the tasks required during the farrowing season. Young pigs were vulnerable animals. Sows often crushed pigs to death. Other piglets succumbed to chills or contracted disease when young. On average, only two-thirds to three-quarters of the pigs born per litter survived. Farmers could improve pigs' chances by separating pigs from the sow, changing bedding, and keeping them warm, but all these tasks took meticulous and round-the-clock care.[35]

Land values also shaped farmers' decisions about whether to maintain hog herds. Until the mid-twentieth century, farmers grazed hogs on pasture during the spring and summer and brought them onto feedlots in the fall to be fattened for market. Housing hogs in separate, movable structures on pasture isolated newborn litters from disease and reduced their exposure to parasites, since the structures were located on fresh pasture each year. But pasture grazing required hog farmers to regularly allocate some tillable lands to pasture. At a time when land values steadily appreciated, many came to see pasture grazing as a less efficient use of land compared to growing corn and soybeans and one that required more work. Furthermore, the ready availability of chemical fertilizers and nitrogen-fixing soybeans made hog manure a less valuable farm asset.[36]

Farm families who continued to raise hogs adapted new feeding and housing strategies that minimized labor and broke from mixed husbandry practices. In 1950, the Food and Drug Administration (FDA) approved the introduction of small levels of antibiotics to animal feeds, a development that stimulated weight gain in hogs and also reduced the prevalence of death among piglets. By reducing the risk of disease, antibiotics encouraged farmers to eschew homemade, temporary pasture shelters and turn toward centralized, confinement-style hog houses.[37] University of Missouri agricultural researchers informed the Senate agricultural committee in 1980 that "Pasture is a thing of the past except for some breeding herds."[38]

Businesses serving Corn Belt agriculturalists adapted. For instance, the Illinois company now known as Morton Buildings switched its product line to accommodate the changing agricultural practices. Founded in 1903 as the Interlocking Fence Company, the company faced a waning market for farm fencing as livestock moved off pasture. Hence, in 1949, it began manufacturing steel-sided post-frame construction to house the ever-more-present farm equipment and animals in confinement. Their manufactured machinery sheds, like the steel grain bin, reflected the new vision for agriculture in the region.[39]

Whereas hogs on pasture distributed manure over a wide space, hogs in confinement produced manure that had to be removed, a toilsome task even on concrete floors designed to facilitate regular cleaning. By the late 1960s and 1970s, engineers promoted slatted floors for hog barns, which allowed manure and urine to drop into shallow pits below hog pens and eliminated the burdensome task of hand-scraping manure to keep hog pens clean.[40] Farm organizations promoted such technologies as hallmarks of industrial hog production. In 1968, for instance, the Michigan Farm Bureau featured hog-raiser Mike Barton, a Michigan State graduate who had a new slatted-floor farrowing house and a feed grinding–mixing plant on their farm tour.[41]

Once cleared from the barn, hog manure had to be applied in the proper amounts and proper season for soil absorption, lest it pollute groundwater with excess nitrates. As manure compounded in confinement settings, some farmers constructed clay-lined pits, called manure lagoons, to store manure until it could be spread on soils that could readily absorb it. Optimally, lagoons protected neighbors from the stench of animal sewage. Overloaded lagoons, however, released offensive odors and endangered surface waterways. By the 1980s and 1990s, hog farmers who could afford it updated their manure facilities and built deep concrete pits below hog barns to avoid this problem.[42]

Even with the trend to confinement feeding, many farmers held on to old practices. In the late 1960s, nearly two-thirds of Illinois hogs spent some time on pasture.[43] In an Indiana study of the early 1970s, a quarter of hog-raising farmsteads lacked a centralized farrowing house, preferring to use individual farrowing houses on pasture.[44] In theory, confinement feeding promised to reduce environmental stresses on hogs, diminish farm people's labor, quicken weight gain, and thereby increase profits. Automated feeding units delivered grain to the hogs more efficiently than farmers could carry feed to houses on pasture. Many labor-saving features of confinement buildings, however, obscured the labor requirements involved in their operation. Erecting confinement buildings for each stage of hogs' life cycle required a massive economic investment. For those who built new confinement operations, hogs were no longer a mortgage-lifter to help offset grain surpluses but the source of mortgages themselves.[45] Hence, the shift toward confinement feeding in hog raising in the Midwest was accompanied by consolidation of hog production during the 1960s and 1970s. Whereas 55 percent of the nation's farms reported hogs and pigs in 1950, only 25 percent reported the animals by 1969.[46]

The story of Ron and Erland Rothenberger, brothers who farmed near Frankfort, Indiana, demonstrates the changes taking place in the Corn Belt. Between the end of World War II and 1962, the Rothenbergers shifted from general farming and crop rotation to specialize on modern corn and hog raising. While the Rothenbergers had once rotated corn with oats and meadow, by 1962 they reported that 95 percent of their cultivatable acreage was in continuous corn. They relied on heavy applications of chemical fertilizers to help offset soil fertility losses and accommodated increased yields of dried shelled corn by remodeling an old horse barn. The Rothenbergers' hog operation also changed. They once used individual farrowing houses on pasture to raise two litters of hogs per year, but by 1962 they invested in concrete-floored barns and a central farrowing building with floor heat. The new setup helped them to raise twice as many litters of pigs each year. In the nursing barn, hogs ate from self-feeding units, providing the Rothenberger brothers with more time to raise corn and tend to cattle raised on feedlot. The brothers, educated in agricultural engineering at Purdue University, welcomed the economic risks that such improvements required. As they explained, "Borrowing and paying—that's the way it is in the farm business."[47]

Removing hogs from the farm eliminated the need for fenced pastures and hog lots and fundamentally altered the experience of farming in the Midwest. Seasonal butchering ceased. Smokehouses and hog houses disappeared apace on farms more reliant on crop raising than meat production. Visitors to rural districts rarely saw hogs before they appeared on the plate, for the animals were cordoned into carefully regulated confinement facilities. Passersby encountered hog farms with their noses, not their eyes.

If the Rothenberger farm represented the shift toward industrial hog raising, the landscape of another Indiana farm, located near Bremen, Indiana, demonstrated how the rise of cash grain production reordered farm landscapes. In the late 1940s, the grounds of this Indiana farmstead included a farm house, silo, barn, hog house, brooder house, corncrib, garage, smokehouse, and milk house, indicating that hogs, chickens, and cattle figured into the farm's balance sheet. An orchard, pasture, and farm garden as well as fields cultivated for corn, hay, oats, spearmint, and wheat graced the grounds. By the 1970s, only three buildings remained: a garage, a farmhouse, and a toolshed-corncrib. Fences, livestock pens, and buildings, as well as the milk house, smokehouse, orchard, and garden, disappeared. One cornfield dominated the area once planted in many farm crops.[48]

Oft-Forgotten Harvests: The Midwestern Fruit and Vegetable Growing Landscape

The features of that Bremen, Indiana, farm as it appeared in the late 1940s, particularly its orchard and spearmint fields, provide a powerful reminder that crops *other* than corn and grown for purposes other than livestock feed thrived in midwestern agriculture in the late 1940s and 1950s. Though often obscured by the focus on USDA commodities, crops such as spearmint, tomatoes, corn, cucumbers, asparagus, pumpkins, beets, and cabbage were important in midwestern agriculture and not simply in areas whose topography disallowed mechanized corn production. In 1950, Indiana was second only to California in tomato production, producing 331,000 tons that year. Ohio ranked not far behind.[49] Michigan and Wisconsin produced half of the nation's pickling cucumbers in 1951.[50] Disease, increased competition, and Cold War policies all played a role in driving some crops to disappear from the Midwest and allowing others to thrive after World War II. These changes left behind an altered agricultural landscape.

One crop whose fortunes in the Midwest changed after 1945 was mint. In the 1940s, the fertile sandy loam soils of Wisconsin, Michigan, and Indiana supplied the bulk of the world's peppermint and spearmint.[51] Most midwestern mint was distilled into oils used for candy, toothpaste, medicine, and chewing gum. Mint districts, then, were marked by the presence of steam-powered distilleries. After midsummer harvests, farm families gathered to cook down mint leaves into a refined product. Steam from boilers passed through cut mint leaves and stems and vaporized the oil. As the vapors condensed, they separated into layers of oil and water, and oil could be skimmed from the top.[52] Larita Killian, whose family grew mint in northern Indiana, remembered a fragrant scent wafting through mint country for five to six weeks each summer.[53]

In the late 1940s, though, midwestern mint plants fell prey to verticillium wilt, a soil fungus that prevented the roots of the mint plant from conducting water to the stem. Fatal to mint plants, the fungus traveled from field to field on rootstocks, water, soil, or equipment that had contact with an infected field. Crop rotation could not prevent its spread because the fungus remained dormant in affected fields for nearly ten years. Verticillim wilt spelled doom for the Michigan peppermint industry by the 1970s, while Indiana also suffered losses. As mint growing foundered in the Midwest, newly established mint crops in Washington and Oregon thrived. When Larita Killian returned to northern Indiana to celebrate the centennial of her hometown's mint-growing history in 2001, the mint industry in the region had all but disappeared.[54]

As Michigan's mint harvests dwindled, its cherry crop grew in importance. Michigan orchardists harvested two kinds of cherries: sweet and sour (or tart). With production centered around Grand Traverse Bay, Michigan dominated the tart cherry industry, producing 50 to 70 percent of the nation's crop during the 1950s and 1960s. Michigan's sour cherries were frozen or canned for use in pies, juice, and jam. Michigan's sweet cherry industry also rapidly grew in the 1960s. From 1959 to 1969, the number of sweet cherry trees in Michigan increased by nearly 45 percent, from 690,000 to over 1 million. Most of Michigan's sweet cherries were brined and then incorporated as maraschino cherries in cocktails, blended into ice cream, or candied in baked goods.[55]

As cherry production expanded, growers adapted new techniques to reduce fruit losses and replace human labor. One step of cherry production that changed in the postwar era was the handling of cherries between the orchard and processing plant. Until the 1950s, fruit pickers filled ten-quart pails in the orchard and then poured full buckets of cherries into lugs. Crews of workers transported these lugs three times—from orchard to trailer, trailer to grower's truck, and at the receiving station, from a grower's to a processor's truck. At the processing plant, unloaded cherries finally soaked in water.[56] The multistep process between pickers' pail and processing plant presented problems. Some cherries spoiled as they awaited transport. Others bruised or spilled during transit. Furthermore, due to heavy demands at the peak times of the harvest, growers had to pay the crews who transferred cherries overtime wages.[57]

By the early 1950s, agricultural experts devised a variety of strategies to speed the trip from orchard to processing plant. Their first recommendation was to use forklifts instead of work crews to transport lugs of cherries. By speeding the transfer from trailer to truck, forklifts promised to reduce spoilage and labor costs alike. They also recommended handling cherries in water. Immersing cherries into trucks with cool water tanks at the receiving station reduced the risk of scalding or bruising. Putting cherries directly into water at the orchard eliminated lugs (and the wages paid to those who heaved them from trailer to truck) entirely.[58]

In the 1960s, cherry growers fully embraced mechanization, turning to harvesting machines to replace the picking crews in Michigan's orchards. In the 1950s, as many as 45,000 men and women served as cherry-pickers in Michigan each year, many of whom also harvested sugar beets, cucumbers, or tomatoes.[59] But labor recruitment foundered, particularly in the wake of the end of the *braceros* program in 1964, a federal program that had legally admitted temporary agricultural workers since 1942.[60] Growers turned to technological solutions. In the late 1950s and early 1960s, engineers developed a machine that shook cherry trees to loosen ripe berries. Harvested cherries fell into a catching frame that gently gathered the crop and could be tipped to roll cherries into tanks of cold water for processing. Only 3 percent of the Michigan cherry crop was mechanically harvested in 1964, but by 1968, 70 percent was harvested by machine.[61] Large orchards with high-yielding trees benefited most from the shift to mechanical harvesting, for large harvests offset the investment and operation costs of using harvesting machines.[62] The purchase of a mechanized cherry harvester, used only for two or four weeks a year, marked growers' commitment to specialization.

Many other vegetables and fruits grown in the Midwest were destined for food processing. During World War II, national companies like Green Giant, McNeill and Libby, and H.J. Heinz built or bought out canneries in the Midwest, especially in northwestern Ohio, southeastern Michigan, northern Indiana, Illinois, and southern Wisconsin. To ensure a steady supply of vegetables for canning, companies contracted with local farmers to grow tomatoes, corn, cucumbers, pumpkins, and beans on a set acreage at a set price. Processors supplied farmers with seeds and machinery and helped recruit labor for the harvest.[63] As farm chemicals and mechanization came to vegetable growing, processing companies provided growers with insecticides, fungicides, and fertilizers to boost yields.[64]

Though national canneries took a broader share of the market, regional companies still commanded some of the canning trade. In southern Minnesota, Owatonna Canning Company's plants sold asparagus, green beans, pumpkin, corn, and peas under the Festal brand. Another regional Minnesota cannery, Minnesota Valley Canning Company, helped maintain its market share by blending canning with frozen food sales.[65] Other regional canneries, however, such as the seasonal tomato canneries that operated in southwestern Missouri's Ozarks, struggled to compete with packers that sold a full line of nationally branded goods. They strained to obtain sufficient tomatoes from local growers, as these residents specialized or shifted to part-time farming.[66] Iowa canneries saw similar declines. Sixty canning factories operated in Iowa in the 1940s, processing sweet corn, tomatoes, green beans, asparagus, pumpkin, squash, beets, carrots, pickles, and sauerkraut. By 1973, only eight remained.[67]

While many midwestern vegetables were canned and processed, some reached the market fresh. Market gardening in the Midwest had a long history. In an age before interstate highways, farms nearest to the region's urban areas sold fresh fruits and vegetables without incurring high transit costs. Southern Illinoisans raised peaches, rhubarb, asparagus, strawberries, beans, cucumbers, potatoes, squash, and even daffodils for the Chicago market, sending their goods on refrigerated train cars to brokers in the city.[68] Ohio tomato growers constructed greenhouses, making it possible to provide fresh tomatoes to residents of Cleveland, Cincinnati, Indianapolis, and Toledo, even in winter.[69]

Market gardeners faced new challenges after 1945. Interstate highways increased competition from growers in western states, many of whom had ready access to irrigation and suffered less from plant diseases that troubled midwesterners. For some, the expanding interstate system turned farms' proximity to urban areas into their greatest curse. As the new roads facilitated suburban development, land prices skyrocketed, forcing many to pay higher property taxes or sell their farms.[70] The rise of supermarkets brought demands for crops of greater volume and consistent quality. Farm families accustomed to sending just a few crates of peaches or strawberries as part of a mixed farming strategy, and who relied on family labor, had to adapt to the new demands of the business or stop raising produce commercially.

Innovative producers sought to make farm crops more attractive to supermarket wholesalers. Vegetable growers in southern Illinois's Little Egypt district founded a cooperative in the early 1950s to improve produce handling. They set up a washer and waxing machine for cucumbers and peppers to meet buyers' demands for uniformity and quality. In the early 1960s, the region's fruit growers followed suit, constructing a new building equipped with cold storage, for packing and marketing fruit. The facility allowed growers to maintain the fruit's condition and also to grade and prepare fruit for market after the harvest's labor crunch.[71] Other growers spurned the wholesale market and turned to direct marketing. While farm stands had long graced the highways and byways of rural districts, the new on-farm markets sought out shoppers who had begun to see the countryside as a site for recreation. On-farm markets reduced farmers' transport costs and pick-your-own orchards slashed labor costs by recasting fruit purchasers as apple, peach, or cherry pickers.[72] Whether selling to wholesalers or directly to buyers, maintaining a small orchard or allocating acreage for a few asparagus or sweet corn plots was no longer enough to stay in the produce business. Plowed-under orchards, like new processing sheds, revealed the fate of small-scale fruit and vegetable growers throughout the region.

Sugar beet production, by contrast, expanded in the postwar era. Important since the turn of the twentieth century in central Michigan, the Minnesota River valley, and the Red River Valley counties of Minnesota and North Dakota, the sugar beet industry grew due to increased worldwide demand for sugar and the Cuban sugar embargo.[73] Upper midwestern farm families turned to sugar beet cultivation as prices for crops like wheat and barley declined. To meet pressures from growers eager to plant beets and consumers with an appetite for sugar, the industry opened new processing plants and initiated technological changes that reordered the labor of sugar beet production.[74] Sugar beet acreage grew steadily. In the Red River Valley, American Crystal Sugar Company contracted 62,000 acres of cropland to sugar beets in 1949. By 1954, the company had 90,000 acres under contract. Acreages under beet contracts increased sharply with the sugar embargo in 1960, reaching 143,000 acres by 1962 and 167,000 acres in 1967.[75] Sugar beet growers who signed contracts agreed to plant a specific number of beets per acre, to tend the crop carefully, and to plant on lands previously fallowed. The processing company supplied growers with access to seeds and equipment and offered them sufficient laborers to carry out the tasks of sugar beet production. Growers paid for labor recruitment services with a per-acre fee assessed and promised to provide worker housing.[76]

As sugar beet production increased, so did the demand for laborers. These laborers undertook a variety of tasks. Their first was to plant the crop. Sugar beets grew not from individual seeds, but from a clump of seeds together. Thus the second step, which took place when the beets were just inches high, was to select the healthiest plant and separate it from the other young plants in the bunch—a process called thinning. As beets grew, the crop had to be weeded two or three times. In the fall, workers lifted beets out from the soil and topped them, which meant removing the leafy part from each beet. Then growers transported the harvested crop to the processing plant.[77] Starting in the 1920s, most of the sugar industry's laborers were Mexican American workers recruited in southern Texas. By the 1950s, upper midwestern labor recruiters had a difficult task convincing workers to weather frigid temperatures in the beet fields. Growers pursued two strategies to alleviate the labor problem, both of which would have a long-term impact on the landscape of sugar beet farms: mechanizing the harvest and improving workers' housing.[78]

The expense of recruiting workers and fear of labor shortages encouraged mechanization. Harvesting equipment of the early 1950s allowed the harvest to take place in four weeks rather than six and eliminated the need for workers to dig and top beets.[79] The technological innovation that most transformed the work of sugar beet farming was the development of the monogerm seed. Unlike predecessors, monogerm beet seeds yielded a single plant. They could be planted mechanically and at uniform spacing, which made it easier for growers to utilize herbicide sprayers to reduce weed growth in the crop. Monogerm seeds eliminated the labor-intensive thinning task and significantly reduced the labor required for cultivating the crop.[80] While mechanization reduced some of the most labor-intensive parts of the beet growing process, it did not eliminate the need for field workers, for the advent of mechanization in the beet fields corresponded with the rapid expansion of acreage devoted to sugar beets.

Thus, growers also addressed labor pressures by improving worker housing. Starting in the late 1940s and early 1950s, sugar companies such as American Crystal urged growers to provide higher quality housing. Until that time, many beet workers lived in retrofitted barns, sheds, or even chicken coops that lacked running water, window screens, adequate sleeping quarters, and electricity.[81] Improvements, the company hoped, would help build worker loyalty and ease labor recruitment challenges. Housing provisions became all the more important in the 1960s, as poor housing conditions became a key target of labor organizers and as state laws for housing standards stiffened. Although enforcement of these standards often was lax, some growers refurbished worker housing, providing mobile homes or moving workers into nearby abandoned farmhouses.[82] While less evident than converted fields or new machinery, the farmhouses with plywood partitioning to allow for multiple occupancy or trailers adjacent to more substantial farmhouses offered physical evidence of a thriving beet sugar industry.

Poultry and Dairy: From Egg Money and Cream Checks to Agro-Industries

Until the late 1940s, chicken coops and cream separators were among the most ubiquitous objects on the midwestern farm.[83] Egg money and cream checks provided one of few steady streams of income between harvests.[84] In the 1950 agricultural census, over 75 percent of farms in the East North Central region and over 81 percent in the West North Central region reported having chickens. Iowa led the nation in dozens of eggs sold. Similarly, many midwestern farm families sent cream to butter-making factories. Seventy-five percent of farms in the West Central region of the country reported cream sales in 1950.[85] If eggs and cream offered year-round income, the sale of poultry for meat took place more sporadically. Turkey sales, for instance, corresponded largely with Thanksgiving.[86]

Starting in the 1950s, new techniques of breeding, feeding, and housing poultry enabled a few farms to make the egg business a mainstay of farm income. As new concerns about dietary fats stimulated Americans' appetite for chicken and turkey and made poultry less tied to Sunday dinners and Thanksgiving, the broiler industry also grew. Most expansion was in the southern United States, but Minnesota and Missouri became important turkey-raising states. Far fewer farms, however, kept hens by the 1960s.[87] Farms supplying the cream trade also saw important changes in the postwar era. After 1945, the butter market slumped and, with it, the demand for farm-separated cream. Improved transportation, though, meant that geographically isolated farmers who had once been cut off from more lucrative fluid milk sales due to transportation challenges could now sell whole milk on the Grade A market. To sell their milk as Grade A, though, farmers had to remodel their dairy barns and milk houses to meet the more stringent health standards required for fluid milk. Farm families who relied on a cream check could either make changes to supply larger processing plants or quit the dairy business entirely. By the 1970s, the agricultural landscape of the Midwest was dotted with two-story henhouses and modern milking parlors. But it boasted far fewer chicken coops and milk houses overall.

Industrialized postwar egg production depended less on natural cycles. Up to the early 1950s, nearly half of midwestern chickens foraged for insects and grubs during the summer, even as poultry raisers utilized poultry houses to protect hens and facilitate egg collection.[88] By the mid-1950s, chickens received a balanced diet in the form of feed supplemented with vitamin B-12, fortified with antibiotics and balanced with soy protein.[89] Egg production had once dropped off as daylight shortened in the fall and winter, but the wider distribution of electric power in the countryside in the 1940s and 1950s made artificial lighting in laying houses the norm, deseasoning the laying cycle. Producers could also artificially end the laying season by shortening the amount of time the lights remained on each day and trimming hens' rations. After about two months of rest, the same hens could be utilized for a second laying cycle—thus making it possible to increase production without purchasing and feeding new pullets (nonlaying hens). Laying houses no longer needed south-facing windows.[90] In new laying houses, hens ate carefully blended concoctions inside cages equipped with wire floors. With the pressure of each new egg, cage floors tilted, rolling the egg onto a conveyor belt and into the processing plant.[91]

Besides mechanical improvements of artificial lights and conveyor belts, the most obvious attribute of modern poultry houses constructed was size and scale. Minnesota poultry raisers in the mid-1950s kept flocks of 500 or 1,000 layers. Henhouses built in the 1960s accommodated as many as 12,000 or 24,000 birds. To service such large flocks, poultry raisers constructed feed mills, manure composting systems, and egg-processing facilities. As in many sectors of midwestern agriculture, poultry raisers traded labor-intensive work for capital-intensive risks. In the process, poultry raising transferred out of the hands of farm women, who increasingly sought off-farm employment, and into those of male entrepreneurs.[92] Investment and returns increased but so did risks, as the threat of disease looms large over facilities of such size and, as with hog confinement operations, processing the waste of these huge flocks of birds requires nearly as much attention as raising the flock itself.[93]

Dairy farmers, too, faced upheaval in the postwar era. Many farmers simply elected to stop milking cows. Those who chose to specialize in dairying reorganized dairy barns, constructed new milk houses, and improved the quality of their herds.[94] One change to the dairy barn was the elimination of the bull pen, and with it, the hulking beast that inhabited it. Artificial insemination (AI) allowed farmers to obtain the benefits of well-bred livestock—sperm from bulls with high production records—at a reasonable cost. Far more cows could be serviced using artificial insemination than naturally by an elite-class bull. By 1949, 10 percent of the nation's dairy cows were enrolled in artificial insemination associations. Numbers grew dramatically in the 1950s, with the discovery of methods to freeze dairy semen. The enhanced genetic profile of midwestern dairy cows accounted for significant increases in production, from an average of 4,622 pounds per cow in 1940 to 7,029 pounds in 1960 and 11,240 pounds in 1978.[95]

A second change promoted in the 1950s was to shift from stanchion barns to loose housing of dairy cattle. Until the late 1940s, most dairy barns confined cows to individual stalls or stanchions. Farmers milked, fed, and bedded cows in their stalls. Stanchion barns were expensive to construct and costly to remodel. As the average size of cows increased, farmers found stalls too cramped or short to accommodate cows' larger bodies. Engineers believed that they could improve cow comfort, reduce farm costs, and relieve laborious barn tasks by altering the layout of the stall barn.[96] After World War II, they experimented with a different kind of dairy barn new to the Midwest: the pen barn. In pen barns, spaces were arranged by function: one section of the barn was used for feeding, another for loafing and bedding of cattle, and a third as a milking parlor. Adult cows were allowed to roam freely, rather than being fixed in place.[97] In a stall barn, farmers provided feed to cows in the feed alley adjacent to their stalls, while in a pen barn cows ate from self-feeding bunks and drank from a common water tank in the feeding area. The biggest change in the loose housing setup for dairy farms, though, was the site where milking took place. In a stanchion barn, a farmer moved from cow to cow during milking. Farmers with loose housing operations milked cows in a central milking parlor. Twice a day, cows filed into the cement-floored room and proceeded into individual milking stalls. Such stalls were elevated, so that the person milking was at eye-level with the cow's udder. As the milker washed udders and hooked cows to the milking machine, the animals ate concentrated feed or grains. When all the cows were through milking, they exited the parlor and allowed the next batch of cows to enter.[98]

In most modern milking parlors, pipeline systems carried the milk directly to the bulk tank, which was also a new technology for chilling milk that debuted in the late 1950s in midwestern dairy districts. Until that time, most farmers chilled milk by pouring it into ten-gallon cans and immersing the cans in cold water in a cement tank. When milk haulers came to pick up the milk, the farmer and the truck driver would hoist the full cans onto the hauler's truck and exchange full cans for empty ones that would be filled the next day. Bulk milk tanks, mechanical refrigerators capable of chilling hundreds of gallons of milk, put an end to these tasks. Rather than heave heavy cans of milk, haulers servicing bulk tanks hooked a special hose between the farmer's bulk tank and pumped milk into the truck's stainless-steel receiving vat, making the chore of milk cooling, transportation, and handling more efficient.[99] Most dairy farmers needed to build new milk houses to accommodate tank truck deliveries. Dairy companies helped finance the construction of new milk houses and the purchase of bulk tanks. For many farmers, though, the improvements required to stay in the dairy business exceeded income and predicted profits. Even in states long central to the dairy industry, many farm families stopped commercial dairying and entered other agricultural sectors or left the farm entirely.[100]

The Remaking of the Great Plains

Like dairying, beef cattle feeding saw great changes by the 1960s. Until the 1950s and 1960s, cattle feeding meshed well with the farming patterns in the Corn Belt. After spending the spring and summer grazing on Great Plains grasses, cattle traveled from western ranches to Corn Belt farms, which supplemented their income by fattening cattle with extra grain and roughage. Farmers purchased a carload or two of steers to feed through the winter, and used the manure the cattle produced to fertilize corn and soybean fields in the spring. The work of cattle feeding, positioned in between the harvest and spring planting, suited farmers' schedules. So compatible did cattle raising and corn growing seem that two historians in 1955 called the Corn Belt the "feedbag of democracy."[101] But between 1950 and 1979, the Corn Belt's share of the cattle raised on feed fell from half the nation's total to just 22 percent. Commercial feedlots that fed a thousand cattle or more, year-round, proliferated in the 1960s. Increasingly, these commercial feedlots were located not in the Corn Belt but in the Great Plains, especially in western Kansas, Nebraska, Oklahoma, and Texas.[102] This westward geographic shift of beef cattle raising rested on a variety of factors, but two were critical—irrigation that yielded a ready grain supply on the plains and the development of a truck transportation system to shuttle cattle from feedlot to processing plant.

First, irrigation turned what was once deemed submarginal land into lush fields of alfalfa, sorghum, and corn and reoriented cattle feeding toward the Great Plains. In 1950, the invention of the center pivot sprinkler allowed farm families to douse hundreds of acres of land in a circular pattern, and to simultaneously enrich soils with commercial fertilizers. The pumps that supplied these center-pivots tapped into the Ogallala Aquifer, a massive groundwater deposit that undergirded the High Plains. The construction of the irrigation infrastructure cost tens of thousands of dollars, and the costs to keep it operating—for fuel, pumps, and fertilizers—compounded the expense. But 1950s droughts made Kansas farmers willing to invest in irrigation, and the resultant high yields inspired others to do the same. In 1950, just 300,000 acres in Kansas were irrigated. By the 1980s, 3.5 million acres attained this status. In Nebraska, irrigated farmland increased from 255,864 acres in 1945 to 3.5 million in 2000.[103]

The record-breaking crops of corn, sorghum, and alfalfa made possible with irrigation reordered the economic and ecological system that had once made the Corn Belt the most logical place to raise feeder cattle. Newly furnished with grain, Great Plains farmers looked to California for inspiration. California feedlots were of much greater scale than the small operations dominant in the Midwest and quickened the pace at which cattle reached weights for slaughter.[104] These feedlots shared many features with the confinement poultry and hog operations. Feedlot operators maintained feed mills to ensure the appropriate scientific balance of digestible, protein-rich rations at the lowest cost, and they supplemented rations with antibiotics to boost weight gains. Even smaller feedlot operators incorporated automated devices like electric-powered augers and silo-unloaders, so that the chore of heaving silage or mixing grain took a worker less time. Even the bodies of animals in the feedlot bore evidence of the shift to industrial feeding. Rather than raise purebred Hereford or Angus, feedlot operators encouraged the introduction of exotic bloodlines that converted feed into flesh more efficiently.[105]

As irrigation unraveled the advantages of Corn Belt feedlot operators, packers who relocated to the Great Plains were able to utilize to their advantage the infrastructure established by prior agribusinesses. For instance, even as the western Kansas sugar beet economy foundered, newly relocated meatpackers convinced former beet growers to provide feedlots' hay, grain, and silage; hired Latino laborers who had first labored in sugar beet fields; and exploited processing centers (like feed mills) established by cooperatives.[106] Great Plains feedlot owners spent less to transport cattle to the feedlot than California competitors. The scale of purchase made by the Plains feedlots allowed them to negotiate more favorable grain transportation rates from shorter distances.[107] By the 1980s, 40 percent of the nation's beef slaughter took place within 250 miles of Garden City, Kansas. Once the beef was packaged, refrigerated trucks hauled meat on interstate highways to market. The new transportation infrastructure, like irrigation, made it possible for the western plains to earn the distinction as the "feedlot belt" of America.[108]

Wheat, the longtime staple commodity of the plains, was also transformed. While some of the most visible changes in wheat production took place before 1945, such as the custom combining operations of the war years, postwar scientific changes boosted wheat yields dramatically.[109] The average U.S. wheat yield in 1949 was 15 bushels per acre but had reached 33.9 bushels per acre by 1971.[110] Adoption of farm chemicals contributed to increases in wheat productivity. By the 1970s, wheat growers utilized herbicides widely, particularly in the Dakotas, Nebraska, Kansas, and Minnesota.[111] Other chemical applications took on greater significance with the adoption of new wheat varieties. Unlike strains developed for dry-land farming, new high-yielding wheat strains responded well to fertilizers and irrigation. The new wheat was shorter and had stronger straw, which minimized the tendency of wheat to lodge, or topple over with the weight of heavy seeds, especially in wind and rainstorms. Semi-dwarf wheats, introduced to Kansas in 1970, constituted over half of the wheat planted by 1982. Shorter varieties were taken up quickly in the more nitrogen-heavy soils of the Corn Belt, and Minnesotans embraced the semi-dwarf variety Era.[112] The Green Revolution touched the nation's midsection even as it revolutionized agricultural practices around the world. In no small way, the Midwest fostered this transformative leap in global agriculture, for the ideas for high-yielding crops first germinated in the mind of Norman Borlaug, an Iowa-raised farmboy and alumnus of the University of Minnesota.

The impact of short and semi-dwarf wheats on the midwestern landscape of the 1950s and 1960s is often overlooked in the context of the more dramatic plow-up of the 1970s. Wheat prices soared in the wake of grain sales to the Soviet Union. Midwestern farmers slashed woodlots, converted fields of rye and flax, eliminated fallow strips, and tilled under pastures to capitalize on wheat.[113] The prospect of increased exports brought more land under production, although the lower quality and fertility of land cultivated meant that yield per acre declined from nearly 34 bushels per acre in 1970 to 30 bushels per acre in 1974. Nevertheless, with so much more land under cultivation, the United States produced 500,000 more bushels of wheat annually by the mid-1970s than it had at the beginning of the decade.[114] The physical imprint of this production increase could be viewed not just in the plowed-up pasturelands but also in the mammoth grain elevators the yields supported. County elevators, no longer able to accommodate record crops, were replaced with fewer, newer structures that extended for nearly a mile.[115]

Conclusion

That the word "Midwest" so often evokes a timeless image of a family farm is truly remarkable, given the changes that have touched the region since 1945. Whether manifest in the corrugated steel of a corn bin, the green circles created by irrigation pivots on the Great Plains, or the shuttered doors of a canning factory, the midwestern rural landscape bears extraordinary evidence of the shift from labor-intensive to capital-intensive agriculture. Often overlooked by outsiders who consider the region "fly-over country," the changes are readily palpable to the rural people who face their direct consequences. Some pay ever-mounting debts to farm lenders, others plant soybeans where their grandfathers grew wheat, while still others worry about the nitrate levels in wells located near feedlots.

The Midwest's continued resonance as the nation's agricultural heartland is also increasingly peculiar as other regions of the country begin to dominate in the production of commodities long associated with the nation's midsection. Between 1988 and 1996, North Carolina's share of the nation's hog production increased from 7 to 17 percent as it challenged Iowa for the status of the number one hog-producing state.[116] Dairy production remains important in the Midwest, but dairy farming's biggest recent gains are in states such as California, Idaho, and New Mexico.[117] Even as rural midwesterners pass ordinances to insulate the reach of corporate agriculture or to control odors from confinements and feedlots, midwesterners cannot deny their central role in these trends of modernization. After all, midwestern farm families and university experts first applied many of the techniques of industrialized production now being implemented around the country and the world. Whether one sees the brightest future for midwestern agriculture in the confinement feedlot or the farmers' market stand, the path to the future of modern farming cannot be forged without considering the dramatic changes to the region's agriculture after World War II.

Notes

1. Eleven of the past seventeen U.S. secretaries of agriculture have hailed from midwestern states: Orville Freeman, Clifford Hardin, Earl Butz, Robert Bergland, John Block, Clayton Yeutter, Edward Madigan, Daniel Glickman, Mike Johanns, Ed Schafer, and Tom Vilsack.

2. James Shortridge, *The Middle West: Its Meaning in American Culture* (Lawrence: University Press of Kansas, 1989), 10–11, 68.

3. Dennis Nordin and Roy V. Scott, *From Prairie Farmer to Entrepreneur: The Transformation of Midwestern Agriculture* (Bloomington: Indiana University Press, 2005), 172–73.

4. Whereas Wisconsin possessed over 1,500 cheese factories in 1945, only 115 such plants operated in 2008. USDA, "National Agricultural Statistics Service, Wisconsin Data—Dairy Products, Total Cheese Plants," <www.nass.usda.gov/QuickStats/Create_Federal_Indv.jsp> (accessed April 1, 2010). Judith Kalbacher, "The Changing U.S. Farm Population," *Rural Development Perspectives* (March 1980): 34.

5. Glenn Trewartha, "Some Regional Characteristics of American Farmsteads," *Annals of the Association of American Geographers* 38 (September 1948): 184–90, 200–204, 215–20.

6. For the second agricultural revolution, see Wayne Rasmussen, "A Postscript: Twenty-Five Years of Change in Farm Productivity," *Agricultural History* 49 (1): 84–86, and Rasmussen, "The Impact of Technological Change in American Agriculture, 1862–1962," *Journal of Economic History* 22 (December 1962): 588; for, less charitably, "the great disjuncture" in American agriculture, see John Shover, *First Majority, Last Minority: The Transformation of Rural Life in America* (DeKalb: Northern Illinois University Press, 1980), 141.

7. Alvin Munn, "Production and Utilization of the Soybean in the United States," *Economic Geography* 26 (July 1950): 232–38.

8. Munn, "Soybean Cultivation in the United States," 223, 225.

9. Shover, *First Majority, Last Minority*, 151. On doubling, see Committee on Agriculture, Nutrition, and Forestry, United States Senate, *Farm Structure: A Historical Perspective on Changes in the Number and Size of Farms* (Washington, DC: GPO, 1980), 296.

10. Alexei Barrionuevo, "Crop Rotation in the Grain Belt," *New York Times*, September 16, 2006, C1.

11. J.L. Anderson, *Industrializing the Corn Belt: Agriculture, Technology and Environment, 1945–1972* (DeKalb: Northern Illinois University Press, 2009), 152–55.

12. Anderson, *Industrializing the Corn Belt*, 165.

13. Merle Prunty Jr., "Soybeans in the Lower Mississippi Valley," *Economic Geography* 26 (October 1950): 311.

14. Ladd Haystead and Gilbert Fite, *Agricultural Regions of the United States* (Norman: University of Oklahoma Press, 1955), 150–51; D. Jerome Tweton, "The Business of Agriculture," in *Minnesota in a Century of Change: The State and Its People since 1900*, ed. Clifford Clark Jr. (St. Paul: Minnesota Historical Society Press, 1986), 281.

15. John Fraser Hart, *The Rural Landscape* (Baltimore: Johns Hopkins University Press), 97–102.

16. Geoff Cunfer, "Manure Matters on the Great Plains Frontier," *Journal of Interdisciplinary History* 34 (Spring 2004): 563.

17. "Pesticide Application Equipment Owned by Farmers," *Agricultural Economic Report* No. 161 (Washington, DC: USDA, 1969), 3.

18. Anderson, *Industrializing the Corn Belt*, 52–54.

19. J. Richard Adams, M.S. Anderson, and Walter Clare Hulburt, *Liquid Nitrogen Fertilizers for Direct Application*, Agriculture Handbook No. 198, Agricultural Research Service (Washington, DC: USDA, 1961), 4.

20. "For Corn—Pour on Fertilizer," *Successful Farming* (November 1963): 36.

21. G.F. Sprague and William E. Larson, *Corn Production*, Agricultural Handbook Number 322 (revised edition) (Washington, DC: USDA Agricultural Research Service, with Minnesota Agricultural Experiment Station, 1975), 10.

22. Anderson, *Industrializing the Corn Belt*, 56; John Schlebecker, *Whereby We Thrive:*

A History of American Farming, 1607–1972 (Ames: Iowa State University, 1975), 301, 313.

23. Anderson, *Industrializing the Corn Belt*, 16–22, 27–29.

24. Anderson, *Industrializing the Corn Belt*, 33–43.

25. W.B. Ennis, "Weeds," *Yearbook of the United States Department of Agriculture* (Washington, DC: GPO, 1962), 126–28.

26. For warnings, see Sprague and Larson, *Corn Production*, 29; Anderson, *Industrializing the Corn Belt*, 49.

27. Loren Neubauer and Harry Walker, *Farm Building Design* (Princeton, NJ: Prentice-Hall, 1961), 244.

28. Laurence Kruckman and Darrell Whiteman, "Barns, Buildings, and Windmills: A Key to Change on the Illinois Prairie," *Journal of the Illinois Historical Society* 68 (3): 257–66.

29. Midwest Plan Service, *Grain Storage Building Plans* (Ames, IA: Agricultural Engineering Department, 1949), 10, 13; Folder 4, Box 7, Records of the Midwest Plan Service, Iowa State Special Collections, MS 48; Midwest Plan Service, "Grain Feed Handling" (Ames, IA: Midwest Plan Service, 1968), G-2, Folder 1, Box 1, Records of the Midwest Plan Service, MS-48, Iowa State Special Collections, Ames, IA.

30. Anderson, *Industrializing the Corn Belt*, 171–79; "Corn-Storage Systems," *Successful Farmer* (July 1962): 38–39, 74.

31. Wayne Kiefer, "An Agricultural Settlement Complex in Indiana," *Annals of the Association of American Geographers* 62 (September 1972): 501.

32. Nineteen of the 192 corncribs in Mclean County, IL, surveyed by anthropologists Kruckman and Whiteman had already met this fate by 1975. Kruckman and Whiteman, "Barns, Buildings, and Windmills," 266.

33. Arthur Anderson, *Swine Management, Including Feeding and Breeding* (Philadelphia: Lippincott, 1950), 3.

34. Mark Finlay, "Hogs, Antibiotics, and Industrial Environments of Post-war Agriculture," in *Industrializing Organisms: Introducing Evolutionary History*, ed. Susan Schrepfer and Philip Scranton (New York: Routledge, 2004), 239. For two-fifths, see Anderson, *Swine Management*, 8; Ladd and Haystead, *Agricultural Regions*, 189; Leonard Odde profile in Hiram Drache, *Creating Abundance: Visionary Entrepreneurs of Agriculture* (Danville, IL: Interstate Publishers, 2001), 258–59.

35. Anderson, *Swine Management*, 147.

36. Finlay, "Hogs, Antibiotics, and Industrial Environments," 240; Anderson, *Industrializing the Corn Belt*, 125.

37. Finlay, "Hogs, Antibiotics, and Industrial Environments," 249–50.

38. V. James Rhodes and Glenn Grimes, "The Changing Structure of the Hog Industry," in *Farm Structure*, 186.

39. Morton Buildings, "About Us," Morton Buildings, Inc., <www.mortonbuildings.com> (accessed June 20, 2011).

40. Chris Mayda, "Pig Pens, Hog Houses, and Manure Pits: A Century of Change in Hog Production," *Material Culture* 36 (Spring 2004): 25–27.

41. "Member Farms among Those on Tour Visit!" *Michigan Farm News* 47 (July 1, 1968), 10.

42. J. Ronald Miner, "Farm Animal–Waste Management," North Central Regional Publication 206, Special Report 67 (Ames: Iowa State Experiment Station, May 1971), 25–31, 33; Mayda, "Pig Pens, Hog Houses, and Manure Pits," 20–21; John Fraser Hart, *Changing Scale of American Agriculture* (Charlottesville: University of Virginia Press,

2003), 227–28.

43. Finlay, "Hogs, Antibiotics, and Industrial Environments of Postwar Agriculture," 254.

44. Kiefer, "Agricultural Settlement Complex," 505.

45. Finlay, "Hogs, Antibiotics, and Industrial Environments of Postwar Agriculture," 248–50.

46. Finlay, "Hogs, Antibiotics, and Industrial Environments of Postwar Agriculture," 185.

47. "Profile of Farming," in *Annual Yearbook of Agriculture* (Washington, DC: GPO, 1962), 74–75.

48. Kiefer, "An Agricultural Settlement Complex in Indiana," 490–91.

49. Haystead and Fite, *Agricultural Regions of the United States*, 143.

50. Deborah Fitzgerald, "Eating and Remembering," *Agricultural History* 79 (Fall 2005): 397.

51. Ralph Green and Homer Erickson, *Mint Farming*, Agriculture Information Bulletin 212 (Agricultural Research Service and Purdue University Agricultural Experiment Station, Washington, DC, 1960), 1–2, 7.

52. Green and Erickson, *Mint Farming*, 18–19; Leroy Barrett, "Mint in Michigan," *Michigan History* 68 (March 1984): 22.

53. Larita Killian, "Mint Farming in Lakeville," *Traces of Indiana and Midwestern History* 16 (January 2004): 46.

54. Barrett, "Mint in Michigan," 23; Killian, "Mint Farming," 46; Green and Erickson, *Mint Farming*, 3.

55. H.W. Fogle, L.C. Cochran, and H.L. Keil, *Growing Sour Cherries*, USDA Bulletin 451 (Washington, DC: GPO, 1974), 1–3; David Smith, Donald Ricks, and William Sherman, *The Michigan and U.S. Sweet Cherry Industry—Present and Future* (Michigan State University Agricultural Experiment Station, East Lansing, MI, 1973), 1–2, 6–7.

56. J.H. Levin and H.P. Gaston, *Grower Handling of Red Cherries*, Agricultural Experiment Station Circular 981 (Washington, DC: GPO, 1956), 4–6.

57. J.H. Levin and H.P. Gaston, *Fruit Handling with Fork Lift Trucks* (Michigan State College Agricultural Experiment Station, East Lansing, 1952), 12; Levin and Gaston, *Grower Handling of Red Cherries*, 7–8.

58. Levin and Gaston, *Grower Handling of Red Cherries*, 10–16.

59. Dennis Nodin Valdés, *Al Norte: Agricultural Workers in the Great Lakes Region, 1917–1970* (Austin: University of Texas Press, 1991), 37, 138–43.

60. Cindy Hahamovith, "'In America Life Is Given Away': Jamaican Farmworkers and the Making of Agricultural Immigration," in *The Countryside in the Age of the Modern State: Political Histories of Rural America*, ed. Catherine McNicol Stock and Robert Johnston (Ithaca, NY: Cornell University Press, 2001), 136–37.

61. Fogle, Cochran, and Keil, *Growing Sour Cherries*, 20–23; Norman Roberts, "Tree Shaker Saves Our Cherry Pies," in *Science for Better Living, Annual Yearbook of Agriculture, 1968* (Washington, DC: GPO, 1968), 84–87.

62. J.S. Bolen, B.F. Cargill, and J.H. Levin, *Mechanized Harvest Systems for Tart Cherries* (East Lansing: Michigan State University Agricultural Experiment Station, 1970), 4.

63. Valdés, *Al Norte*, 90–91.

64. Valdés, *Al Norte*, 137.

65. D. Jerome Tweton, "The Business of Agriculture," in *Minnesota in a Century of Change: The State and Its People since 1900*, ed. Clifford Clark Jr. (St. Paul: Minnesota His-

torical Society Press, 1989), 283.

66. Tom Dicke, "Red Gold of the Ozarks: The Rise and Decline of Tomato Canning, 1885–1955," *Agricultural History* 79 (Winter 2005): 18–21.

67. Deborah Fitzgerald, "Eating and Remembering," *Agricultural History* 79 (Fall 2005): 397; John Etchells, Ivan Jones, and Thomas Bell, "Advances in Cucumber Pickling," *USDA Annual Yearbook of Agriculture, 1951* (Washington: GPO, 1951), 230.

68. Jane Adams, *The Transformation of Rural Life: Southern Illinois, 1890–1990* (Chapel Hill: University of North Carolina Press, 1994), 76.

69. T.H. Short and W.L. Bauerle, "Greenhouse Production with Lower Fuel Costs," *Annual Yearbook of Agriculture, 1980* (Washington, DC: GPO, 1980), 25–26; Allan Stoner, *Commercial Production of Greenhouse Tomatoes*, Agriculture Handbook No. 382 (Washington, DC: GPO, 1970), 1.

70. Mark Friedberger, "The Transformation of the Rural Midwest, 1945–1985," *The Old Northwest* 16 (1992): 15.

71. Adams, *Transformation of Rural Life*, 170–75; H.P. Gaston and J.H. Levin, *On the Farm Refrigerated Cold Storage*, Agricultural Experiment Station Bulletin 389 (East Lansing: Michigan State College, 1954), 6–8.

72. Don Kinsey, "'Colorful as a Rose Garden': Something New and Exciting Is Happening to the Old Roadside Stand," *Michigan Farm News* 43 (November 1, 1965): 6.

73. Valdés, *Al Norte*, 1, 3.

74. Jim Norris, *North for the Harvest: Mexican Workers, Growers, and the Sugar Beet Industry* (St. Paul: Minnesota Historical Society Press, 2009), 98–99, 143, 167.

75. Norris, *North for the Harvest*, 97, 141, 161.

76. Norris, *North for the Harvest*, 31–32.

77. Norris, *North for the Harvest*, 24–25.

78. Norris, *North for the Harvest*, 97–111.

79. Norris, *North for the Harvest*, 104.

80. Norris, *North for the Harvest*, 143–44.

81. Valdés, *Al Norte*, 148–50; Norris, *North for the Harvest*, 107–11.

82. Susan Granger and Scott Kelly, *Historic Context Study of Minnesota Farms, 1820–1960*, Volume II (St. Paul: Gemini Research for Minnesota Department of Transportation and Federal Highway Administration, 2005), 6.270, 6.271. Some such changes were short-lived. By the late 1960s and 1970s, sugar beet processors increased production by extending contracts to new beet cultivators, who lacked any housing structures on their farm and preferred to rely on local laborers. By the 1970s, many growers' contracts no longer required that they provide housing to workers, leaving workers to fend for themselves in finding a place to live near the beet fields. Norris, *North for the Harvest*, 183, 188–89.

83. Trewartha, "Some Regional Characteristics of American Farmsteads," 186.

84. Granger and Kelly, *Historic Context Study of Minnesota Farms*, 6.366.

85. U.S. Bureau of the Census, *U.S. Census of Agriculture, 1950*. Volume II, General Report, Chapter VI: Livestock and Livestock Products (Washington, DC: GPO, 1952), 408, 446.

86. Tweton, "Business of Agriculture," 277; Hart, *Changing Scale of American Agriculture*, 169.

87. For more on these changes, see Katherine Jellison, *Entitled to Power: Farm Women and Technology, 1913–1963* (Chapel Hill: University of North Carolina Press, 1993), 156–60.

88. Robert Hjort and William Manion, *Minnesota's Chicken and Egg Industry* (St.

Paul: Minnesota Department of Food and Agriculture, 1955), 34.

89. William Boyd, "Making Meat: Science, Technology, and American Poultry Production," *Technology and Culture* 42 (October 2001): 639–40; R.E. Cook, H.L. Bumgardner, and W.F. Shaklee, "How Chicken on Sunday Became an Anyday Treat," *Yearbook of Agriculture 1975* (Washington, DC: GPO, 1975), 128–30.

90. Hart, *Changing Scale of American Agriculture*, 153.

91. Hart, *Changing Scale of American Agriculture*, 154.

92. Hart, *Changing Scale of American Agriculture*, 160–68.

93. Boyd, "Making Meat," 641–44.

94. Shane Hamilton, *Trucking Country: The Road to America's Wal-Mart Economy* (Princeton, NJ: Princeton University Press, 2008), 170–86; Susanne Freidberg, *Fresh: A Perishable History* (Cambridge, MA: Belknap Press of Harvard University Press, 2009), 224–25; Kendra Smith-Howard, "Perfecting Nature's Food: A Cultural and Environmental History of Milk in the United States, 1900–1970" (PhD diss., University of Wisconsin–Madison, 2007), 137–51, 179–95.

95. Harry Herman, *Improving Cattle by the Millions: NAAB and the Development and Worldwide Application of Artificial Insemination* (Columbia: University of Missouri, 1981), 7, 14–15, 37; Enos J. Perry, *The Artificial Insemination of Farm Animals* (New Brunswick, NJ: Rutgers University Press, 1945), 7; John William Pou, "A Study of Wisconsin Cooperative Artificial Insemination Associations" (Master's thesis, University of Wisconsin–Madison, 1947), 10–11; H.A. Herman, "Making Artificial Breeding Succeed," *Hoard's Dairyman* 95 (9) (May 10, 1950): 357; G.L. Cole, "Artificial Insemination," *Hoard's Dairyman* 18 (January 10, 1941): 18.

96. S.A. Witzel and E.E. Heizer, "Loose Housing or Stanchion Type Barns? Summary of a 10 Year Dairy Cattle Housing Experiment in Southern Wisconsin," Bulletin 503 (Madison: University of Wisconsin Experiment Station, 1953), 3, 17; H.J. Barre and L.L. Sammet, *Farm Structures* (New York: Wiley, 1950), 219–27; A.M. Goodman, "Remodeling Barns for Better Dairy Stables" (Ithaca, NY: Cornell Extension Bulletin 742, November 1951), 7.

97. Witzel and Heizer, "Loose Housing or Stanchion Type Barns?" 17.

98. Neubauer and Walker, *Farm Building Design*, 57–61; Barre and Sammet, *Farm Structures*, 222–25; Dairy Cattle Housing Subcommittee of the North Central Regional Farm Buildings Committee, "Dairy Cattle Housing in the North Central States," Bulletin 470 (Madison, WI: Agricultural Experiment Station, 1947), 47–50.

99. "Bulk Milk Handling Panel," 1956 Annual Meeting of Consolidated Badger Cooperative, CBC Papers, Mss 104, Box 3, Folder 10; United States Steel Corporation, *Bulk Handling of Milk with Stainless Steel* (Pittsburgh: United States Steel Corporation, 1955), 2–24, Hagley Museum and Library Trade Catalog Collection, Wilmington, DE; Noel Stocker, "Progress in Farm-to-Plant Bulk Milk Handling," Farm Cooperative Service Circular 8 (Washington, DC: USDA, November 1954), 4–5.

100. Hurt, "Ohio Agriculture since World War II," 56.

101. Charles Wood, *The Kansas Beef Industry* (Lawrence: Regents Press of Kansas, 1980), 285; Raymond Dietrich, "Structure and Structural Changes in the United States Cattle Feeding Industry," in *Farm Structure*, 177; Hamilton, *Trucking Country*, 139–40; Geoff Cunfer, *On the Great Plains: Agriculture and Environment* (College Station: Texas A&M University Press, 2005), 48, 53. For "feedbag of democracy," see Haystead and Fite, *Agricultural Regions of the United States*, 140.

102. Dietrich, "Structure and Structural Changes," 173; Wood, *Kansas Beef Industry*,

286; Robert Wuthnow, *Remaking the Heartland: Middle America since the 1950s* (Princeton, NJ: Princeton University Press, 2011), 172.

103. John Opie, *Ogallala: Water for a Dry Land* (2nd edition) (Lincoln: University of Nebraska Press, 2000), 136–45; Frank Bierbely, "Other Crops in the Wheat State," in *Rise of the Wheat State: A History of Kansas Agriculture, 1861–1986*, ed. George Ham and Robin Higham (Manhattan, KS: Sunflower University Press, 1987), 69; James Koelliker, "Water," in *Rise of the Wheat State*, 98; Tim Hiller and Larkin Powell, "Long-Term Agricultural Land-Use Trends in Nebraska, 1866–2007," *Great Plains Research* 19 (Fall 2009): 233.

104. Opie, *Ogallala*, 150–51; Hamilton, *Trucking Country*, 140–43; Dietrich, "Structure and Structural Changes," 177.

105. Hamilton, *Trucking Country*, 144; Wood, *Kansas Beef Industry*, 295; Anderson, *Industrializing the Corn Belt*, 120–21.

106. Wuthnow, *Remaking the Heartland*, 179–80, 186, 196–97.

107. Kenneth Krause, *Cattle Feeding, 1962–1989: Location and Feedlot Size*, Agricultural Economic Report Number 642 (Washington, DC: GPO, 1991), 6–7.

108. Hamilton, *Trucking Country*, 153–55; Opie, *Ogallala*, 151.

109. Dana Dalrymple, "Changes in Wheat Varieties and Yields in the United States, 1919–1984," *Agricultural History* 62 (Fall 1988): 21.

110. J.J. Bond and D.E. Umberger, *Technical and Economic Causes of Productivity Changes in U.S. Wheat Production, 1949–1976* (Washington, DC: GPO, 1979), 7.

111. Bond and Umberger, *Technical and Economic Causes*, 59–62.

112. Bond and Umberger, *Technical and Economic Causes*, 34–38; E.G. Heyne, "The Development of Wheat in Kansas," in *Rise of the Wheat State*, 47; Dalrymple, "Changes in Wheat Varieties," 28–29.

113. Nordin and Scott, *From Prairie Farmer to Entrepreneur*, 191–92.

114. Bond and Umberger, *Technical and Economic Causes*, 70–71, 22, 7.

115. Barbara Krupp Selyem, "The Legacy of Country Grain Elevators," *Kansas History* 23 (March 2000): 44–45; Bonnie Lynn-Sherow, "Beyond Winter Wheat: The USDA Extension Service and Kansas Wheat Production in the Twentieth Century," *Kansas History* 23 (March 2000): 111.

116. Richard Horwitz, *Hog Ties: Pigs, Manure, and Mortality in American Culture* (New York: St. Martin's Press, 1998), 68.

117. Don Blayney, "The Changing Landscape of U.S. Milk Production," Statistical Bulletin 978 (Washington, DC: USDA, 2002), 12–14.

THREE — **BEYOND THE RUST BELT**

The Neglected History of the Rural Midwest's
Industrialization after World War II

Wilson J. Warren

The Rust Belt paradigm is commonly used to explain manufacturing's erosion in the Northeast and Midwest after World War II. The rise and fall of America's manufacturing history is seen as an urban phenomenon, with emphasis on Pittsburgh's steel industry and Detroit's auto industry. Commentators invoke "Rust Belt" in a way that suggests that when manufacturing left urban areas, it disappeared from the country for good. In fact, especially from the vantage point of the late 1960s, the early postwar period saw considerable manufacturing growth. Between 1950 and 1969, total U.S. manufacturing employment increased from just over 13 million to about 19 million jobs.[1]

Obscured by this larger postwar trend is the significant shift in American manufacturing from urban to rural areas of the country, including in the Midwest.[2] From the end of World War II through the 1970s, manufacturing in rural parts of the United States grew rapidly. This was true especially between 1960 and 1970, when manufacturing grew by just 4 percent in urban areas but increased by 22 percent in rural areas. Even after the slowing of this rural manufacturing growth during the 1980s, more manufacturing jobs were located in nonmetropolitan than metropolitan areas of the United States at the end of the twentieth century.[3] This essay will survey the postwar industrial surge by tracing the rise of rural midwestern manufacturing during the prewar period, examining the factors that contributed to its postwar growth, highlighting its distinguishing characteristics, and finally, surveying four representative industrial sectors' evolution through the postwar period.

The rural Midwest's industrialization long predates the post–World War II era. Some historians have characterized the region's industrial emphases in the nineteenth and early twentieth centuries as bulk- or staple-oriented as compared to the specialty work in the East. Perhaps a more useful characterization is "agro-industrialization," whereby manufacturing of agricultural commodities went virtually hand in hand with the Midwest's development as the nation's breadbasket. While Chicago and other large midwestern cities have been seen as the major beneficiaries of this link between farm products and manufacturing, smaller cities and towns in more remote parts of the Midwest were also crucial in a similar respect starting during the nineteenth century.[4]

Agro-industrialization's impact is notable with the rapid development of flour milling, meatpacking, and farm-implement manufacturing in the nineteenth century. These three industries were among the 30 largest in the United States as measured by average number of wage earners by 1900, with significant proportions of workers in each located in the Midwest.[5] Flour milling accompanied the region's development as the nation's center of grain production in the nineteenth century. While Minneapolis became the nation's premier flour-milling center after 1880, considerable milling took place before and after its ascendancy in the region's smaller towns and villages. Between 1860 and 1890, for instance, flour milling was Iowa's most valuable manufacturing sector. Two-thirds of the state's counties had at least one mill, though soon after the Civil War the largest were concentrated in the larger cities along the Mississippi River. At the turn of the twentieth century, Chicago's factories dominated the nation's meat industry, but many significant packing plants had been established in rural midwestern counties. For instance, George A. Hormel opened a meatpacking operation in an old creamery in Austin, Minnesota, in 1891 that quickly became one of the largest independent packing facilities in the country. Several other large packing plants, not owned by the Big Four firms based primarily in Chicago, existed in small-town Iowa and Minnesota during this period. Of the 20 largest cities with significant farm-implement production in 1900, nine had populations between 20,000 and 40,000. Seven of these cities were in the Midwest: three in Illinois, two in Wisconsin, and one each in Ohio and Indiana. In 1901, the Hart-Parr Company, located in the even smaller north-central Iowa town of

Charles City, produced the first successful gasoline-powered farm tractor. By 1907, one-third of all the tractors in the world were produced in Charles City. The company employed nearly 2,000 workers during World War I.[6]

Although agro-industrialization involved a few especially important products, additional diversification occurred in the Midwest's industrial history before the post–World War II era. Railroad construction and repair shops and coal mining were particularly important from the late nineteenth through the mid-twentieth centuries in small towns throughout the rural Midwest. Indeed, several towns of less than 10,000 in the Midwest in the late nineteenth and early twentieth centuries can be classified as railroad towns because of the central importance of this industry in their economies. While manufacturing of rolling stock for the nation's railroads was typically carried out in larger cities of the East and Midwest, construction and repairs were diffused by necessity throughout the country. In Iowa in 1900, railroad construction and repairs shops employed the largest number of wage earners. In that year, there were 58 shops in the state, including two that employed between 500 and 1,000 workers and seven that employed between 250 and 500. Many of these workers belonged to a variety of unions.[7]

Bituminous coal mining accompanied the railroads' movement into the Midwest following the Civil War. The so-called captive mines owned by the railroads constituted a sizable part of the coal business. Ohio, Illinois, Indiana, Iowa, and Kansas all developed significant coal mining in the period between 1870 and 1930, with peak production reached during World War I. Beginning in the late nineteenth century through the mass union building of the New Deal era, the United Mine Workers of America organized thousands of rural midwestern miners. Many of the New Deal–era union organizers across multiple industries first gained union experience in the coal industry.[8]

Some of the region's manufacturing diversity involved other agricultural or extractive commodities also based heavily in rural areas. The furniture, paper, sugar beet, glass, Portland cement, and gypsum industries are notable in this regard. The white pine and hardwood forests of Michigan drew the attention of lumbermen and furniture makers during the mid-nineteenth century. The Grand River, located in the middle of this prime forest belt, allowed easy movement of logs from the forests to the mills located along the river to its mouth on Lake Michigan at Grand Haven. Grand Rapids exploded from a small town to a medium-sized city during the last half of the nineteenth century because of furniture making. By 1910, one-quarter of the manufacturing workers in "Furniture City," as Grand Rapids was known, were employed in the furniture industry.[9]

During the 1870s and 1880s, the paper industry expanded rapidly in several parts of the rural Midwest. In 1875, Middletown, Ohio, was the fourth-largest paper center in the country, producing 15 tons of paper per day. The Miami Valley of Ohio included 27 mills by the 1870s. The industry there had contracted somewhat by 1910 but still produced 900 tons per day. Wisconsin became an even larger center of paper production, while Illinois and the Kalamazoo River valley in southwestern Michigan also had sizable paper production. By World War I, the Kalamazoo River valley's paper industry employed about 6,500 workers—4,500 in Kalamazoo and the rest in surrounding smaller towns.[10]

At the end of the nineteenth century, the sugar beet industry emerged in response to growing American sugar consumption combined with a nationwide entrepreneurial effort to capture a greater percentage of this rapidly growing market away from the Caribbean sugar cane production areas. Michigan, particularly the Saginaw Valley, became the leading beet sugar producer in the Midwest. Between 1898 and 1913, 86 sugar-beet processing factories were built in Michigan, most of which were located in small towns. Sugar beet production also spread into southern Michigan, northwestern Ohio, northeastern Indiana, eastern Wisconsin, southeastern Minnesota, northern Iowa, and the Red River Valley of northwestern Minnesota and eastern North Dakota. The latter area became especially important in the 1920s. After World War I, throughout the Midwest, sugar beet farmers relied on hired labor, the so-called *betabeleros*—either Mexican nationals or Mexican Americans from the Rio Grande valley. Many betabeleros stayed in the Midwest, and by the 1920s and 1930s were moving to the larger cities of the region. Some became railroad workers in Kansas City and Topeka, packinghouse workers in Chicago, and autoworkers in Detroit.[11]

Glass making, after the discovery of new natural gas supplies, expanded significantly in Ohio during the 1880s and 1890s and then into Indiana by the turn of the twentieth century. Portland cement, made by a process of producing cement that began in England in the early nineteenth century, was first produced commercially in eastern Pennsylvania in 1875. Between 1900 and 1910, the industry expanded into the Midwest, particularly in Michigan, Ohio, and Kansas. Huron Portland Cement Company started construction on what would become the world's largest cement manufacturing plant near the small town of Alpena, Michigan, in 1907. The use of Portland cement in the building of new highways further expanded the industry in the Midwest in the 1920s. Very pure gypsum deposits were discovered near Fort Dodge, Iowa, in 1852, and the Fort Dodge Plaster Mill was constructed in 1872. Several other mills followed, producing a variety of building mortar, plaster, roofing, and floor materials after that time. Since the late nineteenth century, the Fort Dodge area has produced a sizable portion of the nation's gypsum supply.[12]

The Warren Featherbone Company was one of the more unusual but notable rural midwestern manufacturing companies based on another agricultural commodity. Established in 1883 in the small town of Three Oaks, Michigan, Warren Featherbone Company processed turkey quills into so-called featherbone, a malleable and durable stiffening material used in the manufacturing of women's undergarments, in a factory employing 300–400 people through the World War II era. Warren Featherbone was the largest industrial employer in Berrien County for much of this 60-year period; typically about three-quarters of its workers were women who came from not only Three Oaks but other towns in the county.[13]

Although not as significant as the agro-industrial or extractive-based manufacturing, some locations in the rural Midwest became production sites for machinery and transportation equipment, including auto and other transportation equipment, before World War II. The auto industry's decentralization push occurred largely after the war, but Ford established 19 "village industries" for automotive component production between 1918 and 1944 in small southern Michigan towns within about a 60-mile radius of Dearborn. Henry Ford anticipated some of the postwar thinking about rural communities. He believed that rural residents, especially surplus farm laborers, could help to decrease production costs. Especially during the 1930s, rural residents were drawn to work in these plants because "they promised well-paying regular jobs to unemployed or underemployed farmers, craftsmen, and other rural folk while allowing them to live and work in their native (or akin) communities." In this way, too, Ford's village industries anticipated much of the appeal of rural manufacturing work after World War II. The Ford plants in the small communities of Milford, Northfield, Waterford, Nankin Mills, Phoenix, Plymouth, Newburg, Cherry Hill, Willow Run, Flat Rock, Ypsilanti, Saline, Sharon Mills, Manchester, Milan, Brooklyn, Hayden Mills, and Dundee each employed between 17 and 1,500 workers and produced a wide variety of components for Ford.[14]

Rural midwestern manufacturing "boosterism," another feature of the post–World War II shift in manufacturing's location in the region, also has a long history. One of the more colorful episodes of this effort was the "palace" building period of the late nineteenth century. During the late 1880s and early 1890s, local business elites and other civic-minded boosters in the Midwest, centered especially in four cities in Iowa, raised money, generally by subscription, to build large and lavish exhibition halls to promote the agricultural, industrial, and commercial specialties of their areas. Sioux City's Corn Palaces (1887–1891) and Ottumwa's Coal Palaces (1890–1891) were situated in medium-sized cities, while Creston's Blue Grass Palace and Forest City's Flax Palace were in small, rural settings. Local entrepreneurs built these halls to celebrate and showcase their region's economic contributions, while hoping to spur further investment in their towns and counties. Myriad displays of local products were a consistent focus in each of these palaces, and the combination of local boosterism, regional development, and architectural grandeur may have influenced later and larger fairs held in the Midwest, such as the 1893 Columbian Exposition in Chicago, the 1898 Trans-Mississippi Exposition in Omaha, and the 1904 Louisiana Purchase Exhibition in St. Louis. At the very least, the "palace" building era strongly suggests that much of the rural Midwest was as eager to attract industry as the region's more urbanized areas.[15]

Both continuity and change characterized rural midwestern manufacturing after World War II. Manufacturing grew especially rapidly from the beginning of the war through the late 1950s throughout the United States. Wartime government contracts both aided existing companies' manufacturing and spurred new growth. Between 1939 and 1958, the East North Central region surpassed the Middle Atlantic region as the country's most significant manufacturing area. By 1958, 26.5 percent of the nation's industrial workers were located in the five states (Ohio, Michigan, Indiana, Illinois, and Wisconsin) that constituted this part of the Midwest. Another 6 percent of the nation's industrial workers in 1958 lived in the seven states (Minnesota, Iowa, Missouri, North Dakota, South Dakota, Nebraska, and Kansas) that made up the West North Central region, an increase of 93.4 percent in industrial employment in these states since 1939. During the early part of the postwar period, much of the absolute growth in manufacturing employment continued to occur in the Midwest's larger cities.[16]

However, the rate of industrialization in rural midwestern counties outpaced that of manufacturing in urban midwestern counties from the end of the war through the early 1970s.[17] Nationwide, post–World War II rural manufacturing employment peaked in 1974. For the purposes of the following analysis, *rural* is defined as a county that had no urban center with a population larger than 10,000. For instance, between 1947 and 1972, the number of industrial production workers grew by just 3.2 percent in the 12 midwestern states. During the same period, value added by manufacturing grew by 139.2 percent (adjusted for 1972 dollars). However, in the rural counties of the

Midwest, the number of industrial production workers grew by 29.8 percent and the value added by manufacturing grew by 208.2 percent in the same 25-year period. The relative contribution of industrial workers from rural midwestern counties to the region's total climbed from 9.5 percent in 1947 to 11.9 percent in 1972, while value added by manufacturing rose from 8.3 percent to 10.7 percent in the same period. The growth of manufacturing in midwestern rural counties is especially impressive given their relative population decline; between 1940 and 1970, the number of midwesterners living in counties with no town or city with a population greater than 10,000 declined by 9.4 percent. After the 1970s, manufacturing declined sharply in the Midwest overall. However, in the region's more rural states (specifically, Iowa, Kansas, Minnesota, Nebraska, North Dakota, and South Dakota, all located in the West North Central region), the number of manufacturing establishments, the number of establishments with 100 or more employees, and the total number of production workers all continued to climb between 1972 and 1997. In 1947, these six states contributed just 8.7 percent of the Midwest's industrial production workers. In 1972, this contribution rose to 12.4 percent. By 1997, the West North Central's contribution had jumped to 18.4 percent (see table 3.1).[18]

Although rural midwestern manufacturing increased rapidly in general after World War II, two of the leading prewar industrial employers—coal mining and railroad construction and repair—both were in severe decline. Coal mining throughout the nation, including the Midwest, had been on the decline since World War I. After World War II, coal sales to the electric utility industry only partially offset huge declines in retail and railroad sales. Between 1919 and 1958, the number of coal miners in Ohio, Illinois, Indiana, Iowa, and Kansas—the Midwest's top five coal-producing states—fell from 157,379 to 22,162. The industry had almost completely disappeared in Iowa and Kansas by the 1950s. Many of the smaller midwestern communities continued to maintain railroad construction and repair shops through the 1960s, but this type of work largely disappeared after railroads transitioned to diesel locomotives. The total number of railroad employees nationwide dropped from 1.7 million in 1928 to 800,000 by 1959.[19]

Multiple factors account for the shift in industrial production from urban to rural midwestern locations. In some industries, this shift occurred because of gradual, long-term developments. In many industries, however, the transition was a result of the new postwar business, government, and social climates. Chief among the various factors were lower labor costs, improved transportation access, increased government incentives, and access to new sources of eager workers. Probably the most important cause was the

TABLE 3.1 — Midwest Manufacturing, 1947–1997

State	Number of Manufacturing Establishments	Number of Establishments with 100+ Employees	Average Number of Production Workers
Illinois	1947: 15,988 1972: 18,638 1997: 17,953	1947: 2,087 1972: 2,465 1997: 1,955	1947: 954,415 1972: 901,200 1997: 629,423
Indiana	1947: 5,408 1972: 7,357 1997: 9,303	1947: 827 1972: 1,142 1997: 1,329	1947: 457,582 1972: 526,500 1997: 478,248
Iowa	1947: 2,965 1972: 3,388 1997: 3,749	1947: 241 1972: 393 1997: 486	1947: 112,490 1972: 157,000 1997: 175,933
Kansas	1947: 1,946 1972: 2,842 1997: 3,309	1947: 125 1972: 286 1997: 361	1947: 59,363 1972: 101,300 1997: 141,169
Michigan	1947: 9,892 1972: 14,463 1997: 16,045	1947: 1,188 1972: 1,464 1997: 1,610	1947: 821,721 1972: 767,900 1997: 630,390
Minnesota	1947: 4,567 1972: 5,699 1997: 8,091	1947: 324 1972: 589 1997: 853	1947: 145,153 1972: 196,100 1997: 260,158
Missouri	1947: 5,725 1972: 6,733 1997: 7,497	1947: 687 1972: 836 1997: 773	1947: 269,711 1972: 300,100 1997: 270,297
Nebraska	1947: 1,344 1972: 1,723 1997: 1,960	1947: 89 1972: 173 1997: 221	1947: 37,338 1972: 63,200 1997: 84,085
North Dakota	1947: 362 1972: 482 1997: 704	1947: 7 1972: 25 1997: 49	1947: 3,823 1972: 7,100 1997: 16,364

Table continued

State	Number of Manufacturing Establishments	Number of Establishments with 100+ Employees	Average Number of Production Workers
Ohio	1947: 12,303	1947: 1,946	1947: 988,446
	1972: 16,369	1972: 2,271	1972: 940,300
	1997: 17,974	1997: 2,084	1997: 730,170
South Dakota	1947: 494	1947: 11	1947: 8,062
	1972: 607	1972: 39	1972: 12,900
	1997: 888	1997: 95	1997: 33,230
Wisconsin	1947: 6,979	1947: 735	1947: 343,008
	1972: 7,849	1972: 988	1972: 360,800
	1997: 9,936	1997: 1,251	1997: 416,254
Totals	1947: 67,973	1947: 8,267	1947: 4,201,112
	1972: 86,177	1972: 10,671	1972: 4,334,400
	1997: 97,409	1997: 11,067	1997: 3,865,721

Note: The Census of Manufactures figures do not include wage earners involved in either coal mining or railroad construction or repairs.
Sources: U.S. Bureau of the Census, *Census of Manufactures, 1947*, vol. III: *Statistics by States* (Washington, DC: GPO, 1950); U.S. Bureau of the Census, *1972 Census of Manufactures*, vol. III: *Area Statistics* (Washington, DC: GPO, 1976); and U.S. Census Bureau, *1997 Economic Census* <http://www.census.gov/epcd/ec97sic/index.html>.

business sector's attempt to decrease its labor costs. Union avoidance was one, and often the major, consideration in the urban-to-rural shift in manufacturing production. Because Section 14(b) of the Labor-Management Relations (Taft-Hartley) Act of 1947 allowed it, some midwestern states passed so-called right-to-work laws, under which no worker could be forced to join unions or pay union dues as a condition of employment. Five of the seven states in the West North Central region—Iowa, North Dakota, South Dakota, Nebraska, and Kansas—passed right-to-work laws in the 1940s and 1950s. Indiana also passed a right-to-work law in 1957 but then repealed it in 1965. The auto industry, for instance, shifted a considerable amount of production away from Detroit in the immediate post–World War II period. In the early 1950s, Ford moved 30,000 jobs away from its River Rouge plant. Other Detroit area plants experienced similar if less dramatic job losses. Much of this production shifted to smaller cities in the Midwest, South, and West. Auto components production became even more scattered. Among the three major U.S. auto makers, General Motors had the most dispersed array of locations for components suppliers by the late twentieth century, including small cities such as Danville, Illinois; Three Rivers, Michigan; and Vandalia, Ohio. Michigan, Indiana, and Ohio were the main states supplying auto components. In Ohio, 60 of the state's 88 counties in 1986 provided employment in motor vehicle parts production, including several rural counties such as Huron, Union, and Williams, each of which employed between 1,000 and 1,999 workers. Much to the surprise of business leaders, however, many workers in rural locations pursued unionization, even as Indiana and Michigan passed right-to-work laws in 2012.[20]

Relocation of foreign companies' manufacturing to the rural Midwest contributed to some of this growth. It involved essentially similar factors as those weighed by domestic companies when they relocated, particularly considerations about wider market access and lower labor costs. When the Japanese auto companies, for instance, started to build production facilities in the Midwest in 1980, they generally chose small cities such as Marysville, Ohio. In addition to union avoidance, these firms believed that rural workers would have lower rates of absenteeism and a work ethic more amenable to Japanese production methods and expectations. Likewise, Japanese auto components suppliers were established in rural locations of the region. By the early 1990s, Japanese auto manufacturers had created an estimated 110,000 jobs. One study conducted in the mid-1970s found a total of 32 factors involved in foreign companies' location decisions. Overall, the five most important decisions involved availability of transportation services, labor attitudes, ample space for future expansion, nearness to markets within the United States, and availability of suitable plant sites.[21]

Location of industrial production in more isolated parts of the country after World War II depended significantly on improvements in transportation, especially the growth of improved highways and the expansion of the trucking industry. Multiple studies of rural industrial growth in the 1960s pointed to the development of the interstate highway system as a key factor in the shift of manufacturing from metropolitan to rural and other non-metropolitan locations. Between 1945 and 1968, for instance, intercity freight moved by trucks grew from 67 billions of ton-miles to 415 billions of ton-miles. During the same period, railroads continued to move more freight than trucks, but the growth rate for railroads was flat: 691 billions of ton-miles in 1945 compared to 755 billions of ton-miles in 1968. Studies made of industrial location decisions following World War II emphasized multiple advantages accruing to sites along the new highways, especially the new interstate highways, including access to wider markets, access to new satellite and ancillary plants, and cost savings due to dispersion.[22]

After World War II, state and local government inducements to industry superseded the local business elite "boosterism" that had dominated much of the prewar industrial recruitment strategies. Five major types of inducement programs began, primarily during the 1950s and 1960s: state industrial finance authorities, local industrial bond financing, tax concessions, and statewide and local development credit corporations. The first three were publicly financed. Statewide development credit corporations were state chartered but privately financed. A 1963 study found that among the 12 midwestern states, the most common state and local inducements were local industrial bond financing and statewide and local development credit corporations. All but Indiana and South Dakota had local industrial bond financing, and only Illinois, North Dakota, and Nebraska did not have statewide development credit corporations. Several hundred local development credit corporations existed in the 12 midwestern states. The 1963 study found that these types of financial inducements were "certainly a secondary location factor in the choice of region and [were] probably also a secondary factor in the choice of location within a region." During the postwar period, state development commissions also provided considerable consulting and educational support for communities hoping to attract industry. Nevertheless, particularly since the 1970s, state and local government intervention on behalf of companies has proved to be no guarantee that businesses will remain located in rural midwestern locations. A revealing case of this occurred in the 1990s with Seaboard Corporation in Albert Lea, Minnesota. After taking over the Farmstead meatpacking plant there and accepting $34 million to upgrade the sewage-treatment system at the plant, Seaboard decided that further improvements would prove too costly and pulled out of town. The State of Oklahoma then paid approximately $90 million for Seaboard's relocation to the small town of Guymon.[23]

The federal government actively promoted rural development programs after World War II. Following publication in 1955 of a U.S. Department of Agriculture report, *Development of Agriculture's Human Resources*, Rural Development Committees were organized to help local communities establish new training programs. Started in 50 communities that year, within five years they had been established in 262 counties in 30 states and Puerto Rico. The Kennedy administration set up the Office of Rural Area Development in the U.S. Department of Agriculture, which then became the Rural Community Development Service. The Johnson administration continued rural development programs with the Economic Opportunity Act of 1964. Between 1961 and 1972, annual funding for rural development projects increased from $575 million to $2.9 billion. Since the Rural Development Act of 1972 passed, the U.S. Department of Agriculture has continued to be the most important federal agent for rural development. Currently, about 10 percent of the department's budget is aimed at rural development.[24]

Postwar manufacturing growth in the Midwest occurred in a context of rapid changes in American agriculture. Agribusiness rapidly replaced more traditional family farming. Technology increasingly replaced human labor on the farm, and farmers looked for other employment on either a full- or part-time basis. Typically, such farm operators or residents sought employment in manufacturing. During the early post–World War II period, widespread acquisition of automobiles and construction of more and better roads enhanced rural residents' ability to drive not only to nearby factories but to industrial employment often quite far away. As early as 1950, approximately one-quarter of the John Morrell and Company meatpacking plant's workforce in Ottumwa, Iowa, came from rural areas surrounding this medium-sized city. Some workers drove as far as 50 miles to work at the plant. By 1982, one-quarter of the farm operators in eastern Iowa worked primarily off-farm, and the rates for farm operators or residents in the eastern part of the Midwest were higher. Another study found that 44 percent of farm families in Iowa had at least one family member working full-time in off-farm employment during the 1980s.[25]

In addition to enticing farmers to work in industry, rural midwestern manufacturing contributed to other ongoing and significant demographic changes. During the mid-nineteenth to mid-twentieth century period, the Great Migration of blacks from the South to the North helped to diversify the rural Midwest's population. Although larger cities attracted most blacks, some also relocated to small- and medium-sized industrial cities like Muncie, Indiana. From the 1890s through World War II, African Americans found steady employment in the city's glass factories. Coal mining and railroad employment also drew blacks from the South to the North. Many settled in small railroad and coal-mining towns in rural areas such as Manly, Iowa, where they worked for the Rock Island Railroad and for Muchakinock and Buxton, Iowa, sites of significant coal-mining operations run by Consolidated Coal Company.[26]

Following World War I, the number of Mexican Americans and Mexican nationals working as agricultural laborers in the Midwest increased rapidly. Many had moved into industrial work in the larger cities of the region before World War II, yet until the late twentieth century, relatively few Mexicans and other Latinos had found industrial employment in the rural Midwest. Especially during the last two decades of the twentieth century, and particularly during the 1990s, Latino immigrants rapidly assumed prominence in several rural midwestern industries, particularly in the meatpacking and food-processing industries. Between 1990 and 2000, the nonmetropolitan Midwest Latino population increased by almost 113 percent, which outpaced Latino growth in all other parts of the United States during this decade with the exception of the non-metropolitan Southeast (232%) and metropolitan West (140%). The economic, cultural, and political impact of this Latino influx of many small communities in the rural Midwest has been enormous. Arguably, the pace of social and cultural change in the rural Midwest associated with particular industries with large Latino workforces has been greater than at any other time in the region's history.[27]

As rural midwestern manufacturing increased between the end of World War II and the mid-1970s, rural and urban areas' manufacturing emphases started to converge. Industrial production in the rural Midwest became more diverse than it had been through the early twentieth century, and these emphases paralleled those of the urban Midwest by the 1960s and 1970s. In 1947, among the 12 midwestern states, the top three industrial production groups in terms of number of large firms (i.e., those with 100 or more employees) were the non-electrical machinery, food products, and fabricated metal industries. These three groups constituted 38.3 percent of the large firms, and at least two of these three were among the top three groups in each of the midwestern states except Kansas, Missouri, and North Dakota. In the same year, in the rural counties of the 12 states, the top three industrial groups as measured by number of large firms (100 or more employees) included two of the three industrial categories that typified the states as a whole: food products (13.2% of large firms) and fabricated metal (10.6%), which ranked first and second respectively. The third-largest industrial group in the rural counties was leather products, especially shoemaking (9.6%), which was particularly prominent in the rural manufacturing economies of Missouri and Illinois.[28]

Twenty-five years later, these trends had converged. In 1972, the top three industrial groups in the midwestern states as a whole as well as the rural counties of these states were the same. Although food products was the top industry in the rural counties compared to non-electrical machinery in the states as a whole, these two industries plus fabricated metals constituted the top three in each as measured by number of large firms (100 or more employees). The percentage of such firms represented by these three industrial groups was a bit higher in the states as a whole, however: 38.5 percent compared to 32.9 percent in the rural parts of the midwestern states' counties. Among the industrial groupings below the top three, changes between 1947 and 1972 in the rural counties also suggested greater convergence with statewide trends. For instance, firms with 100 or more employees in the transportation equipment category increased from 5.6 to 8.6 percent of comparably sized firms in the rural counties. In fact, a greater percentage of auto, truck, and other vehicle assembly plants were located in the rural counties than the states as a whole (5.9%) in 1972. Likewise, the relative number of factories producing electrical machinery in the rural counties had also increased from 5.1 to 6.6 percent in this period. Both of these categories' shifts paralleled statewide trends. At the same time, the number of large-sized firms that produced leather products as well as stone, clay, and glass products shrank in the rural counties between 1947 and 1972, suggesting a decline in some of the traditional agro-industrial and extractive industries that had been significant in this part of the Midwest dating back to the nineteenth century. One exception to this trend was in the lumber and wood products category. The relative number of large-sized factories in this category increased in the rural counties from 4.9 to 6.6 percent between 1947 and 1972.[29]

Manufacturing's growth and diversification was evident in Iowa in the 1950s and 1960s. The Iowa Development Commission's 1955 report noted that 3,376 manufacturing plants existed in the state, with nearly a thousand of them established since 1945. Nearly two-thirds (2,023 to be exact) were located in towns of less than 10,000. But only three of the 54 largest manufacturing plants were located in towns of 10,000 or less: tractor manufacturer Oliver Corporation in Charles City employed 1,800; Amana Refrigeration, manufacturer of home freezers, in Amana employed 1,150; and Thomas D. Murphy Company, a calendar-printing firm, in Red Oak employed about 400. Thirteen years later, the number of companies in Iowa with more than 1,000 workers had grown from 30 to 38, though relatively few of the largest firms were located in small towns. However, 11 of the 31 employers with 500 to 1,000 workers were found in many smaller towns; these firms included traditional agro-industrial companies as well as companies making television components, construction equipment, windows and doors, pharmaceuticals, plastics, and batteries.[30]

After the 1970s, American manufacturing declined dramatically. Nationwide, manufacturing's erosion was especially significant between 1978 and 1982, when a total of 3.5 to 4 million industrial jobs disappeared, and between 2001 and 2004, when another 3 million industrial jobs vanished. In 2001–2004, many of these manufacturing jobs left the country.[31] Not surprisingly, the last quarter of the twentieth century, specifically 1972 to 1997, saw manufacturing employment decline in the Midwest as a whole. In 1947, the 12 midwestern states had a total of 4,201,112 manufacturing workers in 67,973 factories. In 1972, 4,334,400 workers were employed in 86,177 factories. By 1997, 97,409 factories employed 3,865,721 workers, a decline of 10.8 percent in the number of production workers since 1972. The midwestern states with the greatest number of industrial workers, located primarily in larger metropolitan centers in the East North Central region, like Illinois, Indiana, Michigan, Missouri, and Ohio, all lost manufacturing employment between 1972 and 1997.[32] But the more rural states, primarily in the West North Central region, specifically, Iowa, Kansas, Minnesota, Nebraska, North Dakota, South Dakota, and Wisconsin, all continued to add manufacturing jobs during this period, with states like North Dakota and South Dakota adding employment at a particularly striking rate (see table 3.1). As measured by percentage of paid employees, the trend in industrial employment in these more rural midwestern states seems to suggest a continuation of the earlier post–World War II trend toward greater emphasis on machinery-related manufacturing and away from the older agro-industrial and extractive-based manufacturing. The top three industrial categories, as measured by total number of employees, were the same as in 1972, but non-electrical machinery became larger than food products (15.6 versus 14.5% of all employees), and fabricated metal industries were third with 9.1 percent of all employees. These three industries employed 39.2 percent of all manufacturing employees.[33]

Even in the West North Central region of the Midwest, where industrial employment steadily increased after World War II, manufacturing development has proved to be a mixed blessing. When industry replaced agriculture as the leading employer among rural residents by the 1980s across the country, standards of living generally improved. Yet employment growth and economic and demographic diversification have sparked cultural and environmental concerns, particularly in areas such as immigration and water quality. Especially since the 1980s, when industry increasingly fled the United States for foreign countries, rural deindustrialization has created problems not unlike those created by deindustrialization more broadly across the United States.[34]

The history of specific rural midwestern industries provides another perspective on the evolution and impacts of industrialization and deindustrialization. The shoemaking, meatpacking, paper products, and metal fabrication industries illustrate the general trends previously noted, including the trajectories of agro-industrial sectors before and after World War II and the emergence of industries outside this sector.

Manufacturing in some of the agro-industrial sectors had already started to shift from urban to rural midwestern locations before World War II. Shoemaking decentralized considerably from the late nineteenth century through the early post–World War II period throughout the United States, and the evolution of Illinois and Missouri's shoemaking production is illustrative. As Edgar Hoover notes in his study of location theory and the shoe and leather industry, by 1935 "[t]he shoe industry as a whole is not preponderantly an urban one, for a good half of the wage earners are employed in places of less than 20,000 inhabitants." Shoe companies' drive to lower labor costs as well as offers of tax abatements and other inducements to small towns encouraged the shift from urban to rural locations. Before the turn of the twentieth century, St. Louis dominated shoemaking employment in Missouri. However, by 1929, the number of shoemaking factories in Missouri outside St. Louis—in small cities such as Kirksville, Brookfield, Moberly, Mexico, Higginsville, Boonville, Versailles, De Soto, Bland, and Owensville—outnumbered those in St. Louis 37 to 34. St. Louis's shoe production tended to focus on higher quality women's fashions while the state's more rural shoe factories produced cheaper men's and boys' styles. The large St. Louis shoe companies, especially International Shoe Company and Brown Shoe Company, continued to move production to smaller, rural cities from the 1930s through the 1950s. Local chambers of commerce competed aggressively for the shoe companies to relocate their plants. The companies did so with the expectation that workers would not seek union affiliation. They were often wrong about this. For instance, in Moberly, Missouri, many shoe workers had previously been union members in the railroad and coal industries, and they organized a Boot and Shoe Workers (AFL) local. Workers in Salem, Illinois, came largely from the nearby town of Odin, which had militant mining union traditions. International Shoe Company established a plant in an old garment factory in the small town of Anna, Illinois, in 1931 that remained in business, under the Florsheim Company name, until 1992. When it closed as one of the few remaining shoe factories left in the United States, it put about three hundred employees out of work.[35]

Meatpacking was another traditional agro-industry in which significant production occurred in the rural Midwest from an early point. Following the Civil War through the early twentieth century, the industry shifted from locations along the Ohio, Mississippi, and other major rivers in the Midwest to terminal market, or stockyard, centers located at major railroad junctions in the larger midwestern cities, particularly Chicago, Kansas City, and Omaha. But beginning in the late nineteenth century, independent companies as well as the Big Four firms—Armour, Swift, Wilson, and Cudahy, which had dominated the terminal stockyard centers—established plants in locations that allowed them more direct access to animals, and particularly hog supplies. Several small- and medium-sized cities in Iowa, Minnesota, South Dakota, Kansas, and Wisconsin became sites of significant pork production during the late nineteenth and early twentieth centuries. Cedar Rapids and Ottumwa, Iowa, became important interior packing locations in the 1870s; Topeka, Kansas, became significant in the 1880s; Waterloo, Iowa, was briefly important in the 1870s but then developed into a consistently significant site after 1891, when Austin, Minnesota, also emerged; and Mason City, Iowa, was a major site beginning in 1899. Between 1900 and the 1930s, another half dozen interior locations emerged as significant meatpacking sites: Albert Lea, Minnesota; Sioux Falls, South Dakota; Des Moines, Fort Dodge, and Dubuque, Iowa; and Madison, Wisconsin. The independent and Big Four-owned plants in these cities started as pork-packing facilities, but most also added beef and sheep production during the early to mid-twentieth century.[36]

Union building in most of these meatpacking communities commenced successfully during the New Deal era; between the 1930s and 1950s nearly all of the largest rural locations became important labor union strongholds, particularly for the United Packinghouse Workers of America (CIO) and, to a lesser degree, the Amalgamated Meat Cutters and Butcher Workmen (AFL). With better wages and improved standards of living, which benefited workers in industries other than meatpacking as well, these communities grew and prospered. However, after the emergence of the technologically innovative production and marketing strategies of Iowa Beef Packers (later, Iowa Beef Processors, then IBP, and finally Tyson) as well as ConAgra (Swift) and Excel (Cargill), the older independents and the remnants of the older Big Four firms faced competition that resulted in the closing of many of the older rural meatpacking plants. Between the early 1960s and the beginning of the twenty-first century, the beef- and pork-packing industry shifted to even smaller and more isolated midwestern locations in the West North Central region. For instance, IBP's Finney County, Kansas, plant was built outside Holcomb, a town of just over two thousand people, in 2000. By that date, the Midwest's largest cattle-slaughtering plants were located in counties with average populations of just over thirty thousand. Meatpacking's transformation contributed significantly to rural industrial growth in the Midwest's western half.[37]

The newer meatpacking firms have been much more aggressive than their predecessors in opposing workers' efforts to join labor unions. Although some union building has occurred, particularly with the United Food and Commercial Workers (UFCW), which in 1979 replaced the new Amalgamated Meat Cutters and Butcher Workmen union that had formed in 1968 out of the earlier CIO and AFL unions, the UFCW was unable to stave off huge wage and benefits cuts in the industry during the 1980s. IBP and the newer meatpacking firms used widespread recruitment of Mexican and other Latino workers to cut labor costs as well. Massive influxes of these workers into the rural midwestern meatpacking communities created a variety of social concerns during and after the 1980s and 1990s. Educational and social service demands have put stress on local communities in which packing plants are located, partly because the latest phase of the industry's development has often been associated with declining populations and rising poverty rates in many counties. The most recent phase of the industry's history has also created severe environmental problems, particularly in terms of water pollution.[38]

The paper industry in the Kalamazoo River valley of southwestern Michigan illustrates both the economic benefits of pre–World War II industrialization as well as the tragic effects of late-twentieth-century deindustrialization. The paper industry has caused even more environmental damage than meatpacking. Kalamazoo Paper Company established the first mill in the area in 1867. By 1890, there were four paper mills along the Kalamazoo River in both Kalamazoo and Allegan Counties. The industry expanded rapidly through World War I. In 1910, there were 23 mills with a total of 26 paper machines, which then jumped to 49 machines by 1917. The area's mills were well-known nationwide for high-quality rag, book, and stationery paper products as well as specialty items like playing cards. The industry became the dominant industrial employer in the two counties, and unionization helped to boost wages considerably during and immediately after World War I in Kalamazoo County and then in Allegan County during World War II.[39]

Allegan County, which was the rural half of the pair of paper-producing counties, had two small towns, Otsego and Plainwell, where mills had been established in the late nineteenth century. All were started by former employees of the Kalamazoo paper mills. The owners used the Kalamazoo River as both a power source and a convenient waste disposal system. The Bardeen Paper Company in Otsego and Michigan Paper Company in Plainwell both went into operation in 1887. The third major mill in Allegan County, owned by MacSimBar Paper Company in Otsego, opened in 1906. By the turn of the twentieth century, the paper industry was the main manufacturing employer in both communities. Otsego's paper industry grew to seven mills by 1906, which included manufacturing of coated paper, tissue, and waxed paper. The three largest mills in the two towns following World War II—United Biscuit Company (which acquired MacSimBar in 1944), Menasha Wooden Ware Company (which purchased the old Bardeen mill that had first been acquired by Allied in 1922, followed by Otsego Falls in 1935, and then Menasha in 1939), and Michigan Paper Company—produced over 10 percent of the state's paper products. The two Otsego mills had primarily focused on production of paperboard, mostly from straw, before the 1940s. During these same years, the Plainwell mill produced high-quality paper and newsprint.[40]

Through the mid-twentieth century, each of the three major Allegan County mills employed 200 to 400 production workers, a significant proportion of the two communities' populations; in 1940, the total population of Allegan County was 41,839. The mills were run in paternalistic fashion under local ownership, with both the detriments and the benefits that typically accompanied this style of management. Workers at MacSimBar routinely worked 11- to 13-hour days in the 1920s. At the same time, the mill generated enough electricity to provide power for the cities of Allegan, Otsego, and Plainwell. In 1944, when the Chicago-based United Biscuit Company acquired MacSimBar, employees voted to join the AFL's International Brotherhood of Firemen and Oilers.[41]

After World War II all three mills continued operations, but each became part of larger national corporations. Menasha operated the Otsego mill from 1939 to 2005. Hoerner Waldorf Corporation acquired the United Biscuit Company's Otsego mill in 1960, and then Mead Corporation purchased it in 1968. Finally, Rock-Tenn Corporation bought it in 1988. Michigan Paper Company was purchased by Hamilton Paper Company in 1956, which then became part of Weyerhaeuser Company in 1961 before Simpson Plainwell Corporation bought the plant. The new companies tended to invest in new production technologies, which increased the mills' efficiency, but these investments usually decreased the number of production workers needed for operations. Still, through the 1970s, overall industrial employment increased and diversified in Allegan County. Between 1947 and 1972, the number of industrial employers increased from 64 to 137. The number of large-scale employers (with more than one hundred workers) more than doubled from nine to twenty.[42]

During the post–World War II era, as fewer residents of both Allegan and Kalamazoo Counties found paper industry employment, they also became increasingly aware of the paper industry's hazardous effects on the environment, especially the water quality of the Kalamazoo River. This fact earned the area national notoriety when a photo of a massive fish-kill in the Kalamazoo River caused by the paper industry was featured on the cover of *Life* on October 5, 1953. Even before the outcry stemming from this negative publicity, the Michigan Water Resources Commission sponsored public meetings in Kalamazoo to discuss the river's extensive pollution. Burnett J. Abbott, an industry representative on the commission, said: "The people around here, if the paper mills were not here, would not be employed. The city would not be the fine city it is." After the *Life* article's publication, at a Michigan Sewage and Industrial Waste Association meeting in June 1955, R.J. Seuss of Menasha in Otsego explained that when the company transitioned after World War II from using straw to more hardwood pulp for its paperboard production, it significantly increased the amount of waste that it disposed in the river. But Seuss claimed the company was starting to recycle its waste products into materials that could be used for road-building materials. Nevertheless, by the early 1960s, a 30-mile stretch of the Kalamazoo River centered on Kalamazoo was almost completely dead. Due no doubt in large part to public pressure, the various Allegan and Kalamazoo County paper companies increasingly invested in waste treatment facilities. United Biscuit Company installed a new treatment system at Otsego during the 1960s. The Kalamazoo Water Reclamation Plant opened in 1986 at a cost of $122 million.[43]

While the river appeared to be much healthier due to these efforts, a new problem emerged when massive amounts of polychlorinated biphenyls (PCBs), considered a potentially dangerous human carcinogen, were discovered in the river and around the various paper mills. PCBs were initially produced in 1929 as chemical stabilizers used in many industrial processes, including paper making. Until it was banned in 1976, companies, including those in Allegan and Kalamazoo Counties that made paper, routinely dumped them into rivers. An 80-mile-long stretch of the Kalamazoo River was declared a Superfund site by the Environmental Protection Agency in 1990. Remediation efforts have been ongoing since that date, with considerable contention surrounding the best way to clean up the estimated 120,000 pounds of PCBs that are primarily found behind six dams in the river. In the meantime, the paper industry has almost completely disappeared in the two counties. In Allegan County, the Plainwell mill closed in 2000, and Rock-Tenn Corporation closed its Otsego mill in 2004. The Menasha plant closed in Otsego in 2005, putting two hundred employees out of work, before state financial incentives enticed USG Corporation to reopen it in 2006. The plant, which now makes paper-backing for gypsum wallboard, employs only about 110 workers. Nationwide, between 2000 and 2006, 95 paper mills closed and 123,000 workers lost their jobs.[44]

Metal fabrication industries were among the largest and fastest-growing manufacturing employers in the rural Midwest after World War II. They were an important contributor to the region's industrial diversification. Behlen Manufacturing Company, based in Columbus, Nebraska, provides an important illustration. In 1936, Walter Behlen and his brothers began making spring-action husking hooks in the family garage in this town of nearly 7,000 in Platte County, about 80 miles west of Omaha. Behlen then grew rapidly starting in 1944 when it moved its production of rubber rollers for corn pickers to the former Columbus Brick Works. Forty-four people worked for the company that year. The following year, the Behlen brothers developed a corn dryer system that then blossomed into the core of their manufacturing business for the next two decades: grain bins and dryers. These innovations contributed significantly to the postwar mechanization and more technologically advanced production and storage systems that transformed family farming into agribusiness. Although Behlen Manufacturing Company also made a variety of custom and standard metal buildings for both farm and nonfarm uses, by the 1960s their grain bins and dryers along with augers, elevator legs, heat blowers, and perforated bin floors were the heart of their business. Immediately after the war, Behlen moved just northeast of Columbus to a new plant built on the planned but never developed site for a wartime aluminum extrusion facility. By the end of the 1950s, the plant reached a peak of nearly 1,000 employees. Columbus likewise grew steadily during this period and reached a population of 12,476 by 1960 and 15,471 ten years later. Between 1947 and 1972, the number of industrial employers in Platte County jumped from 14 to 47.[45]

During the 1960s, Behlen Manufacturing Company's workers remained nonunion despite efforts by some of their employees to promote unionization. In both 1962 and 1965, the Sheet Metal Workers Union lost National Labor Relations Board certification elections. During the same decade, Behlen further diversified its production to include a variety of building systems, power steering units for farm vehicles, and hydraulic presses. As the founding family members neared retirement age, they decided in 1969 to allow Wickes Corporation to buy them out. As it turned out, Wickes, primarily a lumber company for most of its history, wanted to use Behlen's assets to expand its home and furniture construction and sales goals. Little new investment was put into Behlen's operations through the early 1980s. In 1975 the Sheet Metal Workers Union finally won an NLRB certification election at the Behlen plant. Then, in 1982, Wickes filed for bankruptcy protection after its expansion plans ran afoul during the recession years. A small cadre of Behlen employees, led by Tony Raimondo, convinced workers to decertify their union with promises of better local management and purchased the company back from Wickes. According to the new Behlen leadership, a completely new decentralized system of time management and profit sharing was implemented, which has allowed the company to rebound and prosper. From the 1980s to the present, Behlen Manufacturing Company reoriented its manufacturing away from grain storage systems to livestock equipment, due in part to federal government payment-in-kind programs that idled acres in the early 1980s and consequently limited the storage market. The company also continues to make custom metal buildings and grain storage systems, the latter especially for international customers.[46]

Rural deindustrialization is now a popular topic among academics and journalists. Midwestern rural communities' decline is linked to the erosion of manufacturing in much the same way that the Rust Belt paradigm was invoked in the 1980s to explain urban problems. Yet in some of the contemporary studies of the rural Midwest, industry is no longer seen as the central determinant of economic growth and development for rural communities. For instance, one study of rural Kansas communities' survival strategies mentions manufacturing but places just as much emphasis on economic diversity through a mix of emphases that include K–12 and higher education, telecommunications, medical and health care facilities, fine arts, tourism, recreation, alternative energies, and more specialized natural and organic agriculture.[47] Assuming small midwestern communities do survive through strategies of economic diversity, it is likely that manufacturing will still remain part of the economic base necessary for towns to prosper.

The current debate about the growth of the ethanol industry underscores the continued importance of agro-industrial manufacturing in the rural Midwest. In 1980, relatively little ethanol was produced in the United States. Beginning in the 1990s, advocates touted ethanol production for its potential rural-job-creation benefits. Production gradually increased and has soared since 2002. The number of ethanol plants in the United States increased from 54 in 2000 to 171 in 2008, with the majority located in the Midwest. In October 2007, eight midwestern states, especially Iowa and Nebraska, produced 78.4 percent of the nation's ethanol. As researchers have noted, however, federal energy, environmental, and tax policies sparked much of the industry's growth. High tariffs also protected the nation's ethanol industry from foreign competition, particularly Brazilian ethanol. The industry requires low corn prices and considerable supplies of cheap water to remain competitive against other types of fuel. Because corn and water are the main inputs, ethanol plants are located primarily in rural parts of the Midwest close to ready supplies of both. A typical 100-million-gallons-per-year ethanol plant employs about 40 workers, a rather small figure but nevertheless a total seen as desirable in many rural areas, particularly in the context of declining manufacturing opportunities. Yet it is unclear just how viable the ethanol industry is over the long term, given its dependence on the current volatile mix of federal policies and incentives as well as fluctuation in global petroleum demand and production.[48]

Ethanol and other biofuel industries are one among several types of manufacturing that illustrate the enduring importance of midwestern agro-industrialization. Although often misunderstood and neglected in American economic history and the history of the rural Midwest, manufacturing has been one of the most important elements of the rural Midwest's history and appears likely to continue to contribute to its development in the future.

Notes

1. Academic references to the Rust Belt paradigm to explain manufacturing's flight from the Midwest's larger cities include Jon C. Teaford, *Cities of the Heartland: The Rise and Fall of the Industrial Midwest* (Bloomington: Indiana University Press, 1993), 211–52; and Daniel Nelson, *Farm and Factory: Workers in the Midwest, 1880–1990* (Bloomington: Indiana University Press, 1995), 165–94. Sean Safford, *Why the Garden Club Couldn't Save Youngstown: The Transformation of the Rust Belt* (Cambridge, MA: Harvard University Press, 2009) is a sophisticated comparative examination of responses to the Rust Belt manufacturing crisis in the medium-sized cities of Youngstown, Ohio, and Allentown, Pennsylvania. For post-1950 manufacturing employment statistics, see Congressional Budget Office, "What Accounts for the Decline in Manufacturing Employment?" February 18, 2004, <www.cbo.gov/doc.cfm?index=5078&type=0>.

2. The Midwest comprises the 12 states included in the Bureau of the Census's classification of North Central states: Ohio, Michigan, Indiana, Illinois, Wisconsin, Minnesota, Iowa, Missouri, North Dakota, South Dakota, Nebraska, and Kansas. The federal government uses a variety of definitions to distinguish between urban and rural populations. A metropolitan area must contain one or more central counties with urbanized areas, defined as a population of at least 50,000, and hence, a nonmetropolitan area has no central counties with urbanized areas of more than 50,000. The federal government also uses the term "urban clusters" to include populations between 2,500 and 50,000. Within this category of urban clusters, a micropolitan area is an urban cluster of 10,000 or more persons. In general, for the purposes of distinguishing between urban and rural in this essay, counties with urban clusters of less than 10,000 are classified as rural while counties with urban clusters larger than 10,000 are classified as urban. For an overview of manufacturing em-

ployment in the United States after World War II, see E. Willard Miller, *A Geography of Manufacturing* (Englewood Cliffs, NJ: Prentice-Hall, Inc., 1962), 31–38; and Congressional Budget Office, "What Accounts for the Decline in Manufacturing Employment?" February 18, 2004. Jefferson Cowie's *Capital Moves: RCA's 70-Year Quest for Cheap Labor* (Ithaca, NY: Cornell University Press, 1999) is a notable case study of American manufacturing relocation strategies.

3. Dennis Roth, "Thinking about Rural Manufacturing: A Brief History," *Rural America* 15 (1) (January 2000): 15, 17; and Claude C. Haren, "Rural Industrial Growth in the 1960s," *American Journal of Agricultural Economics* 52 (3) (August 1970): 431–37.

4. Especially during the peak of post–World War II rural industrialization in the 1960s and 1970s, some commentators argued that this development was unprecedented in American history. See, for instance, Richard E. Lonsdale, "Background and Issues," in *Nonmetropolitan Industrialization*, ed. Richard E. Lonsdale and H.L. Seyler (Washington, DC: V.H. Winston, 1979), 3. On midwestern industrialization's nineteenth-century origins, see David R. Meyer, "Emergence of the American Manufacturing Belt: An Interpretation," *Journal of Historical Geography* 9 (2) (April 1983): 145–74; and David R. Meyer, "Midwestern Industrialization and the American Manufacturing Belt in the Nineteenth Century," *Journal of Economic History* 49 (4) (December 1989): 921–37. William Cronon, *Nature's Metropolis: Chicago and the Great West* (New York: W.W. Norton and Company, 1991), explains the role of agro-industrialism, especially in terms of the grain, lumber, and meat industries, in the growth of Chicago in the late nineteenth century. In fact, agro-industrialism was important in the growth of a wide range of cities throughout the Midwest during the same period. Philip Scranton outlines differences in the industrial character of the East versus the Midwest in "Multiple Industrializations: Urban Manufacturing Development in the American Midwest, 1880–1925," *Journal of Design History* 12 (1) (1999): 45–63. Brian Page, "Across the Great Divide: Agriculture and Industrial Geography," *Economic Geography* 72 (4) (October 1996): 376–97, makes a powerful theoretical case for the importance of agro-industrialization in the Midwest's history.

5. Agricultural implements, flour and grist milling, and wholesale meatpacking employed an average of 143,489 wage earners in 1900. See U.S. Bureau of the Census, *Manufactures: 1905*, Part I (Washington, DC: GPO, 1907).

6. On the development of flour milling, see Herman Steen, *Flour Milling in America* (Minneapolis: T.S. Denison, 1963); and Keach Johnson, "Iowa's Industrial Roots, 1890–1910," *Annals of Iowa* 44 (3) (Winter 1978): 176–79. On midwestern meatpacking during its frontier, wholesale period from the 1840s through the Civil War, see Margaret Walsh, *The Rise of the Midwestern Meat Packing Industry* (Lexington: University Press of Kentucky, 1982). On meatpacking's economic evolution in both urban and rural midwestern locations in the nineteenth and twentieth centuries, see Wilson J. Warren, *Tied to the Great Packing Machine: The Midwest and Meatpacking* (Iowa City: University of Iowa Press, 2007), 7–28. On the farm-implement industry and its rural midwestern industrial history, see Mary Beth Pudup, "From Farm to Factory: Structuring and Location of the U.S. Farm Machinery Industry," *Economic Geography* 63 (3) (July 1987): 219; Miller, *Geography of Manufacturing*, 397–402; and Mark R. Finlay, "Systems and Sales in the Heartland: A Manufacturing and Marketing History of the Hart-Parr Company, 1901–1929," *Annals of Iowa* 57 (4) (Fall 1998): 338, 344.

7. Shelton Stromquist, *A Generation of Boomers: The Pattern of Railroad Labor Conflict in Nineteenth-Century America* (Urbana: University of Illinois Press, 1987), 142–

87; and Johnson, "Iowa's Industrial Roots," 179–82. Meyer, "Midwestern Industrialization and the American Manufacturing Belt in the Nineteenth Century," 931–32, emphasizes that even though one-half of the region's industrial production was concentrated in the eight largest cities in 1880, this production was already highly diversified.

8. Dorothy Schwieder, *Black Diamonds: Life and Work in Iowa's Coal Mining Communities, 1895–1925* (Ames: Iowa State University Press, 1983). On the importance of former UMWA members in the packinghouse industry in the 1930s, see Warren, *Tied to the Great Packing Machine*, 63–64.

9. Rolland H. Maybee, *Michigan's White Pine Era, 1840–1900* (Lansing: Michigan Historical Commission, 1960); and Christian G. Carron, *Grand Rapids Furniture: The Story of America's Furniture City* (Grand Rapids, MI: The Public Museum of Grand Rapids, 1998).

10. David C. Smith, *History of Papermaking in the United States, 1691–1969* (New York: Lockwood Publishing Company, 1970), 221–25, 236–37, 240, 325.

11. Dennis Nodin Valdés, "Betabeleros: The Formation of an Agricultural Proletariat in the Midwest, 1897–1930," *Labor History* 30 (4) (Autumn 1989): 536–62; Valdés, *Al Norte: Agricultural Workers in the Great Lakes Region, 1917–1970* (Austin: University of Texas Press, 1991); Kathleen Mapes, *Sweet Tyranny: Migrant Labor, Industrial Agriculture, and Imperial Politics* (Urbana: University of Illinois Press, 2009); and Jim Norris, *North for the Harvest: Mexican Workers, Growers, and the Sugar Beet Industry* (St. Paul: Minnesota Historical Society Press). On the movement of Mexican agricultural laborers into urban midwestern industries, see Zaragosa Vargas, *Proletarians of the North: A History of Mexican Industrial Workers in Detroit and the Midwest, 1917–1933* (Berkeley and Los Angeles: University of California Press, 1993); and Juan R. García, *Mexicans in the Midwest, 1900–1932* (Tucson: University of Arizona Press, 1996).

12. On the expansion of glass making into Ohio and Indiana in the late nineteenth century, see Pearce Davis, *The Development of the American Glass Industry* (New York: Russell and Russell, 1970 [1949]), 124–25, 175. On the Portland cement industry, see Miller, *Geography of Manufacturing*, 430–34; and George W. Stark, *The Huron Heritage: Fifty Years of Concrete Achievement by the Huron Portland Cement Company, 1907–1957* (Detroit: Denman and Baker, Inc., 1957), 7, 12–17. On the Fort Dodge gypsum industry, see Raymond R. Anderson, "Fort Dodge Gypsum: A Salt from Iowa's Jurassic Sea," *Iowa Department of Natural Resources Geological Survey*, <www.igsb.uiowa.edu/browse/ftdodge/ftdodge.htm> (accessed February 26, 2013).

13. Although the Warren Featherbone Company's history in Three Oaks, Michigan, deserves more historical study, useful information about its development can be found in Sally Helvenston, "From Feathers to Fashion: How the Turkey Revolutionized Women's Clothing," *Michigan History* 80 (5) (September 1996): 28–35; Eric Morgenthler, "A 19th Century Firm Shifts, Reinvents Itself and Survives 100 Years," *Wall Street Journal*, May 9, 1989; and Robert Burgh, *The Region of Three Oaks* (Three Oaks, MI: The Edward K. Warren Foundation, 1939). The Charles Lee Collection, Western Michigan University Archives and Regional History Collection, Kalamazoo, Michigan, holds extensive records pertaining to the Warren Featherbone Company.

14. James M. Rubenstein, *The Changing U.S. Auto Industry: A Geographical Analysis* (New York: Routledge, 1992), 102–3; and Howard P. Segal, "'Little Plants in the Country': Henry Ford's Village Industries and the Beginning of Decentralized Technology in Modern America," *Prospects* 13 (1) (1988): 181–223, quote from Segal on 187.

15. On nineteenth-century midwestern town boosterism, see Timothy R. Mahoney,

River Towns in the Great West: The Structure of Provincial Urbanization in the American Midwest, 1820–1870 (Cambridge, UK: Cambridge University Press, 1990); Mahoney, "'A Common Band of Brotherhood': The Booster Ethos, Male Subcultures, and the Origins of Urban Social Order in the Midwest of the 1840s," *Journal of Urban History* 25 (5) (July 1999): 619–46; and Mahoney, "The Rise and Fall of the Booster Ethos in Dubuque, 1850–1861," *Annals of Iowa* 61 (4) (Fall 2002), 371–419. A large body of literature exists on the Iowa Palaces. Some of the more important sources include John Ely Briggs, "The Sioux City Corn Palaces," *Palimpsest* 3 (1922): 315–26; E.W. Irish, *Sioux City's Corn Palaces* (Sioux City: Pinckney Book and Stationery Co., 1889); Carl B. Kreiner, "The Ottumwa Coal Palace," *Palimpsest* 46 (December 1963): 572–78; Clara B. Rouse, *Iowa Leaves* (Chicago: Illinois Printing and Binding Company, 1891); and Dorothy Schwieder, "The Sioux City Corn Palaces," *Annals of Iowa* 41 (Spring 1973): 1209–27. On the national exhibition movement of the era, see Robert W. Rydell, *All the World's a Fair: Visions of Empire at American International Expositions, 1876–1916* (Chicago: University of Chicago Press, 1984).

16. Miller, *Geography of Manufacturing*, 31–38.

17. Between 1962 and 1978, the North Central region added 564,000 non-metropolitan manufacturing jobs, which constituted 30 percent of the non-metropolitan industrial employment in the United States. This contribution was second only to that of the South, with 46 percent of the nation's non-metropolitan industrial jobs. See Claude C. Haren and Ronald W. Holling, "Industrial Development in Nonmetropolitan America: A Locational Perspective," in *Nonmetropolitan Industrialization*, ed. Lonsdale and Seyler, 27.

18. Sources on the more rapid growth of rural (or nonmetropolitan) manufacturing compared to metropolitan manufacturing in the United States after World War II include Roth, "Thinking about Rural Manufacturing," 12–19; and John Fraser Hart, "Small Towns and Manufacturing," *Geographical Review* 78 (3) (July 1988): 277–81. On the differentiation in manufacturing development in the eastern and western parts of the rural Midwest after 1969, see Demese Chanyalew, "Industry Structure in Rural America: The Effect of Change in Industry Structure on Job Loss in the Rural Counties of the North Central Region" (PhD diss., Department of Agricultural Economics, Kansas State University, 1990), 81–84, 145.

19. On the decline of the coal industry, see Reed Moyer, *Competition in the Midwestern Coal Industry* (Cambridge, MA: Harvard University Press, 1964), 41, 66; U.S. Bureau of the Census, *Sixteenth Census of the United States: 1940, Mineral Industries, 1939*, Vol. I: General Summary and Industry Statistics (Washington, DC: GPO, 1944), 231; and U.S. Bureau of the Census, *U.S. Census of Mineral Industries, 1958*, Vol. I: Summary and Industry Statistics (Washington, DC: GPO, 1961), 12A-7. On the railroad industry's post–World War II erosion, see Richard Saunders Jr., *Merging Lines: American Railroads, 1900–1970* (DeKalb: Northern Illinois University Press, 2001), 103, 110, 121; and Stephen B. Goddard, *Getting There: The Epic Struggle between Road and Rail in the American Century* (New York: Basic Books, 1994), 164–94.

20. On post–World War II union avoidance strategies, see, for instance, Bennett Harrison and Barry Bluestone, *The Deindustrialization of America: Plant Closing, Community Abandonment, and the Dismantling of Basic Industry* (New York: Basic Books, 1982), 164–70; Bennett Harrison and Barry Bluestone, *The Great U-Turn: Corporate Restructuring and the Polarizing of America* (New York: Basic Books, 1988), 48–49; and Norman Caulfield, *NAFTA and Labor in North America* (Urbana: University of Illinois Press, 2010), especially 32–33 on the Taft-Hartley Act's impact on right-to-work laws, and 90–141 on

more recent union avoidance strategies. On the impact of right-to-work laws on business relocation to the Midwest and South, see Mark Drabenstott and Lynn Gibson, eds., *Rural America in Transition* (Kansas City, MO: Federal Reserve Bank of Kansas City, 1988), 46–48; and Robert J. Newman, *Growth in the American South: Changing Regional Employment and Wage Patterns in the 1960s and 1970s* (New York: New York University Press, 1984), 51–67. On the auto industry's union avoidance strategies, see Harrison and Bluestone, *Deindustrialization of America*, 166–67; Thomas J. Sugrue, *The Origins of the Urban Crisis: Race and Inequality in Postwar Detroit* (Princeton, NJ: Princeton University Press, 1996), 153–77; Rubenstein, *Changing U.S. Auto Industry*, 20, 234–50. On the geography of auto industry decentralization, see Rubenstein, *Changing U.S. Auto Industry*, especially 99–133, 174. On the impact of globalization on the auto industry, see Caulfield, *NAFTA and Labor in North America*, 142–65.

21. Phyllis A. Genther and Donald H. Dalton, *Japanese Direct Investment in U.S. Manufacturing* (Washington, DC: U.S. Department of Commerce, June 1990); Martin Kenney and Richard Florida, *Beyond Mass Production: The Japanese System and Its Transfer to the U.S.* (New York: Oxford University Press, 1993), 95–154; William L. Casey Jr., *Beyond the Numbers: Foreign Direct Investment in the United States* (Greenwich, CT: JAI Press, 1998), 77–105; Rubenstein, *Changing U.S. Auto Industry*, 161–65, 172–82; and Teaford, *Cities of the Heartland*, 227–28. For a systematic analysis of survey results regarding foreign companies' location decisions in the mid-1970s, see Hsin-Min Tong, *Plant Location Decisions of Foreign Manufacturing Investors* (Ann Arbor, MI: UMI Research Press, 1979).

22. Richard B. Carnes, "Productivity Trends in Intercity Trucking," *Monthly Labor Review* 91 (1) (1974): 53–57; Haren, "Rural Industrial Growth in the 1960s," 431; Ronald J. Dorf and M. Jarvin Emerson, "Determinants of Manufacturing Plant Location for Nonmetropolitan Communities in the West North Central Region of the U.S.," *Journal of Regional Science* 18 (1) (April 1978): 109–20; and J. Edwin Becht, *A Geography of Transportation and Business Logistics* (Dubuque, IA: William C. Brown Company Publishers, 1970), 27, 45–48. On the link between the rise of the trucking industry and the growing power of agribusiness, see Shane Hamilton, *Trucking Country: The Road to America's Wal-Mart Economy* (Princeton, NJ: Princeton University Press, 2008).

23. Benjamin Bridges Jr., "State and Local Inducements for Industry: Part I," *National Tax Journal* 18 (1) (March 1965): 1–14; and Bridges, "State and Local Inducements for Industry: Part II," *National Tax Journal* 18 (2) (June 1965): 175–92, quote on 191. I am grateful to Coreen Derifield for allowing me to read her unpublished essay, "'Industry's Road to Opportunity Leads to Iowa': Industrial Recruitment and Capital Mobility in the Midwest, 1950–1965," which focuses on the postwar Iowa Development Commission's efforts to entice manufacturing to the state. Harrison and Bluestone describe how corporations played off state and local tax inducements to their advantage in plant relocations after World War II. See Harrison and Bluestone, *Deindustrialization of America*, 180–88. Osha Gray Davidson, *Broken Heartland: The Rise of America's Rural Ghetto* (Iowa City: University of Iowa Press, 1996), 132–51, criticizes state and federal rural development programs for contributing to rural community decline, especially since the 1980s. On state initiatives in the 1980s to require corporations to provide various types of compensation when they closed plants, see Antone Aboud and Sanford F. Schram, "Overview of Legislation," in *Deindustrialization and Plant Closure*, ed. Paul D. Staudohar and Holly E. Brown (Lexington, MA: Lexington Books, 1987), 279–91. On Seaboard Corporation and Albert Lea, Minnesota, see especially Donald L. Bartlett and James B. Steele, "The Empire of the Pigs," *Time*

152 (November 30, 1998): 52–64; and Warren, *Tied to the Great Packing Machine*, 171–72.

24. Wayne D. Rasmussen, "90 Years of Rural Development Programs," *Rural Development Perspectives* 2 (1) (October 1985): 2–9; Drabenstott and Gibson, *Rural America in Transition*, 6–8, 73–74; and Richard E. Wood, *Survival of Rural America: Small Victories and Bitter Harvests* (Lawrence: University Press of Kansas, 2008), 144–47.

25. Jon Lauck, *American Agriculture and the Problem of Monopoly: The Political Economy of Grain Belt Farming, 1953–1980* (Lincoln: University of Nebraska Press, 2000); Paul Conkin, *A Revolution down on the Farm: The Transformation of American Agriculture since 1929* (Lexington: University Press of Kentucky, 2008); Alan L. Olmstead and Paul W. Rhode, *Creating Abundance: Biological Innovation and American Agricultural Development* (Cambridge, UK: Cambridge University Press, 2008); and J.L. Anderson, *Industrializing the Corn Belt: Agriculture, Technology, and Environment, 1945–1972* (DeKalb: Northern Illinois University Press, 2009). On farmers and off-farm employment, see Hart, "Small Towns and Manufacturing," 281–85; Mark Friedberger, *Shake-Out: Iowa Farm Families in the 1980s* (Lexington: University Press of Kentucky, 1989), 122; and Warren, *Tied to the Great Packing Machine*, 64.

26. James N. Gregory, *The Southern Diaspora: How the Great Migrations of Black and White Southerners Transformed America* (Chapel Hill: University of North Carolina Press, 2005); and Teaford, *Cities of the Heartland*, 189–97, 230–39. On black migration to Muncie, Indiana, see Jack S. Blocker Jr., "Black Migration to Muncie, 1860–1930," *Indiana Magazine of History* 92 (4) (December 1996): 297–320. On blacks in Manly, Iowa, see William J. Maddox, "Blacks and Whites in Manly: An Iowa Town Overcomes Racism," *Palimpsest* 63 (September/October 1982): 130–37. On blacks in Muchakinock and Buxton, Iowa, see Pam Stek, "Muchakinock: African Americans and the Making of an Iowa Coal Town," *Annals of Iowa* 68 (1) (Winter 2009): 37–63; Dorothy Schwieder, Joseph Hraba, and Elmer Schwieder, *Buxton: Work and Racial Equality in a Coal Mining Community* (Ames: Iowa State University Press, 1987).

27. Rogelio Saenz and Cruz C. Torres, "Latinos in Rural America," in *Challenges for Rural America in the Twenty-First Century*, ed. David L. Brown and Louis E. Swanson (University Park: Pennsylvania State University Press, 2003), 57–70; and Martha Crowley and Daniel T. Lichter, "Social Disorganization in New Latino Destinations?" *Rural Sociology* 74 (4) (December 2009): 573–604. Saenz and Torres report a figure of 113 percent for nonmetropolitan Midwest Latino population growth between 1990 and 2000, while Crowley and Lichter calculate 122 percent. On Latinos in the modern meatpacking industry, see Warren, *Tied to the Great Packing Machine*, 66–72.

28. U.S. Bureau of the Census, *Census of Manufactures, 1947*, Vol. III: Statistics by States (Washington, DC: GPO, 1950). Allan Rodgers, "Some Aspects of Industrial Diversification in the United States," *Economic Geography* 33 (1) (January 1957): 16–30, notes the continued heavy emphasis on machinery, metal fabrication, and transportation in the urban Midwest between 1940 and 1950. On the increasing structural diversity of rural Midwest industries after World War II, see Haren, "Rural Industrial Growth in the 1960s," 433; and Miller, *Geography of Manufacturing*, 33, which point out that fabricated metal products and non-electrical machinery were two of the leading manufacturing industries during the early postwar period throughout the United States.

29. U.S. Bureau of the Census, *1972 Census of Manufactures*, Vol. III: Area Statistics (Washington, DC: GPO, 1976).

30. George S. May, "Recent Industrial Development," *Palimpsest* 37 (5) (May 1956):

229–89; Lawrence O. Cheever, "Comments on 11 Years," *Palimpsest* 48 (3) (March 1967): 93–145; and Lawrence O. Cheever, "Industries of Iowa, Part II," *Palimpsest* 49 (1) (January 1968): 1–41.

31. On the contraction of U.S. manufacturing during the late 1970s and early 1980s, see Harrison and Bluestone, *Deindustrialization of America*, especially 25–48; Harrison and Bluestone, *The Great U-Turn*, especially 21–52. On the 2001–2004 manufacturing job loss and movement of manufacturing out of the country, see Congressional Budget Office, "What Accounts for the Decline in Manufacturing Employment?" February 18, 2004; and Caulfield, *NAFTA and Labor in North America*, 112–41.

32. *Census of Manufactures, 1947*, Vol. III; *1972 Census of Manufactures*, Vol. III; and U.S. Census Bureau, *1997 Economic Census*, <www.census.gov/epcd/ec97sic/index.html> (accessed February 26, 2013). Between 1973 and 1980, Michigan's total manufacturing job loss of 17.3 percent was among the worst in the nation. See Barry Bluestone, "In Support of the Deindustrialization Thesis," in Staudohar and Brown, *Deindustrialization and Plant Closure*, 48. Over the slightly longer period of 1972 to 1986, Michigan's manufacturing job loss of 9.0 percent was actually outpaced by Illinois (28.0%), Ohio (17.6%), and Indiana (15.0%). See Ann R. Markusen and Virginia Carlson, "Deindustrialization in the American Midwest: Causes and Responses," in *Deindustrialization and Regional Economic Transformation: The Experience of the United States*, ed. Lloyd Rodwin and Hidehiko Sazanami (Boston: Unwin Hyman, 1989), 42.

33. From 1972 to 1986, only Iowa (9.7%) and Missouri (4.4%) lost manufacturing jobs. The other states in the West North Central region all added manufacturing jobs: Nebraska (0.9%), Minnesota (19.0%), Kansas (20.4%), North Dakota (42.6%), and South Dakota (53.8%). See Markusen and Carlson, "Deindustrialization in the American Midwest," 42. Some of this job gain in the West North Central states seems to have come at the expense of the East North Central states during the 1970s. For instance, in the metalworking subset of the non-electrical machinery category of manufacturing jobs, between 1973 and 1979 the East North Central region's contribution to national employment declined from 48.1 to 46.6 percent, while the West North Central region's contribution rose from 3.6 to 4.8 percent. See Marie Howland, *Plant Closings and Worker Displacement: The Regional Issues* (Kalamazoo, MI: W.E. Upjohn Institute for Employment Research, 1988), 33. During the particularly grim manufacturing slump from 1980 to 1986, though, Wisconsin was the only state in the North Central region that experienced relative growth in manufacturing employment. See Chanyalew, "Industry Structure in Rural America," 131. Note that the *1997 Economic Census* does not provide disaggregated data on the number of production workers per industrial category. Only data on all paid employees (production and salaried) per industrial category are available.

34. For a comparative economic analysis of employment sectors in the rural United States after World War II and manufacturing's leading role by the 1980s, see Drabenstott and Gibson, *Rural America in Transition*, 16–28. On the links between the 1980s farm crisis and midwestern deindustrialization, see Davidson, *Broken Heartland*, 57–59.

35. On the leather and shoemaking industry in Missouri, see Edgar M. Hoover Jr., *Location Theory and the Shoe and Leather Industries* (Cambridge, MA: Harvard University Press, 1937), 248–51, 274, 278–80, quote on 240. On the labor struggles of workers in the small Missouri towns with shoe factories, see Rosemary Feurer, "Shoe City, Factory Towns: St. Louis Shoe Companies and the Turbulent Drive for Cheap Rural Labor," *Gateway Heritage* 9 (2) (Fall 1988): 2–17. On the Anna, Illinois, shoe factory and its

impact on rural employment, see Jane Adams, *The Transformation of Rural Life: Southern Illinois, 1890–1990* (Chapel Hill: University of North Carolina Press, 1994), 141, 195–96, 216, 240, 247.

36. Warren, *Tied to the Great Packing Machine,* 17–23.

37. On the post-1960 evolution of the rural location of midwestern meatpacking, see Warren, *Tied to the Great Packing Machine,* 23–28. An excellent study of the impact of meatpacking plant closings in Iowa is Mickey Lauria and Peter S. Fisher, *Plant Closings in Iowa: Causes, Consequences, and Legislative Options* (Iowa City: Institute of Urban and Regional Research, University of Iowa, 1983).

38. Warren, *Tied to the Great Packing Machine,* esp. 35–46, 66–72, 82–98, and 175–77; and Donald D. Stull and Michael J. Broadway, *Slaughterhouse Blues: The Meat and Poultry Industry in North America* (Belmont, CA: Thomson/Wadsworth Learning, 2004). Useful contemporary studies that focus on the modern meat industry's economic and cultural impacts on specific rural midwestern communities include Stephen G. Bloom, *Postville: A Clash of Cultures in Heartland America* (New York: Harcourt, 2000); and Dale Maharidge, *Denison, Iowa: Searching for the Soul of America through the Secrets of a Midwest Town* (New York: Free Press, 2005).

39. *Paper Trade Journal* (February 10, 1910): 157, 159; Smith, *History of Papermaking in the United States,* 240, 325, 599; and Larry B. Massie and Peter J. Schmitt, *Kalamazoo: The Place behind the Products* (Woodland Hills, CA: Windsor Publications, 1981), 149–52.

40. Ryan Wieber and Sandy Stamm, *Otsego and Plainwell* (Charleston, SC: Arcadia Publishing, 2006), 85–98; and Paper Mill Folders, box 11, Local History Files, Otsego Public Library, Otsego, Michigan.

41. *Census of Manufactures, 1947,* Vol. III, 300; and Paper Mill Folders, box 11, Local History Files, Otsego Public Library.

42. Paper Mill Folders, box 11, Local History Files, Otsego Public Library; *Census of Manufactures, 1947,* Vol. III, 312; and *1972 Census of Manufactures,* Vol. III, 23–32.

43. Bill Gilbert, "Of Time and the River," *Sports Illustrated,* July 24, 1989, <sportsillustrated.cnn.com/vault/article/magazine/MAG1068620/1/index.htm> (accessed February 26, 2013); and Paper Mills Folders, box 11, Local History Files, Otsego Public Library. Abbott quoted in Gilbert.

44. Gilbert, "Of Time and the River"; U.S. Environmental Protection Agency Region 5, Allied Paper, Inc./Portage Creek/Kalamazoo River, NPL Fact Sheet, EPA ID#MID006007306, November 2009, <www.epa.gov/region5superfund/npl/michigan/MID006007306.html>; *Kalamazoo Gazette,* April 23, 2006. Steven High and David W. Lewis, *Corporate Wasteland: The Landscape and Memory of Deindustrialization* (Ithaca, NY: ILR Press, 2007), 150–54, includes haunting photographs of the abandoned Allied paper mill in Kalamazoo.

45. William H. McDaniel, *Walt Behlen's Universe* (Lincoln: University of Nebraska Press, 1973), 19–101. On the importance of new grain storage and drying systems for agribusiness, see Anderson, *Industrializing the Corn Belt,* 179–88. On Platte County's industrial employers in 1947 and 1972, see *Census of Manufactures, 1947,* Vol. III, 371; and *1972 Census of Manufactures,* Vol. III, 28—15.

46. McDaniel, *Walt Behlen's Universe,* 123–67; Behlen History, Company Information, and Culture, <www.behlenmfg.com> (accessed February 26, 2013); and "Reaping the Harvest," Behlen Manufacturing Company, *Industry Today* 9 (4) (2006), <www.usitoday.com/article_view.asp?ArticleID=1664> (accessed February 26, 2013).

47. Woods, *Survival of Rural America*.

48. Mindy Petrulis, Judith Sommer, and Fred Hines, "Ethanol Production and Employment," Economic Research Service, USDA, Agriculture Information Bulletin 678 (July 1993); and Sarah A. Low and Andrew M. Isserman, "Ethanol and the Local Economy: Industry Trends, Location Factors, Economic Impacts, and Risks," *Economic Development Quarterly* 23 (1) (February 2009): 71–88.

FOUR — MIDWESTERN RURAL COMMUNITIES IN THE POST–WWII ERA TO 2000

Cornelia Butler Flora and Jan L. Flora

The end of the Second World War resulted in an economic boom in midwestern rural communities. Local retailers satisfied pent-up demand for consumer goods. Farmers came to town to shop and visit on Saturday nights and all the stores were open late. New service clubs emerged, movie theaters expanded, and local baseball and basketball teams drew large crowds. Yet numerous changes were under way that undermined the economic and social viability of midwestern small towns. Television broadcasting and viewing expanded, moving entertainment from the public to the private sphere. By the end of the 1950s, many small-town movie houses had closed and local semipro and church sports leagues folded. At the same time, America's suburbs, facilitated by government highway construction and a robust auto industry, attracted the young people who might otherwise commute from rural towns to urban areas for their jobs. School consolidation, railroad deregulation resulting in the massive closure of rail lines, the consolidation of retail and creation of shopping malls, the collapse of local newspapers, and the industrialization of agriculture all contributed to the decline of many small towns. Historian Richard Davies, in his study of his hometown of Camden, Ohio, noted the importance of conservative, low tax, and limited government spirit as well as male dominance that drove the town into gradual decay.[1]

By contrast, sociologist Robert Wuthnow, also inspired by his midwestern roots, claimed that the rural American Middle West has "undergone a strong, positive transformation since the 1950s." Instead of a post–WWII boom described by Davies, Wuthnow claimed that the situation in midwestern communities was worse than the residents, whose measuring point was the Great Depression, realized. By focusing on the relationship between rural communities and urban centers and the ways in which rural communities developed new collective identities and economies to overcome the difficult economic situations, Wuthnow offered a much more optimistic assessment of the rural Midwest.[2] Which view is correct? Did rural midwestern communities decline or regenerate between 1945 and 2000?

A good starting point for assessing change in the postwar period is to examine the United States Department of Agriculture (USDA) rural community studies conducted on the eve of World War II. USDA leaders contracted with sociologists to assess the stability of America's rural communities after several years of New Deal programs devoted to shoring up farmers and communities. Two of these studies focused on the Midwest—Irwin, Iowa, and Sublette, Kansas—representing different versions of midwestern communities.[3]

In many ways, Irwin, in Shelby County, with a population of 345 at the time of the study, represented an ideal rural community. Good soil and a dependable rainfall regime supported the agricultural dominance of the county and the town, typical of Corn Belt communities. Agriculture was highly diversified mixed crop and livestock farming, with the crops fed to animals to add value. Farm owners and renters shared common values of planting straight corn rows and maintaining farmsteads. Increased use of tractors facilitated the concentration of farmland. There was no single dominant ethnic group in Irwin. Much social activity was carried out on Main Street on Saturdays when the farm families came to town to shop. Due to the Depression of the 1930s, land had changed hands and there was a high rate of farm tenancy, with a concomitant decrease in attachment to the land and the community of Irwin. Community institutions were strong in Irwin. Residents were willing to tax themselves to support schools, even if the majority of high school graduates left Irwin for city employment. Churches were considered the most important institutions in the community, contributing greatly to the residents' quality of life.[4] In 1940 there was a fairly complete institutional structure to support the agricultural economy, and the families related to it by providing for the production of goods and services in Irwin, although even then there was a concern about lost businesses.

Sublette and Haskell County, Kansas, presented a somewhat different picture. The population of Sublette, like that of Irwin, was completely non-Hispanic whites, and survey data showed a great deal of mutual support within the community. According to the authors of the study, however, "Instability has been the dominant theme in the history of Haskell County."[5] The largest challenge for rural Sublette was aridity, which consistently challenged the community assumption that adequate rainfall to sustain wheat farming was a normal condition. The boom-and-bust nature of wheat monoculture meant that population turnover was high and that it was difficult to sustain a stable rural community.

The rural Midwest of the 1950s consisted of thousands of communities like Sublette and Irwin where, in spite of their differences, farm production was booming, farmers were still numerous, Main Street prospered, and a robust civil society prevailed. There was a reasonable balance among local government, community institutions and voluntary organizations, and locally competitive markets. This system of local markets, state, and civil society was heavily influenced by industrial corporations from which residents bought and to which they sold their products, and by government programs, particularly the Farm Bill, which prompted commodity farmers of the Midwest to face toward Washington rather than their own state capitals. Industries that had quickly geared up to produce war matériel beginning in 1940 just as quickly transitioned to the manufacture of civilian products such as cars, tractors, and washing machines following the war.[6] Chemical industries shifted from making nitrogen-based explosives to making nitrogen fertilizer, which helped spur farm production.[7]

World War II was a watershed for the rural Midwest and for the nation as a whole. During the war, diverse farming enterprises were converted to grain production to feed the troops and the animals that fed the troops. That specialization contributed to land concentration and a decline in the number of farms. Plant breeders developed new corn and wheat varieties that responded better to fertilizers and herbicides and made monoculture on larger and larger plots of land more feasible. Further, manufacturing shifted back to the production of farm machinery, giving an extra impetus to mechanization. The concentration of landholdings and the move to less differentiated farming systems was mirrored in rural communities, as creameries, canneries, and small meat lockers that processed and stored local animals closed across the rural Midwest. Many of the enterprises in rural midwestern communities became redundant or obsolete. Similarly, it became easier to expand the amount of land farmed by a single individual. New technology, rural electrification, and demand for foodstuffs propelled by European relief and recovery facilitated this change. Furthermore, urban industry and commerce quickly employed midwestern youths who shared a strong work ethic and acceptance of authority. Those who remained on the land with family farms in the Midwest viewed the land as financial capital. Farming increasingly became a way of earning a living rather than a way of life. These changes had an enormous effect on rural communities. As farm size grew, counties not experiencing that growth and that did not discover other options began to experience declines in population.[8]

The 1970s represented a hiatus in that trend as cheap money was available to purchase farms, and many younger persons (often with the help of their elders) took advantage of the opportunity to get into farming. The average age of farmers actually declined during the decade of the 1970s, reversing a long-standing trend. The new farmers of the 1970s were able to make payments on land purchased at unprecedented per-acre prices (in relation to the productive capacity of the land) only if land and farm commodity prices continued to increase.

The rural renaissance of the 1970s was an aberration of the postwar period that actually accelerated the trend of consolidation. Although the political and economic power of middling farmers was on the decline before, the farm crisis of the 1980s sealed their fate. Commodity prices and land values collapsed in the early 1980s, bankrupting many farmers. Farm bankruptcies impacted rural banks that had loaned them money. Although the land remained in production, the new landowners and management companies did not use local goods and services, putting many small towns in peril.

Midwestern farmers and the communities that serviced them were increasingly subordinate to other parts of the agricultural value chain, losing market share with declining margins, making fewer independent decisions, and increasingly pushed to run faster on the agricultural treadmill. Rural communities in agriculturally dependent counties faced a declining economic base as the new larger farmers bypassed the locality in their input purchases and in the marketing of an ever-increasing volume of product. While the effect of agriculture on local communities and counties was diminished, other economic activities grew relative to agriculture in their effect on the local community. Local governments took on new functions of the welfare state (mental health care, for instance), retail activities grew, and services that previously were not purchased became a larger part of the economy. Rural communities competed for industrial activity that was leaving the high-cost metro areas known as the Rust Belt. For all of these reasons and more, the numbers of farm-dependent counties declined sharply from mid-century to 2000.[9]

Industrial Development and Rural Communities

In 1950, most rural counties in the Midwest, including Haskell and Shelby, were classified as farming-dependent, with 20 percent or more of labor's and proprietors' income coming from farming. Counties that were not dependent directly on agriculture included towns that served as trade centers for an agricultural hinterland or were dependent on some other sort of natural resource extraction. By 2000, most of the farming-dependent communities were in the Great Plains. Those communities created far fewer service and manufacturing jobs than other rural communities in the region and their populations shrank sharply.[10]

Credit continued to be the means for economic development. The independent banks that survived the Great Depression thrived after World War II. The community banker often made "character loans," based not on collateral or even a good business plan but on generational knowledge of the individual and his family (the loans almost always went to men). The newly regulated banking system was bound by the 3-6-3 rule: pay investors 3 percent, charge borrowers 6 percent, and be out on the golf links by 3:00 every afternoon (which was when banks were required by law to close). This predictability as well as limitations on interest charged by banks favored slow growth of small businesses, while industrial corporations found more agile investment funds with development banks.

This conservative commercial banking system fostered the emergence of a new group of rural entrepreneurs after the war. The combination of ambitious entrepreneurs and available local capital allowed Main Streets to display a new generation of shops selling a variety of goods and services. Local bankers were the key leaders. Their willingness to invest locally made the difference between community stagnation and community vitality. Such leadership was not only in economic development but also in a variety of civic ventures aimed at increasing the quality of life in the community, from homegrown carnivals to public libraries.[11]

Bank deregulation and consolidation in the 1980s and 1990s led to the decline of community banks. Loan officers during that time looked for "a pretty piece of paper," not for the known human and social capital that had once served as loan guarantees. By the 1990s, new financial instruments were available in rural communities in the Midwest, including limited partnerships and venture capital—both nearly nonexistent in 1980.[12]

Between 1950 and 1980, more jobs were created than lost in non-resource-based industries in the rural Midwest, while jobs in resource-based industries such as agriculture, mining, and fishing decreased. Communities on the western side of the region (the plains states) were more dependent on resource-based employment than on the eastern side (the lakes states) in 1940 and were less successful in replacing them with service and industrial jobs by 1980. Sublette, Kansas, was an exception, with the arrival of the meatpacking industry and the industrial jobs it generated.

Manufacturing growth came from internal and external financial capital. Local entrepreneurs built plants in their local community. These men and women were often returnees who had worked for major companies in urban areas and discovered a way to manufacture a particular piece of the larger process and to convince the larger company to outsource to their new plant. They continued to innovate and to diversify their product line, creating a community climate that encouraged innovation and difference. However, in other communities the growth in manufacturing was due to larger companies locating branch plants in areas with cheap land and labor and local governments eager to provide inexpensive capital. Furthermore, they were less likely to encounter environmental regulations and enjoyed a more dispersed rural population that had not experienced the level of environmental contamination of some communities in the East.

Both new and branch plant construction continued through the 1970s, but with the farm crisis of the 1980s, the balance tipped toward recruitment of branch plants that were unrelated to the resource base of the rural communities in which they came to be located. That separation of ownership from place meant that the firms could threaten to leave if they did not receive tax abatements and other favors from the local government. By 2000, many of those plants were gone, having migrated to lower-wage parts of the globe. Most non-metro manufacturing counties were located near metropolitan counties or counties that were adjacent to metro counties that did not reach the threshold for manufacturing classification.[13]

Firms that located in rural communities tended to be labor-intensive because the larger share that payroll represented in the costs of the firm, the greater the comparative advantage of locating in places where unionization was low and labor organizers would experience open hostility from both local elites and the general population. The attraction of low-wage employers in the 1980s made it difficult for rural communities to attract high-tech and computer-age jobs in the succeeding decade. The most educated rural sons and daughters found it difficult to return to their home communities because there were few jobs that were commensurate with their education. They often went to "edge cities"—communities near metropolitan areas, such as Olathe, Kansas, near Kansas City, Missouri, that attracted talented young people from the rural Midwest and formed innovative centers of high-tech industries.[14]

By 2000, those "isolated" (not adjacent to a metro area) rural manufacturing counties that remained in the region were of two types: those which recruited footloose branch plants and those with firms started by local entrepreneurs who, decades earlier, had succeeded in building a national market. Winnebago Industries in north central Iowa is an example of such an industry. In the postwar period the most common example was the large meatpacking plant, especially in southwestern Kansas (including Sublette), central Nebraska, southern Minnesota, Iowa (including Denison, Iowa, adjacent to Shelby County), and western Illinois into Missouri. Common to most of these counties were the interrelated features of distance from metro areas and the absence or weakness of organized labor.

These communities and counties were beneficiaries and victims of what is known as the IBP revolution that began in Denison, Iowa, with the establishment of the first Iowa Beef Packers plant in 1960. Meatpacking in the Midwest was restructured by placing the plants near beef cattle feedlots, which had sprung up in the vicinity of the Ogallala Aquifer on the southern Great Plains, or later, by co-locating concentrated animal feeding operations (CAFOs) and pork-packing plants. Retail cuts of meat were boxed at the plant rather than cutting the meat to the taste of the customer at retail outlets. Labor was thus deskilling from packinghouse to grocery store. The strong meat-packing unions were broken, and mergers and buyouts further concentrated the industry.[15]

Oberlin, the county seat of Decatur County in northwest Kansas, is an example of a creative community far away from urban centers that attempted to develop a homegrown industrial base during the farm recession of the 1980s. One local Oberlin wag, no doubt thinking about the dictum that private sector success is *location, location, location*, commented dryly that "we are strategically situated half way between Interstates 70 and 80."[16]

Oberlin, with a population of 2,019 in 1950, like many other communities experiencing agricultural decline, entered the industrial park business. In order to understand why Oberlin did so, it is important to recognize how tightly the concept of industrial development gripped local rural elites in the Midwest, particularly those in more isolated parts of the Great Plains. There was a consensus among small-town leaders that industrial parks were critical for economic development, even though in the 1960s the evidence was clear that they were not cost-effective in attracting industry. The Oberlin Industrial Development Corporation was formed in 1962. Shortly thereafter, with the money raised through the sale of stock, 15 acres of land, a total of four parcels, was purchased. The park was not filled until the mid-1970s.

In 1970, Phil Finley, a dynamic and organizationally minded county extension director, organized a meeting of the Decatur County Planning Commission (established two years earlier), and the Chambers of Commerce of Oberlin, and of Norcatur and Jennings, the two smaller communities in the county. The result was the abolition of the individual Chambers of Commerce and the establishment of the Decatur County Area Chamber of Commerce (DCCC). A number of projects, including the community carnival, an investor-run dairy, a feedlot, and several smaller ones that included the development of attractive canopies draping the stores on Main Street, were all projects of the DCCC. The Amusement Authority (to run the carnival and give out the funds generated from the carnival for social and economic development projects) was an arm of the DCCC and sought to assist projects in all three communities. The creation of the DCCC moderated conflicts common among the towns in many midwestern counties.

In the early 1970s, Decatur County citizens organized a feedlot and a dairy by selling shares of stock to local persons. Similarly, in the mid-1980s in response to the farm crisis, community investors put up the seed money to establish a bus coach factory and a boat factory. The leadership in Kansas Coach Manufacturing, the bus coach firm, included several individuals who had been involved in the feed yard and dairy.

There was considerable controversy among investors as to how the dairy should be run, and it was not clear who was in charge. Kent Reinhardt resigned his position as county extension director to take on the management of the faltering dairy, but he became manager too late to save the enterprise. Investors received partial repayment of their investment. The investors in the feedlot would have lost money in that venture had not the owner of an auto dealership agreed to buy out his partners at one hundred cents on the dollar. Community investors were willing to take the plunge again during the crisis of the mid-1980s. Considerable amounts of volunteer time were given to these private for-profit community efforts as well as to the carnival.

When the dairy failed, Reinhardt became a partner in a local elevator and feed, seed, and fertilizer store. He was an example of an outsider who obtained positions of leadership in the community, but he was the exception that proves the rule in that he married into a local family. Generally in a midwestern farming-dependent community it was difficult for outsiders to break in to positions of leadership.

A younger group of leaders emerged to organize the Decatur Manufacturing Company, a boat-building company that began production in January 1987 and ceased operation as a collectively run enterprise in August 1988. The company gathered pledges of $170,000 from community investors, which facilitated getting a Small Business Administration loan of $90,000 and a $200,000 Community Development Block Grant. These were followed by a $200,000 line of credit from a local bank.

The story of the Decatur Manufacturing Company illustrates the reasons that people in rural communities became wary, or at least should have been wary, of outsiders who lacked enduring ties to the community. Dick Schroeder, representing Paragon International of Laramie, Wyoming, learned of Oberlin's desire for economic development. A Denver attorney and former Oberlin resident pointed Schroeder toward Oberlin as a source of financing. Schroeder, described in hindsight by community members as a "real bullshitter," had patented the design for a family boat/ floating trailer combination and convinced Oberlin investors to put up the funds to begin manufacturing.[17]

Production of the boat itself was straightforward, but the "innovative" trailer, which was made of fiberglass and was to serve as both a trailer and a floating dock, had not been market tested and proved to have little consumer appeal. According to one informant, the product "looked awful and [when towed] drug like a dead hog." Production of the trailer was discontinued after several months, but the enterprise was already hemorrhaging. The boat factory had to stop production 18 months after it opened because it ran out of capital, with the precipitating factor being a client who reneged on a contract to take 80 boats and trailers. The firm also had problems with poor ventilation of the workplace, and an employee reported the facility to the federal Occupational Safety and Health Administration. The large order for boats resulted in the firm putting all its resources into production and little into market development. When the order fell through, the bank was obligated to take over. Outsiders walked away from the project when they saw that it was not going well and escaped with investing only their time. The local banks were protected by taking collateral. Oberlin investors and the federal government, by contrast, bore the entire financial risk.

By the mid-1980s, the Oberlin industrial park was nearly empty and rural communities, especially those in the hinterland of regional trade centers, were increasingly desperate to generate employment to ensure the survival of their communities as they had known them. Oberlin promoters attempted to buy an existing bus coach factory in Fort Worth, Texas, and bring it to Oberlin. Before that could be accomplished, however, the company went bankrupt. Believing they now had a comparative advantage due to their education in bus coach production and marketing, the "stockholders" who had collectively pledged $315,000 as seed money for the new venture decided to organize their own bus coach company. They were able to parlay those funds into $500,000 from the Kansas Public Employees Retirement System, which in turn opened the door to another $400,000 Community Development Block Grant. A $400,000 line of credit from a local bank topped off the financial package. In June 1987, about a year and a half after the first contact was made with the Fort Worth firm, the new industry opened its doors. In November 1988, less than a year and a half later, the firm closed with $500,000 of unfilled orders, having exhausted its financial capital.

Decatur County leaders showed a willingness to invest their private funds in what turned out to be rather risky ventures. The approximately $500,000 raised from among local citizens through contributions that averaged approximately $1,000 each for the bus coach and for the boat companies was remarkable. Even after the loss of some $500,000 of citizens' money in the bus and boat schemes, a number of participants reported that there were few recriminations, perhaps because no one had invested more than they could afford to lose.

Decatur County did an excellent job of generating both vertical and horizontal linkages with federal and state governments as well as peers. There was rarely a state government program that leaders in the county did not know about and apply for. Decatur County leaders reached out to other communities for knowledge about how to accomplish a particular project. They sent carloads and even busloads of people to inspect a home-grown carnival, feed yards, dairies, bus coach factories, and other enterprises and have adapted what they learned to their own circumstances.[18] However, they were more successful in social enterprises than in commercial ones that tended to depend on outside expertise.

Oberlin also invested in social infrastructure. Their concern with economic development did not divert them from recognizing and acting on the fact that schools, hospitals, and other infrastructure were important for attracting businesses and preserving quality of life. During the oil boom of the 1970s, Halliburton, one of the world's largest oil field service companies, located a regional office in Oberlin because of its location near the center of several oil fields and also because of Oberlin's good school system. Halliburton was not recruited (although it did locate in the industrial park), but Oberlin's preparedness paid off. For its size and location, Oberlin had numerous high-quality health care facilities, including a county hospital, five medical doctors, and two long-term care facilities, one skilled and one intermediate. In 1989, a bond issue to expand the hospital passed when other rural community hospitals were struggling merely to survive. The bond issue passed in the same period that the bus coach and the boat factories were in serious trouble and investors were in danger of losing their money.

Why was Oberlin, Decatur County, which had more than three decades of experience—and overall success—in self-development efforts, unable to successfully launch either of two locally controlled industrial firms? Leaders failed to follow certain key rules of social organization, and although the effort came from within the community, they followed a model of industrial recruitment whose time had passed.

The local workers were accustomed to a more artisanal labor process, which was a poor fit with contemporary industry. In both the bus and boat factories, labor costs were a substantial portion of the total cost of the product. Many workers were former farmers who had left agriculture during the farm crisis or were part-time farmers. Either way, farmers are often artisans or jacks-of-all-trades who underestimate labor costs in their farm accounting. On the farm, the worker who could be mechanic, fabricator, botanist, veterinary technician, broker, and bookkeeper helped reduce out-of-pocket costs for the farm and home and could consequently make a profit from a modest number of livestock and grain units at a higher margin than a more specialized competitor. Those workers were not likely to adapt well to repetitive work in which production processes were divided into smaller and smaller segments. Artisanal work was appropriate for niche markets but not for mass markets.

The more appropriate model for growth was that of the entrepreneurial artisan and businessperson, not that of the larger industrial firm. Unfortunately, government economic development policy and community expectations under conditions of severe economic distress led community-based industrial firms to follow the wrong model. Their vision led to an incompatible amalgam of development. Oberlin and Decatur County leaders believed they could exercise some control over their collective destinies. The community exhibited collective entrepreneurship, but the means they chose were not compatible with their skills and experience. Although Oberlin gradually increased in population up to 1980, by 2000 it had only 1,994 residents. The population of Decatur County declined even more precipitously, from 6,185 in 1950 to 3,472 in 2000.

Rural Communities and Cultural Conflict

The rural Midwest, in contrast to the rural South and West, was marked by a more egalitarian social structure that allowed the growth of a rich community life. In midwestern rural communities, each adult played a variety of roles, and no single role was the one that defined such a person for members of other groups in the community. An individual might have owned and operated a clothing store on Main Street, pitched for the softball team, volunteered at the local hospital, sung in their church choir, led a 4-H Club, and belonged to a civic club. This role heterogeneity—that one might be a leader in one organization and a follower in another—resulted in a high density of acquaintanceship. Not only did everyone know everyone else, it was also possible to know who could be counted on for what. Density of acquaintanceship was also a major mechanism of social control, reducing both deviance and innovation.[19]

Organizations of all kinds thrived in rural midwestern communities after World War II. Women who had gone to college during the war formed chapters of the American Association of University Women, which met regularly and worked to be sure that young women in rural communities were encouraged to further their education and to use it for the benefit of their communities. Service organizations such as fraternal orders and their female auxiliaries continued to function in postwar communities, although their membership was increasingly elderly. County-level Democratic and Republican party organizations were also important community groups. Clubs and organizations, with chapters at the town and county level, provided the basic social infrastructure for civil society to thrive.

While social and cultural capital in rural America had many positive features, the end of the war marked a reassertion of dominance by northern European males in the nation as a whole. African American and other minority soldiers who came back from the war confronted persistent racism. Rosie the Riveter became a homemaker, and in the rural Midwest, women often became unremunerated helpmates on the farm and on Main Street. Men took advantage of the G.I. Bill, agricultural colleges and teachers' colleges became full-blown universities, and community colleges (then called junior colleges) flourished. It would be several decades before women would come to equal and then outnumber men as undergraduates. These negative aspects of social and cultural capital have important rural manifestations.

Native American communities were driven out of most of the Midwest by the end of World War II, except on or near reservations in the Dakotas, Nebraska, Minnesota, Wisconsin, and northern Michigan. Members of these communities lived uneasily with their European American neighbors, who continued the animosity toward these Native American Indian communities and their fear of them from the days of their ancestors' moving onto Indian lands. Devils Lake, North Dakota, is very near the Spirit Lake Reservation. During fieldwork in 2005, residents told the authors how uncomfortable they felt on the reservation and what courage it took for a few from the community to even attend a pow-wow, a tribal event that encourages outsiders to come to observe. Previously, they reported, community members did whatever they could to avoid the reservation, despite tribal efforts to establish a tourism center there. Tribal members told of the discrimination they faced when they went to town, from the time they were children to the present, and they also feared physical violence from local residents and thus avoided going to town.[20] Although leaders in both communities were working to heal the rift, most of the post–WWII era had perpetuated the separation.

Population loss was a problem for communities across the region. Towns that managed to keep their post offices maintained a core where people could pick up mail and socialize. Other midwestern communities, such as Irwin, survived during the 1950s and 1960s and thrived during the rural renaissance in the 1970s, when a weak dollar fueled rural industrialization through the location of branch plants. The rise in the value of the dollar and subsequent globalization and economic consolidation undermined the industrial, commercial, and agricultural base of those communities in the 1980s.[21]

The cultural homogeneity that prevailed in the rural Midwest for most of the postwar period encouraged the growth of institutions to serve the goal of community improvement, including schools, parks, and public libraries. These institutions were locally controlled, and to a large degree locally funded, but they mirrored the values of the local elites. School consolidation and the resulting decline in the social boundaries between communities through blended school districts and high schools increased after the Second World War. With consolidation came pressure for uniform curricula at least on a statewide basis. As midwestern communities prided themselves on the quality and the universality of education, there were more objections to losing the high school football team than in changing the social studies or science curriculum.

Cultural homogeneity was a distinguishing feature of the postwar rural Midwest, due in part to the decline in European immigration during the 1920s through the 1940s. But the second and third generation descendents of German, Finnish, Danish, Swedish, Norwegian, Dutch, and English who had moved to the region often maintained a degree of separation, if not through their churches and other organizations then through a shared sense of belonging. In the mid-1990s, a blonde undergraduate from rural Iowa reported her pain in growing up a Finn in a Swedish community. Ethnic prejudice and tension were real in some communities. A Wisconsin native recalled a childhood conversation with a school busdriver from the early 1960s: "One time our school bus driver told me he would give me a dollar for each Norwegian I could find who was worth anything…. I found him ten, and he said only two counted because the rest were dumb Norwegians, just like me."[22]

Religious homogeneity persisted to 2000, with many midwestern counties over 50 percent Lutheran, Catholic, Methodist, Christian and Missionary Alliance, Anglican, or Mennonite. In southern Missouri and downstate Illinois, Baptists made up over 50 percent of the population in rural communities, which much more closely resembled the South than most of the Midwest.[23]

Counties were often a checkerboard of Protestant and Catholic communities, and the rivalries among sports teams were echoed in the strong norms against dating—and worse, marrying—a person of the "opposite" religions. This checkerboard pattern of community religious predominance in the Midwest led to greater intermarriage than occurred in the more homogeneous South, where Southern Baptists were the majority in most communities and counties. Religious endogamy began declining in the 1950s when the Baby Boomers began to come of age.[24]

After attracting new residents in the 1970s largely around the booming agricultural economy, rural communities in the Midwest reverted to their long-term trend of out-migration in the 1980s and into the 1990s. Only the new immigrants, primarily from Mexico and Central America, who began arriving in significant numbers in the 1990s kept populations from declining further.[25] That was the case in Sublette, Kansas.

The de-unionization of industry during the postwar period changed the complexion of the labor force. Meatpacking plants, which once paid good wages that attracted local men and women from farms and towns, reduced pay and benefits and speeded up the meatpacking line. Packinghouse wages in Iowa declined more than 40 percent between 1978 and 1992. As wages plummeted, it became increasingly difficult to recruit so-called corn-fed (white male) Iowa workers, so the large meatpacking companies began to recruit workers in Mexico and later Africa and Southeast Asia. In Iowa the downward spiral in real wages in meatpacking preceded the massive in-migration of Latinos to work in the plants.[26]

The fact that declining wages preceded the recruitment of outside workers did not prevent people in those communities from blaming the newcomers, both documented and undocumented, for the deterioration in pay and in the quality of jobs on the meatpacking line. This was not a propitious beginning for relations between immigrants and long-term residents in meatpacking communities that were accustomed to racial and ethnic homogeneity dating back to World War I, when German Americans were compelled to reject their ethnicity. The new immigrants, often of different language, racial, and religious background than those who had previously held the jobs, upset the comfortable cultural balance that had developed between descendents of Western and Northern European immigrants.[27] Changes in places like Sublette required a lot of effort and adjustment.

Response to the new immigrants was sharply divided. Legalists demanded that everyone speak English and have all their documents in perfect order before arriving in town. Pluralists valued diversity in otherwise homogeneous settings and stressed social justice. Pragmatists viewed the new immigrants as necessary for the economy in order to replace the local youth who migrated to areas with more amenities.[28]

The Creative Class in Midwestern Rural Communities

Some midwestern rural communities proved innovative in terms of accepting difference, which is critical for nurturing entrepreneurs. Despite the many obstacles, a number of creative communities developed in the Midwest after the farm crisis of the 1970s and 1980s thanks to an entrepreneurial culture that stimulated economic development and the growth of amenities.[29]

Aurora, Nebraska, was one of these rural places that managed to successfully negotiate postwar changes. Aurora, located in the rich bottomland of the Platte River about five miles off Interstate 80 in Hamilton County, grew from a city of 2,455 inhabitants in 1950 to 4,225 in 2000, while the county population increased slightly from 8,778 in 1950 to 9,403 in 2000.

By 2000, the town boasted a first-class library, an excellent community center, a hands-on science center, two moderate-income housing corporations, and a farm museum. It developed a lively industrial park and a farmers' cooperative that included 29 communities in central Nebraska and northern Kansas. In September 2006, groundbreaking occurred on the Aurora West Project, a joint venture between the Aurora Coop and private firms that when completed will include grain-handling facilities, an automated fueling station, an agronomy center, and a 220 million gallon-per-year ethanol plant. In a previous joint venture in the early 1990s, the Coop was a partner in a 50 million gallon-per-year ethanol plant, sited next to the new larger plant, although Aurora Coop sold its interest in the original facility.

Hamilton Telecommunications provided sophisticated electronic communication for its customer base and received the contract with the state for a "translation" center for deaf and hearing-impaired telephone customers throughout the state. The firm trained and employed 45 skilled translators.

Citizens still called it "the telephone company" in the early 2000s out of habit or out of affection for the thriving locally owned telecommunications firm. This misnomer frustrated CEO Phil Nelson because he worked vigorously to make it much more than just a telephone company. The company also managed a telemarketing firm that employed two hundred people in 1996 at modest wages. Hamilton Telecommunications was a key factor in attracting a Denver-based software company in 1998. The president of the software company affirmed that the telecommunications company provided more options and better transmission power than was available in Denver. Aurora also recruited an Iams pet food plant in 1985 that utilized corn purchased from area farmers.

Aurora was more successful in building a collective life for its people and generating a sense of optimism about its future than was Irwin or Oberlin. Aurora's success was due, in part, to its location in a prosperous farming area with irrigated agriculture, its proximity to an interstate highway, and its success in attracting or initiating a number of manufacturing firms.[30]

A number of individuals paved the way for long-term changes in local culture and organization by reinvesting in the community. For instance, Aurora had 12 community-based foundations, the first of which was established in 1964. In the late 1960s, the culture of giving was enhanced by a banker and his wife who died without progeny. They became benefactors of the foundation that funded construction and maintenance of the library. Other donors—large and small—followed suit, and it became the norm for financial advisors to suggest that people consider a bequest to one of the community's foundations, along with providing for their children and grandchildren. By the early 2000s the community's foundations possessed over $44 million of physical and cash assets, including a library, museum, educational center, leadership training center, senior center, community center, hospital expansion, home care, and independent living facilities. The original community foundation continued to fund university scholarships for local students.

Ken Wortman was a leader of Aurora's creative class. Wortman established a car dealership in Aurora in 1948 with funds borrowed from his family after he was mustered out of the army. He was a founder of the Aurora Development Corporation (ADC), which brought community leaders together. He cajoled and maneuvered to make sure that individuals representing all major local economic interests were at the table and, with others, devised a mechanism for bringing promising young men (few women have been groomed for leadership in the town) into leadership roles in the ADC.

But there are other more subtle aspects to the Aurora story, including a willingness to generate money locally for a project, rather than first seeking a grant. Compared to Oberlin, which also generated internal investments, Aurora residents were overtly suspicious of government investments and the resulting strings attached. Similarly, and in contrast to Oberlin, Aurora promoters preferred to spend resources for locally owned enterprises rather than engage in subsidizing outside firms to locate in Aurora, known as "smokestack chasing." A community-minded banker explained Aurora's approach to economic development:

> A lot of towns will give them [businesses] a building, give them land, give them this. Our story is, everything's paid for here; you don't have to pay for it. All you got to do is come here and create jobs. We've paid for everything else. You don't have to pay for the schools and the libraries and this city's infrastructure is all paid for and is in place. A lot of communities—they expect them to help pay for it all, you know, so that's been a big selling point—plus the quality of life.[31]

Leaders in Aurora recognize the importance of both community development and economic development. The focus on making the community a good place to live—assuring good health care, adequate housing, quality schools, and recreational and cultural opportunities, and, yes, a low tax ideology—are better economic development tools than are tax abatements.

Aurora city government is a facilitator, not an initiator. One of the community's goals articulated in the 1989 strategic plan was "To continue to develop the new and enhanced facilities needed to provide a high quality of life for our citizens from private funds rather than tax dollars."[32] The city could have proposed a bond issue to build a library, but these "conservative collectivists" preferred, when possible, to keep government out, even if it meant using private funds for maintenance of the building, as in the case of the library.

The city administrator offered his explanation for Aurora's success by contrasting Aurora with Hays, Kansas, the city of 20,000 where he worked prior to Aurora. He stated that Aurora possessed "a great attitude." Hays was "factionalized" in the sense that "if somebody got something and some other group perceived it to be at their expense...we don't have that here," he claimed. "Not that we don't have disagreements. But that they're left at the table, they're never personal."[33]

Conclusion: Sublette and Irwin at the Turn of the Century

Capital-intensive technology made Sublette more stable as a community since the 1940 USDA study. A 1964 follow-up study found that local residents utilized irrigation to overcome (at least temporarily) environmental limitations, but instead of developing a diversified agriculture they simply used it to raise corn to the exclusion of other crops. Government programs undergirded the irrigation and corn prices, but local residents who voice distrust of government do not acknowledge the government's role in supporting the local economy. In local politics, new professionals had increasing influence and a different agenda, with more concern about city parks and schools than farm prices and safety nets.[34]

The changes in Sublette between 1945 and the turn of the twenty-first century align with Wuthnow's view of a generally positive remaking of rural communities, despite new sources of social tensions. By 1993, the results of yet another sociological community study were published, showing that the Hugoton gas field, one of the largest known gas reserves in the world, provided employment that reduced the community's dependence on agriculture. Agriculture remained essential to the community, but by the late twentieth century it was irrigated agriculture, which enhanced the stability of the population even as doubts arose about the long-term future of the Ogallala Aquifer. Irrigation increased feed grain production, which in turn attracted feedlots and meatpacking plants. Originally locally owned, the meatpackers transitioned to transnational corporations, responsive to global trends in the demand for meat. The population was about 1,400. Hispanics, employed mostly at feedlots and meatpacking plants, comprised 13 percent of the population in 1990. By 2000, the population had increased to 1,592 and Hispanics were over 21 percent, yet all elected and appointed officials were Anglo males. Hispanic workers from Sublette were active in unions at the meatpacking plants in other communities and were active in churches but were largely absent from other aspects of civic life.[35]

Irwin had experienced significant change since 1940. The population of the town remained about the same as it had been in the late 1930s (372), but it had lost more businesses, and its schools had consolidated into IKM (Irwin-Kirkman-Manila), despite the long-term rivalry between Irwin and Manila. Agriculture was more specialized, with an emphasis on corn, soybeans, hogs, and cattle, and the decline in the number of farmers was significant. Median income in Irwin was below that of Iowa and of Sublette, but the cost of living was 20 percent below the U.S. average. There is still excellent support for the schools, although parents feel that their children have no future in Irwin. For all of their doubts about the future of Irwin, residents wonder whether the cities are really better.[36]

The Farm Services Cooperative of Irwin and the Farmer's Elevator dominated the town's physical landscape. Robinson Implement Inc. greatly expanded its service area and was doing well. There were numerous local service providers, including auto body shops, mechanics, beauty shops, a gunsmith, a veterinary clinic, a corn sheller, an independent insurance agency, a tank wagon, a bulldozing service, plumbing and electric shops, and a local branch of the Shelby County State Bank, which purchased the local Irwin bank in the 1980s. The locker plant still butchered local meat and added a deli. There were few retail establishments, however. A convenience store with grocery, deli, movie rentals, and gasoline met many basic needs in the community. The Godfather's Pizza at Irwin Country Store seated 80 patrons and was used for social events as well as family dining. The majority of the working population left Irwin for their jobs.

In 1989, Irwin founded its own Chamber of Commerce, but by 2000 it had become part of the Shelby County Chamber of Commerce. The three remaining local churches were an important source of community interaction. All were branches of mainstream denominations, and they tended to seek pastors who favor individual solutions within the current institutional and social structures.[37]

Oberlin, Kansas, and Aurora, Nebraska, both cities with a high degree of internal leadership and willingness to invest locally, chose different paths to development. While both started with social investments—the carnival, a community cafe, and movie house in Oberlin and Decatur County, and a library and scholarship in Aurora and Hamilton County, Oberlin sought outside investment from both the state and markets sectors while Aurora focused on internal market investment. As a result, Aurora was able to maintain the enterprises it began through local investment, while most failed in Oberlin.

Irwin residents of the early 1990s reported that they felt "somewhat or very much at home in Irwin" and very attached to the community.[38] Farm residents expressed less attachment. Almost everyone surveyed listed high numbers of relatives and friends in Irwin, and most found this to be a good thing. Town residents were active in their community, which was similar to the situation in 1940. Despite the impact of the 1980s farm crisis, Irwin fits Wuthnow's hypothesis of a town re-creating itself to survive in the twenty-first century.

At the beginning of the twenty-first century the fortunes of small towns and rural communities varied, based on whether they faced persistent poverty, amenity-led rapid growth (rural and remote), or rapid exurban growth. Rural midwestern communities were particularly vulnerable to the debilitating impacts of increasing monoculture, consolidation of farms, and loss of community vitality. The promise of amenity- and service-based rural economies and the loosening of the tie between job and residence brought on by the digital age offered some hope but did not fully materialize. Industrialization and consolidation of agriculture have contributed to increasingly uneven rural community development.[39]

Midwestern rural communities changed dramatically from the end of World War II to the turn of the twenty-first century. Their populations were older. Ethnic diversity and acceptance of diversity increased. While many small communities had disappeared, county government and the consolidated school districts helped redefine and broaden the boundaries of rural midwestern communities. These changes might support the pessimistic view expressed by Richard Davies. However, those communities that have expanded their boundaries and made them more permeable, and more accepting of innovation and newcomers, maintain participatory local institutions that support the optimism expressed by Robert Wuthnow. Residents of midwestern rural communities may have had lower incomes than those in urban areas, but they also appreciated their pace of life and their ability to work with neighbors to improve their local area.

Notes

1. Richard O. Davies, *Main Street Blues: The Decline of Small Town America* (Columbus: Ohio State University Press, 1998), 162.

2. Robert Wuthnow, *Remaking the Heartland: Middle America since the 1950s* (Princeton, NJ: Princeton University Press, 2011), ix.

3. E.O. Moe and C.C. Taylor, *Culture in a Contemporary Rural Community: Irwin, Iowa. Rural Life Studies 5* (Washington, DC: USDA, Bureau of Agricultural Economics, 1943); E.H. Bell, *Culture of a Contemporary Rural Community: Sublette, Kansas. Rural Life Studies 2* (Washington, DC: USDA, Bureau of Agricultural Economics, 1942); C.C. Taylor, C.P. Loomis, J.Provinse, J.E. Huett Jr., and K. Young, *Cultural, Structural and Social Psychological Study of Selected American Farm Communities: Field Manual* (Washington, DC: USDA, Bureau of Agricultural Economics, 1940); L. Bloomquist, D. Williams, and J.C. Bridger, "Sublette, Kansas: Persistence and Change in Haskell County," in *Persistence and Change in Rural Communities: A 50-Year Follow-Up to Six Classic Studies*, ed. A.E. Luloff and Richard S. Krannich (New York: CABI Publishing, 2002); E.O. Hoiberg, "Irwin, Iowa: Persistence and Change in Shelby County, " in *Persistence and Change in Rural Communities*; C.B. Flora, J.L. Flora, and S. Fey, *Rural Communities: Legacy and Change* (2nd edition) (Boulder, CO: Westview Press, 2004); "Rural Communities: Legacy & Change," <www.learner.org/resources/series7.html> (accessed February 26, 2013); Scott Robinson, director, and Jan L. Flora, project director, "The Invisible People" (Mexico City: Grupo Cine

Labor, 1975), 16 mm, 32 min., available from Kansas State University Minorities Center, Farrell Library.

4. Moe and Taylor, *Culture in a Contemporary Rural Community*, 70, 60.

5. Bell, *Culture of a Contemporary Rural Community*, 109.

6. Katherine Jellison, *Entitled to Power: Farm Women and Technology, 1913–1963* (Chapel Hill: University of North Carolina Press, 1993).

7. M.M. Kroma and C.B. Flora, "Greening Pesticides: The Presentation of an Agricultural Tool over Time," *Agriculture and Human Values* 20 (2003): 21–35.

8. F. Hines, M. Petrulis, and S. Daberkow, "An Overview of the Non-Metro Economy and the Role of Agriculture in Non-Metro Development," in *Interdependencies of Agriculture and Rural Communities in the Twenty-First Century: The North Central Region*, ed. P. Korsching and J. Gildner (Ames, IA: North Central Regional Center for Rural Development, 1986); Sonya Salamon, *Prairie Patrimony: Family, Farming, and Community in the Midwest* (Chapel Hill: University of North Carolina Press, 1992).

9. Allan Schnaiberg and Kenneth Alan Gould, "Treadmill Predispositions and Social Responses: Population, Consumption, and Technological Change," in *Environment and Society: The Enduring Conflict* (New York: St Martin's Press, 1994); D.C. Monchuk, J.A. Miranowski, D.J. Hayes, and B. Babcock, "An Analysis of Regional Economic Growth in the U.S. Midwest," Working Paper 05-WP392, April 2005, Center for Agriculture and Rural Development, Iowa State University.

10. "Understanding Rural America," *Agriculture Information Bulletin No. 710* (Washington, DC: Economic Research Service, USDA, 1995).

11. J.L. Flora and C.B. Flora, "Local Economic Development Projects: Key Factors," in *Rural Community Economic Development in the Midwest*, ed. Norman Walzer (Westport, CT: Praeger Publishers, 1991).

12. Stephen Prowse, "Equity Capital and Entrepreneurs," in *Equity for Rural America: From Wall Street to Main Street*, ed. Mark Drabenstott and Larry Meeker (Kansas City, MO: Federal Reserve Bank of Kansas City, 1999).

13. William P. Browne, *The Failure of National Rural Policy: Institutions and Interests* (Washington, DC: Georgetown University Press, 2001).

14. Wuthnow, *Remaking the Heartland*, 214–53.

15. Deborah Fink, *Cutting into the Meatpacking Line: Workers and Change in the Rural Midwest* (Chapel Hill: University of North Carolina Press, 1998); D.D. Stull, M.J. Broadway, and D. Griffith, eds., *Any Way You Cut It: Meat Processing and Small Town America* (Lawrence: University Press of Kansas, 1995).

16. Interview by authors, 1987.

17. *Oberlin Herald*, December 11, 1986.

18. They also used the trips to generate publicity and community support. In the case of the visit to Hydro, Oklahoma, to see the home-grown carnival, the participants were carefully chosen. They included, among others, a local banker and the wife of the newspaper publisher. Not surprisingly, the newspaper became a strong supporter of a similar project in Decatur County, and the bank contributed $2,000 toward initiation of the carnival; other bankers in the county followed suit.

19. Perhaps it is most like the Northeast, although early on much of the rural Northeast was more closely linked to its metropolitan cities than was true for most of the rural Midwest. Max Pfeffer, "Social Origins of Three Systems of Farm Production in the United States," *Rural Sociology* 48 (4) (1983): 540–62; W.R. Freudenberg, "The Density of Acquain-

tanceship: An Overlooked Variable in Community Research?" *American Journal of Sociology* 92 (1982): 27–63.

20. C.B. Flora and A. Thiboumery, "Devils Lake, Ramsey County Capitals Assessment," unpublished paper, North Central Regional Center for Rural Development, Ames, IA, 2005.

21. C.B. Flora, "Rural Peoples in a Global Economy," *Rural Sociology* 55 (2) (1990): 157–77.

22. Personal conversation, Ames, IA, July 2010.

23. *Major Religious Families by Counties of the United States: 2000* (Nashville, TN: Glenmary Research Center, 2002).

24. D.E. Sherkat, "Religious Intermarriage in the United States: Trends, Patterns, and Predictors," *Social Science Research* 33 (2004): 619; E.L. Lehrer, "Religious Intermarriage in the United States: Determinants and Trends," *Social Science Research* 27 (1998): 245–63.

25. "Understanding Rural America," *Agriculture Information Bulletin No. 710* (Washington, DC: Economic Research Service, USDA, 1995).

26. U.S. Census Bureau. "County Business Patterns (CBP): U.S., States, and Counties in the U.S. (1998–2007)"; "County Business Patterns: State Data 1977–1997," Geospatial and Statistical Data Center, Charlottesville, VA, 2008 (see figure 1); J.L. Flora, C. Prado-Meza, H. Lewis, C. Montalvo, and F. Dunn, "Impact of Immigration and Customs Enforcement Raid on Marshalltown, Iowa," in *Latinos in the Midwest*, ed. Rubén O. Martinez (East Lansing: Michigan State University Press, 2011).

27. Dale Maharidge and Michael Z. Williamson, *Denison, Iowa: Searching for the Soul of America through the Secrets of a Midwest Town* (New York: Free Press, 2005); James W. Loewen, *Sundown Towns: A Hidden Dimension of American Racism* (New York: New Press, 2005); Eileen Diaz McConnell and Faranak Mraftab, "Sundown Town to 'Little Mexico': Old-Timers and Newcomers in an American Small Town," *Rural Sociology* 74 (4) (December 2009): 605–29.

28. C.B. Flora, J. Flora, and R.J. Tapp, "Meat, Meth, and Mexicans: Community Responses to Increasing Ethnic Diversity," *Journal of the Community Development Society* 31 (2000): 277–99; David J. McGranahan, "Natural Amenities Drive Rural Population Change," *Agricultural Economics Report* No. 781 (Washington, DC: USDA, 1999).

29. Richard L. Florida, *The Rise of the Creative Class: And How It's Transforming Work, Leisure, Community and Everyday Life* (New York: Basic Books, 2002); D.A. McGranahan and T.R. Wojan, "The Creative Class: A Key to Rural Growth," *Amber Waves* 5 (2) (2007): 17–21; J.L. Flora, J.S. Sharp, C.B. Flora, and B. Newlon, "Entrepreneurial Social Infrastructure and Locally Initiated Economic Development," *Sociological Quarterly* 38 (4) (1997): 623–45; C.B. Flora and J.L. Flora, "Entrepreneurial Social Infrastructure: A Necessary Ingredient," *The Annals of the American Academy of Political and Social Science* 529 (1993): 48–58.

30. Jeff S. Sharp, "Locating the Community Field: A Study of Interorganizational Network Structure and Capacity for Community Action," *Rural Sociology* 66 (3) (2001): 403–24; see also J. Flora's observations from having conducted research in Aurora and the two other communities compared in Sharp's article.

31. Personal interview conducted by Jan Flora and Jeff Sharp, August 16, 1996.

32. "Strategic Plan of the City of Aurora: 1989," Aurora, NE, approved October 1989, p. 2.

33. Personal interviews conducted by Jeff Sharp and Jan Flora, July 23, 1996, City of

Aurora Information Center, Aurora, Nebraska, <www.cityofaurora.org/> (accessed February 26, 2013). It should be noted that Hays is much larger than Aurora, and originally founded by German Russians, it had developed strong ethnic and class divisions over the years as it shifted from agriculture to petroleum and back again.

34. W.E. Mays, *Sublette Revisited: Stability and Change in a Rural Kansas Community after a Quarter Century* (New York: Floram Park Press, 1968); Bloomquist et al., "Sublette, Kansas: Persistence and Change," 38.

35. D.D. Williams, "From Dustbowl to Green Circles: A Case Study of Haskell County, Kansas" (unpublished PhD diss., Kansas State University, Manhattan, Kansas, 1995).

36. Hoiberg, "Irwin, Iowa," 62.

37. J.L. Flora, C.B. Flora, and E. Houdek, with M. Weinberg and M. Lapping, *Rural Communities: Legacy and Change: Faculty Guide* (Boulder, CO: Westview Press, 1992).

38. Hoiberg, "Irwin, Iowa," 63.

39. Flora et al., *Rural Communities: Legacy and Change*, 274.

FIVE — **UNEASY DEPENDENCY**

Rural and Farm Policy and the Midwest since 1945

J.L. Anderson

In 1973 a chemical company had inadvertently delivered polybrominated biphenyl (PBB), a fire retardant, to a Michigan Farm Bureau livestock feed yard instead of magnesium oxide, a livestock feed additive. A worker at the feed yard mistook the fire retardant for the feed additive and subsequently mixed the PBB with livestock feed. The contaminated feed was sold and distributed to farms across the state. Millions of people consumed the tainted milk, meat, and eggs that came from the tens of thousands of dairy cows, thousands of other large farm animals, and over a million chickens that ingested contaminated feed. Farm losses from destroyed livestock were estimated to be as high as $100 million, with an unknown cost to human health. The incident attracted attention from around the world and resulted in legislative and congressional hearings, numerous lawsuits, and the cessation of PBB manufacturing in 1976. That same year the Centers for Disease Control initiated a multi-agency, long-term study of possible health effects of PBB exposure.[1]

What happened to the farmers who used the contaminated feed on their farms? In 1979 researchers investigating health consequences of the incident found that these farmers experienced depression and guilt about their inadvertent role in the incident. Bureaucrats, scientists, and chemical industry representatives assumed that farmer error was to blame and failed to consider the possibility that contaminated feed was the problem. One of the researchers related that one farmer had a recurring dream in which a government representative approached the farmer's house and handed him a check for one million dollars. "In another dream," the doctor reported, "that Government agent comes to the door and the farmer blows his head off." The role of the government man in this person's dream life was extreme, but it reflects the fact that farmers found that in their waking lives the government was ever-present in the countryside.[2]

The dream also highlighted the tension between government as friend and government as enemy. Regardless of individual opinions about the wisdom or legality of the New Deal reach into everyday life, government quickly became a critical means of support for rural people, even as it failed to solve the worst of America's rural problems. World War II strengthened the government's position in the countryside. Farmers who became accustomed to commodity programs during the 1930s and 1940s encountered an ever-widening scope of government action in the postwar period. This expanding reach of government resulted in an uneasy dependency between rural people and government that characterized the postwar period.[3]

This essay addresses the ways in which rural midwesterners and their governments—federal, state, and local—attempted to form rural policies to meet changing social, technological, economic, and environmental conditions. It is a story of farmers, farm organizations, government institutions, and policy makers as they grappled with seemingly intractable problems. To what extent would the New Deal rural and farm programs be maintained, if at all? How would politicians, United States Department of Agriculture (USDA) officials, advocacy groups, state and local authorities, and farmers behave? How would governments shape the social, economic, and physical landscape of the rural Midwest?

Changes that transformed the rural Midwest after 1945 unhinged some old assumptions about the relationship between governments and farmers. In one sense, midwestern farmers confronted what historian R. Douglas Hurt described as "problems of plenty": a continuation of the surpluses of the first half of the twentieth century. Journalist Loren Soth observed in 1957 that more than 25 years of federal farm policy to support farm income and align farm production with demand for commodities had not yielded the expected fruit. Soth, editor of the *Des Moines Register and Tribune*'s editorial page, lamented that "Acreage controls have not been successful yet we continue to employ them. Price supports limited to a few basic crops have not done a good job of stabilizing total farm income." Protecting commodity prices disrupted foreign trade and was costly for taxpayers. But for Soth, issues of plenty were only part of the story. The federal government only offered "timid" efforts to deal with the one-third of rural families in poverty—those who were "outside the stream of twentieth century progress." As farmers became more productive due to the substitution of capital for labor, surpluses compounded and the divide between rural haves and have-nots widened, compelling farmers and policy makers alike to rethink government farm programs.[4]

Government action subsequently expanded into new areas. President Lyndon Johnson's War on Poverty struck rural targets as well as urban ones. An emerging consumer movement brought government attention to issues of food quality and production. Critics raised environmental concerns about pesticides, chemical fertilizers, and livestock waste and asked for governmental solutions. America's newest minority, rural Americans, found themselves at odds with the growing urban and suburban population.

Part of the solution to the problems associated with this new minority status was to seek action at the state and local level. State-level involvement was not new, but some of the objects of regulation and action were. Tax credits, environmental regulation, and efforts to curb corporate farming all were important issues for state legislatures, governors, and bureaucrats. Local governments, including the county and township, were bulwarks for people who viewed themselves as victims of corporations and failures of state and federal governments.

The Farm Bill

Farmers were concerned about the direction of federal farm policy at the end of World War II. They dreaded a repeat of the post–World War I collapse of farm commodity prices in 1919–1920 and the end of wartime prosperity. In 1942, Congress passed the Steagall amendment to maintain price supports until 1948 and forestall a postwar collapse, but it was an open question if the surpluses and low prices that plagued farmers during the interwar period would return with peace. Farm organizations with significant constituencies in the region argued over farm policy, with groups such as the American Farm Bureau Federation (AFBF) often squaring off against the National Farmers Union (NFU). More recently, commodity-based organizations have risen to prominence in shaping farm policy.[5]

The New Deal system of supporting farm commodity prices attracted attacks from the left and right. President Truman's secretary of agriculture Charles Brannan maintained that preserving farmers was the most important task, and he proposed supporting farm income rather than commodity prices. Brannan hoped to maintain viable family farms and urged capping support for the largest farms that had been the biggest beneficiaries of commodity programs. From the right, President Eisenhower's secretary of agriculture, Ezra Taft Benson, hoped to free agriculture from what he viewed as costly un-American programs that undermined freedom. While some farmers were comfortable at the ends of this ideological spectrum, the most common reaction to federal farm policy was much less ideological. Specifically, a farmer's financial condition at election time was often the most important consideration for supporting a secretary of agriculture, congressman, or presidential candidate.[6]

The Korean War shifted attention away from the Brannan Plan and back to maximizing production. Dwight Eisenhower's campaign message to farmers was "...a Better Day for the farmer..." that was to consist of "Full 100% of Parity for all farm products...not just 90%."[7] Farmers could be excused if they were surprised when Secretary Benson advocated introducing more of a free market system of flexible price supports that would range from 75 to 90 percent of parity. In 1953, wheat farmers voted to end acreage allotments and in 1958 corn farmers followed suit. Both of these free market solutions yielded bitter fruit. Farm income suffered in the Eisenhower years, sliding 27 percent from 1951 to 1955 due to massive surpluses and a cost-price squeeze. To help ease surpluses, the administration proposed and Congress enacted the Soil Bank program, which allowed farmers to retire land from production in exchange for cash payments. Still, farmers wanted less Benson and more government assistance. Both Democratic and Republican farmers in Iowa overwhelmingly wanted production payments to make up the difference between the support price and the record low market price for hogs. Iowa Republican congressman Ben Jensen, fighting for his political life in what had been a reliable Republican district, claimed that the Benson plan was "almost a complete failure."[8]

Widespread dissatisfaction with Benson led some farmers to search for an alternative vision. In 1955, a group of Iowa farmers formed the National Farmers Organization (NFO), led by Oren Lee Staley of Missouri. Headquartered in Corning, Iowa, NFO quickly gained popularity in the Midwest. NFO leaders testified before Congress about the power that processors had over individual producers. By 1957, the NFO embraced collective bargaining, an indirect appeal to the left by invoking union language but also made an attempt to appeal to the right by emphasizing self-help and rejecting government handouts. In 1962, the NFO initiated withholding action to compel processors to sign contracts with NFO members in hopes of gaining income security.[9]

The Eisenhower years left midwestern farmers ambivalent about the future of federal involvement in agriculture. Nationally, 78 percent of *Farm Journal* subscribers wanted lower government supports and controls.

Figure 5.1: During a 1967 NFO holding action, Minnesota dairy farmer Dale Rommes scoured and disinfected his cement mixer to churn butter on the farm. According to Rommes, "We gave a lot of butter away and also dumped a lot of milk on the ground. We were milking about 100 cows at the time and for two weeks no milk left the farm." Source: Mary A. Mitchell. Used with permission.

Midwestern subscribers voiced the most significant support for commodity programs, with 53 percent favoring some degree of support and 47 percent wanting none. Iowa farm opinion polls also indicated the rural divide. One-fifth of Iowa farmers surveyed wanted government out of agriculture, and two-thirds favored some kind of government program. Younger farmers tended to favor less involvement. As one older farmer stated, "We've been thru it. And these youngsters haven't. They're too hopeful that a little bitty program will take care of a whopper of a problem." Similarly, a *Des Moines Register* farm poll indicated that 44 percent favored a price support program based on parity while only 24 percent supported an AFBF proposal for supports based on a three-year moving average of market prices.[10]

President Kennedy and his secretary of agriculture Orville Freeman advocated a stricter program of production control. In 1963, wheat farmers conducted a nationwide referendum on a USDA proposal for a 10 percent acreage cut accompanied by high price supports. If the program failed to receive a two-thirds majority then a low support program and low restriction program would be enacted. The program only gained the required majority in six states, all but one of them in the South. Midwesterners east of the Mississippi who tended to vary crop strategies overwhelmingly rejected the plan, while a majority of farmers east of the river who were more heavily committed to one or two cash grain crops favored it, but only North Dakota farmers gave support even close to the necessary two-thirds.[11]

The rejection of stricter government controls in 1963 mirrored the position of the AFBF. Charles Shuman, Illinois farmer and AFBF president, wanted to get the government out of farming to prevent the American farmer from becoming "a member of a permanently subsidized peasantry." Shuman carried on the vision of his predecessor, Iowa farmer Allan Kline, who led the charge for "less government, not more" during his tenure as president from 1947 to 1954. Shuman once claimed that the federal farm program "denies the unmistakable pattern of God's law" and that federal payments were an addictive drug used by socialistic government bureaucrats. Shuman's primary critic from the left, Kansan and NFU president Jim Patton, contended that "What Charlie Shuman doesn't realize is that we've got the welfare state and we've had it for 30 years. And we're not going to give it up unless we lose the ballot box."[12]

Shuman was at odds with some Farm Bureau members in his own state. DeKalb County Farm Bureau president Howard Mullins was unique among Farm Bureau presidents in his outspoken opposition to parts of the AFBF agenda. President Kennedy appointed Mullins to the National Agricultural Advisory Commission because he was a Republican who supported Kennedy's feed-grain program and acreage restrictions. Mullins used his position on the commission to move administration policy away from mandatory restrictions toward a voluntary program.[13]

Farmers were suspicious of the Johnson administration due to its efforts to control rising food costs by releasing government surpluses. As one midwestern farmer claimed in 1966, "The Democrats are obviously appealing to the great mass of consumers. I think farmers have to accept the fact that they are a very small minority."[14] Nonfarm issues dominated national politics in the 1960s, and farm opinion was increasingly irrelevant in national elections.

President Nixon alienated many farmers from 1969 to early 1972 but ultimately managed to offer farmers inducements to vote Republican in the 1972 election. Farm income was low in early 1972 thanks to surpluses and high production costs. By fall, however, Nixon had authorized a massive increase in government payments to farmers, from $3.1 billion in 1971 to

$4.1 billion in 1972. Furthermore, the administration had negotiated the sale of 30 million bushels of wheat to the Soviet Union, which endeared Nixon to grain farmers in the Dakotas, Kansas, Nebraska, and Minnesota. But Nixon's eleventh-hour efforts did not sway all farmers. An Ohioan commented prior to the election, "Farmers from South Dakota elected George McGovern to two terms in the U.S. Senate....I'm sure if McGovern was the extremist the Republican party is trying to claim that he is, he would not be in the Senate today." Upon reelection, Nixon initiated price controls on meat to placate urban consumers but again alienated farmers. Favorable farm prices in 1973, however, eased the pain.[15]

Many midwestern farmers supported Georgia farmer Jimmy Carter in 1976, but Carter failed to sustain that support. Carter made a strong showing in the Iowa caucuses, impressing people with his sincerity and knowledge of farm issues, but he was the victim of high expectations on the part of farmers as well as his own political miscalculations. Low target prices for the 1977 crop, modest administration proposals for the 1977 farm bill, and a cheap food policy angered farmers. A 1978 *Farm Journal* poll indicated that 64.5 percent of midwestern farmers viewed consumers and farmers as natural antagonists. Carter's support among midwestern farmers fell from over 50 percent at his inauguration to under 30 percent six months later and hovered there through 1979. In response to the Soviet invasion of Afghanistan in 1980, the president declared a grain embargo of the USSR, which depressed prices and further alienated farmers. Administration offsets in the form of government buyouts of unfulfilled contracts, enhanced purchases for food relief, increased ethanol funding, and subsidized storage for unsold grain did not salvage Carter's reputation.[16]

The election of Ronald Reagan promised a conservative retreat from government involvement in agriculture. Jaded by Benson's apparent lack of sympathy with farm conditions, impatient with Nixon's inconsistencies, and frustrated by Carter's apparent concern for consumers over farmers, many farmers who supported Reagan would have been justified in believing that no involvement was better than insincerity, opportunism, and incompetence. But Reagan was no farm-policy free-market ideologue. In 1981, dairy farmers benefited from the administration's massive government milk purchases and continued support for commodity programs in exchange for votes on tax and budget bills. Reagan allowed extensive Soviet grain purchases in 1982 and offered farmers a $1.5 billion plan for interest-free and government-backed credits to foreign governments for U.S. grain purchases. American farmers received $12 billion in price supports in 1982, three times the amount paid in 1981. Midwesterners supported the Payment-In-Kind program, which paid farmers with grain from government storage in exchange for idling land. Just weeks before the 1984 presidential election, Reagan used a rural Iowa campaign stop to announce an extended repayment schedule for indebted farmers who had borrowed from the government or had private loans guaranteed by the federal government, reminding voters that he could deliver the goods better than Democrat Walter Mondale.[17]

A full-blown farm crisis developed in Reagan's second term. Chronic high inflation led the Federal Reserve to limit credit, which resulted in higher interest rates and caused a rapid decline in land prices. Farmers had borrowed heavily based on high land values, leaving them with debt they could not repay. Furthermore, the U.S. dollar surged in the early 1980s, which hurt farm exports and exacerbated commodity surpluses. By the mid-1980s, the Midwest was enduring the worst crisis since the Great Depression. Young educated farm operators who had leveraged assets to gain economies of scale were the most severely affected by the crisis, which caused a severe decline in quality of life and even led some to question the value of landownership, a cornerstone of agrarian ideology. At least one hundred farm groups formed in the region during the 1980s to assist farmers.[18]

Reagan's budget director David Stockman and leaders of the federal farm credit system expressed little sympathy for debt-plagued farmers. While lenders had aggressively sold credit to farmers in the 1970s, they were often equally aggressive about foreclosures in the 1980s. Nebraska Democratic senator J. James Exon exclaimed that the administration "doesn't give a cocklebur for rural America," expressing the frustration that some midwesterners felt as Reagan threatened to veto farm relief. Yet rural midwesterners were divided about financial assistance for farmers. A survey of North Dakota farmers and rural residents indicated that approximately 45 percent still favored some kind of federal or state financial program, while approximately 35 percent were opposed. Reagan was slow to respond to indebted farmers, but annual federal commodity payments during the 1980s exceeded those of the 1970s.[19]

In the midst of the farm crisis, Congress passed the Food Security Act of 1985, a program that apparently pleased no one but was a bill that all could live with. It provided for a continuation of the federal commodity programs, including increases in cash subsidies as well as easing the $50,000 cap on payments to individual farmers. A survey of Illinois and Ohio farmers in 1984 and 1985 indicated that only about one-third of farmers wanted to continue the current program and one-fourth wanted no federal commodity programs. Current programs were most popular with farmers who reported sales over $200,000 per year and were least satisfactory to those with sales under $40,000. Just 22 percent of the higher income farmers reported a desire to be rid of commodity programs, while 29 percent felt that agriculture would be better without them. The Food Security Act of 1985 included several conservation provisions that were popular with farmers. The Conservation Reserve Program allowed farmers to take highly erodible land out of production for ten-year periods, in theory advancing the conservation cause and reducing production. The "swampbuster" section required that farmers who converted wetlands to agricultural use developed or preserved wetlands somewhere else. Noncompliance resulted in the loss of other federal farm payments.[20]

Subsequent commodity policy debates followed established forms of more government/less government until the deregulation debate on the 1996 Farm Bill. Kansas congressman Pat Roberts introduced the Federal Agriculture Improvement and Reform Act, commonly known as Freedom to Farm, to eliminate subsidies and allow farmers to plant what they wanted. Senator Robert Dole proclaimed that "Farmers will finally plant for the market and not for the government." As one Kansas farmer explained, "I'm locked into wheat because the Government won't let me change," claiming that he could make more money raising corn for a local feedlot. The act provided for seven years of transition payments to ease farmers away from subsidies and would expire if Congress did not reauthorize it in 2002.[21]

Since 1996, farmers experienced varying degrees of freedom, including the freedom to fail. Congress was free to deal with the inevitable contingencies such as crop failures, natural disasters, and low prices due to soaring production and collapsed international markets. Commodity prices were at record highs in the mid-1990s when Freedom to Farm became law, but a price collapse in the late 1990s inspired emergency measures that pumped ever-larger sums into the countryside starting in 1998. In 1999 hog prices were at the lowest level since the 1930s, prompting hog industry representatives to ask for help. Missouri farmer Blake Hurst supported Freedom to Farm in 1996 but six years later was still participating in federal commodity programs, conceding that as long as he qualified for them he would continue to cash the checks.[22]

Even as midwestern farmers disagreed about the role of the federal government in agriculture, they were major beneficiaries of federal commodity payments. Midwestern states frequently ranked among the top ten states receiving government payments from 1995 to 2010. During those years, Iowa ranked number one; Illinois, Nebraska, Minnesota, and Kansas were third, fourth, fifth, and sixth, respectively; Indiana ranked eighth and North Dakota tenth. Missouri, South Dakota, Ohio, and Wisconsin ranked twelfth through fifteenth, and Michigan ranked twentieth. Furthermore, federal farm credit, crop insurance, and disaster relief all provided major props to the rural Midwest. New Deal production and commodity programs proved to be remarkably enduring.[23]

Electrification

Federal support for another New Deal venture, rural electrification, also proved to be enduring and popular. The Rural Electrification Administration (REA), created in 1935, provided low-cost loans to farmers who organized cooperatives to establish service to rural areas and to construct power-generating and transmission stations. The program had barely begun before World War II, but by the late 1950s approximately 90 percent of rural people had access to electricity. The co-ops managed to pay back almost all of their loans, making it an anomaly in accountability.

The Eisenhower administration paid little attention to the REA because the agency supported small scale co-ops that served a long-ignored constituency, but Eisenhower also believed that public power had a chilling effect on private enterprise. When an Indiana cooperative applied for a $42 million REA loan to construct a power plant to provide energy for an aluminum smelter, the Eisenhower administration replied that industrial use was contrary to the purpose of the REA and denied the loan. Encouraged, private power companies extended "spite lines" into co-op areas and offered lower rates to drive out the co-ops in the 1960s. In Michigan co-ops responded during the 1970s and organized the Michigan Electrical Cooperative Association to gain a higher profile in the state legislature and to combat private spite lines. Public power was a critical tool for enhancing rural quality of life and economic development.[24]

Even as public power remained popular, a surprising controversy arose in the upper Midwest in the 1970s. Minnesota's two electric generation and transmission organizations, United Power Association and Cooperative Power Association, obtained REA loans to construct a power plant in North Dakota to serve rural markets in western Minnesota. Two years of hearings on power line corridor and route selection resulted in tremendous friction between many rural people and the co-ops. Project opponents claimed that state and federal governments did not adequately consult with landowners in the corridor, project costs were excessive, payments for farmland were too low by comparison to other land, and bureaucrats were more concerned about wildlife and highways than rural people and farmland. When some rural residents refused to grant easements, the state intervened. Approximately one thousand farmers arrived in Minneapolis to demand a construction moratorium while others harassed survey crews, blocked construction machinery, vandalized equipment, and intimidated work crews.[25]

Opposition continued after the power lines were erected. Rural Minnesotans expressed frustration that they had been victimized by oil companies, chemical companies, power company representatives who compromised their property rights, and the state officials who let it happen. The governor mobilized state police to protect the lines, but it was difficult to provide security for 176 miles of power lines and 685 towers. On February 15, 1978, in the "Battle of Stearns County," farmers sprayed state troopers with anhydrous ammonia fertilizer. Rifle fire destroyed the glass insulators that kept the electricity from discharging into the ground through the 180-foot tower. More extreme measures were taken by "bolt weevils," farmers who removed the bolts that secured the towers to the supporting piers. Once unsecured, it was possible either to push the tower over or let it fall in high winds. Ten towers toppled due to vandalism. By the time the controversy subsided, 170 protesters were arrested, although 75 of them did not go to trial; 14 pled guilty to reduced charges, and 31 went to trial; 27 of those tried were acquitted, and only four were convicted. Rural regulators failed to halt the construction of the line.[26]

Rural Development

New Deal programs that promoted community building were quickly defunded during World War II, but this did not mean that the rural social and economic problems those programs addressed disappeared. A midwesterner, True D. Morse of the farm management firm Doane Agricultural Service in St. Louis, recognized that a major adjustment in agriculture was imminent and that community planning would be important in the postwar period. In a 1944 speech to community leaders in Dallas, Morse was likely the first person to use the phrase "rural community development," contending that planning was necessary to create "permanently progressive" communities. Morse understood the importance of rural industry for sustaining communities, even as he maintained that agriculture would always be the backbone of rural life. In 1948, Secretary Brannan echoed this concern and advocated for the creation of federal programs to encourage rural industry and education to check rural underconsumption, which impeded national growth.[27]

The Eisenhower administration began the first postwar federal pilot projects in rural development. True D. Morse, now an assistant secretary of agriculture, convinced Secretary Benson to create such a program to assist low-income farmers. Morse asked Don Paarlberg, formerly of Purdue University, to lead a task force, which resulted in a 1955 report titled *Department of Agriculture's Human Resources: A Report on Problems of Low-Income Farmers*. The report indicated that small farmers, especially in the South, had substandard income and that solutions should rely on education and development. That year Congress authorized funds for pilot programs at the county level. By the end of 1960, two hundred counties participated in the program.[28]

Perry County, Indiana, was one of the areas targeted in the spring of 1960. Like many rural areas, Perry County suffered from high unemployment, poor educational attainment, and relatively low standards of living. Local residents recognized the complex nature of these issues. As one Perry County community leader claimed, "You can't say it's all [a] farm problem or lack of industry or inadequate education." The program was not intended to simply provide bricks-and-mortar or make-work projects, which frustrated some residents. One of the early projects was a health survey that identified a high incidence of cancers, which subsequently triggered more study.[29]

Presidents Kennedy, Johnson, and Nixon continued Rural Development programs and expanded their scope. Southern Indiana received federal money again in 1963 when Secretary of Agriculture Orville Freeman announced federal lending programs to help communities attract industry, improve marketing facilities for local products, and create new outdoor recreational venues such as swimming pools and golf courses. Towns of less than 2,500 people were eligible for these loans. In 1965, at least 16 recreation projects in Iowa had received funding, including a golf course. One area teacher claimed that but for the golf course "I'd have taken a job elsewhere." Also in 1965, the USDA created a Rural Community Development Service to help other federal agencies extend their reach to rural areas by allowing large rural areas to cooperate to improve access to hospitals, libraries, and educational facilities. President Nixon asked Congress for $1.3 billion in rural development money in 1972, mostly in the form of federal loan guarantees for businesses, industrial parks, recreational facilities, and improvements in rural water and sewer systems.[30]

Since 1965, the Farmers Home Administration has been authorized to provide grants and long-term, low-interest loans for rural water facilities for municipalities of under ten thousand people. Rural people believed that water costs should be a small percentage of total household expenses, but they could not afford private capital. Funding for this program surged in the 1970s, and although Congress made sharp cutbacks in 1981 and 1982, the program continued. In Ohio, for example, the USDA provided loans and grants to local governments and rural water districts to enhance services for hundreds of thousands of households. From 1996 to 2008, USDA grants in Ohio ranged from a low of $11.7 million in 2007 to a high of $18.8 million in 1999, while total loan amounts ranged from a high of $57.9 million in 2007 to a low of $23.3 million in 1996.[31]

Rural development diversified in the postwar period. In 2001, rural housing loans in Ohio totaled over $133 million, including loans for purchases, repairs, and construction of single-family and multi-family housing. The ripple effect of this was significant, considering real estate commissions, title insurance purchases, appraisals, and inspections, as well as income for local vendors and contractors. Ohio's rural community facilities grants totaled $10.6 million in 2001, with funds allocated for seven fire trucks, an ambulance, construction of a fire station, as well as renovations to a nursing home, public library, community center, and numerous other projects. Millions of dollars have been used to enhance rural broadband Internet access. Business and Industry Program loans totaled $44.4 million, including a $1.6 million loan for the largest flag manufacturer in the United States, located in Coshocton, a small city that had experienced significant population decline since 1970.[32]

Parts of the rural Midwest obtained more resources from the federal government than was paid in taxes. Downstate Illinois relied on the government in the form of federal aid for road construction and maintenance, mental health facilities, education, and prisons. Approximately 27 percent of personal income in Union County, Illinois, came from government employment in 1969, with 31.6 percent in 1986 and 30 percent in 1990. When Social Security is included, Union County's personal income derived from government sources was 41.5 percent in 1990. This was in contrast to the statewide percentage of government-derived income, which remained under 23 percent in 1990.[33]

Midwestern congressmen with rural constituencies advocated for generous ethanol subsidies to consume surplus grain and create jobs in rural areas. The Energy Tax Act of 1978 encouraged the manufacture of ethanol to be blended with gasoline by providing a tax exemption of 40 cents per gallon of pure ethanol. By the mid-1980s, the exemption had been raised to 60 cents per gallon thanks to the Surface Transportation Assistance Act of 1983 and the Tax Reform Act of 1984. The Clean Air Act amendments of 1990 required reductions in ozone-producing hydrocarbons and improvement in engine emissions, both of which gave ethanol a boost. Federal money also flowed to research and development of biofuels, ranging from $50 billion to

Figure 5.2: Low-interest USDA financing was crucial for the construction of the PioneerCare Center in Fergus Falls, Minnesota. Approximately $18 million of the total $23 million for this 105-bed, nonprofit nursing home came from the federal government. The facility opened in 2011. Source: Photo by Steve Guttormson. Used with permission.

$100 billion per year from 1978 to 1998. The USDA provided rural development grants through its Value Added Producer Grant program, authorized in 2000, for feasibility studies, start-up funds, and construction of plants to promote a "rural renaissance."[34]

States also joined the biofuel boom. Midwestern states frequently required state-owned vehicles to run on gas with ethanol. In 2010, Wisconsin enacted a law to promote biofuels by offering a $5,000 per station pump credit to retailers to encourage them to offer blended fuel, established new goals for state biofuel use, and allowed the biofuel industry to qualify for industrial revenue bonds and state grants.[35]

Both federal and state governments have promoted tourism in the region. The National Park Service hoped to add a grassland park in the central states to preserve a grassland ecosystem and "for the education and enjoyment of the general public." From 1958 to 1963, Park Service leaders promoted a tract of land in Pottawatomie County, Kansas, located in the Flint Hills.

Local opposition, however, was intense, partly due to the recent controversy over the establishment of the nearby Tuttle Creek Reservoir. A delegation from the Department of the Interior, led by Secretary Stewart Udall, had been authorized by a local landowner to visit the site and land their helicopter on private property, but the renter confronted the delegation and asked the party to leave. The Twin Mound incident, as it became known, helped galvanize local opposition to the park. Opponents believed that tax revenue losses would be significant, ranchers would be displaced, and local people and their indigenous knowledge were better suited than federal bureaucrats to managing grassland. These arguments resurfaced in the late 1980s and early 1990s in the controversy over the establishment of another grasslands national monument in the Flint Hills. A compromise public-private partnership proposal emerged, however, and in 1996 President Clinton signed the legislation that created the Tallgrass Prairie National Preserve.[36]

Research and Extension

Federal and state governments collaborated to provide a major indirect subsidy to rural people through research and outreach. Among the many accomplishments of the experiment stations in the rural Midwest prior to 1945 was the development of wheat varieties suited to the conditions of central and western Kansas. During the immediate postwar years, this kind of applied research continued, but since then funding has increasingly come from institutions such as the National Science Foundation rather than from direct appropriations, which compelled station staff members to focus on short-term problems such as marketing.[37]

Nevertheless, the first 30 years of the postwar period was a positive time for agricultural research at land grant universities and the state experiment stations. Damon Catron joined the Iowa State faculty in 1945 as professor of animal husbandry and helped facilitate tremendous changes in hog farming through the promotion of antibiotics in feeds, lifecycle housing, and year-round breeding to minimize the impact of commodity price fluctuations. In North Dakota, the immediate postwar years brought an influx of federal investment that resulted in improved facilities and increased personnel. North Dakota Experiment Station scientists developed rust-resistant durum wheat in the 1950s, which helped keep the state's wheat economy intact and endeared the station to farmers and powerful rural legislators. The station responded to farmer demand for high-yielding dwarf wheat by developing the Olaf variety in 1973. In 1981, the state established the Central Grasslands Experiment Station to meet the needs of cattle producers in the high plains.[38]

After a boom in the 1940s through the early 1970s, experiment station funding declined during the late 1970s and 1980s. The Food and Agriculture Act of 1977 decreased formula funds for the stations and increased the emphasis on competitive funding. The collapse in the farm economy during the mid-1980s compounded funding problems. It was difficult for station personnel to continue research programs in this environment, and the Kansas and North Dakota stations focused more on marketing, value-added processing, and economic development. In the late 1980s, the Ohio station experienced a 30 percent cut in programs and staff. A notable exception to the decline in funding was Minnesota's authorization of grape research in 1984, which provided for the state experiment station to develop cold-hardy and herbicide-resistant wine grape varieties. In spite of a generally favorable perception of publicly funded research, some midwesterners were skeptical, especially as it related to alternative agriculture. When asked about the value of hoop structures for hogs, a sustainable agriculture practice, approximately 40 percent of Iowa farmers surveyed were in favor, 40 percent were opposed, with 20 percent undecided.[39]

Cooperative Extension represented one of the most intimate and least controversial manifestations of federal and state government presence in the lives of rural Americans. Extension personnel, most often the county agent (later county extension director), home economist, and youth director carried the information generated at agricultural experiment stations and land-grant universities to the people. They did so by coordinating field days, offering workshops in subjects as varied as food preservation techniques and integrated pest management, and reaching out to young people through 4-H. The emphasis on self-help, education, and the voluntary nature of these programs made them the most palatable expressions of government in everyday life.[40]

Extension work continued to focus on enhancing production and quality of life for rural people, but it was also transformed in the postwar period. One of the most important shifts was the separation of the extension service from the Farm Bureau. In 1954, Secretary of Agriculture Ezra Taft Benson ordered that the extension service could no longer accept funds or program direction from private organizations. This ended the relationship that had developed since 1913, when county organizations known as Farm Bureaus provided half the funds to hire county agents, with the other half paid by the state, although federal funds were sometimes appropriated to flow through the states to support extension staff. This change was partly due to criticism that the county agent was in the pocket of partisan and partial Farm Bureau organizations that favored dues-paying members. For their part, Farm

Bureau leaders were also ready to move on from the historic arrangement to better pursue profitmaking ventures such as insurance, livestock pharmaceutical manufacture, pesticide sale and distribution, and direct marketing of commodities.[41]

Midwestern extension services pioneered the movement toward consolidation of services. The growing sophistication of agricultural technology such as synthetic fertilizers, pesticides, pharmaceuticals, animal nutrition, and countless other developments meant that county directors could not offer a consistent level of expertise. In 1961, Iowa Cooperative Extension organized TENCO, a ten-county region that would focus resources on an area in need, in this case ten counties in southeastern Iowa that had experienced decline in mining and agriculture. The entire state was organized into extension regions by 1969. Minnesota created its first five-county program area in 1964 and Missouri created extension regions in 1965.[42]

Extension also responded to social problems. In 1984 the Iowa Extension Service developed programs to help farmers understand the developing farm crisis and their particular financial issues. Collaboration with the state Department of Human Services and the United Way of Central Iowa resulted in the implementation of a toll-free service called the Iowa Rural Concern Hotline to help farmers locate needed social services, including emotional and mental health services.[43]

Governing the Rivers

Midwestern farmers received yet another major boost from the federal government in the form of the development and maintenance of a navigation channel to facilitate the flow of midwestern grain to the Gulf of Mexico. Barges, not railcars or trucks, carried most of the midwestern corn crop to terminal markets in New Orleans. The U.S. Army Corps of Engineers constructed and maintained the dams, locks, and channels for navigation and flood control in the Mississippi basin. Some of the most persistent debates in the rural Midwest related to the management of the Mississippi River and its tributaries, most significantly the Ohio and Missouri Rivers. Corps actions to maintain water levels behind dozens of dams across the region and its efforts to channelize the rivers remain lightning rods for criticism. Farmers argued for a steady slack pool for navigation while critics contended that such a pool is harmful to ecosystems.

Midwestern governors and commercial leaders wanted to develop the Missouri River basin to improve market access for their commodities, generate low-cost hydroelectric power, and obtain relief from devastating

Figure 5.3: The U.S. Army Corps of Engineers developed and maintains a system of locks and dams to preserve a nine-foot-deep navigation channel in the region's major rivers to facilitate the flow of midwestern grain to terminal elevators. This is an aerial view of Melvin Price Locks and Dam near Alton, Illinois, looking upstream on the Mississippi River toward the Missouri shore. Photo Name: 2528-23. Original ID: 1177. Source: U.S. Army Corps of Engineers. Used with permission.

floods. Congress passed the Flood Control Act of 1944, merging plans from the Army Corps of Engineers and the Bureau of Reclamation for navigation, power, and flood control but also for irrigation of up to 4.7 million acres of new farmland and the creation of 53,000 farms. The Pick-Sloan plan, named for the Corps's Major Lewis A. Pick and the Bureau's W. Glenn Sloan, included plans for five new large dams on the Missouri, with four of them planned for South Dakota and numerous other dams on the Missouri's tributaries. Urban promoters favored the Pick-Sloan plan to boost their economic fortunes and avoid costly floods.[44]

Rural people were not always in favor of the plan. An intense debate erupted in Kansas over the construction of the Tuttle Creek dam on the Blue River in the 1940s. Farmers and the townspeople who lived in the area to be flooded organized the Blue Valley Study Association (BVSA) in 1945 to oppose the plan. Although U.S. Senator Clyde Reed of Kansas successfully blocked appropriations for the dam throughout the late 1940s, widespread flooding across Kansas galvanized support for funding the construction of the Tuttle Creek reservoir among downstream residents. Blue Valley opponents became more aggressive in opposing what they viewed as tyranny. They held local information meetings, campaigned to unseat a congressional supporter of the project, and even chartered a bus for a BVSA women's delegation to meet with President Truman and Republican candidate Dwight Eisenhower. The BVSA claimed that if the dam were built "there is a shadow and a threat over every fertile valley in the Missouri Basin." The Army Corps of Engineers claimed that the dam was critical to water management on the Kansas River, given that the Blue River watershed accounted for one-third of all the water in the basin, which ultimately fed the Missouri River.[45]

Blue Valley residents were not strictly opposed to federal intervention. Their target was "Big Dam Foolishness," specifically the loss of their homes and productive farmland. The BVSA promoted soil conservation as flood control, primarily through smaller, upland check dams, with the maxim "Stop the Water Where It Falls." The USDA, however, did not endorse soil conservation alone as an adequate flood control strategy, and the BVSA was left in a desperate fight without allies.[46]

The Tuttle Creek controversy ended in victory for the Corps and its supporters in Congress and urban, downstream Kansas. Work continued on the reservoir, which began to fill in 1962. In the Republican River valley, just west of the Blue River, residents learned that the Flood Control Act of 1954 authorized the construction of Milford dam on the Republican. People from the farms and towns in the reservoir site chose not to fight and instead worked to document the stories of their communities and each farmstead.[47]

Further to the north another dam controversy raged, but this dispute was not over the creation of a dam. The completion of South Dakota's Oahe dam in 1959 allowed the U.S. Bureau of Reclamation to commence the Oahe Irrigation Project to carry Missouri River water approximately 125 miles east via canal to irrigate land in the James River valley. Proponents of the Oahe Project, including U.S. Senator George McGovern, argued that it would bring millions of dollars to the regional and local economies for canal construction, not to mention the prospect of new jobs to support the anticipated growth in the farm population. As with any dam, some South Dakotans would be losers, and Native Americans were among those who lost the most. Approximately 309,584 bottomland acres to be flooded belonged to the Sioux. The final settlements to the tribes amounted to $34 million.[48]

Questions about the Oahe Irrigation Project arose even as the dam was under construction. Successful dry land farmers could not understand why

Figure 5.4: Many residents in the Blue River Valley of Kansas opposed the construction of the Tuttle Creek dam on the Kansas River and actively organized and protested the project through lobbying and a public relations campaign. This sign was erected in Randolph, Kansas, in 1955. Source: DaRT ID: 211596. KansasMemory.org. Used with permission.

their property would be sacrificed for a reservoir to bring other land under irrigation. The 1971 draft Environmental Impact Statement, a new federal requirement mandated by the National Environmental Policy Act of 1970, indicated that 110,000 acres of land, 100,000 of which was pasture or under cultivation in wheat, would be condemned to irrigate approximately 190,000 more acres, making irrigation appear to be a poor bargain. Environmental groups and local residents feared that water quality would be compromised and that fish and wildlife habitat would be destroyed. Newer government estimates revised downward the number of acres that could be brought under cultivation, which raised per-acre costs of the project. In the early 1970s some South Dakotans formed the United Family Farmers to oppose the Oahe Project, labeling it "The Oahe Problem" and the BOR the "Bureau of Wrecklamation." Irrigation opponents scored a victory in 1978 when they won control of the Oahe Conservancy Sub-District board and ultimately secured de-authorization of the Oahe Project.[49]

The Corps, under pressure from rural midwesterners, retreated from several projects in the 1970s. The planned flood control dam on the Kickapoo River at La Farge, Wisconsin, was one such project. Once again, the Environmental Impact Statement was controversial. For the La Farge dam, the statement failed to account for water quality issues. Construction continued as the controversy raged between local advocates who favored the dam and environmental and recreation enthusiasts who opposed it, but ultimately political will in Congress collapsed after Senator William Proxmire pulled his support and Congress eliminated project funding in 1975. A generation later, local residents still recalled the controversy with disdain because floods continued to plague La Farge.[50]

Dam opponents also frequently claimed that the proposed benefits did not always match the reality. An official of the Iowa Conservation Commission reported, "sometimes when you build a lake for flood control, what you get is controlled flooding." Farmers who initially supported dams for flood control later learned that rivers ran bank-full for a longer part of the year as water was released from reservoirs. This resulted in poor drainage in the bottomlands that had been the most productive acres on the farm. Farmer Elmer Dobson of Carroll County, Iowa, led a successful fight against the proposed Jefferson reservoir, which would have flooded approximately 20,500 acres. Dobson cultivated support among downstream communities as well as that of the Sierra Club and the Iowa Confederation of Environmental Organizations. The state ultimately denied funds for the development of recreational facilities on the proposed lake, which deflated the economic justification for the reservoir. Inspired by the success in Carroll County, farmers in a neighboring county successfully protested another proposed Army Corps of Engineers reservoir.[51]

Navigation has proved to be the most persistent economic concern relating to midwestern rivers and has justified continued government expense to maintain the nine-foot channel and the attendant system of dams and locks. Starting in the 1930s, the Army Corps of Engineers began a modernization project on the Ohio River to replace 53 low, movable dams with 20 fixed dams, facilitating an increase in barge traffic. According to a Corps study, Ohio River traffic doubled between 1955 and 1977 as a result of river improvements and the increasing productivity of midwestern farms. In 1989, the Corps began to study the feasibility of extending the length of locks on the Upper Mississippi-Illinois Waterway system from 600 feet to 1,100 feet to accommodate larger barge tows. In 2000, controversy arose over the $50 million as-then-unfinished study when critics charged that the Corps manipulated data to justify the expansion program. Most farmers continued to support the maintenance and expansion of the locks and dams, claiming that most urban people would not accept the increased interstate traffic and costs of relying on trucks and railroads, given that barges carried approximately 60 percent of American grain exports to market.[52]

Interstate Highways

The river system carried most of the midwestern grain harvest to market, but roads were also critical to farmers. The passage of the Federal-Aid Highway Act of 1956 brought a major transition to the old system of farm-to-market roads and for the lives of rural people. In 1959 University of Illinois attorney N.G.P. Krausz informed farmers that interstate highway construction would directly affect them in multiple ways, including the ability to move farm products to market more quickly and at less expense, an increase in urban-to-rural migration, and the ability of part-time and full-time farmers to get to their city jobs faster. Interstate right-of-way would account for as much as 40 acres of land per mile of road, with interchanges requiring up to 65 acres. Ultimately, the U.S. government would spend $6 billion to acquire the land needed for the 41,000 miles of planned interstates.[53]

In the shorter term, debates over the planned routes often pitted rural communities against each other to gain the best access to the roads and anticipated economic benefits. In Nebraska, a group representing communities south of the Platte River advocated for the east–west route to run between Hastings and Grand Island, which would be shorter and would require fewer bridges. According to one state senator, a northern route would "divide large ranches and disrupt economically significant hay and cattle feeding operations," while a representative of the Platte Valley Irrigation District contended that the northern route would disrupt a main irrigation channel and numerous laterals. Supporters of a north bank route contended that a larger population north of the river warranted a northerly route and, turning the claims of south bank promoters on their head, that a southern route would cut off ranch lands from access to water and destroy woodlands. The Federal Bureau of Public Roads ultimately decided on a southern route for Nebraska's portion of Interstate 80.[54]

In addition to the obvious changes of land purchases, local job creation for the construction of culverts, bridges, and road surfaces, and the travel and tourism industry, there were other major shifts in the midwestern landscape. The interstates liberated meatpackers and processors from the rail network, resulting in a fragmentation of that industry away from cities and into the country. The creation of Iowa Beef Processors in 1960 is the best-known example of how the industry was able to move closer to producers and low-cost labor to break the power of urban-based labor unions.[55]

Regulation: Corporations, Environment, and Health

Government actions to ensure the health of ecosystems and the food supply helped make both government and environmentalism four-letter words for many rural midwesterners. Farmers were accustomed to periodic changes in the Farm Bill and expected Congress and the USDA to set price and conservation policy, but there were new agencies and administrators, including the Federal Food and Drug Administration (FDA) and the Environmental Protection Agency (EPA). New regulations shaped the ways in which farm products were raised, from the location of feedlots to the chemicals used in crop production and livestock husbandry. Writers for *Successful Farming*, a widely read farm magazine, reminded farmers that "He's peering over your shoulder, into your back hog lots, under the lids of your feeders and even inside your hogs. He's your Uncle Sam, the federal government."[56]

By the early 1970s, farmers' traditional ideas about stewardship and man's dominion over earth encountered new consumer and environmental movements. In 1970, U.S. Secretary of Agriculture Clifford Hardin argued that environmental quality was a "new crusade." He recognized that productive technology was capable of "offending and polluting our environment" and that farmers needed to adapt to new conditions and expectations. One farm editor argued that farmers were in a "fight for survival" against intrusive government bureaucrats, meddlesome congressmen, and a hypersensitive public arrayed to challenge the farmers' assumptions about technology and the often unanticipated consequences of its use. As one Illinois farmer complained in 1973, "If they [environmentalists] got everything that they now ask for in regulating pesticides, herbicides, hormones, and waste management, my costs of hog production would increase 50%, and my soybean yield could drop 75%."[57]

The federal government restricted or banned many of the technologies that facilitated industrial agriculture, despite pushback from the powerful agribusiness interests. The FDA banned the use of the feed additive diethylstilbestrol, a growth-promoting hormone widely used in Corn Belt beef production, and the USDA cancelled the registration of DDT. The FDA restricted the use of antibiotics in dairy production. Elaborate procedures were established to ensure that livestock producers carefully sited their feedlots and confinements far enough away from watercourses and constructed them to reduce the risks of manure runoff and contamination of surface and groundwater.[58]

Yet pesticides, feed additives, and confined animal-feeding operations did not disappear. In spite of complaints by farmers during the 1960s and 1970s that it would become impossible to farm in the new regulatory climate, farming continued to be big business in the Midwest, with a growing percentage of production conducted by a shrinking number of producers. Some regulations proved to be remarkably porous. Throughout the 1970s, 1980s, and 1990s, midwestern governors, legislators, and bureaucrats refused to alienate agricultural interests by enforcing laws to reduce the risk of ground- and surface-water contamination by livestock producers. In 2001, the State of Iowa gave farmers a five-year amnesty period to install manure control facilities that had been mandated in the 1970s. At the end of the amnesty period, dozens of farmers faced state and federal punishment, including fines of tens of thousands of dollars.[59]

Environmental regulation was not simply a matter of farm versus non-farm interests. Farmers who expanded faced opposition, most often from their neighbors who also happened to be farmers or retired farmers. The Pork Motel, a finishing operation with a capacity of four thousand head of hogs located near Salina, Kansas, faced opposition soon after it opened in 1974. The first complaint was about odor, not about water quality. A neighboring farmer who lived approximately 1.5 miles away did not like the smell. At a public hearing in 1976, there were numerous complaints of odor nuisance, and by 1978 the Pork Motel was empty and out of business. The frustrated owner of the Pork Motel stated, "I can't diaper every pig." In Iowa, farm neighbors of Garner Pork claimed that approximately 40 percent of the time they were overwhelmed with odor, with only a slight respite in the winter. One plaintiff raised five hundred hogs but claimed that he "kept his odor at home," while another described the smell as "nauseating." In 1978, residents of a rural southwestern Minnesota community fought the development of a hog-breeding facility, this time before the farmer could break ground. Opponents wanted assurances that there would be no groundwater contamination, and they demanded a state environmental impact statement. Rural residents turned out en masse at hearings, drafted a petition, and created new zoning ordinances to block the proposed operation.[60]

Environmental regulation at the state level was rooted in efforts to control corporate farming and ownership of farmland. The technological transformations in agriculture rewarded farmers who could specialize, gain economies of scale, and substitute capital for labor. Farmers were caught in a cost-price squeeze in which the prices they received for their commodities did not keep pace with expenses, exposing them to greater risk by increasing debt-to-asset ratios. Most farm families would not or could not manage this change and instead moved to the cities and suburbs or became part of the rural nonfarm population. The rise of the new agriculture and the associated demographic trends were unsettling for many rural people who witnessed their way of life vanish.

Rural and urban midwesterners responded to these structural changes with anticorporate rhetoric and legislation. Campaigning in 1960, South Dakota's George McGovern claimed that a Republican victory meant that "the family farm is doomed as an institution and corporate agriculture will sweep the country." There had been earlier attempts to legislate against corporate farming in Minnesota, Nebraska, North Dakota, and Kansas, but in the postwar period Missouri, South Dakota, Minnesota, Wisconsin, Iowa, and Nebraska all enacted new corporate farming statutes due to concerns about corporate takeover of agriculture. At hearings of Wisconsin senator Gaylord Nelson's Small Business Committee on Monopoly in 1968, the president of the South Dakota Farmers Union testified that corporations owned over 16 million acres of land in the state, the equivalent of five counties.[61]

Missouri and Nebraska enacted versions of anticorporate farming laws to preserve the family farm and limit industrial-scale agriculture within their borders. Missouri's 1975 law prohibited nonfamily corporations from farming or purchasing farmland. In 1982 Nebraska voters approved Initiative-300 (I-300), which prohibited corporations from engaging in farming or ranching or owning agricultural land. Yet large-scale hog farming came to Missouri in 1988 with Premium Standard Farms (PSF), located over three counties in north central Missouri, which managed about 80,000 sows in expectation of raising approximately 1.7 million pigs per year. Officials from Missouri's Department of Economic Development, state legislators, and the state's congressional delegation were eager to attract economic activity. Murphy Family Farms began operations in southwestern Missouri in 1992, and Continental Grain opened facilities in northwest Missouri in 1994. These companies were allowed to operate under exemptions to the 1975 law, which defined family farm corporations as having at least one-half of voting stock held by members of the same family, with one stockholder either living on the farm or actively managing it. Nebraskans also saw the rise of big swine, in spite of I-300. Operations such as Nebraska Premium Pork and Premium Farms with 130,000 hogs in four counties could operate legally as long as the producers raised their own animals. In both Nebraska and Missouri the anticorporate farming statues did little to protect citizens, natural resources, and other industries such as tourism from harm.[62]

Local and state governments began a process of re-regulation due to negative environmental consequences. Local governments positioned themselves as the protectors of property values, health, ecosystems, and agrarian values. In response to a 1997 request to the Nebraska Department of Environmental Quality (NDEQ) to construct a 34,000-hog operation in Harlan County, county supervisors denied the company the easements to carry liquefied manure under county roads to center pivot systems. The town of Alma hired an independent engineer to assess the impact of the hog facility, but in the meantime the NDEQ had granted the construction permit. Alma's appeal went all the way to the Nebraska Supreme Court. At least six Missouri counties created ordinances regarding CAFOs, including Linn County's health ordinance, which required locating facilities at least 4.5 miles from existing homes and 5.5 miles from towns as well as requiring bonding for producers. The Missouri Court of Appeals upheld the Linn County ordinance in 1996. Township zoning regulations in Missouri were ultimately held to be unlawful regulations of farm structures (barns and manure lagoons), reinforcing the primacy of state governments in the regulatory scheme.[63]

Meanwhile, advocates and state legislators debated various means of facilitating large-scale farming and its environmental consequences while also preserving rural quality of life. Numerous fish kills and complaints about odor problems led Missouri to create more stringent regulations in 1996. A Kansas advocate suggested moving away from uniform, design-based rules to actual monitoring and performance-based standards. In 1998, Nebraska legislators debated a bill that would allow counties the right to enact emergency zoning to halt construction of CAFOs, but it was ultimately withdrawn after unfriendly amendments undermined the intent of the bill. When the NDEQ director issued a report that raised concerns about the reliability of manure lagoons and the impact of runoff into surface waters in 1998, there was little evidence that the Nebraska legislators even read the report. One farmer-legislator conceded that most farmers would not monitor phosphorus levels on their farms, unless required to do so by law, but still favored minimal regulation.[64]

In contrast to Nebraska and Missouri, Michigan had no anticorporate farming statute. When a 1983 state Department of Commerce study determined that rural Jackson County would be suitable for operations to prepare 90,000 hogs for market annually and construction began, many people in Parma Township were surprised and began to ask questions of company and government representatives, but construction proceeded. When the facility was finished, local residents experienced the sharp smell from the three manure lagoons and witnessed the degradation of nearby Rice Creek, which no longer supported fish and was soon covered with foam and algae and choked with alligator grass. Township and county officials, state bureaucrats, the governor, and the state's congressional delegation professed impotence; the facility was legal. Frustrated residents organized, gathered documentation, hired lawyers, and filed suit against Sand Livestock and the Department of Natural Resources. In 1992 Sand Livestock declared bankruptcy and vacated the premises, but the experience left those who led the attack on Sand embittered. As one opponent reflected, "Our own state government really let us down."[65]

The lack of effective government oversight is the most remarkable aspect of agriculture in the postwar period. The underfunded and understaffed NDEQ relied on citizen "poop police" to notify the agency of potential hazards and infractions. In Ohio, EPA officials did not know that the state's largest cattle operation with 9,000 head stored massive amounts of manure on a concrete slab that leached into the Little Miami River for three years. In Licking County, Ohio, an egg producer was cited for 87 environmental violations in 2002 but remained in business. Ohio's EPA director explained that "We couldn't keep up with the large farms. They just kept coming and snowballed us."[66]

Conclusion

The U.S. government has been responsible for sustaining much of the rural Midwest since 1945. Participants in farm commodity programs are only the most obvious examples of the dependency that characterized the region in the second half of the century. The federal government was there with loan deficiency payments and purchase programs to ease the regular shock of low prices. Similarly, federal disaster relief and crop insurance programs cushioned the blow of the periodic crop damage or loss. Federal funds to maintain a navigation channel in midwestern rivers and the creation of an interstate highways system aided farmers and rural people. Federal and state research funds helped farmers utilize new productive technology. Government investment in rural social and infrastructure programs such as drinking water and sanitation projects, job training and economic development, not to mention grants and loans for fire trucks, ambulances, housing, child care facilities, and nursing homes made a major difference in sustaining quality of life on farms and in small towns. Government support of these programs is ubiquitous but remains invisible to most people.

Yet the government man was an ambivalent figure, just as he was for the farmer with the bad dream in the aftermath of the Michigan PBB incident. Rural midwesterners were typically numbered among the most vocal critics of the federal government. In 2004, journalist Thomas Frank asked, "What's the Matter with Kansas?" in an attempt to explain why rural midwesterners opposed government involvement in the economy even though doing so was contrary to their economic self-interest. Historian Shane Hamilton replied that many postwar midwesterners rejected New Deal–style government involvement in the economy because they had been economic losers in the managed economy. In short, Hamilton's answer to the question "What's the Matter with Kansas?" was that traditional assumptions about economic self-interest were at worst incorrect and at best incomplete. Hamilton demonstrated the complex ways in which policy, economics, socioeconomic status, and identity intersected in shaping political behavior and reminded us that it is possible for people simultaneously to express multiple and contradictory behaviors.[67]

Rural midwesterners have also been angry and frustrated with state and local governments because those entities, like the federal government, let them down. In 1994 Blaine Nickles, a retired Iowa farmer turned activist, was appointed to a state task force to draft guidelines for hog industry legislation, but the final recommendations largely ignored his input as well as the suggestions of many other stakeholders. Nickles, a former hog farmer, favored rules to minimize risk to ground- and surface-water and air quality, and to hold industry accountable for pollution. But Nickles contended that the threat to agrarian values posed by corporate, large-scale hog operations was a greater threat than pollution. "We now have corporate neighbors who think first about their profits," Nickles asserted, neighbors who "care little about the needs of the community, and are leaving a trail of waste for our grandchildren to inherit." The fact that state legislators, governors, congressmen, and bureaucrats encouraged this kind of rural growth exposes some of the reasons that so many rural midwesterners on the political right and left are uneasy about their continued dependence on government.[68]

Notes

1. Luther J. Carter, "Michigan's PBB Incident: Chemical Mix-Up Leads to Disaster," *Science* 192 (4236) (April 16, 1976): 240–43; Edwin Chen, *PBB: An American Tragedy* (Englewood Cliffs, NJ: Prentice-Hall, Inc., 1979); Joyce Egginton, *The Poisoning of Michigan*, revised edition (East Lansing: Michigan State University Press, 2009); Edward C. Lorenz, "Containing the Michigan PBB Crisis, 1973–1992: Testing the Environmental Policy Process," *Environmental History Review* 17 (2) (Summer 1993): 49–68; Michael R. Reich, "Environmental Politics and Science: The Case of PBB Contamination in Michigan," *American Journal of Public Health* 73 (3) (March 1983): 302–13.

2. "Farmers Shaken by Poison Case," *New York Times*, August 8, 1979, A12.

3. Theodore Saloutos, *The American Farmer and the New Deal* (Ames: Iowa State University Press, 1982), 270.

4. R. Douglas Hurt, *Problems of Plenty: The American Farmer in the Twentieth Century* (Chicago: Ivan R. Dee, 2002); Lauren Soth, *Farm Trouble* (Princeton, NJ: Princeton University Press, 1957), v.

5. John Mark Hansen, *Gaining Access: Congress and the Farm Lobby, 1919–1981* (Chicago: University of Chicago Press, 1991). For examples of farm organizations in the Cold War context, see Bruce Field, "The Price of Dissent: The Iowa Farmers Union and the Early Cold War, 1945–1954," *Annals of Iowa* 55 (1) (Winter 1996): 1–23; and Bruce E. Field, *Harvest of Dissent: The National Farmers Union and the Early Cold War* (Lawrence: University Press of Kansas, 1998).

6. Virgil W. Dean, *An Opportunity Lost: The Truman Administration and the Farm Policy Debate* (Columbia: University of Missouri Press, 2006); Allen J. Matusow, *Farm Policies and Politics in the Truman Years* (Cambridge, MA: Harvard University Press, 1967); Edward L. Schapsmeier and Frederick H. Schapsmeier, "Eisenhower and Ezra Taft Benson: Farm Policy in the 1950s," *Agricultural History* 44 (4) (October 1970): 369–78; Edward L. Schapsmeier and Frederick H. Schapsmeier, "Eisenhower and Agricultural Reform: Ike's Farm Policy Reappraised," *American Journal of Economics and Sociology* 51 (2) (April 1992): 147–59.

7. "Why Iowa Farmers Like Ike," advertisement, *Wallaces' Farmer and Iowa Homestead*, October 18, 1952, 31.

8. Willard W. Cochrane and Mary E. Ryan, *American Farm Policy, 1948–1973* (Minneapolis: University of Minnesota Press, 1981), 30–31; "Support Hogs, Farmers Say," *Wallaces' Farmer and Iowa Homestead*, January 7, 1956, 31; "Ezra Benson's Harvest," *Time*, Monday, November 23, 1959 (quote).

9. Patrick H. Mooney and Theo J. Majka, *Farmers' and Farm Workers' Movements: Social Protest in American Agriculture* (New York: Twayne Publishers, 1995), 93–97. On the NFO, see John T. Schlebecker, "The Great Holding Action: The NFO in September, 1982," *Agricultural History* 39 (4) (October 1965): 204–13; and Jon Lauck, *American Agriculture and the Problem of Monopoly: The Political Economy of Grain Belt Farming, 1953–1980* (Lincoln: University of Nebraska Press, 2000).

10. "Agriculture: Louder for Less," *Time*, April 6, 1959; "How Farmers Vote on the Kind of Farm Program They Want," *Wallaces' Farmer*, May 16, 1959, 46; "Uncle Sam, Leave Me Alone!" *Wallaces Farmer*, October 17, 1959, quote on 62; Lauren K. Soth, "Farm Policy, Foreign Policy, and Public Opinion," *Annals of the American Academy of Political and Social Science* 331 (September 1960): 109.

11. "The Wheat Vote," *Time*, May 31, 1963; James N. Giglio, "New Frontier Agriculture Policy: The Commodity Side," *Agricultural History* 61 (3) (Summer 1987): 53–70.

12. "Agriculture: How to Shoot Santa Claus," *Time*, September 3, 1965.

13. Eric W. Mogren, *Native Soil: A History of the DeKalb County Farm Bureau* (DeKalb: Northern Illinois University Press, 2005), chapter 5.

14. "Are U.S. Farmers Now Getting Rich?" *U.S. News and World Report*, May 16, 1966, 54.

15. "The Nation: Frustrations of a Rural Republican," *Time*, November 22, 1971; "Inflation: Changing Farm Policy to Cut Food Prices," *Time*, April 9, 1973; "How Farmers Say They'll Vote," *Farm Journal* (November 1972): 26–27 (quote).

16. "History of Agricultural and Price-Support Programs, 1933–1984: Background for 1985 Farm Legislation," Economic Research Service, USDA, *Agriculture Information Bulletin* 485 (Washington, DC: U.S. GPO, 1985), 31–35; Gilbert C. Fite, *American Farm-*

ers: The New Minority (Bloomington: Indiana University Press, 1981), 228; "Farmers Disenchanted with Carter Farm Policy," *Farm Journal* (August 1977): B-2; "Despite All the Sweetening—Farm Policy Still Hasn't Won Farmers," *Farm Journal* (October 1978): 17; Monte Sesker, "Kennedy vs. Reagan in 1980?" *Wallaces Farmer*, October 13, 1979, 16–17; "Grain Becomes a Weapon," *Time*, Monday, January 21, 1980.

17. Walter Isaacson, "Mixing Politics with Parity," *Time*, November 2, 1981; "Grim Reapings," *Time*, November 22, 1982; Gisela Bolte, Susan Tifft, and Lee Griggs, "Going against the Grain," *Time*, April 4, 1983; Laurence I. Barrett, Kurt Andersen, and Douglas Brew, "Christmas on the Hustings," *Time*, October 1, 1984.

18. Mark Friedberger, *Shake-Out: Iowa Farm Families in the 1980s* (Lexington: University Press of Kentucky, 1989); Mooney and Majka, *Farmers' and Farm Workers' Movements*, 106–19; Kathryn Marie Dudley, *Debt and Dispossession: Farm Loss in America's Heartland* (Chicago: University of Chicago Press, 2000); Neil E. Harl, *The Farm Debt Crisis of the 1980s* (Ames: Iowa State University Press, 1990); Barry J. Barnett, "The U.S. Farm Financial Crisis of the 1980s," in *Fighting for the Farm: Rural America Transformed*, ed. Jane Adams (Philadelphia: University of Pennsylvania Press, 2003); Kenneth L. Peoples, David Freshwater, Gregory D. Hanson, Paul T. Prentice, and Eric P. Thor, *Anatomy of an American Agricultural Credit Crisis: Farm Debt in the 1980s* (Lanham, MD: Rowman and Littlefield, 1992); Gordon Bultena, Paul Lasley, and Jack Geller, "The Farm Crisis: Patterns and Impacts of Financial Distress among Iowa Farm Families," *Rural Sociology* 51 (4) (Winter 1986): 436–48; William C. Pratt, "Using History to Make History? Progressive Farm Organizing during the Farm Revolt of the 1980s," *Annals of Iowa* 55 (1) (Winter 1996): 24–45.

19. Mark Friedberger, *Farm Families and Change in Twentieth-Century America* (Lexington: University Press of Kentucky, 1988), chapters 5, 8; "Real Trouble on the Farm," *Time*, February 18, 1985 (quote); F. Larry Leistritz and Brenda L. Ekstrom, "North Dakota Farm and Nonfarm Residents' Views on Financial Assistance Policies," *North Central Journal of Agricultural Economics* 10 (1) (January 1988): 128–29; Dennis S. Nordin and Roy V. Scott, *From Prairie Farmer to Entrepreneur: The Transformation of Midwestern Agriculture* (Bloomington: Indiana University Press, 2005), 195–96.

20. Carl R. Zulauf, Harold D. Guither, and Dennis R. Henderson, "Government and Agriculture: Views of Agribusiness and Farm Operators concerning Selected Issues of the 1985 Farm Bill Debate," *North Central Journal of Agricultural Economics* 9 (1) (January 1987): 87–88.

21. Lyle P. Schertz and Otto G. Doering III, *The Making of the 1996 Farm Act* (Ames: Iowa State University Press, 1999); Barnaby J. Feder, "Sowing Confusion on the Farm," *New York Times*, February 11, 1996 (Dole quote), E5; James Brooke, "Farm Bill in Congress Offers Kansan Visions of Choice for His Open Fields," *New York Times*, September 26, 1995, A18 (farmer quote).

22. "Freedom to Farm? Not Likely," *USA Today*, January 2, 2002; Daniel Eisenberg, Christopher Burbach, Alison Jones, and Dick Thompson, "Lean Times on the Farm," *Time*, January 11, 1999.

23. Environmental Working Group, States Receiving Commodity Payments, 1995–2010, <farm.ewg.org/progdetail.php?fips=00000&progcode=totalfarm&page=states> (accessed June 27, 2011).

24. Wyatt Wells, "Public Power in the Eisenhower Administration," *Journal of Policy History* 20 (2) (2008): 228, 235–36; Raymond G. Kuhl, "On Their Own Power," *Michigan History Magazine* 84 (5) (September/October 2000): 53.

25. James E. Fogerty, "Oral History and Environmental Controversy: The Minnesota Powerline Project," *Oral History Review* 13 (1985): 77–91; "Tension over a Power Line," *Time*, February 6, 1978; Paul Wellstone and Barry M. Casper, *Powerline: The First Battle of America's Energy War* (Amherst: University of Massachusetts Press, 1981).

26. Wellstone and Casper, *Powerline*, 286, 288–90.

27. Dennis Roth, "True D. Morse and the Beginnings of Post-War Rural Development Work," in *Federal Rural Development Policy in the Twentieth Century*, ed. Dennis Roth, Anne B.W. Effland, and Douglas Bowers (Washington, DC: Economic Research Service, USDA, 2002), links modified July 2008, <www.nal.usda.gov/ric/ricpubs/rural_development_policy.html> (accessed July 12, 2011); Tadlock Cowan, "An Overview of USDA Rural Development Programs," Congressional Research Service, May 3, 2010.

28. Roth, "True D. Morse."

29. "One Farm Program That Works," *Time*, August 12, 1957; William M. Blair, "Rural Help Plan Tested in Indiana," *New York Times*, May 8, 1960, quote on 83.

30. "Indiana Will Get a Resources Area," *New York Times*, May 28, 1963, 22; "Freeman Widens Agriculture Aim," *New York Times*, November 25, 1964, 23; "Recreation for Rural Communities," *Wallaces Farmer*, September 4, 1965, quote on 68; "Agriculture: The Great Society, Country Style," *Time*, February 12, 1965; "The Administration: Room at the Bottom," *Time*, February 4, 1966; "Nixon Asks Fund for Rural Areas," *New York Times*, February 2, 1972. For a full discussion of rural development from 1972 through the Clinton administration, see Anne B.W. Effland, "From the Rural Development Act through the Twenty-First Century," in *Federal Rural Development Policy in the Twentieth Century*.

31. Paul H. Gessaman and Terese M. Janovec, "Operational Characteristics of Rural Water Systems in Five North Central States," Department of Agricultural Economics, University of Nebraska–Lincoln, January 31, 1982, 5–8. Dollar amounts for Ohio are not in constant figures. USDA, *Ohio Rural Development, Annual Reports*, 1996–2008.

32. USDA, *Ohio Rural Development, Annual Report, 2001*.

33. Jane Adams, *The Transformation of Rural Life: Southern Illinois, 1890–1990* (Chapel Hill: University of North Carolina Press, 1994), 230–34.

34. Doug Koplow, *At What Cost? Government Support for Ethanol and Biodiesel in the United States* (Winnipeg: International Institute for Sustainable Development, 2006), 11–15; "USDA Grants Support Home-Grown Fuels," *Rural Cooperatives* 71 (4) (July–August 2004).

35. "Wisconsin Bill Promotes Biofuels," *Feedstuffs* 82 (22) (May 31, 2010).

36. Gary Baldridge, "Pottawatomie County Says No to Prairie Preservation," *Kansas History: A Journal of the Central Plains* 16 (2) (Summer 1993): 94–107.

37. Bonnie Lynn-Sherow, "Beyond Winter Wheat: The USDA Extension Service and Kansas Wheat Production in the Twentieth Century," *Kansas History: A Journal of the Central Plains* 23 (1) (2000): 100–111; Alan I Marcus, "The Wisdom of the Body Politic: The Changing Nature of Publicly Sponsored American Agricultural Research since the 1830s," *Agricultural History* 62 (2) (Spring 1988): 4–26.

38. Mark R. Finlay, "Hogs, Antibiotics, and the Industrial Environments of Postwar Agriculture," in *Industrializing Organisms: Introducing Evolutionary History*, ed. Susan R. Schrepfer and Philip Scranton (New York and London: Routledge, 2004); David B. Danbom, *"Our Purpose Is to Serve": The First Century of the North Dakota Agricultural Experiment Station* (Fargo: North Dakota Institute for Regional Studies, 1990), 127–28, 134–35, 150–51.

39. Danbom, *"Our Purpose Is to Serve,"* 159, 166; Christopher Cumo, *A History of the Ohio Agricultural Experiment Station, 1882–1997* (Akron, OH: Midwest Press, 1997), 116–17; Penelope Krosch, "Grape Research in Minnesota," *Agricultural History* 62 (2) (Spring 1988): 267–69; Julie T. Sharp and Clare C. Hinrichs, "Farmer Support for Publicly Funded Sustainable Agriculture Research: The Case of Hoop Structures for Swine," *American Journal of Alternative Agriculture* 16 (2) (2001): 81–88.

40. Dorothy Schwieder, *Seventy-Five Years of Service: Cooperative Extension in Iowa* (Ames: Iowa State University Press, 1993); Roland H. Abraham, *Helping People Help Themselves: Agricultural Extension in Minnesota, 1879–1979* (St. Paul: University of Minnesota Extension Service, 1986).

41. Abraham, *Helping People Help Themselves,* 162, 239–40; Schwieder, *Seventy-Five Years of Service,* 135–39.

42. J.L. Anderson, "The People's University: Iowa State Cooperative Extension and Outreach," in *A Sesquicentennial History of Iowa State University: Tradition and Transformation,* ed. Dorothy Schwieder and Gretchen Van Houten (Ames: Iowa State University Press, 2007), 260–61; Abraham, *Helping People Help Themselves,* 199; C. Brice Ratchford, "Knowledge in Action: The University of Missouri's Extension Network," *Annals of the American Academy of Political and Social Science,* Volume 529, Rural America: Blueprint for Tomorrow (September 1993), 66.

43. Schwieder, *Seventy-Five Years of Service,* 202–12.

44. Robert Kelley Schneiders, *Unruly River: Two Centuries of Change along the Missouri* (Lawrence: University Press of Kansas, 1999); John Ferrell, "Developing the Missouri: South Dakota and the Pick-Sloan Plan," *South Dakota History* 19 (3) (Fall 1989): 310–14.

45. The precursor to the Tuttle Creek controversy was the debate over the planned Kiro Dam on the Kansas River. See Dale E. Nimz, "Damming the Kaw: The Kiro Controversy and Flood Control in the Great Depression," *Kansas History: A Journal of the Central Plains* 26 (Spring 2003): 14–31; "Missouri Valley: Land of the Big Muddy," *Time,* September 1, 1952; Homer E. Socolofsky, "The Great Flood of 1951 and the Tuttle Creek Controversy," in *Kansas: The First Century, Volume II,* ed. John D. Bright (New York: Lewis Historical Publishing, 1956), 497–98, 502; Philip E. Meyer, "Tuttle Creek Dam: A Case Study in Local Opposition" (Master's thesis, University of North Carolina at Chapel Hill, 1962).

46. Homer E. Socolofsky, "The Great Flood of 1951 and the Tuttle Creek Controversy," 499.

47. Robin A. Hanson, "'If the Lord's Willing and the Creek Don't Rise': Flood Control and the Displaced Rural Communities of Irving and Broughton, Kansas," *Great Plains Quarterly* 30 (Fall 2010): 260–61.

48. Ferrell, "Developing the Missouri," 314–21; Michael L. Lawson, *Damned Indians: The Pick-Sloan Plan and the Missouri River Sioux, 1944–1980* (Norman: University of Oklahoma Press, 1982).

49. Hugh Gardner, "McGovern vs. the Farmers: South Dakota's Water Showdown," *The Nation,* April 16, 1977, 456–61; Peter Carrels, *Uphill against Water: The Great Dakota Water War* (Lincoln: University of Nebraska Press, 1999).

50. Lynne Heasley, *A Thousand Pieces of Paradise: Landscape and Property in the Kickapoo Valley* (Madison: University of Wisconsin Press, 2005), chapter 6. For more on the Wisconsin context for environmental regulation, see Thomas R. Huffman, *Protectors of the Land and Water: Environmentalism in Wisconsin, 1961–1968* (Chapel Hill: University of North Carolina Press, 1994).

51. Gene Logsdon, "The Battle over 'Big Dam Foolishness,'" *Farm Journal* (August 1972): 20, 48.

52. David P. Billington, Donald C. Jackson, and Martin V. Melosi, *The History of Large Federal Dams: Planning, History, and Construction in the Era of Big Dams* (Denver: U.S. Department of the Interior, Bureau of Reclamation, 2005), 373; Mary Losure, "Army Corps of Engineers' Plan for the Upper Mississippi River, Tainted by Scandal, Leaves Environmentalists a Chance to Defeat It," *Morning Edition*, broadcast transcript, May 8, 2000; "Corps Told to Consider Alternatives before Extending Locks on Upper Mississippi-Illinois Waterway System," *Feedstuffs* (March 12, 2001): 31.

53. N.G.P. Krausz, "Interstate Highways Will Affect You, Too!" *Successful Farming* (January 1959).

54. James C. Creigh, "Constructing the Interstate Highway in Nebraska: Route and Funding Controversies," *Nebraska History* (Spring 1991): 44–53, quote on 50.

55. Shane Hamilton, *Trucking Country: The Road to America's Wal-Mart Economy* (Princeton, NJ: Princeton University Press, 2008); Wilson Warren, *Tied to the Great Packing Machine: The Midwest and Meatpacking* (Iowa City: University of Iowa Press, 2006); Jimmy M. Skaggs, *Prime Cut: Livestock Raising and Meatpacking in the United States, 1607–1983* (College Station: Texas A&M University Press, 1986), chapter 6.

56. Gene Johnston and Deborah M. Clubb, "Uncle Sam: Down on YOUR Hog Farm," *Successful Farming* 76 (October 1978): H20.

57. Clifford M. Hardin, "Environmental Quality: The New Crusade," in *The 70s: Challenge and Opportunity* (Ames: Iowa State University Press, 1970), 59–64; Fred Bailey Jr., "From DES to Fertilizer—We're In a Fight for Survival," *Successful Farming* (May 1972) (quote); "Inflation: Changing Farm Policy to Cut Food Prices," *Time*, April 9, 1973.

58. Alan I Marcus, *Cancer from Beef: DES, Federal Food Regulation, and Consumer Confidence* (Baltimore: Johns Hopkins University Press, 1994); Kendra Smith-Howard, "Antibiotics and Agricultural Change: Purifying Milk and Protecting Health in the Postwar Era," *Agricultural History* 84 (3) (Summer 2010): 327–51; J.L. Anderson, *Industrializing the Corn Belt: Agriculture, Technology, and Environment, 1945–1972* (DeKalb: Northern Illinois University Press, 2009).

59. Perry Beeman, "Many Cattle Feedlots Lack Needed Manure Controls," *Des Moines Register*, April 4, 2006.

60. "Odor Complaints Force Custom Feedlot Shutdown," *National Hog Farmer* (April 1978); "New Lagoon Settles Odor Suit," *National Hog Farmer* (June 1978) (first quote); "Pollution Issue Used to Block Large Unit," *National Hog Farmer* (July 1978) (second quote).

61. Jon Lauck, "The Corporate Farming Debate in the Post–World War II Midwest," *Great Plains Quarterly* 18 (Spring 1998): 142, 146.

62. Douglas H. Constance, Anna M. Kleiner, and J. Sanford Rikoon, "The Contested Terrain of Swine Production," in *Fighting for the Farm: Rural America Transformed*, ed. Jane Adams; Jan Stout, "The Missouri Anti-Corporate Farming Act: Reconciling the Interests of the Independent Farmer and the Corporate Farm," *UMKC Law Review* 64 (1996): 835–60; Carolyn Johnsen, *Raising a Stink: The Struggle over Factory Hog Farms in Nebraska* (Lincoln: University of Nebraska Press, 2003), 56–65; John Walter, "Nebraska's Dilemma," *Successful Farming* (December 1985).

63. Johnsen, *Raising a Stink*, 29–43; Constance et al., "Contested Terrain of Swine Production," 89; Benjamin A. Joplin, "Can Townships Really Smell? Coping with the Malodorous Problems of Hog Farms in Rural Missouri," *Missouri Environmental Law and*

Policy Review 5 (2) (1998): 83–92. For state level environmental regulation campaigns, see Karen A. Bradley, *The Missouri Natural Streams Act (1990): How An Environmental Campaign Was Waged and Lost* (Lewiston, NY: Edwin Mellen Press, 2007).

64. Keynen J. Wall, "Knowing When to Say When to Hog Waste: Do State Lagoon Regulations Adequately Protect Ground Water in Kansas?" *Kansas Journal of Law and Public Policy* 11 (1) (Fall 2001): 113–39; Johnsen, *Raising a Stink*, 45–47.

65. Laura B. DeLind, "Parma: A Story of Hog Hotels and Local Resistance," in *Pigs, Profits, and Rural Communities*, ed. Kendall M. Thu and E. Paul Durrenberger (Albany: State University of New York Press, 1998), 35.

66. Mike Wagner and Ben Sutherly, "The Supersizing of America's Livestock Farms," *Dayton Daily News*, December 1, 2002.

67. Hamilton, *Trucking Country*, introduction.

68. Blaine Nickles, "An Iowa Farmer's Personal and Political Experience with Factory Hog Facilities," in *Pigs, Profits, and Rural Communities*, 137.

SIX — FARM WOMEN IN THE MIDWEST SINCE 1945

Jenny Barker Devine

In 1950, Clara Fenstermann of Delaware County, Iowa, penned a letter to the *Iowa Bureau Farmer*, a periodical of the Iowa Farm Bureau Federation, explaining the new responsibilities of farm women in the postwar economy. "The modern farm wife does not stay 'cooped up' in a house," she asserted, "but is helping her husband decide which crop to plant, which heifers to keep... when to sell the hogs, and also what would be the best way to spend the money." Fenstermann envisioned her daughter's future as a farmwife, mother, and housekeeper but added "farm partner" to that list and encouraged her daughter to participate in 4-H livestock programs. Raising, showing, and selling livestock provided valuable "training" that would "come in handy as she and her future mate plan their herds, dairy, beef, or hogs."[1]

Fenstermann's expectations for her daughter demonstrate how, in the years after 1945, rural midwestern women encountered both continuity and change in their work lives, families, and communities. For generations, rural midwestern women had identified as helpmeets and contributors to family farms and small communities. They created rich social networks and emphasized their roles as community builders. In her study of European and Native women on the Wisconsin frontier, historian Joan Jensen found that women shared roles as household laborers, healers, educators, spiritual leaders, and local political actors. Though patriarchal social structures and gendered divisions of labor limited women's participation in public activities, women created complex kinship and neighborhood networks for shared labor and exchange that encompassed churches, businesses, schools, welfare agencies, and social and political clubs. These networks persisted well into the twentieth century and remained a defining feature of rural life in the decades after 1945. In these years, depopulation and agricultural mechanization dramatically altered rural landscapes and demographics. Rural electrification eased the physical labor required for household chores, and trends toward large-scale poultry, egg, and milk production eliminated traditional women's work in the farmyard. Yet, even as these transformations unfolded and outward migration to urban areas led to the rapid decline of female kinship and neighborhood networks, women continued to seek out new "sisters," as well as social, economic, and political opportunities that stressed their importance as farm partners, business owners, landowners, and economic contributors.[2]

The geographic expanse and economic diversity of the 12-state midwestern region lends itself to unique experiences based on location, occupation, social class, ethnicity, and race. As a result, generalizations about the Midwest prove difficult given the significant differences between the diversified farms in the Corn Belt, the small dairy farms of the Great Lakes region, and the extensive cattle-ranching and wheat-growing operations of the Great Plains. Historians Andrew R.L. Cayton and Peter S. Onuf have argued that despite these regional variations, a midwestern identity emerged in the nineteenth century that emphasized capitalism, consumerism, and middle-class values central to the creation of "responsible, earnest, industrious citizens." Women's activities played a significant role in fostering this regional identity that was rooted in agricultural production, but relied less on geographic similarities and more on idealized standards of behavior and aspirations for economic independence. Rural women active in religious, social, political, voluntary organizations upheld such values, often drawing upon agrarian ideals that distinguished rural midwesterners as stalwarts of democracy and providers of the nation's food supply, even if their own circumstances did not necessarily reflect such romanticized visions of country living.[3]

The nuclear family, patriarchy, and gendered hierarchies rest at the heart of this emerging midwestern identity, leading most women to identify as members of families: as dependent wives, mothers, and daughters who relied on male heads of household for their livelihood. Within this framework, women utilized neighborhood and community networks to find intrinsic and economic value in their labor. In so doing, they "championed human worth based on labor and gender interdependence" to assert the importance of their work on family farms. After 1945, however, the mechanization of agriculture and a greater orientation toward specialized, capital-intensive, large-scale agribusiness operations appeared to remove women from agricultural production. This seemed to compromise the mutual valuations of labor that had characterized family farming for generations. Historian Mary Neth asserted that women sought new strategies to maintain their involvement in family farm labor because as housewives, or even as wage earners, women engaged in "urban wage work or housework, which was the least valued form of women's labor."[4]

This transition in women's work unfolded rapidly in the years following the Second World War. Electricity and indoor plumbing became common features in midwestern farm homes, though their extent varied across the region. By 1950, electrification reached 90.9 percent of all Iowa farms, 77.7 percent of all farms in Nebraska, and 69 percent of farms in Missouri. As home appliances became more affordable, farm women enthusiastically adopted labor-saving devices such as refrigerators and vacuums to ease the burden of household chores. Electric ovens proved easier to control than wood-burning stoves, while preserving garden produce in a deep freeze unit saved time and resources when compared with canning. The automatic washing machine quickly became the most sought-after appliance, and by 1960, washing machines could be found on 93 percent of all midwestern farms, surpassing freezers, telephones, and televisions in popularity. These allowed women to wash any day of the week, in all seasons, without having to haul and boil water. If they purchased a dryer, this further reduced the time required for hanging and ironing clean clothes. A 1956 article in *Wallaces' Farmer* declared, "You can wash on rainy days," and reminded readers that for a relatively low cost, women could be free from an "aching back from lifting dripping clothes to the wringer."[5]

While the availability of electricity and plumbed water eased the labor-intensive nature of housework, the large gardens and poultry operations that characterized women's work also became obsolete. During the 1920s, midwestern farm families raised 70 percent of the food they consumed. By 1960, as consumer prices fell and commercially packaged produce became affordable, the average farm family raised just 40 percent of their own food. Rather than a cost-saving measure, canning and freezing produce became more of a hobby for those who enjoyed the tradition or the taste of fresh produce. In 1966, as more women reported working in the fields, with livestock, and off the farm, a *Wallaces' Farmer* poll asked, "What's Happened to the Farm Garden?" Though over 90 percent of women from all income levels said they continued to raise and preserve produce for home consumption, they devoted less and less time to working in large gardens. Gardens were increasingly expensive to maintain and, unlike commercially packaged produce, could not guarantee results. Poor weather or an insect infestation could destroy a season's work and, as one woman stated, she didn't "save enough money to pay for the work."[6]

In the case of poultry and eggs, tighter state regulations geared toward standardized egg production coupled with the introduction of large-scale facilities required poultry producers to make significant capital investments and increase the size of their flocks in order to turn reasonable profits. Furthermore, supermarket chains that purchased poultry products in bulk overtook the local grocers that typically purchased eggs from nearby farms. Without ready markets and unable to compete with corporate producers, women gradually abandoned small flocks. In 1945, approximately 94 percent of American farms maintained flocks of hens, but by 1959 this number declined to 75 percent. Within a decade, in 1969, only 24 percent of farms devoted resources to raising hens and producing eggs. This dramatic decline continued throughout the 1970s and 1980s, so that by 1982, only 4 percent of farms continued poultry operations. This had serious implications for farm women, who typically raised chickens and gathered eggs for urban markets. Profits from egg and poultry sales often provided families with much-needed cash for children's education, clothing, and other household expenses. Women's "egg money" also paid for additional land, farm equipment, and outstanding farm debts. By the end of the 1950s, however, large-scale poultry and egg production were considered specialized men's work and a primary source of farm income.[7]

As modernization altered traditional female work roles, women seemed to disappear not only from the farmyard but from the farm press and popular agricultural discourse as well. Anthropologist Jane Adams noted that rural women were not immune to the "feminine mystique" that shaped the public discourse during the 1950s and upheld domesticity and leisure as ideals for women. Immediately following the Second World War, the widely popular magazine *Farm Journal* and its women's insert *Farmer's Wife* featured articles that encouraged farm women to participate in politics and community activism as well as articles that recognized women's contributions as workers on the farm. By the mid-1950s, however, articles focused more on domesticity and defined women's economic contributions to the farm as "'a sideline' providing money for luxuries and extras." Over time, fewer articles featured women engaged in productive labor. Women pictured in illustrations and photographs became "more shapely and fashion conscious," while images of farm homes featured modern ranch houses furnished with the latest consumer goods.[8]

By the end of the 1960s, many of the major farm periodicals, including *Successful Farming*, completely dropped women's sections because they had declined in popularity and advertisers were no longer interested in supporting them. In 1973, when asked about the demise of *Farmer's Wife*, an insert in the widely read *Farm Journal*, one *Farm Journal* editor explained that, "general women's magazines were cutting too much of the advertising base from under specialized women's magazines." In other words, publishers believed that farm women no longer desired a magazine, or even a special section, that emphasized their distinct roles on family farms. According to market research by major publishing firms, midwestern farm women favored the same magazines as urban women, such as *Good Housekeeping* and *The Ladies' Home Journal*, because they preferred to read about consumer products and modern homemaking and no longer exhibited rural distinctiveness.[9]

What the editor failed to note was that women were still engaged in agricultural production but in very different ways from the previous generation. When rural and urban women were grouped together, it was assumed that farm women utilized modern household appliances as a means to gain leisure time. Yet more often, rural women increased their involvement with field work, raising livestock, bookkeeping, farm management, and wage-earning jobs that provided the family with much-needed cash income. Historian Sarah Elbert found that even as agricultural production changed, most midwestern farming operations still relied on a family labor force. On modern farms, even those that were highly specialized, women often ran the business and directed or coordinated "farm tasks on CB radios." Women maintained commitments to the farming enterprise and were not "self-sacrificing so much as they have been self-actualizing through the sense of 'us' and 'ours' that characterizes family farms." A 1960 article in *Wallaces' Farmer* recognized that "labor-saving" did not necessarily correlate with actual reductions in work, especially for women. Though women expressed varying degrees of enthusiasm for field work, the article concluded, "When modern appliances were first introduced it looked like an end to the old adage, 'Women's work is never done.' But along with the time-savers inside, came the increased use of machinery outside and women were right back where they started."[10]

Even seemingly mundane activities like bookkeeping became progressively more complicated as farm families confronted state and federal regulations, rising costs of production, and changing inputs. Women who took charge of the business aspects of farming devoted several hours each day not only to keeping accounts but to fielding phone calls, discussing finan-

Figure 6.1: Betty Sirles oversees the harvesting crew at Rendleman Orchards in Union County, Illinois. In addition to twelve different varieties of peaches, Sirles also directs the harvest and care of nectarines and apples. Courtesy of the Illinois State Museum. Used with permission.

cial matters with lenders, ordering parts, supplies, chemicals, and feed, and working closely with agribusinesses and government agencies. In 1971, Opal Reiff of Burnettsville, Indiana, described the volume of materials she managed for the family dairy farm, including financial documents, cattle registrations, lifetime histories for individual cows, and detailed records pertaining to breeding and calving, crop production, gasoline usage, and their participation in the Dairy Herd Improvement program, a national regulatory plan designed to promote standards in milk production. Though she managed complex sets of records that required in-depth knowledge of dairy farming, legal obligations, and financial management, Reiff saw her role as a bookkeeper to be consistent with her regular duties as a farmwife. Having completed secretarial training prior to marriage, Reiff assumed "it automatically falls to my lot to keep all records for the farm."[11]

Discussions in the agricultural press as to how midwestern farm women should adapt to these changes mirrored greater debates about the roles of women in the American workforce, demonstrating the complexity of the transition. Generally, articles in farm magazines portrayed field work as an opportunity for women to expand their involvement with farming and enhance their status in the agricultural community. Implicit within these same articles was the fact that women were still responsible for housework, cooking, child rearing, and if time permitted, gardening and food preservation. Therefore, it was not simply a matter of whether women should work in the fields, with livestock, or on financial matters but how they should balance the demands of housework and child rearing, whether they should be involved with business decisions, how they should manage the cash they earned from off-farm employment, and how they should negotiate new work roles with their husbands. In 1959, an article in *Wallaces' Farmer* asked, "Who Baby Sits When You Are in the Field?" Acknowledging that "life is more complicated for the modern homemaker," the article assumed that women could easily care for children while performing the traditional chores associated with poultry and gardening. This became impossible once women began "plowing or planting the 'back forty.'" Like urban women seeking employment, farm women had to find creative solutions for child care. Suggestions included finding older children, relatives, or neighbors to babysit, postponing field work until young children started school, devising makeshift playpens out of leftover fencing, or simply leaving children to nap in the back of station wagons parked in the field. Similar articles occasionally hinted that husbands should "help" around the house if women worked in the fields, but the basic assumption that women should be entirely responsible for balancing child care with other work implied the flexibility inherent in women's traditional work on family farms.[12]

Striking a balance between work and family responsibilities became even more contentious for those women who chose to take paid employment off the farm. Growing numbers of women took jobs in factories or as office workers, nurses, teachers, and retail clerks in order to pay for farming and household expenses. In 1960, nearly 20 percent of midwestern farm women over 14 years of age held jobs off the farm, compared to just 13 percent in 1950. In the late 1950s, Luella Zmolek of Black Hawk County, Iowa, found a job as a secretary at a nearby manufacturing plant in order to provide a cash income while her husband worked to build a purebred Angus operation. Though her youngest child was just two years old, Zmolek and her husband had taken on a mortgage to purchase 80 acres and she reasoned, "We had to have more income, and so I decided, well, I guess I would go to work." A 1962 study of employed farmwives in Greene County, Iowa, revealed that Zmolek's desire to support the farm was hardly unique. In keeping with regional trends, one 1962 study found that approximately 10 percent of married farm women in Greene County sought employment primarily to earn a cash income to support family farming operations.[13]

The growing number of women seeking employment drew the attention of researchers and reporters, who asserted that wage labor off the farm led to greater personal autonomy for women. The authors of the 1962 Greene County report, for example, found that families with wage-earning wives experienced a "decline in patriarchal authority patterns." Their surveys indicated that husbands and wives increasingly shared child care and household chores, and wives demanded a greater say in the purchasing and business decisions for the farm. That women should retain control over their wages and utilize earning power to assert their opinions within their marriages was further reflected in the farm press. A 1965 article in *Successful Farming* advised women to open their own bank accounts in order to maintain control over their wages. Otherwise, their hard-earned money would only go toward "gasoline, a tax bill, or the cost of machinery repairs," and their "hoped for goals of education, medical expenses services, and a better home are never reached." Three years later, in 1968, *Successful Farming* asked once again, "Should a Farm Wife Work outside the Home?" The author discounted the popular notion that women worked to support the farm and emphasized that most women who sought paid employment simply wanted to "thrive and grow in a new atmosphere" where their identity was not dependant upon their husbands and children.[14]

The authors of the 1962 study in Greene County and those in the farm press who praised women for their off-farm employment may have been overly optimistic in asserting that wage labor led to greater economic and marital equality. Women encountered significant limitations when seeking employment and earned significantly less income than men. In 1979, for example, the average income for Iowa farm women was just $3,926, a mere 34 percent of what farm men earned in their off-farm jobs. After surveying farm women in one Iowa county during the early 1980s, anthropologist Deborah Fink concluded that men still considered women's work, whether it be on the farm or in town, peripheral and of lesser value. In the modern Midwest, "the woman as a full partner on a family farm was rarely, if ever, a reality." In other words, women's work on the farm or in town rarely resulted in greater equality and "did not automatically mean that they were business partners" with their husbands.[15]

In the agricultural press, articles praising women for their work on and off the farm quietly noted that women's changing work roles could potentially heighten marital tensions. Instructional articles for farm couples on sharing responsibilities and maintaining happy marriages appeared with increasing frequency. In 1962, *Farm Journal* ran two articles titled, "How to Stay on Speaking Terms...Though Married," and "Things a Man Should

Never Tell His Wife...Or Should He?" Both articles clearly indicated that women were capable of taking on farmwork if provided with information from patient husbands. If wives were expected to work in the fields, for example, husbands needed to keep machinery in good working order to ease the physical labor. Husbands also had an obligation to keep wives informed about the day-to-day aspects of farming, including unpleasant news of disease among the livestock or insect infestations in crops. Rex Gogerty of Hardin County, Iowa, stated, "Many farm women say they don't want to know and don't have the time to understand the business. But in this day and age, I'll bet it's rather that their husbands don't give them the chance." Even after 1945, as women increased their participation in the actual business of farming, articles such as these indicate that patriarchal social structures did not fall away easily and women remained largely marginalized in the masculine world of agriculture.[16]

The process through which women began to assert their authority within the agricultural community was largely personal and private, requiring that they negotiate work roles with husbands and family members. By the 1970s, however, growing numbers of women began to express their concerns, and their desires for greater recognition as agricultural producers, in the public forums provided by agricultural organizations. During the 1960s and 1970s, the public discourse associated with social and political movements, such as those for civil rights, environmentalism, and gender equality, was very present in the midwestern countryside. Demands for civil, social, and political rights resonated with many rural midwesterners as congressional reapportionment during the 1960s compromised the political power long held by the farm bloc. Agricultural leaders claimed that depopulation created a rural minority whose voices lost out to urban consumers. In 1900, 61 percent of midwesterners lived on farms and in small towns with populations of less than 2,500. On the Great Plains, this number was considerably higher: 73 percent of Kansans and 93 percent of North Dakotans lived in rural areas. By 1950, 35 percent of midwesterners lived in rural areas and only four states (Iowa, North Dakota, South Dakota, and Nebraska) had rural populations just over 50 percent. In 1980, 29 percent of midwesterners lived in rural areas and only a small fraction claimed "farming" as a full-time occupation.[17]

Women activists readily employed the rhetoric that emphasized the minority status of rural and farm families, often raising concerns that low commodity prices and growing costs of production occurred as a result of unreasonable demands by consumers. For instance, during the late 1970s, the female-led organization American Agri-Women published a pamphlet titled, "How to Be a Vocal Farm Wife OR How Are They Gonna Find Out If

WE Don't Tell Them?" The pamphlet's author, Laura Heuser, a national organizer for American Agri-Women and an orchard manager from Hartford, Michigan, asked women, "Are you committed to the profession of agriculture? Do you and your husband, if you have one, choose to be food producers? If both answers are yes, you are a member of a minority group and you must defend your profession."[18]

Most rural midwesterners blamed the economic instability of agriculture for the steady flow of young people out of the countryside. By the early 1970s, unstable fuel prices, consumer boycotts, price caps, and skyrocketing costs of production forced midwestern farmers either to "get big" by investing in land and specialized equipment, or to "get out" of farming altogether. Operating a modern farm required extensive capital and resources unavailable to many rural midwesterners. Female members of the Iowa Farm Bureau Federation Women's Committee often expressed alarm at the rising start-up expenses of farming for young families and, as early as 1953, advocated job training in rural areas to help marginal farmers find "opportunities outside of agriculture." In 1970, a young farmwife, Mrs. D. Hutson of Logan, Iowa, explained that she and her husband could not compete with established farmers. Local insurance companies and banks withheld credit and benefits because Hutson and her husband had only been farming in the area for a few years. She pessimistically concluded, "The odds are greatly against anyone starting to farm."[19]

Economic instability drew many farm women together to form new female forums, organizations, and political outlets that allowed them to speak publicly on behalf of their families. Rural midwestern women had a time-honored tradition of organizing under the banner of agriculture and for generations had been active members of groups such as a Grange, the Farm Bureau, the Non-Partisan League, and the Farmers' Union. In 1980, a nationwide survey revealed that 72 percent of farm women were active members of a community organization of some kind, while approximately 40 percent were involved in a general farm organization or an auxiliary to a general farm organization. Another 21 percent belonged to marketing or farm supply cooperatives, and 14 percent belonged to a commodity producers' association or an auxiliary of a commodity producers' association. For the majority of these women, however, active membership meant serving in supportive roles that mirrored gendered divisions of labor practiced on most farms. They typically met in members' homes for presentations from local authorities, socializing, and shared work. Women rarely attained leadership positions, swayed public policy, or moved beyond domestic settings.[20]

By the early 1970s, farm women recognized that they needed to develop new strategies that emphasized their roles as agricultural producers. Leading farm magazines had all but eliminated women's content due to market research reports indicating dwindling interest. In this same period, however, female-authored newsletters and publications flourished at the local, regional, and even national levels. Midwestern women readily supported this trend. In 1970, publisher Roy Reiman of Greendale, Wisconsin, found instant success when he developed *Farm Wife News*, a monthly, ad-free, reader-driven magazine that depended only on subscriptions for financing. Rather than offering instruction or idealized accounts of rural life, Reiman wanted to offer a "forum" for farm women to share their experiences. Readers authored the majority of the articles, and editors regularly asked readers to respond to questions, including women's opinions on agricultural policies, farming practices, consumer products, or current events. Within its first three weeks, 38,000 women subscribed, and by 1975 the small, 50-page magazine enjoyed a circulation of over 500,000. By the early 1980s, this number reached 2.3 million, and the magazine was renamed *Country Woman*.[21]

Because farm women directed the content, *Farm Wife News* reflected farm women's broad interests and illustrated that women had not adopted urban ideals or changed their identity, as suggested by trends in other farm periodicals. *Farm Wife News* presented a wide variety of material, from recipes and sewing patterns to the latest news on agricultural policy from Capitol Hill and information on caring for livestock. Articles also helped women navigate the complexities of modern agriculture. In July 1975, for example, a story titled "Who's Liable for Shared Farm Workers?" informed readers that the time-honored tradition of sharing work was now subject to federal regulations. Under the Job Safety Act, families could be held responsible if a neighbor or a neighbor's farmworker was involved in an accident on their farm. As a result, farmers and their wives needed to carefully negotiate contracts and work agreements that defined liability. Stories like these spurred lively debates, and each month readers engaged such topics as the Equal Rights Amendment, diet and weight loss plans, the introduction of Universal Product Codes (UPC) in grocery stores, and farm management methods. The all-female editorial staff encouraged reader participation by continuing conversations over several months and by persuading women to recognize the value of their work. In 1975, an article in *Farm Wife News* estimated that, if they were salaried employees, farmwives would earn more than $17,000 for their work as nurses, cooks, housekeepers, laundresses, gardeners, chauffeurs, hired hands, and veterinarians. In an era when farm profits were quickly consumed by rising costs of production, the author urged women to add up their total worth and "spring a few figures" on their husbands.[22]

Moving beyond mere rhetoric, however, the editors of *Farm Wife News* put considerable effort into fostering women's activism. In 1973, editors secured an official proclamation from Secretary of Agriculture Earl Butz to designate November as National Farm Wife Month. The following year, *Farm Wife News* partnered with Women for the Survival of Agriculture in Michigan (WSAM) to sponsor the first National Farm Women's Forum. Held in Milwaukee, Wisconsin, the conference attracted more than 1,600 women from 30 states and culminated in the creation of American Agri-Women, a coalition of more than 20 women's organizations located throughout the Midwest and the West. The coalition included commodity groups, such as the Associated Milk Producers, as well as political action groups like the United Farm Wives, formed in Missouri in 1973 as a response to consumer beef boycotts. Members of American Agri-Women gave presentations to the Department of Agriculture, testified before Congress, and served on the Agriculture Council of America, a nonprofit organization devoted to consumer education. At the local levels, *Farm Wife News* reported that members gained new insights at the National Farm Women's Forum that allowed them to "revitalize their programs" in existing organizations such as Farm Bureau Women's Clubs and county commodity groups.[23]

Meetings like the National Farm Women's Forum drew large audiences because, as farm women communicated their concerns within regional and national forums, they began to understand the complexity and systemic nature of their problems. This shift was largely precipitated not only by concerns about depopulation and economic instability but also by the realization that women's work and economic contributions to the farm provided no legal protection if their marriages ended through divorce or the husband's death. Most midwestern states attributed all farm property and income to husbands, leaving women destitute in cases of divorce, or requiring women to pay estate taxes on the farms they inherited. Even in "separate property" states like Wisconsin, where husbands and wives retained their own property over the course of a marriage, ownership of joint property was typically granted to men. Unless a couple signed formal partnership agreements, the State of Wisconsin attributed all farm income to the husband. Women rarely bought or sold equipment, maintained separate bank accounts, or kept detailed work diaries that clearly documented their work on the farm. As a result, rising land and equipment values throughout the 1960s and 1970s forced many widows to sell off parcels of land, or even the entire farm, to pay estate taxes.[24]

A growing awareness of the problem fueled calls for reform that required women to identify as producers and laborers rather than mere helpmeets. Many women took their concerns to major farm organizations with an established lobby in Washington, DC, but when male leaders failed to act, they realized "they would have to organize on their own." Throughout the decade, women across the Midwest formed several new groups at the national, state, and local levels to address tax law, economic woes, environmental issues, and other concerns. Many of the activists who took on tax reform and farm policy had some experience in women's clubs, but few had ever worked as professional organizers, lobbyists, or spokespersons. They ventured into new roles as activists due to personal experiences and concerns. In 1975, Doris Royal of Springfield, Nebraska, experienced a personal epiphany after a day's work with her husband, Lloyd, on their 240-acre farm. When they returned to their home after dark, Doris turned to her husband and said, "Lloyd, do you realize that I haven't contributed a dime to the farm today, according to the IRS?" The couple purchased the farm in 1960 for $72,000, but in 1975 rising land values drove up the assessment of their farm to $300,000. In the same period, their actual income had remained about the same. Were her husband to die suddenly, Royal would owe $32,000 in estate taxes. This prompted Royal and several friends to begin a national awareness campaign and gather the signatures of 500,000 farm women from across the country. Royal's leadership garnered national attention, and with the assistance of the editorial staff at *Farm Wife News*, she led a delegation to Washington, DC, where they personally delivered the petitions to Congress. This not only provided the impetus for new guidelines in the Tax Reform Act of 1976 but compelled Royal to become more involved with organizations such as American Agri-Women.[25]

In 1979, economist Frances Hill declared that public recognition of economic inequalities had fueled a new rural women's movement. Hill believed that by coming together over issues such as tax law, ownership, and inheritance, farm women's situation was actually advantageous because agricultural problems were "non-threatening" and enabled them to act while asserting that they were not "libbers," or "man-hating, bra-burning feminists." Hill noted that while these new women activists sought equality and respect, they also made a concerted effort to "distinguish themselves and their organizations from what they take to be the feminist movement." Most amazing to Hill, however, was not the fact that women started these new groups but that these were the first new general farm organizations "founded in a quarter century." They ran "counter to the trend toward increased commodity specialization" by forming organizations to address the wide range of problems facing all farm families.[26]

The success of new female-led organizations, coupled with the intensity of the debate over farm women's economic rights, led to greater acknowledgment of women's contributions to farming and the realities of women's dependence on men. By the end of the 1970s, leading farm magazines revived women's content with a new understanding that farm women wanted to read about their roles in agriculture rather than homemaking. A 1978 article in *Farm Journal* titled, "You Have Fewer Rights Than You Think," departed from the usual rhetoric that promoted positive valuations of women's household labor as the author declared, "the role of farm wife and homemaker, valuable as it is, does not offer any guarantee of economic security for women." The author encouraged women, in addition to familiarizing themselves with the family and finances, to become active in politics, contact their legislators, work for the Equal Rights Amendment, and keep a detailed diary that clearly demonstrated their "contribution to the business."[27]

Monthly articles in *Farm Journal* continued to remind readers of women's presence in agriculture, including one article from November 1978 that featured sketches of female farm and ranch owner-operators. Rather than portray these women as unusual, the author pointed out that most were widows or were daughters who inherited a farm and who learned the business of farming through experience. They tended to weather rocky transitions from "helpers" to "owners" as they took on responsibility for the farm, and they continued to experience discrimination in their own communities. Betty Harms of Monona County, Iowa, who began managing the family grain-farming operation following the death of her husband, encouraged women to "believe in yourself." She held that women had to overcome significant social hurdles once they took over the farm, saying, "Independence is great, but not all people appreciate that you're a woman. When someone says, 'You're getting more independent,' it isn't always meant as a compliment."[28]

The following year, nearly a decade after *Successful Farming* dropped its women's section, Cheryl Tevis, a native Iowan and experienced farm journalist who began her career as a reporter for *Farm Wife News,* joined the staff of *Successful Farming* as the associate editor of farm management. Responsible for women's content, she devoted her inaugural column titled "Woman Interest" to the estate tax problem. She encouraged women to take decisive action by writing and speaking to politicians. Evoking language influenced by the women's movement, Tevis wrote, "The expression, 'I'm just a farm wife,' has no place in the farm woman's vocabulary today," and she demanded that women be taken seriously as full partners on family farms. Reader response to Tevis's writing was overwhelmingly positive, reflecting farm women's desires to identify as more than mere "helpers."

Laura Beane of Ft. Atkinson, Wisconsin, wrote, "It's about time! So glad *Successful Farming* has awakened to the fact that farm wives are a real part of the farming business."[29]

Even as women gained greater recognition for their contributions to agriculture, few eagerly integrated themselves into the masculine worlds of production, agribusiness, and farm politics. Rather, most women continued to seek out transformative and collaborative experiences that had shaped women's work and community service for more than a century. A 1984 study on women's leadership traits found that farmwives valued cooperation, emotional stability, and discretion over actual knowledge of agricultural policy. This distinctive leadership style, well established in rural communities by the 1970s, became more and more important throughout the early 1980s as the economic situation in agriculture deteriorated and much of the Midwest was mired in the farm crisis.[30]

The farm crisis unfolded throughout the 1980s as farm families struggled to pay mounting debts. During the 1970s, farmers aspiring to compete in the modern marketplace took out loans to finance land acquisitions, new machinery, and specialized equipment. By the early 1980s, however, unstable commodity prices and mounting interest rates precluded families from making loan payments and forced thousands into foreclosure. Farm families had little choice but to allow their debts to roll over year after year, and between 1981 and 1983, farm indebtedness soared 130 percent. Leaders of major agricultural organizations recognized the severity of the situation, but collective action evaded activists because the crisis affected individual families at different times and in varying ways. Between 1982 and 1992, the number of farms in the United States fell from 2.2 million to 1.9 million, and the crisis was particularly severe in the grain belts of the Midwest. Yet those who had not borrowed heavily managed to weather these critical years, while those who drew on credit to expand their operations suffered varied degrees of hardship based on the amount of their debt. Those facing foreclosure often blamed themselves rather than the lenders and policies that created the situation. They attempted to readjust loans and negotiate with creditors in isolation from friends and neighbors, generating severe stress within marriages and families.[31]

As women contended with the realities of the farm crisis, they defined the political and financial aspects of the situation as distinctly personal. Pat Eddy, a farm woman from Stuart, Iowa, believed women turned to activism in order to "keep their families together and survive." Though few women attained leadership positions in well-established national farm organizations, they came to define grassroots activism by joining and forming new groups. Building on past experiences working within agricultural organizations, women often continued to work in predominantly female groups and form special task forces specifically for women. The difference in the 1980s, however, was a new rhetoric among female activists that questioned men's abilities to act effectively. Eddy noted that the private nature of the farm crisis paralyzed men who had previously taken tremendous pride in their abilities as farmers and managers. Many husbands were simply unable to deal with the stress, forcing their wives to take their roles as caretakers and nurturers into the political arena.[32]

As families confronted poverty and the possibility of displacement, it was often the women who sought financial and legal assistance, applied for food stamps, called hotlines, and reached out to the community. In doing so, they encountered others suffering from similar problems. In a 1985 speech to female activists in Wisconsin, Anne Kanten, the Minnesota assistant commissioner of agriculture, persuaded women not to be ashamed but to channel their anxiety and frustration into activism. In the midst of a crisis, personal experience trumped financial and political expertise, and she encouraged women to "believe in yourself and have courage." Kanten concluded, "[Activism] has to start at home. Women must become the catalysts around our own table. It has to be all right to talk about what hurts. Say it. Wherever you are, tell the story and let people know." This shift in political strategy that valued women's lived experiences was certainly unique to the farm crisis, leading the historian Mark Friedberger to assert that, in many ways, women benefited personally from economic instability. He believed that because husbands were unable to cope, "it was the wife who was able to grow in stature and to discover a new role for herself." No longer satisfied by their "duties as homemakers and nurturers," women took on leadership roles that garnered real power within families and communities. Ultimately, Friedberger asserted, "the farm crisis that ruined her husband's career gave his wife a new dimension and meaning."[33]

Other women, especially those displaced from their farms, dealt with the crisis by seeking paid employment and fostering efforts to stimulate the local economy. In 1989, following the loss of her farm, a succession of odd jobs, and a tragic trucking accident that nearly killed her husband, Jeannie Williams of Lucerne, Missouri, decided to start her own business. Devastated by the farm crisis and the decline of the coal-mining industry and by the bleak economic conditions in her northeastern Missouri village of 51 residents, this mother of two young sons was compelled to market old family recipes under the name Aunt Nene's Specialty Foods. With so few employment opportunities in the area, Williams believed her entrepreneurial venture had greater significance as a symbol of community stability than as an effort to achieve personal success. Between 1980 and 1990, Lucerne lost 61 percent of its population and nearly 80 percent of all high school graduates left the community. Businesses abandoned Main Street one by one, leaving derelict buildings to collapse from neglect. By 1991, Williams moved her business from her home into an abandoned elementary school, where she employed 14 women and produced gourmet pickles and jellies for markets in New England, Canada, and the United Kingdom. Despite numerous setbacks, she hoped to hire seven or eight more employees within the year. "This is against all odds," she told a reporter from the *St. Louis Post-Dispatch*, "but I want to create jobs. We need it so badly up here."[34]

Many women like Williams chose to start unique, female-centered businesses because they provided personal independence, authority over their work space, and employment for other women. During the mid-1980s, Diane Niebuhr and her husband purchased an Iowa farm that included a bridal boutique housed in a massive pink dairy barn. Niebuhr transformed Hope's Bridal Boutique, opened by Hope Kolsto during the 1970s, into one of the "top five bridal businesses in the Midwest." She employed two dozen local women and offered them the rare opportunity to work in a female-dominated industry characterized by glamour and affluence. In rural areas, where women often lamented their inability to partake in popular feminine consumer activities, Niebuhr provided "a big city selection and big city service but a small town atmosphere." The big pink barn bound young girls to the community as they dreamed of growing up and one day selecting their gown from Hope's Bridal Boutique.[35]

Despite this undeniable influence on grassroots action and community development, historian William Pratt cautioned against overestimating the equalizing influence of the farm crisis. Pratt rightly pointed out that "older attitudes and the traditional division of labor" remained well entrenched in most rural midwestern communities. The farm crisis simply presented one more moment in time, much like the Great Depression, when women used their domestic skills to maintain the family and assert their authority. Furthermore, few of the women who experienced foreclosures, loan readjustment, marital stress, and dire poverty would have agreed that the crisis was personally advantageous. The farm crisis simply drew greater public attention to women's activism and legitimized feminine leadership styles in the public arena. Historian Sarah Elbert argued that, as early as the late 1960s and early 1970s, farm women asked male political leaders and agricultural economists for a "progressive public policy" that took into account women's participation in farming and familial work patterns. It was not until the farm crisis that these political leaders, policy makers, and popular media outlets finally took notice.[36]

In the years following the farm crisis, women continued to serve as spokespersons for agricultural organizations, while gaining ground as agribusinesses professionals, policy makers for state and federal agencies, and farm owners and operators. By the end of the twentieth century, women owned more than half of the farmland in the Midwest, and growing numbers described themselves as farm operators. According to the 2002 Agricultural Census, women served as principal operators on 237,819 (11 percent) of the more than 2.1 million American farms. Of those, 84 percent of the women were full owners and operators, and 52 percent reported farming as their primary occupation. Though the actual numbers of women in agriculture remained relatively low, the numbers continued to rise. In 1992, just ten years earlier, only 145,156 women were reported to be principal farm operators. By 1997, however, the number reached 209,784. This was especially unusual given the fact that in general, over the previous two decades, the total number of farms in the United States had declined.[37]

The mainstream media picked up on what they termed the "feminization of agriculture," wherein women were engaged in actual farmwork: cultivating crops, raising livestock, operating heavy equipment, and managing the business. A 2001 article in the *Omaha World Herald* reported "dramatic" changes throughout Nebraska. The reporter was astonished not only that the number of women in farming and ranching was growing but that in Cherry County, Nebraska, in the heart of cattle country, the 91 ranches owned and operated by women averaged 5,800 acres—equal to the average size of those owned and operated by men. On the other hand, the article was also careful to point out that women who actually farmed were not to be confused with the increasing number of women landowners. Females owned nearly half of the farmland in both Nebraska and Iowa, but this trend was easily explained by the fact that most of these women were the widows and daughters of farmers, and they rented the land and left the work to male relatives, neighbors, or tenants.[38]

Despite their growing numbers, female farm operators continued to struggle in a predominantly masculine profession. In 2001, Jacque Trumbull, who operated a 3,200-acre ranch near Stapleton, Nebraska, said that auctioneers at bull sales occasionally ignored her because they "weren't used to women doing the buying." In 2006, Nan Bonfils, an owner-operator of an organic farm in Madrid, Iowa, told a reporter, "[Women as farmers] is not how agriculture was in Iowa, and it's not how most people imagine agriculture to be. To actually give full credit to women as producers, landowners, and decision makers, I think that's still a challenge in Iowa." Likewise, April Hemmes, who owned and operated a farm near Hampton, Iowa, said that, while she had never been denied a loan, she always had to earn the respect of male farmers, bankers, and merchants. She said, "It seems like you have to keep proving yourself. I just take that for granted now."[39]

For women like Bonfils and Hemmes, creating female support networks through agricultural organizations specifically geared toward women offered training and solidarity they did not find in traditionally male organizations. Hemmes, for example, served as the president of the board of the Iowa Women in Agriculture. She found all-female organizations provided important services for women and that even women who farmed "thousands and thousands of acres" simply did not feel comfortable going to meetings with men. Founded in 2003, Iowa Women in Agriculture offered a number of services—including in-depth seminars on topics including farm management, agricultural business, marketing, intergenerational communication, and estate planning. Ultimately, the organization's goal was to provide women in agriculture, whether they were primary operators or workers on family farms, with the information they needed to be successful. As a group, members also hoped to extend friendship and support. Hemmes hoped that the group could help more women establish themselves as farmers and overcome stereotypes that women were not able to do farmwork. When asked whether women might face difficulties performing certain tasks, Hemmes simply said, "Corn doesn't care who plants it, and a cow doesn't care who feeds it."[40]

Female farmers found working with other women to be helpful because they believed that their identities as women shaped how they approached production, marketing, and conservation. In 2002, Ruth Hambleton, a farm operator and Extension educator in Illinois, developed "Annie's Project," an educational program for midwestern women in agriculture that emphasized personal instruction, collaboration, and participant-guided curriculum. Hambleton asserted that unlike male farmers, women tended to focus more on families, to take a risk-adverse approach to marketing, and to see cultivating and marketing as an open, community-based activity. Women were also more likely to focus on conservation and sustainability, not only for their own families but also for the overall economic health of nearby rural communities. When asked to forecast new trends in agriculture, Hambleton hoped that women's voices would continue to grow in strength and influence policy as more land came under female ownership and cultivation.[41]

Hambleton's observations from the early twenty-first century would have made perfect sense to Clara Fenstermann, who in 1950 foresaw that her daughter would one day enjoy a full partnership with her husband. In many ways, Fenstermann's prediction seemed unlikely as new technologies, agribusinesses, and rural depopulation appeared to marginalize midwestern women from agricultural production. Yet, the demands of modern agriculture required not only a family workforce but greater capital and liquid assets. So rather than retreating from family farming operations and seeking idealized lives of leisure, women adapted their work roles to incorporate bookkeeping, business management, field work, raising livestock, wage work, and activism. While entering public spaces and taking on new roles required women to renegotiate gendered divisions of labor and identify as agricultural producers, they also maintained time-honored female strategies of shared work and community building. By the beginning of the twenty-first century, the "feminization of agriculture" became a noticeable trend that required policy makers, educators, and agribusinesses to recognize women as a transformative force in the rural Midwest.

Figure 6.2: Ruth Hambleton, who raises beef cattle on a farm near Mt. Vernon, Illinois, developed Annie's Project through the University of Illinois Extension Service to educate farm women and strengthen women's voices in shaping agricultural policy. Since 2002, Annie's Project has been implemented in several states. Courtesy of the Illinois State Museum. Used with permission.

Notes

1. Clara Fenstermann, *Iowa Bureau Farmer* (August 1950): 4.

2. Joan Jensen, *Calling This Place Home: Women on the Wisconsin Frontier* (St. Paul: Minnesota Historical Society Press, 2006), 147; John Mack Faragher, "History from the Inside-Out: Writing the History of Women in Rural America," *American Quarterly* 33 (Winter 1981): 553–54; Rachel Ann Rosenfeld, *Farm Women: Work, Farm, and Family in the United States* (Chapel Hill: University of North Carolina Press, 1985), 26; Deborah Fink, *Open Country, Iowa: Rural Women, Tradition, and Change* (Albany: State University of New York Press, 1986), 218.

3. Andrew R.L. Cayton and Peter S. Onuf, *The Midwest and the Nation: Rethinking the History of an American Region* (Bloomington: Indiana University Press, 1990), 56–57, 118; Deborah Fink, *Agrarian Women: Wives and Mothers in Rural Nebraska, 1880–1940* (Chapel Hill: University of North Carolina Press, 1992), 21–29.

4. Mary Neth, *Preserving the Family Farm: Women, Community, and the Foundations of Agribusiness in the Midwest, 1900–1940* (Baltimore: Johns Hopkins University Press, 1995), 217, 178–80. See also Katherine Jellison, *Entitled to Power: Farm Women and Technology, 1913–1963* (Chapel Hill: University of North Carolina Press, 1993).

5. *Census of the Population: 1950, Volume II: Characteristics of the Population, Part 15: Iowa, Part 25: Missouri, Part 27: Nebraska* (Washington, DC: U.S. GPO, 1952); *United States Census of Agriculture 1950, Volume I, Part 9: Iowa, Part 10: Missouri, Part 12: Nebraska* (Washington, DC: U.S. GPO, 1952); Jellison, *Entitled to Power,* 169; "You Can Wash on Rainey Days," *Wallaces' Farmer and Iowa Homestead,* December 1, 1956, 26.

6. "Does Home Canning Save You Money?" *Wallaces' Farmer,* July 11, 1970, 24–25; "What's Happened to the Farm Garden?" *Wallaces Farmer,* October 8, 1966, 41.

7. Fink, *Open Country, Iowa,* 136, 142, 148–59.

8. Jane Adams, "The *Farm Journal's* Discourse of Farm Women's Femininity," *Anthropology and Humanism* 29 (1) (2004): 49, 56; Jellison, *Entitled to Power,* 172–74.

9. Janet Galligani Casey, "'This Is YOUR Magazine': Domesticity, Agrarianism, and *The Farmer's Wife,*" *American Periodicals* 14 (2) (2004): 206.

10. Sarah Elbert, "Women and Farming: Changing Roles, Changing Structures," in *Women and Farming: Changing Roles, Changing Structures,* ed. Jane B. Knowles and Wava G. Haney (Boulder, CO: Westview Press, 1988), 261–62; "Women Who Work in the Field," *Wallaces Farmer,* December 3, 1960, 29.

11. "Farm Wives Tell: 'How I Help My Husband,'" *Farmer's Digest* 34 (9) (March 1971): 72.

12. "Who Baby Sits When You Are in the Field?" *Wallaces Farmer,* April 18, 1959, 52.

13. USDA, *Agricultural Statistics: 1967* (Washington, DC: GPO, 1967), 443, 573; Luella Zmolek, interview by Doris Malkmus, September 10, 2001, transcript, Voices from the Land Oral History Collection, Iowa Women's Archives, University of Iowa, Iowa City; Lee G. Burchinal, "Factors Related to Employment of Wives in a Rural Iowa County," *Research Bulletin* 509 (Agricultural and Home Economics Experiment Station, Iowa State University, Ames, Iowa, 1962), 659, 662, 666; Janet H. Fithian, "Should It Be Off To Work for You?" *Successful Farming* (June 1965): 82.

14. USDA, *Agricultural Statistics: 1967* (Washington, DC: GPO, 1967), 443, 573; Luella Zmolek, interview by Doris Malkmus Burchinal, "Factors Related to Employment of Wives in a Rural Iowa County," 659, 662, 666; Janet H. Fithian, "Should It Be Off To Work

for You?" *Successful Farming* (June 1965): 82; Joan McCloskey, "Should a Farm Wife Work outside the Home?" *Successful Farming* (September 1968): 57, 71.

15. Fink, *Open Country, Iowa*, 135–61, 188, 195.

16. "How to Stay on Speaking Terms…Though Married," *Farm Journal* (November 1962): 38–39; "Things a Man Should Never Tell His Wife…Or Should He?" *Farm Journal* (November 1962): 62D–62F.

17. "Urban and Rural Population: 1900 to 1990," United States Bureau of the Census (October 1995), <www.census.gov/population/censusdata/urpop0090.txt> (accessed October 25, 2009).

18. Laura Heuser, "How to Be a Vocal Farm Wife OR How Are They Gonna Find Out If WE Ddon't Tell Them?" (American Agri-Women pamphlet, n.d.), WIFE Records, University of Nebraska–Lincoln.

19. Hanson et al., "Agriculture in Iowa: Trends from 1935 to 1997," 25, 32; "Farm Bureau's 10-Point Program for Agricultural Prosperity" (Des Moines: Iowa Farm Bureau Federation, 1953), Iowa Farm Bureau Federation Records, Special Collections, Iowa State University; *Iowa Farm Bureau Spokesman* 36 (39) (May 30, 1970): 4.

20. Rosenfeld, *Farm Women*, 193, 196–98. See also Donald B. Marti, *Women of the Grange: Mutuality and Sisterhood in Rural America, 1866–1920* (New York: Greenwood Press, 1991); Nancy K. Berlage, "Organizing the Farm Bureau: Family Community, and Professionals, 1914–1928," *Agricultural History* 75 (4) (2001): 406–37; and Mary Neth, "Building the Base: Farm Women and the Rural Community and Farm Organizations in the Midwest, 1900–1940," in Knowles and Haney, *Women and Farming*.

21. Chris Beam, "The Reiman Reason: Reiman Publications' Magazines Are the Radio Call-In Shows of the Publishing World, Allowing Readers to Chat with Their Neighbors," *Folio: The Magazine for Magazine Management* (September 15, 1996): 18; Matt Neznanski, "Publisher Reiman Addresses Aspiring Entrepreneurs," press release in "Greenlee School of Journalism and Communication News" (March 9, 2006), <www.jlmc.iastate.edu/news/2006/spring/reimantalk.shtml> (accessed October 4, 2007).

22. "Who's Liable for Shared Farm Workers?" *Farm Wife News* 5 (7) (July 1975): 9; "Farm Wife Worth More than $17,000 in '75!" *Farm Wife News* 5 (11) (November 1975): 17.

23. "The Voice of the American Agri-Woman," American Agri-Women Annual Report and Directory, 1980, WIFE Records, University of Nebraska–Lincoln; "You Have a Right to Be Proud!" *Farm Wife News* (5) (11) (November 1975): 42–43.

24. Marygold Shire Melli, *The Legal Status of Homemakers in Wisconsin* (Washington, DC: Center for Women Policy Studies, May 1977), 2–4.

25. Roy Reed, "Death Taxes Compelling Heirs to Sell Farm Land," *New York Times*, February 15, 1976, 1; Linda F. Little, Francine P. Proulx, Julia Marlowe, and Patricia K. Knaub, "The History of Recent Farm Legislation: Implications for Farm Families," *Family Relations* 36 (4) (October 1987): 402–6; Cheryl Tevis, "Family," *Successful Farming* (March 1991): 35.

26. Frances Hill, "Women and Farm Politics—National Level," *Nebraska's New Land Review* (Summer 1979): 10.

27. Laura Lane, "You Have Fewer Rights than You Think," *Farm Journal* (June/July 1978): 35–37.

28. Jean Gillies, "When a Woman Runs the Farm," *Farm Journal* (November 1978): 37–39.

29. Cheryl Tevis, "Woman Interest," *Successful Farming* (August 1979): 14; Cheryl Tevis, "How Does Estate Tax Law Cut the Cake—Equal Partner or Marital Helpmate?"

Successful Farming (September 1979): 30–31; Cheryl Tevis, "Woman Interest," *Successful Farming* (November 1979): 18.

30. Karen Freiberg, "Supportive Role Still Suits Farm Wives," *Farm Journal* (October 1984): 32; William C. Pratt, "Using History to Make History? Progressive Farm Organizing during the Farm Revolt of the 1980s," *Annals of Iowa* 55 (Winter 1996): 40–42.

31. "Farmers Home Administration: An Overview of Farmer Program Debt, Delinquencies, and Loan Losses" (Washington, DC: U.S. General Accounting Office, January 1986); Kathryn J. Brasier, "Spatial Analysis of Changes in the Number of Farms during the Farm Crisis," *Rural Sociology* 70 (4) (Winter 2005): 541.

32. Pat Eddy, interview by Doris Malkmus, September 20, 2001, transcript, Voices from the Land Oral History Collection, Iowa Women's Archives, University of Iowa, Iowa City.

33. Carol Hodne, "Women's Strategic Role in the Farm Movement," *North American Farmer* (January 1989): 4; Mark Friedberger, *Shake-Out: Iowa Farm Families in the 1980s* (Lexington: University Press of Kentucky, 1989), 112, 82. See also Peggy F. Barlett, *American Dreams, Rural Realities: Family Farms in Crisis* (Chapel Hill: University of North Carolina Press, 1993).

34. William Robbins, "In Depressed Farm Belt, Cultivating Self-Reliance," *New York Times*, December 21, 1989; Peter Hernon, "Fighting Back for Small Town: Cottage Industries May Be Salvation," *St. Louis Post-Dispatch*, December 31, 1991.

35. Katherine Jellison, *It's Our Day: America's Love Affair with the White Wedding, 1945–2005* (Lawrence: University Press of Kansas, 2008), 100–101.

36. Elbert, "Women and Farming," 261–62.

37. *2002 Census of Agriculture*, vol. I (Washington, DC: USDA, 2004), 2, 50, 56; *1992 Census of Agriculture*, vol. 1 (Washington, DC: USDA, 1994), 24.

38. Bill Hord, "'Love for the Land' Has Women Running Farms," *Omaha World Herald*, July 8, 2001.

39. Hord, "Love for the Land"; Heidi Marttila-Losure, "Farmwork Network: Farm Women Help Each Other Learn and Succeed," *Facets*, published by the *Ames Tribune* (August 2006): 12–19.

40. "Anne Fitzgerald, "In Large Part, the Land's Future Is Up To Women," *Des Moines Register* (July 17, 2005); Marttila-Losure, "Farmwork Network," 12–19.

41. Ruth Hambleton, interview by Michael Maniscalco, April 15, 2008, transcript, Oral History Project of Illinois Agriculture, Illinois State Museum, Springfield. Illinois State Museum Audio-Visual Barn, <avbarn.museum.state.il.us/BioID/11> (accessed January 14, 2010).

SEVEN — CHILDHOOD IN THE RURAL MIDWEST SINCE 1945

Pamela Riney-Kehrberg

Our understanding and expectations of midwestern rural childhood owe a great deal to both Norman Rockwell and Grant Wood. When we think about the contours of that way of life, we imagine blue skies and sunshine. We see apple-cheeked children studying in one-room schools, working side by side with mothers and fathers, and romping in lush woodlands and rolling hills. Interspersed throughout the picture are dogs, cats, horses, maybe the occasional goat, patched overalls, tire swings, fishing holes, blackberry brambles, and numerous other indicators that this is the location of the rural good life. We may also envision small-town America in earlier days, where children walked and rode their bikes to school, climbed trees afterward, and seemingly maintained carefree innocence, fostered by loving adults.[1] This is not an imagined world that leaves much room for unpleasant intruders such as abandoned schools, tractor accidents, and meth labs. The world in our mind's eye is one, instead, that our parents, grandparents, and great-grandparents could have conjured. Our imaginary picture of rural midwestern childhood has largely remained static in spite of vast transformations that have occurred in the years since the Second World War.

For midwestern rural children, the second half of the twentieth century meant enormous change. The imagined world of rural childhood—if it ever truly existed—would be gone forever by the century's end.

Although the lives of rural and urban children were far different in the early days of the twentieth century, they moved closer to convergence during the postwar era. Changes in education and work habits brought rural children closer to their urban and suburban counterparts. By the 1960s, the vast majority of midwestern youth attended consolidated schools, signaling the end of the little red schoolhouse and many of the idiosyncrasies of midwestern rural education. Educational expectations would also converge with more and more rural children graduating from high school and attending colleges and universities. Another area of convergence would be children's working lives. While farm children would continue to spend at least some time laboring for their parents, the overwhelming work hours faced by previous generations of farm children would increasingly become a relic of the past. Perhaps not surprisingly, however, farm children would face new threats due to farm mechanization. In the world of the tractor, the young would bear a disproportionate burden of injuries and fatalities. The technology of leisure would also bring rural childhood closer to urban childhood with television and, later, computers playing an increasing role in children's lives, no matter where they lived.

Change, however, is a relative term. It is important to remember that the elements of change in children's lives have not been distributed evenly across the region. Time and circumstances transformed some communities more quickly than others, and some areas of change were more thorough than others. Economic change and development progressed unevenly across the region, meaning that some of the area's children were quite privileged, or quite deprived, relative to others. Additionally, some new elements of rural life in the late twentieth century, such as exposure to methamphetamine, altered children's lives in particular communities quite radically, and the degree of damage done has yet to be fully assessed. There is no single story of growing up rural in the post–World War II Midwest. The focus in this essay will balance areas of change with areas of stasis and will highlight areas of diversity, in order to enhance understanding of the ways in which the lives of rural children and youth conformed with or diverged from the midwestern mainstream.

One of the greatest areas of convergence between rural and urban children's lives has been education. In the pre–World War II era, many rural children received their education in country schools, often of the one-room variety. These schools enrolled children from the local neighborhood, and the teacher might educate as few as two or three students or as many as fifty. Generally young, minimally trained teachers taught in these schools, and students received an education that ranged from very bad to very good. Turn-of-the-century reformers isolated a "rural school problem," which they defined as being a poor education caused by children attending small, poorly supported schools, taught by young underprepared teachers. They believed that these concerns could be resolved by consolidation. Consolidation involved the closing of small rural schools and replacing them with larger, central schools, sometimes in rural areas but more often in cities and towns.[2]

The midwestern states began consolidating their schools before the end of the nineteenth century, in response to a desire for a higher quality, less expensive, and more uniform education for all of their children. The process, however, would not be completed until after the Second World War. States like Iowa, for example, began the process in the 1910s but lost momentum with the onset of the agricultural depression in the 1920s. Iowans would see their last one- and two-room public schools close in the late 1950s and early 1960s, and most rural communities closed their small high schools, moving instruction to cities and towns.[3] In many places, the process of improving rural education also involved the creation of local, easily accessible high

Figure 7.1: In the 1940s country schools were common in rural areas, but the trend toward consolidation led to fewer and larger rural schools that more closely resembled urban institutions. This school photograph was taken of the students, grades one through eight, at Prairie Flower School, located in Gentry County, Missouri, during the 1951–1952 school year. Source: J.L. Anderson. Used with permission.

schools. In the 1950s, for example, students in the vast majority of Michigan's school districts did not have access to local high schools and had to rely upon the ability and willingness of neighboring districts to accept them as tuition pupils. Sometimes there was room for interested students, but other schools were full. Improving education in that state, as in most, meant consolidating districts, enlarging high schools, and making secondary education more accessible to all rural children.[4]

Attending high school in town changed the cultural orientation of rural youth. The authors of a study of Hardin County, Iowa, found that "the rural child in high school finds his interests in town. School activities themselves are the predominate excuse for going to town in the evening." High school attendance opened up opportunities for social activities unavailable closer to home. High school sports could bring the whole family to town as well, not just the older children. In these communities, "Basketball games take on great importance.... Other sports conflict, in their season, with farm work, but around basketball is formed a community of interest which extends even to adults."[5] In Iowa, high school basketball was not just for boys but for girls too. Astonishing numbers of girls played six-on-six basketball, a game specifically adapted for play in rural communities. In the 1950s, 70 percent of Iowa's high school girls were on basketball teams, the vast majority of them playing in small-town and rural schools.[6] Schools, more than ever, became the social centers of their communities.

Consolidation could provide rural children with better-equipped schools and more choice of classes, but it did not necessarily offer them an experience identical to that of their town and city peers. Large numbers of rural children traveled to school by bus, which often meant that they could not participate in extracurricular activities such as sports and dramatics. Additionally, the chores that farming parents still expected often cut into time for after-school activities as well. A 1950 study of youngsters in Hamilton County, Iowa, found marked disparities between farm and nonfarm youth in participation in school activities. While 41.2 percent of nonfarm boys participated in athletics, only 22.9 percent of farm boys did. There were similar results for girls, with 49.2 percent of nonfarm girls involved in athletics as opposed to 37 percent for farm girls. Work and access to transportation were most likely the determining factors. The same study found that nearly 10 percent of rural boys and girls were working more than 40 hours a week on their parents' farms.[7] This may have been part of the impetus for farm states to allow lower driving ages for young people commuting to and from farms to consolidated schools. States such as Kansas and Iowa maintained a driver's license age of 14 for rural youth who needed to drive to school and home again on a daily basis.

By the 1950s and 1960s, the majority of the Midwest's children received their primary and secondary educations in consolidated schools located in cities and towns. Any treatment of this subject, however, should not over-emphasize the universality of this movement. One-room schools persisted, especially in the more westerly reaches of the Midwest. In the mid-1980s, a five-state study found 385 one-room schools in Nebraska and 87 in South Dakota. (The researchers also found one-room schools in several other midwestern states: North Dakota, Michigan, Ohio, and Kansas. They exam-ined only public one-room schools and did not consider private endeavors such as Amish schools.) The schools generally enrolled fewer than a dozen children, with approximately five families providing the entire enrollment. Unlike in earlier years, their teachers had more than ten years' experience and most had a bachelor's degree. Better-trained teachers, televisions, and computers aside, these schools offered children instruction much like that of their pre–World War II forebears. Individualized lessons and cooperative learning in a multi-grade environment featured heavily in their educational experiences.[8] These children remained in a minority, however, with the rural majority receiving their educations in consolidated schools of varying sizes.

There is still substantial disagreement about the advisability of school con-solidations. For every researcher or administrator who applauded the results of moving children into larger schools, there was another who upheld the im-portance of small schools in fostering children's educational and social de-velopment. Those who favored small rural schools usually stressed their co-operative aspects in general and individualized educational opportunities in particular. What seemed to be universal, however, was the acknowledgment that losing a school meant the potential (or likely) death of the affected small town. Because of issues of convenience, young adults planning on raising fam-ilies would be unlikely to settle in small towns without schools, and towns without an infusion of young adults would wither and die as their populations aged. Schools also often provided a significant portion of the economic base, employing teachers, janitors, and other support staff. When schools closed, jobs disappeared and property values plummeted. The inevitable result was more children living in progressively larger places.[9]

Just as rural children's educations changed, their working lives did as well. This provided another important point of convergence between the rural and the urban. Prior to World War II, laxity in enforcement of compulsory schooling laws as well as low levels of enrollment in high schools meant that rural youth spent long hours working on behalf of their parents' agricultur-al enterprises. Children often completed extensive chores before and after school or instead of going to school. Many rural districts also shortened their school years in order to synchronize with the rhythms of the agricultural work cycle. School began late in the fall, in order to accommodate harvest, and ended early in the spring so students (largely older boys) could help with plowing and planting. Over time, however, this changed. Increasing numbers of rural youth were from non-agricultural families, meaning that their parents generally did not require long hours of farm labor. They, in comparison with their farm peers, made increasingly "individualistic and discretionary" decisions about whether to work or not.[10] Also, with advancing mechanization, farm youth completed less total hours of work than in the past. They generally attended consolidated schools and had as long an academic year as their peers in town. Families with sufficient resources allowed their children the opportunity to participate in the same activities as their nonfarm peers. As historian David Danbom noted, the decline of child labor on the farm meant the decline of farms as institutions of vocational education. "The farm today is mainly a place where people grow up. When they have reached adulthood, they are more likely to leave and become accountants or computer programmers or retail clerks than they are to follow in their parents' footsteps."[11]

The working farm child, however, did not disappear completely. Even in the late twentieth century, farm children worked for their parents after school as well as on the weekend. Unlike in urban areas, child labor laws did not protect them from work on their parents' farms. Summer work in particular remained an important part of children's lives. Many youngsters spent long hours in the summer "walking beans," the colloquial term for clearing the weeds out of soybean fields either by hand or with a long, sharp hook. Some of these youngsters walking beans were from town, hired for the task, while others were farm kids, whose parents often expected them to work without pay. It was a hot, wet chore, done at the height of the summer. Dannie Weir Larsen, who grew up on a farm in southern Iowa, described the task: "we literally walked through the rows of soybeans, bending low to pull the weeds from the earth with our gloved hands. After a couple of hours of this our backs felt like they were ready to snap in half, our shoulders ached and our arms seemed to weigh fifty pounds each."[12] Walking beans was a tedious task.

Painful or not, these and other chores had to be done. Researchers examining children's work on farms in the 1980s found that families continued to value their children's labor, and children continued to feel a responsibility to their parents. They commented, "Farm children are brought up to view what they do in terms of their families. They are counted on, and this nurtures a sense of significance. The family suffers if a child does not come through on an assignment or task."[13] Late twentieth-century children still plowed, planted, harvested, and cared for animals. They worked in gardens and in the house. Youngsters often gained a sense of pride and mastery from their work. They grew up with a sense of being needed.[14]

Walking beans was not the only farm task consuming children's summer hours. Thousands of boys and girls spent three weeks of their summer working as corn detasselers. Detasseling is essential to the production of hybrid corn, and because corn is not uniformly tall, mechanical detasseling produces imperfect results. Seed corn companies hired armies of teenagers to complete the job. Because of the short-term nature of the work, boys and girls could take detasseling jobs as early as age 12, 13, or 14, depending on the state. The 20-day detasseling season employed (and still employs) roughly 100,000 rural and urban midwestern youngsters each season. Even at minimum wages, in 2000, the most diligent and experienced workers could earn up to $4,000 for their efforts. The money helped many a young person pay for clothes, cars, and a college education.[15]

The work, like walking beans, was tedious and painful. Although adults thought of detasseling as character building, many workers remembered it as just plain miserable. Jonathon Bergman, who grew up in Nebraska and worked summers as a detasseler, described his experience:

> You get up before the sun comes up, meet at the high school and get on the yellow school bus that takes you to the field. You know that your first 10 steps into the corn are going to be anything but pleasant because it's full of dew. You're wet head-to-toe no matter what you're wearing. The corn is tall, you're walking through mud and engaged in repetitive physical exertion for the next 10 hours. In the morning, it's wet and chilly. By 10 a.m., steam is rising from the field. By noon it's darn hot, and by three, it's extremely hot and you're exhausted.[16]

Bergman and his compatriots held on to the end, working for the paycheck that would make it all worthwhile. These sources of summer income were precarious, however. Herbicide-resistant soybeans eliminated the need for walking beans, and detasseling may soon succumb to scientific change as well. Scientists at seed companies are working to produce male-sterile corn, which does not produce viable pollen and does not require detasseling.

Just as agricultural science affected young people's work opportunities, so did technology. One of the primary changes on midwestern farms since World War II has been the proliferation of machines, particularly tractors. Mechanization made the work of farming easier for youngsters but also more dangerous. No longer was most farmwork done with a hoe or behind a team of horses. Tractors in particular reduced the muscle power necessary for much agricultural work, making it possible for workers to start younger and for adults to work later in life. This, of course, posed safety hazards for individuals both young and old. Despite safety campaigns beginning during World War II and extending through the rest of the century, tractor accidents continued to account for the highest number of farm fatalities, with the greatest numbers of deaths concentrated in the groups aged 15 and under and over age 65.[17]

Parents were not unaware of the dangers associated with their children's use of farm machinery but weighed those risks against other concerns. Researchers studying the decision-making processes of farm parents discovered that economic considerations often clouded their judgment. "When the risks imposed by farm hazards are weighed against the farm's economic well-being or a child's potential future in agriculture, the hazards may be overlooked."[18] Organizations such as Farm Safety 4 Just Kids and the American Academy of Pediatrics attempted to get too-young children out from behind the wheel, but parents' perceived needs as well as children's eagerness to help meant that accidents continued to kill and injure children every year.

Technological developments were altering children's lives in other ways as well. They changed their working lives, but they also changed the way in which youngsters played. In the years before World War II, farm children spent their limited leisure time in significantly different ways than urban chil-

Figure 7.2: Detasseling corn was a common job for rural and urban young people in the Midwest. Detasseling is dirty, demanding work, often performed in adverse conditions. These youths were photographed in the mid-1990s in Eastern Nebraska. Source: Lisa McNeel, Schernikau Detasseling. Used with permission.

dren. Although they had increasing access to the radio and its children's programming, they had much more limited access to other forms of popular culture. Distance often limited children's exposure to the movies; tight budgets limited their access to comics and children's literature. New technology and better incomes in the postwar period served to bridge the entertainment gap.

When automobiles became widely and relatively inexpensively available in the immediate post–World War I era, farm families purchased them in large numbers, valuing the mobility that came with the car.[19] In the decades between the 1920s and 1950s, roads improved significantly, making automobiles even more useful to rural families. Getting to town in the muddy weather of winter and spring became less of an ordeal. Declining population in the countryside also made the access to town that cars allowed more of a social necessity. Community activities in the countryside were succumbing to town-oriented sociability, often organized around consolidated schools. As early as 1940, researchers found rural families in Iowa allowing themselves at least one trip to the movies a week, as well as trips to town for other social and economic activities. The researchers commented, "The automobile has also been responsible for releasing the farmer from the necessity of social intercourse with any of his immediate neighbors…the total amount of visiting of all sorts has declined in favor of motion pictures, shopping, or simply driving."[20] Better vehicles and better roads connected youngsters ever more tightly to the world of town, be it for school activities such as dramatics and sports or for other forms of group activity, such as parties, dances, bowling, movies, and church.[21] Access to town dramatically increased rural youths' participation in other programs as well, such as scouting. Before school consolidation and better roads, boys' and girls' ability to join the Boy and Girl Scouts was severely limited. Problems such as troop size and the availability of adult leaders limited access, and neither organization saw rural children as their primary focus. Instead, they sought to bring appreciation of nature and a structured program of self-improvement to urban youngsters who, reformers believed, needed this kind of direction more than farm youth.[22] The increasing orientation of farm children toward town meant that they, too, could take part in scouting.

Transportation was not the only technological innovation changing the lives of rural youth. Television would have an equally dramatic effect on the contours of rural children's lives. By the 1950s, television was remaking child life all across the United States, changing patterns of leisure from active to inactive. Television programming targeted children from the very young to teens. Youngsters could watch *Romper Room* and *Captain Kangaroo*, as well as *Howdy Doody*, *The Mickey Mouse Club*, and *Leave it to Beaver*. As historian Steven Mintz has commented, "Television broadcasting produced a shared children's culture unprecedented in history, one that stretched across all social classes and regions."[23] For the vast majority, location ceased to dictate access to the most common form of popular culture, and programming with nationwide appeal undercut regional differences in children's culture.

Television's spread across the rural Midwest was relentless but somewhat uneven. As early as 1954, 59.4 percent of Indiana farm homes had television, as did 54.9 percent in Iowa. In North Dakota and South Dakota, however, the numbers were 18.1 percent and 17.0 percent respectively. By 1960, though, the numbers of televisions in farm homes, like the number of televisions nationwide, had grown significantly. While just over 80 percent of farm homes in Missouri had television (the lowest number in the region), more than 90 percent in Iowa did.[24] Problems of poor reception aside, farm children had access to roughly the same world of televised kid-culture as their peers in towns, cities, and suburbs. Children across the country would share a set of cultural references as never before. Those in the countryside would be just as familiar as city children with characters such as Oscar the Grouch, the Teenage Mutant Ninja Turtles, and Bob the Builder. Over the second half of the twentieth century, other communication technologies would become available in the country as well, with rural children gaining access to computers and the Internet, although at a somewhat slower rate than in urban areas.[25]

Some activities for youth retained a more distinctively rural flavor. Although there is considerable debate about where and when 4-H clubs had their origins (several midwestern states claim credit), by 1914 the organization was a part of the Cooperative Extension Service and midwestern children's lives. The organization sought to promote progressive farming and farm homemaking by educating the nation's youth. In the early post–World War II period, 4-H clubs maintained their focus on traditional topics such as crop and animal projects for boys and animal and household projects for girls. 4-H club work gave youngsters opportunities for social interaction, pursuit of interesting projects, and recognition for work well done. 4-H even began broadcasting by television to its young audience, attempting to build greater membership. Although in the mid-1960s 4-H clubs shifted their focus to increase their appeal to urban youth, the bulk of the clubs' work remained in rural communities, with rural youth. Animal projects involving horses, cows, pigs, and other livestock continued to be particularly popular and almost demanded a rural location.[26] Even in 2000, individual youngsters' projects made up a large proportion of the exhibits at the heartland's state fairs.

The Future Farmers of America (FFA) also flourished in rural areas of the Midwest. Founded in the 1920s, the organization sought to promote progressive farming by expanding on the school activities of young men age 14 to 21 studying vocational agriculture. Although conceived as an organization for young white men, FFA eventually expanded to include minorities (1965) and young women (1969).[27] FFA members participated in livestock judging contests, attended agricultural education events, and pursued projects of interest to individual members. The list of organizational objectives grew over time, with the FFA encouraging young people to develop their leadership skills, love of nature, patriotism, scholarship, and thrift, in addition to their commitment to some variety of agricultural pursuit. Although the organization had its first urban-based African American president in 1994 and expanded its reach to youngsters interested in pursuing "more than 300 careers in the science, business, and technology of agriculture," the organization retained its largely rural character. In Iowa, for example, FFA members showed animals at the state fair, as well as restored tractors and other farm equipment, among other activities.[28] Involvement in FFA and 4-H remained dear to the hearts of rural teens, and a significant number chose to attend college at land-grant universities such as Kansas State in order to foster the ties and continue the interests developed in these organizations.[29]

Figure 7.3: Vocational Agriculture programs and 4-H were designed to train rural youth to be productive, efficient, and enlightened farmers. Many young people, however, like this teenager from Audubon County, Iowa, photographed around 1950, grew up and left the farm. Source: J.L. Anderson. Used with permission.

In the years since World War II, the education, work, and play of rural children have changed dramatically (although not always consistently), with rural children's lives becoming far more like those of their urban and suburban counterparts. Although these children might have had elements of their lives that marked them as firmly rural, like membership in organizations such as FFA, most parts of their lives converged with those of the urban majority. They spent most of their time in school. Farm children worked for their parents, but to a far more limited degree than the children of the pre–World War II period. Rural children gained increasing access to a national youth culture of television, sports, movies, and scouting. It was becoming more difficult to argue that rural youngsters had a culture separate from that in the region's urban and suburban centers.

The Midwest's rural children were also unremarkable economically, having more in common with their urban and suburban counterparts than with rural children in other parts of the nation. At the century's end, rural children nationwide were overrepresented among the nation's poor. Over 2.5 million children in rural communities were poor, making up more than one-third of the total population of the rural poor. Minority children were also overrepresented; 46 percent of African American and 43 percent of Native American children in rural communities were poor. Midwestern rural children, however, were less likely to suffer from persistent poverty than their counterparts in other locations, as measured by the USDA's Economic Research Service. In fact, the rate of poverty among families and children in rural areas of the United States declined markedly in the 1990s, much more quickly than in urban areas. Areas of persistent poverty, however, remained an entrenched problem.[30] In the last 30 years of the twentieth century, the majority of persistently poor counties were in the southern United States—280 of 386. There were no persistent poverty counties in Indiana, Iowa, Kansas, Michigan, Minnesota, Ohio, or Wisconsin. There were three in southern Illinois and one in Nebraska. North Dakota had five, and both Missouri and South Dakota had thirteen.[31]

Perhaps unsurprisingly, the persistent poverty counties in the Dakotas clustered around reservations.[32] Shannon County, South Dakota, for example, is a part of the Pine Ridge Reservation. In 2000, 18 percent of the labor force was unemployed, the median age of the population was only 20.8 years, and a full 61 percent of children were members of families living below the poverty line.[33] As rural sociologists have pointed out, children growing up in these circumstances were highly likely to continue to live in poverty as adults, given depressed local economic conditions, substandard schools and social services, and a lack of employed adult role models.[34] There was no clear path out of these disadvantaged communities.

In three midwestern states—South Dakota, North Dakota, and Missouri—child poverty was significantly higher in rural communities than in urban ones. In most parts of the rural Midwest, however, the situation was not so dire. In Wisconsin, Indiana, Ohio, and Michigan, rural child poverty was lower than urban, and in Iowa, Minnesota, and Illinois, there was a less than 1 percent difference in the levels of poverty between rural and urban children.[35] At the century's end, as compared to those in other parts of the country, the Midwest's rural children were more likely to live in two-parent households and were less likely to be Latino, Native American, or African American, all factors affecting child poverty rates.[36] In 2000, the economic outlook for the Midwest's rural children was relatively positive, and fairly unremarkable.

In one very unfortunate way, however, the rural Midwest of the late twentieth century became quite remarkable. On the eve of the twenty-first century, disturbing developments threatened the region's children. In the last years of the twentieth century, levels of methamphetamine use and manufacture skyrocketed across the Midwest. While in 1997, Illinois police seized only 24 methamphetamine labs, by the early years of the twenty-first century, the numbers had soared into the hundreds.[37] Rural midwestern communities were particularly hard hit by this drug crisis because of a cluster of factors peculiar to their location. Rural depopulation and a limited police presence made it easy to hide meth laboratories, and easy access to anhydrous ammonia, a key component of the drug, facilitated production.[38] Additionally, falling wages in industries such as meatpacking encouraged some individuals to pursue more lucrative, if illegal and dangerous, economic activities.[39] By the beginning of the twenty-first century, approximately 25 percent of all child neglect/abuse calls taken by rural social welfare field offices involved methamphetamine manufacture and use by parents.[40] The meth epidemic dramatically increased the number of rural midwestern children in foster care, because of either parental arrest or parental addiction.

Children raised in meth-affected families faced and continue to face a bleak future. Because their parents often converted their homes into "mom and pop" meth labs, they lived in toxic environments, prone to fire and explosions. These homes were often filthy and remote, and their parents often neglected to provide them with even the bare minimum of food, water, and shelter. Their parents were so addicted to meth that they often forgot, or little cared, that they had children to support. Young children acted as surrogate parents to their younger siblings and even assumed the role of caregiver for their incapacitated and violent parents.[41] Many experienced significant problems overcoming the poor socialization they received in their parents' homes.[42] No one knew then, or even knows today, what the long-term problems associated with early methamphetamine exposure will be.

Affected communities struggled with an enormous burden of endangered children, facing problems that seemed to belong more to inner cities than the countryside. In rural Illinois, one bright spot, however, were the local schools. Teachers and administrators took it upon themselves to offer informal support to children dealing with parental meth addiction. Educators helped local officials to spot abuse and neglect. Teachers enlisted youngsters to "help" them after school, in order to keep them in a safe environment as long as possible, in a given schoolday. One school stockpiled food, clothing, and toiletries for children whose parents were meth addicts.[43] Even so, it remains unlikely that schools, social service agencies, and foster parents will be able to undo the damage done to so many of the rural Midwest's most vulnerable residents.

At century's end, the midwestern rural communities most clearly upholding an old-fashioned Rockwellian version of childhood were those of the Amish. These traditional religious communities continued to value the one-room school and in most states maintained a separate school system. The purpose of these separate schools was to ensure that children learned the values of the community in the classroom. The vast majority of children left school at the conclusion of eighth grade, in order to begin their working lives, a cultural practice upheld by the United States Supreme Court in the 1972 case *Wisconsin v. Yoder*.[44] Children continued to labor beside their parents and to serve a vital function in the continuation of family farms. As a scholar of Amish childhood and youth recently commented, "all Amish parents want their children to be diligent workers. This virtue is a cultural distinctive as much as plain clothes and horse-drawn transportation." Boys and girls continued to combine work with leisure, taking part in work bees, barn raisings, and quilting bees. While many of their peers spent hours in front of televisions and computers, Amish children went outside to play. Although the rules governing leisure activities varied from community to community, youngsters filled their somewhat meager playtime with ball games, hunting, fishing, bird-watching, bicycling, skating, swimming, and other outdoor pursuits.[45] This is a rural childhood that would have been recognizable, even in 1900.

In the late twentieth century, however, more modern concerns began to impinge upon Amish youth. Being born Amish does not guarantee an Amish adulthood. Young people must freely choose to join the church and signify this choice through baptism. Parents expect that between their sixteenth birthday and their baptism, youths will engage in behavior not officially sanctioned by the group as they test the limits of their Amish identity. This period is called *Rumspringa*, or "running around." Youngsters may cut their hair, drive automobiles, listen to rock music, and even drink. They have the opportunity to decide whether or not they want to be Amish, and somewhere between 20 and 25 percent of Amish youngsters will decide to leave the group prior to baptism. Generations of Amish parents expected the same behavior of their young adults. In the latter years of the twentieth century, however, the temptations available in rural communities became significantly more dangerous. Meth made its appearance in Amish country, as well as the rest of the rural Midwest, bringing experimentation and unwelcome national attention to Rumspringa in the form of documentary films and discussions on television programs such as *Oprah*. In some communities, this led to a previously unheard-of level of adult supervision of older teens.[46] No community, no matter how traditional, seemed to be immune to the scourge.

Methamphetamine-affected children, however, were not the face that rural midwestern communities wanted to present to the nation. Exposure to drug abuse did not fit into a traditional understanding of what rural childhood should be. It also challenged rural communities' ability to grow and prosper by damaging their image—one of their most important and salable assets in the late twentieth century. A number of small communities decided to use the image of a sheltered, old-fashioned rural childhood as a selling point in the battle to maintain population. In spite of changes threatening the vision of an idealized rural midwestern childhood, that vision remained for many a true representation of what childhood *should* be. Childhood should be leisurely. It should be experienced in close proximity to grass, trees, open fields, and blue skies. Children should have the opportunity to play outdoors, unafraid of being accosted by malicious strangers. They should be able to ride their bicycles in the streets and walk home from school at the end of the day. Whether or not rural children did these things more often than urban children is unclear; the possibility that they might, however, seemed promising.

From the perspective of children's needs, late twentieth-century rural communities had other appealing features as well. Midwestern rural communities with their high levels of stability, homogeneity, and two-parent families helped to produce relatively law-abiding, well-adjusted children. Small populations and close community connections reduced the opportunity for juvenile delinquency.[47] Rural communities remained places where close connections between the generations prevailed. Researchers found this in 1950 and again half a century later. These relationships manifested themselves in strong working partnerships with parents in 1950 and close emotional bonds between children and their grandparents 50 years later.[48] In spite of change, rural places continued to represent what many parents wanted for their children.

Hoping to cash in on these sentiments, at the close of the twentieth century a number of midwestern communities initiated what were called "free land" programs, offering free lots in residential neighborhoods to individuals willing to build moderate- to high-value homes. In Minneapolis, Kansas, not far from the much larger town of Salina, a number of families moved in and took advantage of the offer, while others lured in by the promise of free land bought inexpensive but substantial older homes for renovation. Local leaders observed that this influx of population was largely young adults looking for a good place to raise their children: "a safe place for kids to walk, ride, and play."[49] While the programs in Kansas communities were perhaps the best-known, communities in North Dakota, Nebraska, and other states largely in the western reaches of the heartland began similar initiatives. Rural communities have had small to moderate luck in luring families to them, for "the children's sake."

The free land movement as well as other back-to-the-land impulses did not stop the movement of individuals and families from rural areas into cities, towns, and suburbs. Many of those who made the move were young. In the closing years of the twentieth century, very few rural youths expected that they would remain in rural communities as adults. Most planned to move on to larger communities, and many planned to make that transition by way of an education achieved at one of the region's colleges or universities. Increasingly, all roads led out of the rural Midwest. But was that the case at mid-century, at the close of World War II? When rural sociologists studied the problem of out-migration in 1949, the answer was more equivocal. In a survey of 2,622 rural boys and girls in Minnesota, the sociologists found that more than 40 percent of farm boys hoped to remain on the farm as adults. Nearly 8 percent of nonfarm boys wanted to go into agriculture as well.[50] Whether girls wished to remain in agriculture was less obvious, since none listed "farmer" as a career choice. Large numbers of farm girls listed vocational choices that indicated a possible departure from agriculture, including secretary, nurse, teacher, or beauty operator. More than 20 percent, however, wanted to be housewives, a career choice that might very well lead back to the farm.[51] As had been the case since the pre–World War II period, more girls were leaving the countryside than boys, creating "a definite shortage" of marriage partners.[52]

The economic traumas of the second half of the twentieth century, combined with other major national and international events, conspired to encourage rural youth to leave the countryside. This out-migration was not new in the postwar period; it simply accelerated. Parents who came of age during the Great Depression and dust bowl years remembered their struggles and encouraged their own children to go to college, giving them additional options should hard times come again. Pursuing an education, not surprisingly, led many youngsters out of the countryside for good.[53] The farm crisis of the 1980s produced similar results. Parents took stock of the economic stress that they and their neighbors were experiencing and encouraged their children to think twice if they thought at all about a life on the farm. In one 1989 study, 26 percent of parents said they "would not recommend farming to a young man under any circumstances." Their sons, in turn, made plans to pursue other options. Many wanted to farm, but only if conditions were ideal. No one could argue that such conditions existed in the late 1980s.[54] Youngsters headed to college and then on to midwestern urban centers such as Chicago and Minneapolis, bypassing the opportunity to return to their parents' farms or neighboring rural communities.

Changes in the structure of other types of rural employment such as meatpacking have also encouraged working-class rural youngsters to look elsewhere. While meatpacking jobs in the 1940s, 1950s, and 1960s provided high wages and good benefits, those wages and benefits declined significantly in the 1970s and 1980s, making meatpacking low-wage, undesirable work. The demography of meatpacking communities changed significantly, with large numbers of new immigrants (both legal and not) moving in.[55] For example, in Storm Lake, Iowa, the packing plant attracted large numbers of both Laotian and Mexican immigrants. In Worthington, Minnesota, ConAgra recruited both Asian and Latino workers for its meatpacking plant. Increasingly, the new rural youth in the Midwest's small communities came from outside the region, and outside the United States.[56] Economic change, combined with the meth epidemic, increased the likelihood that midwestern rural childhood in the twenty-first century would be less privileged than it was in the twentieth.

The story, however, was not one of economics only. In addition to the lack of opportunities in rural areas, there were also problems of perception. Rural communities had become places where, from the point of view of many young people, there was nothing to do and nowhere to go. A child's enjoyment of outdoor play, the benefits of a small school, and the joys of a plethora of pets did not necessarily translate into a teenager's or young adult's desire to remain in their community of origin. Once the years of early childhood were over, youngsters began looking for social opportunities that went beyond Boy Scouts, Girl Scouts, 4-H, and the activities they offered. They wanted access to a world that looked brighter and more active than Main Street, just as their grandparents had in the 1910s and 1920s.[57] In the period following the Second World War, however, more young people acted upon their dissatisfactions and chose to live their adult lives in more urban locations. Because of improvements in rural education and greater access to higher education, these possibilities were available to more rural youth than ever before.

By the end of the century, it had become unclear what a rural childhood had to offer, beyond a difference in venue. Size aside (and not even that, in some large consolidated schools), rural schools were not markedly different from their suburban counterparts. Rural and urban children worked similar hours, although farm children might have a few more responsibilities at home. Both groups generally pursued the same goals: a college education, followed by work and family in an urban or suburban context. Children's leisure activities—rural, urban, and suburban—became more and more oriented toward what could be viewed on a screen and less oriented toward the outside world. Although enough differences remained in certain communities, in certain places, to provide texture, childhood in the rural and urban contexts had largely converged to become a part of a single story, one that was far less affected by the vagaries of place.

So, what should we make of those iconic midwestern images of childhood that Americans so cherish? The setting is still there—blue skies, green fields, and rolling hills. Many of the barns and houses, however, are gone, casualties of the rural depopulation of the last half century. The characters in the landscape, also, are no longer so clearly visible. The rural children who once inhabited this landscape are, for the most part, absent. We have to look much harder than our parents and grandparents did to find the boys wading in the creek or the little girl playing with her kittens on the lawn. No one is sailing high above the floor of the barn on a rope swing; the barn is long gone, and the pastime, from the perspective of modern parents, is simply too dangerous. The children have moved to town or are taking the bus to a consolidated school. They are going to pack and troop meetings in town or are playing basketball in the high school gym. They are no longer playing in the brook but have gone inside to watch the television and to use the computer, out of sight, and out of this distinctively rural picture.

Notes

1. For an exceptional description of such a small-town setting, see Roger G. Barker and Herbert F. Wright, *One Boy's Day: A Specimen Record of Behavior* (Hamden, CT: Archon Books, 1966).

2. Tracy L. Steffes, "Solving the 'Rural School Problem': New State Aid, Standards, and Supervision of Local Schools, 1900–1933," *History of Education Quarterly* 48 (2) (May 2008): 188.

3. David R. Reynolds, *There Goes the Neighborhood: Rural School Consolidation at the Grass Roots in Early Twentieth-Century Iowa* (Iowa City: University of Iowa Press, 1999), 240–41.

4. J.F. Thaden, *Equalizing Educational Opportunity through Community School Districts* (East Lansing: Michigan State University Agricultural Experiment Station, 1957), 3–4.

5. Horace Miner, *Culture and Agriculture: An Anthropological Study of a Corn Belt County* (Ann Arbor: University of Michigan Press, 1949), 74.

6. Max McElwain, *The Only Dance in Iowa: A History of Six-Player Girls' Basketball* (Lincoln: University of Nebraska Press, 2004), 5.

7. Walter A. Lunden, "The Farm and the Non-Farm Youth: The Parental Relationships, Organizational Participation, Patterns of Work, Leisure Time Activities and Means of Earning Money for 903 Farm and Non-Farm Youth in Hamilton County, Iowa, in 1950" (unpublished report, Iowa State College, Ames, 1953), 58, 87.

8. Bruce Barker and Ivan Muse, "One-Room Schools of Nebraska, Montana, South Dakota, California, and Wyoming," *Research in Rural Education* 3 (3) (1986): 127–30.

9. See Leah Fran Tookey, "Maintaining *Gemeinschaft* during a Century of Change: Rural School Consolidation in Iowa, a Case Study" (Master's thesis, Iowa State University, Ames, 2003), 99–113.

10. Glen H. Elder Jr. and Rand D. Conger, *Children of the Land: Adversity and Success in Rural America* (Chicago: University of Chicago Press, 2000), 87.

11. David Danbom, *Born in the Country: A History of Rural America* (Baltimore: Johns Hopkins University Press, 1995), 251.

12. Dannie Weir Larsen, "How Our Dog Got His New Name," in *Walking Beans Wasn't Something You Did with Your Dog: Stories of Growing Up in and around Small Towns in the Midwest*, ed. Jean Tennant (Everly, IA: Shapato Press, 2008), 15.

13. Elder and Conger, *Children of the Land*, 87.

14. Elder and Conger, *Children of the Land*, 104, 242–43.

15. Ellen Byron, "Detasseling, a Midwest Rite of Passage, Faces Extinction," *Wall Street Journal*, August 9, 2002, <www.mindfully.org/Farm/Detasseling-Faces-Extinction-9aug02.htm> (accessed May 12, 2010).

16. Byron, "Detasseling."

17. U.S. Department of Labor, "Farm Safety," Fact Sheet No. OSHA 91–39, <ehs.okstate.edu/training/oshafarm.htm> (accessed October 8, 2009). For a discussion of the larger farm safety movement, see Derek Oden, "Selling Safety: The Farm Safety Movement's Emergence and Evolution from 1940–1975," *Agricultural History* 79 (4) (Autumn 2005): 412–38.

18. William Pickett, Barbara Marlenga, and Richard L. Berg, "Parental Knowledge of Child Development and the Assignment of Tractor Work to Children," *Pediatrics* 112 (1) (July 2003): 15.

19. Katherine Jellison, *Entitled to Power: Farm Women and Technology, 1913–1963* (Chapel Hill: University of North Carolina Press, 1993), 54.

20. Miner, *Culture and Agriculture*, 37, 50.

21. Danbom, *Born in the Country*, 248–50.

22. For a discussion of the urban origins and orientation of scouting, see David I. Macleod, *Building Character in the American Boy: The Boy Scouts, YMCA, and Their Forerunners, 1870–1920* (Madison: University of Wisconsin Press, 1983).

23. Steven Mintz, *Huck's Raft: A History of American Childhood* (Cambridge, MA: Belknap Press of Harvard University Press, 2004), 298.

24. Jellison, *Entitled to Power* 161, 169.

25. The USDA found that by 2001, 55 percent of American farms had computers, and 43 percent had Internet access, showing significant growth in service from 1999. On larger farms, 73 percent had computers and 58 percent had Internet access. USDA, National Agricultural Statistics Service, "New Report Shows Increase in Farm Computer and Internet Access," <www.nass.usda.gov/Newsroom/archive/comp_use_announcement. htm> (accessed October 15, 2009).

26. For a comprehensive history of 4-H, see Thomas Wessel and Marilyn Wessel, *4-H: An American Idea, 1900–1980: A History of 4-H* (Chevy Chase, MD: National 4-H Council, 1982).

27. Girls also had the option of joining the Future Homemakers of America, founded in 1944. Within a year, it had 92,000 members. Unlike Future Farmers of America, the organization appealed as much to urban as to rural youth. The goal of the organization was to promote vocational home economics in the schools. See Megan J. Elias, *Stir It Up: Home Economics in American Culture* (Philadelphia: University of Pennsylvania Press, 2008), 119–23.

28. Future Farmers of America, *Official Manual for Future Farmers of America, the National Organization of Boys Studying Vocational Agriculture* (Baltimore: French-Bray Printing, 1947), 4–6; Ralph E. Bender, Robert E. Taylor, Chester K. Hansen, and L.H. Newcomb, *The FFA and You: Your Guide to Learning* (Danville, IL: Interstate Printers, 1979), 1–9; National FFA Organization, "Key Historical Moments," <www.ffa.org/documents/ about_keymoments.pdf> (accessed October 16, 2009).

29. David Danskin, James M. Foster, and Carroll E. Kennedy Jr., *The Attitudes and Ambitions of Students at a Land Grant College of Agriculture and Their Implications for Curriculum Planning and for Teaching*, Bulletin 479 (Manhattan: Kansas Agricultural Experiment Station, 1965), 20–21.

30. Daniel T. Lichter and Kenneth M. Johnson, "The Changing Spatial Concentration of America's Rural Poor Population," *Rural Sociology* 72 (3) (2007): 331–58.

31. Economic Research Service (USDA ERS), "Rural Poverty at a Glance," Rural Development Research Report Number 100, July 2004, 3–4.

32. Economic Research Service (USDA ERS), "Rural Poverty at a Glance."

33. William P. O'Hare and Kenneth M. Johnson, "Child Poverty in America," *Reports on America* 4 (1) (March 2004): 13, <www.prb.org/pdf04/ChildPovertyRuralAmerica.pdf> (accessed July 24, 2009).

34. Lichter and Johnson, "The Changing Spatial Concentration of America's Rural Poor Population," 353. 35. O'Hare and Johnson, "Child Poverty in America," 10.

36. USDA ERS, "Rural Poverty at a Glance," 2–3.

37. Wendy Haight et al., *Children of Methamphetamine-Involved Families: The Case*

of Rural Illinois (Oxford, UK: Oxford University Press, 2009), 9.

38. Haight et al., 'In These Bleak Days," 27.

39. See Nick Reding, *Methland: The Death and Life of an American Small Town* (New York: Bloomsbury, 2009), 15–18.

40. Wendy Haight et al., "'In These Bleak Days': Parent Methamphetamine Abuse and Child Welfare in the Rural Midwest," *Children and Youth Services Review* 27 (2005): 956.

41. Haight et al., 'In These Bleak Days," 958–59.

42. Haight et al., 'In These Bleak Days," 967.

43. Haight et al., 'In These Bleak Days," 956.

44. For a discussion of *Wisconsin v. Yoder*, see Shawn Francis Peters, *The Yoder Case: Religious Freedom, Education, and Parental Rights* (Lawrence: University Press of Kansas, 2003).

45. Richard A. Stevick, *Growing Up Amish: The Teenage Years* (Baltimore: Johns Hopkins University Press, 2007), 61–67, 105–19.

46. Stevick, *Growing Up Amish*, 151–70. See also Denise M. Reiling, "The 'Simmie' Side of Life: Old Order Amish Youths' Affective Responses to Cultural Prescribed Deviance," *Youth & Society* 34 (2) (December 2002): 146–71.

47. D. Wayne Osgood and Jeff M. Chambers, "Community Correlates of Rural Youth Violence," *Juvenile Justice Bulletin* (May 2003): 1–8, <www.ncjrs.gov/pdffiles1/ojjdp/193591.pdf> (accessed October 23, 2009).

48. Lunden, "Farm and the Non-Farm Youth," 92; Valerie King, Merril Silverstein, Glen H. Elder Jr., Vern L. Bengston, and Rand D. Conger, "Relations with Grandparents: Rural Midwest versus Urban Southern California," *Journal of Family Issues* 24 (8) (November 2003): 1065–67.

49. Richard E. Wood, *Survival of Rural America: Small Victories and Bitter Harvests* (Lawrence: University Press of Kansas, 2008), 94–95.

50. William H. Dreier and Burton W. Kreitlow, "The Educational Plans of Minnesota Rural Youth," *Journal of Educational Sociology* 23 (1) (September 1949): 38.

51. Dreier and Kreitlow, "The Educational Plans of Minnesota Rural Youth," 37.

52. Miner, *Culture and Agriculture*, 59.

53. Danskin et al., *Attitudes and Ambitions of Students at a Land Grant College*, 5.

54. Kazi Aziz Ahmed, "The Impact of the Farm Economic Crisis on the Career Aspirations of Iowa Farm Youth" (unpublished PhD diss., Department of Sociology, Iowa State University, Ames, 1989), 146–47.

55. Deborah Fink, *Cutting into the Meatpacking Line: Workers and Change in the Rural Midwest* (Chapel Hill: University of North Carolina Press, 1998), 39–71.

56. Rochelle L. Dalla and Shirley L. Baugher, "Immigration and the Rural Midwest," in *The Hidden America: Social Problems in Rural America for the Twenty-First Century*, ed. Robert M. Moore III (Selinsgrove, PA: Susquehanna University Press, 2001), 220–21, 226.

57. See Mary Neth, *Preserving the Family Farm: Women, Community, and the Foundations of Agribusiness in the Midwest, 1900–1940* (Baltimore: Johns Hopkins University Press, 1995), 244–66.

EIGHT — "THE WHITEST OF OCCUPATIONS"?

African Americans in the Rural Midwest, 1940–2010

Debra A. Reid

Few African Americans called the rural Midwest home prior to World War II, and fewer still lived in the region after 1945, yet African Americans farmed in every midwestern state and lived in several persistent rural enclaves in Illinois, Kansas, Missouri, and Ohio. Certainly the number could not compare to the concentrated populations of African Americans in the rural South or in the industrial North. Less than 159,000 African Americans, or 1.2 percent of the entire black population in the nation, lived in the rural Midwest by 1940. At the same time, only 7,466 or 1.1 percent of all black farmers in the nation tilled midwestern soil. These numbers indicate the extreme minority situation of blacks in the region. Studies of rural midwestern black life tend to concentrate on antebellum community building or post–World War I community decline rather than post–World War II survival. The few studies that document experiences between 1940 and the present indicate that race relations between residents of rural black communities and the majority white world depended on attitudes of residents and evolved in tandem with generational transition. As one scholar noted, "while on the surface it would appear that [the black residents] were not barred from participating in the American Dream…it is certain that their very real accomplishments were due primarily to individual tenacity and to the continued presence of several black mutual support kinship networks, rather than to any inherent openness in the…class structure."

The choices that rural black midwesterners made after World War II can teach powerful lessons about race relations, rural and farm modernization, and the enduring lure of the land.[1]

Racism tempered social and economic relationships between African Americans and the white majority population in the rural Midwest even as both forged mutually dependent relationships to survive. Rural residents had to be aware of subtle individualized expressions of white supremacy and also had to negotiate places where racially restrictive ordinances prevented them from sharing space or status, property or markets. Different contexts resulted in different encounters; residents of open country settlements and biracial communities attended schools with their white neighbors, while residents of separatist communities sought control over their own social and cultural outlets, including schools. Rural Kansans contributed to the landmark U.S. Supreme Court case, *Brown v. Board of Education*, an indication of rural commitment to civil rights. The strategies black farmers adopted likewise indicated intolerance for the status quo despite the risks of change. Minority farmers specialized much as their white neighbors did, that is, they operated dairy farms in urban milk sheds and raised corn and hogs, beef cattle and soybeans. For these farmers, production agriculture represented the model for success. But sometimes lenders refused to extend credit, neighbors refused to sell land, and both de facto and de jure segregation constrained personal liberty. That said, one-half of all black farmers owned their farms by World War II. While ownership did not protect them from injustice, it provided some security. Some entered niche markets, such as growing vegetables, tending orchards, or raising goats for consumption by Black Muslims. Some minority youth joined their white peers in the out-migration from the country to college and off-farm jobs, but others participated in a back-to-the-country movement that accelerated as the growing middle class retired and veterans returned from war and looked for alternatives to city life. Investors bought land for hobby farms near historically black communities or purchased retreats near recreation areas that catered to a black clientele. This kind of rural development sometimes worried established residents, white and black alike, given their trepidation about newcomers. Sometimes the communities devolved into dens of iniquity through no fault of the residents. In general, however, African Americans engaged in quintessential American pursuits in the countryside: they sought happiness via their rural retreats, property and profit through their investment in production agriculture, isolation from troubles they associated with urban life, and full citizenship as the civil rights movement matured.

Race and Rural Life

During the 1950s *Wallaces' Farmer and Iowa Homestead* commented on "the kind of segregation" practiced in the North, which prevented blacks from living where they wanted to, working at their chosen trade, or getting service in the restaurant of their choice. Theorists in the 1960s argued that "the white man's sense of group position [was] just as strong [in northern towns and small cities] as it [was] in the South, although more subtly manifested." Mark Schultz differentiated between southern rural and northern urban white supremacy in *The Rural Face of White Supremacy*. White northerners protected their space and status with restrictive covenants, "sundown" laws, and discriminatory employment practices that virtually eliminated cross-race exchange. Southerners, by contrast, constructed rural white supremacy on a foundation of selective intimacy, expecting people they knew well to practice "ritualized deference" or else face the consequences of "highly personalized violence."[2]

Inadequate research exists to draw definitive conclusions about the applicability of Schultz's theory to the rural Midwest, but similar relations existed in the most culturally deep-southern counties of the Missouri Bootheel, along the Missouri River in the "Little Dixie" area of central Missouri, and in Alexander, Massac, and Pulaski Counties in southern Illinois along the Ohio River near its confluence with the Mississippi. Evidence from other parts of the Midwest indicated that racism tempered the opportunities open to residents, whether they descended from French-held slaves, free blacks, or fugitive slaves. Regardless of their origins, rural blacks encountered race prejudice. They often had to tread carefully or else suffer repercussions from white neighbors; but the more personal the relationships, the less heinous the encounters. Owen Whitfield, a leader of the Southern Tenant Farmers Union (STFU) and international vice president of the United Cannery, Agricultural, Packing and Allied Workers of America (UCAPAWA) in 1941, identified the heart of the problem when he spoke at the UCAPAWA Cotton States Convention in Harviel, Missouri: "When men and women lay aside race hatred and organize and make up their minds we're going to do something, then something is done." Race hatred, however, consumed many midwesterners, as it did southerners.[3]

Most African Americans who owned farmland in the rural Midwest descended from families that had settled during the antebellum years on farms clustered near each other in a dispersed pattern or open-country settlement. They generally owned farms of 40 to 100 acres that tended to be smaller and less capital-intensive than those operated by their white neighbors. Residents knew that their property helped preserve their economic independence, and they protected this investment, sometimes choosing that security over the risks associated with challenging racist whites who did not believe blacks were equals. Ironically, rural blacks who lived in relative isolation from kin regularly turned to white neighbors for labor exchange and interaction, and vice versa, even as both races maintained social and cultural distance.[4]

Many rural whites opposed post–Civil War migration of freed slaves into the Midwest, and their resistance effectively diverted many migrants from rural areas. Violence was infrequent in the widely dispersed settlements in the region, but this might have resulted from the interest among rural blacks to remain separate and from the common goals of farmers, regardless of race, who shared labor to clear land and harvest or to process crops and stock. Residents of biracial communities that existed before the war or that began immediately afterward united against common threats, as did blacks and whites in the Quaker area of Calvin Township in Cass County, Michigan. When newcomers from cities began to arrive after World War II, residents used the term "Calvinites" to distinguish residents of the traditional black community from newcomers, and the Calvinites united in their cool welcome of the seasonal residents and hobby farmers who invested in the community in the postwar era.[5]

Pernicious racism helped explain why the rural Midwest did not attract more African Americans despite its proximity to northwestern Mississippi and eastern Arkansas, the area most densely settled by black farm families in the South. The Illinois Central Railroad and U.S. Routes 61 and 51 funneled folk north from this area and into the rural Midwest, but migrants did not stop there. Instead, they made their way to northern cities. Demographer Calvin Beale of the U.S. Department of Agriculture (USDA) claimed that southerners migrating north "avoided like the plague the farm work they had been used to back home." Few had any capital to invest in farmland or even tools to help them negotiate a tenant contract. But racism also influenced them to avoid the rural Midwest. Rural black families found white farmers unwilling to sell them property, and those who secured land found their mobility constrained by sundown laws enacted in nearby communities. Small midwestern cities such as Rock Island, Illinois, and Davenport and Fort Madison, Iowa, became their social and cultural outlet as a result of these restrictions. Rural race prejudice and white supremacy explain why few blacks considered the rural Midwest a destination.[6]

Social separation and community custom characterized race relations until newcomers arrived or outside forces threatened the status quo. Then

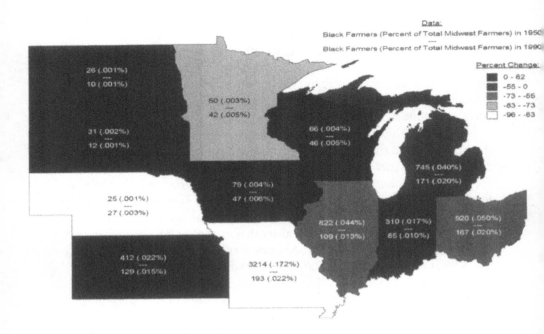

Figure 8.1: From 1950 to 1990 the number of African American farmers declined in every midwestern state except Kansas, although the number of African American farmers as a percentage of the total number of farmers in the region varied considerably from state to state. Map created by Logan Bruce, Department of History, Eastern Illinois University. Used with permission.

whites often reinforced their supposed racial superiority. For example, in 1942 farm families near Seymour, Indiana, lost their land when the U.S. government seized it to construct Freeman Field as a training ground for U.S. Army Air Force pilots. Only about 75 blacks called the 8,000-person city of Seymour home at the time, and they worked as farm laborers, porters, and janitors. Time-honored race relations in the community in transition endured until members of the 477th Bombardment Group made up of Tuskegee Airmen arrived for training in March 1945. Locals refused to socialize with them, grocers refused to trade with airmen's wives, and bar and restaurant owners and hotelkeepers refused to serve black troops. The tension between rural residents, those stationed at the airbase, and those living in the small city culminated in a mutiny when black officers entered the all-white officers club. Residents took the opportunity to try to impose the separate-but-equal doctrine, but officers refused to accept it. African

American resistance to inequality, combined with sustained military and civilian pursuit of equality, had a cumulative effect.[7]

Less sensationalized but more persistent challenges to segregation made race relations anything but static in the rural Midwest. Most midwestern states passed laws that prohibited school segregation in the aftermath of the Civil War. Then, as black populations in towns and cities increased, state and local officials selectively reinstituted race segregation. For example, in 1868, Kansas legislators authorized the formation of boards of education only in cities of the first class (over 15,000 inhabitants) and gave only those boards the authority to organize and maintain separate schools for white and black children. Urban expansion precipitated conflict when residents in rural townships who supported integrated education refused to comply with city policies. Citizens in small towns and rural townships across the Midwest, in fact, challenged both de jure and de facto school segregation. Cases launched against the Board of Education of Topeka, Kansas, during the 1890s, 1910s, and 1920s sought to protect the interests of African American children who had attended integrated country schools before Topeka annexed rural townships.[8]

School segregation continued after World War II despite sustained challenges. Residents in Topeka, Kansas, continued their resistance after the Kansas legislature amended rather than repealed the school segregation law. Many of the lawyers and litigants involved in *Brown v. Board of Education* (1954) had been born and raised in Topeka, but others, including local NAACP branch leaders and petitioners, shared rural backgrounds and had personal connections. Some had been educated in integrated schools, and they intended for their children to have the same experience. Even though African Americans had relocated to the city for jobs, their rural experiences with integrated education inspired them. They recognized the greater inequity they encountered in the city, and they made use of personal relationships forged in the country to effect change.[9]

The *Brown v. Board* decision did not change racial attitudes among the Midwest's majority white population. It was possible to be in favor of constitutional rights in the abstract and civil rights gradualism but still retain negative stereotypes about African Americans. The words and actions of President Dwight D. Eisenhower, who was raised in Abilene, Kansas, indicate the complexity of the situation. Eisenhower's oft-quoted apologia expressed to Earl Warren, Chief Justice of the U.S. Supreme Court, conveyed the interests of southern whites who did not want to see "their sweet little girls…required to sit in schools alongside some big overgrown Negroes" but showed no concern for African American children.[10] In the years following the *Brown* decision, white midwesterners did not consistently support black equality. Surveys indicated that more than one-third of rural white Iowans hoped that blacks would not purchase a farm in their area. Some rural whites believed that "If the Negroes start moving in, the value of your property decreases. The whites do everything possible to keep them out." Other respondents, however, noted that if they "got acquainted with [a Negro] we got along fine." Twenty percent of rural Iowans surveyed, mostly older and uneducated, believed that blacks were less intelligent than whites. Yet, 65 percent believed that blacks should secure civil rights gradually. These responses indicate the persistence of race prejudice by many midwestern whites.[11]

In the aftermath of *Brown*, Wisconsin's Commission on Human Rights investigated the ways in which its residents responded to the decision. The Commission found that no other northern state had documented its rural black populations or inquired about their well-being. Commission members worked with local officials, county agricultural extension agents, and black families to identify African American residents and sampled 150 black families to record their economic and social relationships with white residents in the rural communities. Social scientists also interviewed 365 white community residents to document their attitudes and interactions with the black families.[12]

The 1959 Wisconsin report emphasized the intelligence, dignity, maturity, skill, dependability, and community engagement of rural black Wisconsinites and claimed that no negative racial attitude existed. The authors of the study implied that common enemies—infertile land, demanding physical labor, and inadequate finances—helped forge an alliance across race. As an elderly white resident near the black community of Pleasant Ridge noted, "we got to know each other—the colored people and the white people. They helped us, we help them. Life wasn't so easy those days clearing the land, homesteading. We had no time for hatred." Some blacks noted that race relations in Wisconsin were better than in Chicago or the South. Newcomers, however, indicated that they had to tread carefully. Resort owners did not borrow money locally because "no one knew us." A printer indicated that "sometimes people make statements they don't really mean deep down and you can take offense if you want.... You know, when you're a stranger in a small community people look at you regardless of who you are." The Commission acknowledged that "the Ku Klux Klan may have been partly responsible for the fact that some Wisconsin communities had no early Negro populations." Black residents recalled barbers who would not cut their hair, antagonistic neighbors who circulated petitions to have them removed, landowners who would not sell property to them, and employers who refused to extend equal opportunity to them.[13]

Years of residency in an area may have shielded African Americans from ritualized and frequent violence, but they experienced other aspects of rural white supremacy just the same. John M. Smith's family had lived in Champaign County, Illinois, since 1876, along with the Wards, another black family. The families farmed fertile soil in an area with some of the highest land values in the nation. Smith capitalized his operation, investing $12,000 in equipment to mechanize production. Yet, the prosperous farm family faced racism. The family had always taken pride in its prize horses, and in the years preceding World War I, horse breeding had been a big business in central Illinois. By 1954, at 69 years of age, Smith reminisced about the barriers he had faced when he began to show horses in 1912. White horse owners did not want him to participate, judges refused to award his mounts the prizes that they deserved, and he could not participate in the annual stock show at the University of Illinois or at the county fair during the 1940s because of his race. Eventually Smith earned a place because of his fine horses and his skill as a horseman, but it took hard work and dedication on the part of the entire family as well as some fair-minded acquaintances to intercede with judges and fair boards. "Pretty soon I was completely accepted as just another exhibitor," Smith recalled. Grandson John, however, remembered that once he asked his grandfather why he didn't ride in the University's stock show, and he was told to "be quiet." The elder John Smith gained a reputation for hosting his own horse shows, which drew 1,500 spectators but few black exhibitors. Only his grandson rode in 1954, but at six years of age he won first place in the youth riding class. The next year the grandson assumed more duties on the farm. His mother taught him to drive the grain truck in and out of the field, and when he mastered that, she taught him how to drive the tractor. Young John and his sister, Brenda, both participated in county-yield contests and livestock shows as they came of age in the years after *Brown v. Board of Education* and the Civil Rights Act, but Brenda did not date during high school in the 1960s because "you didn't do that then."[14]

Rural racism needed to be studied, argued the USDA's Calvin Beale, because "three-fourths of the total Negro population" still lived in rural areas during the 1960s. He also believed that "many of the problems that beset the Negro everywhere occur in their most severe, undiluted and least hopeful settings in the countryside," including the "subtle" sort that the Smith family encountered and the more overt that created sundown towns. Beale's plea coincided with a growing concern among scholars and activists to document causes of inequality and poverty and look for models of integration in the context of the Civil Rights era. The 1960 census indicated that rural African Americans in the Midwest had an economic advantage over rural black southerners, but even the affluent faced discrimination and threats to their personal security, and this affected their daily decisions as well as their life choices.[15]

The experiences of Lloyd Johnson, a retired farmer from Alton, Illinois, perhaps best summarize the complexity of rural race relations in the racially homogenous postwar Corn Belt. Johnson downplayed his race when discussing his inclusion in an oral history project conducted by the Illinois State Museum in 2009. "There ain't a lot of black farmers.... I suppose I'd be considered—although I don't see it that way—as a different perspective on farming." Johnson credited his own stubborn determination and good neighbors for his success in an uncertain business, but he also acknowledged that he had to "be a fixture in the area" and maintain a good reputation. Evidently, not all community members supported him as he recounted the story of a banker who, during the 1980s, reversed his decision to extend an agricultural loan to Johnson "as soon as he saw me." To survive, farmers who intended to succeed at agriculture as national policy urged them to "get bigger, get better, or get out" had to overcome *de facto* segregation and selective racism but also economic disadvantages and cultural isolation that resulted from rural white supremacy.[16]

Minority Farmers and the Production Revolution

In 1940, blacks operated 680,000 farms (11.2%) of the 6.1 million farms in the United States. Most farmed in the South (98.6%), with the remainder operating in the Midwest (1.1%), Northeast (0.2%), and West (0.1%). Between 1940 and 1997, the number of black farmers in the nation dropped to 18,451, a decline of 97.3 percent. Black farmers in the Midwest left the business at a less precipitous rate than southern blacks (89% compared to 97.5%), but they left farming at a higher rate than midwestern whites during the same time period (89% compared to 64.4%), even as the Midwest remained a dominant agricultural region. More than one-third of all farmers in the nation farmed in the Midwest (34.4% in 1940, 42.2% in 1970, 39.2% in 2000). Black farmers, however, accounted for a minuscule proportion of the total (0.128% on average since 1970). Farming in the Midwest truly was "among the whitest of occupations."[17] (See this chapter, appendix 8.1.)

Mechanization played an important role in making midwestern agriculture a predominantly white occupation. Farm equipment radically changed the mutual dependency that linked farm families. Prior to World War II, farmers often had to cooperate to realize their goals, trading labor to facilitate harvest and raising diverse crops to ensure they could support a community infrastructure that sustained their operations. White farmers were as vested in this as blacks, but black farmers had fewer kinship, community, and infrastructure resources to draw on to weather the transition. Farmers mechanized to increase production to meet their operating costs as crop prices dropped and their costs increased. This created competition among farmers over land, and expansion was beyond the reach of many. Black farmers protected the land they owned; it offered them some autonomy in decision making and some economic security. They willed it to their children to provide a stable financial basis for the next generation. But the land they owned could not protect them when they reached retirement age if their children did not want to take over the operation. Too few blacks continued in the family occupation to keep the tradition alive. By the mid-twentieth century, the "authentic, black landowning class" that Manning Marable described was dying.[18]

Arthur McWorthy represented the passing of a way of life that had sustained rural black midwesterners. McWorthy left farming in 1949 at the age of 74 and moved to Chicago, ending a 115-year family farming tradition begun by his grandfather Free Frank McWorthy in 1830 in Pike County, Illinois. The family had lost most of Free Frank's original 800 acres during the Great Depression, but Arthur and two of his sisters farmed during their adult lives, two in Pike County and one in Alton, Illinois. When they left farming it marked more than the passing of a generation. The families that had settled in Pleasant Valley, Wisconsin, experienced similar generational loss. Migration of freed slaves from Virginia and fugitive slaves from Missouri populated the community in southwestern Wisconsin during the 1840s to 1860s. Two generations farmed, but the third generation that came of age between the 1910s and 1930s left for urban opportunities. By World War II, no longer did farm ownership and rural communities act as insurance against civil rights abuses; instead professional occupations, steady paychecks, and civil rights legislation acted as safeguards.[19]

Not all black farmers, however, left the business. Some who remained in farming participated fully in the production revolution and adopted the same strategies as their white peers to succeed. Champaign County, Illinois, farmer John Smith purchased land to secure the collateral needed to mechanize. Others devised new technologies to increase yields. Matt Jordan, a berry grower in central Wisconsin, installed an irrigation system during the 1950s. Jordan also planted hybrid strawberries developed at the University of Wisconsin that could better withstand packing and shipping. By doing

Figure 8.2: George Green, the "last survivor of the African American colony at Pleasant Ridge (near Lancaster, WI) looks out over the colony graveyard." The community began in 1848 and ceased to exist in 1959. Source: Wisconsin Historical Society, WHS-2204. Used with permission.

so he could take advantage of lucrative urban markets in Wisconsin and northern Illinois. Civic engagement allowed others to become indispensable to community stability and growth, and this also helped them keep their accomplishments visible. William Sallee, the only black farmer in North Dakota in 1957 and a descendent of a Missouri family that homesteaded in the state in 1902, operated a 640-acre dry-land livestock farm, led a 4-H club, and chaired the county board. The U.S. Department of the Interior's Bureau of Reclamation selected Sallee to sharecrop an experimental irrigation farm. In the postwar era, few cash-strapped farmers, black or white, could do what these three farmers did. Smith, Jordan, and Sallee all extended their credit and increased their scale of production, thus keeping pace with USDA agricultural policy that encouraged farmers to "get bigger, get better or get out."[20]

Many African American farmers with the largest acreages in the Midwest lived near Nicodemus, Kansas. They descended from Exodusters who had participated in an earlier separatist movement to the Plains. The region's population peaked prior to World War II, and by 1950 only 14 families remained in Nicodemus, but 50 black farm families still owned 12,000 acres in the area and raised wheat on farms that ranged from 50 to 1,000 acres. Residents expressed pride in their connection to the freedom town, but they acknowledged that, without good wheat crops and favorable prices during the 1940s, Nicodemus would have been deserted. During the late 1940s and early 1950s, some farmers invested in oil wells to diversify their business portfolios, but individual farmers' choices did little to slow the rural community's decline. Instead, their experiences represent the ways that mechanization undermined the mutual dependency that had helped hold rural and farm communities together prior to World War II, and it heralded the coming of competitive production agriculture.[21]

Government support for farm modernization expanded after 1945. The Farmers Home Administration (FHA), created in 1946 to help farm families acquire and develop their own farms, offered low-interest, long-term insured loans. Applicants often had to prove that they had trouble securing a loan from a commercial bank to qualify. The Clarence Haines family, owners of a 95-acre dairy farm in Calvin Township, Michigan, received the first FHA development loan awarded to an African American family in Michigan, and the first loan issued by an African American lender in the United States. Supreme Liberty Life Insurance Company of Chicago financed the $5,500 insured loan for construction of a farm home; Haines paid 4 percent interest. Haines grew up in Cass County and he and his father, Loda Haines, and siblings would have been considered "Calvinites" (longtime black residents of the community), well-known by both their white and black peers. Family members planned to use their own skills to build most of the cement-block bungalow that the FHA loan financed. They had to make a 10 percent down payment either with their own funds or with equity equal to 10 percent of the total real estate investment, which included a new dairy barn they constructed in 1945. The FHA loan program expanded with the Housing Act of 1949, which authorized the USDA to help farmers pay for sanitary housing for themselves and their tenants, sharecroppers, and laborers. Under this rural housing loan program, farm families could build new houses or repair or remodel existing homes with indoor plumbing and electrical appliances. In 1950, the FHA picked the first black families in the country to receive these loans from areas more heavily populated with black farmers, even though the Supreme Liberty Life Insurance Company of Chicago remained a lender.[22]

Black farmers who contributed to the postwar production revolution participated in government programs, made good management decisions, and hoped to preserve the farm for future generations. William Coleman purchased 80 acres near Detroit in 1933. He enrolled some of his cropland to take advantage of government subsidies and installed the first mechanical milking system in the state. His wife, Essie, operated the system when emergencies arose. Coleman's pure-bred herd of Guernsey cattle produced 14,000 pounds of milk a week, marketed through the 400-member Twin Pines Cooperative. He worked with experts from the College of Agriculture at Michigan State University to artificially inseminate his cows. He invested in four tractors, a silage chopper and pneumatic silo filler, and a combine. Coleman had the resources to operate at this scale because of lucrative urban business connections (he held one of two liquor licenses issued to black bar owners in Detroit during Prohibition). He parlayed that income into his model "pushbutton dairy farm." Vaida L. Baker, another successful businessman turned farmer, invested his stock-market earnings into beef calves. Over time he accumulated 3,200 acres of bottomland and a reputation for holding the largest single cattle sale in Missouri by 1952. Neither of these black farmers could afford to remain isolated from their majority white neighbors. Coleman depended on white dairy farmers to maintain the marketing infrastructure that the cooperative facilitated and on white consumers to purchase the product. Baker depended on white farmers to sell him their calves, white sharecroppers to till his acreage, white auctioneers to work his sales, and white buyers to purchase 2,500 head of cattle each fall. Baker planned to distribute his farmland in 80-acre parcels to African Americans in Lewis County when he retired, a hint at an old agrarian ideal of racial solidarity.[23]

Agrarian idealism caused many black farm families to remain committed to race-centric pursuits that included physical separation from urban capitalist society. They chose farm life rather than starvation in the city. Harvey Adams and his family left Milwaukee for this reason during the Great Depression, and they purchased cutover land in rural Wisconsin on contract. They turned the 160-acre farm into a successful dairy farm with 20 milk cows, grain fields, and large vegetable gardens to feed themselves. Other farmers secured college educations, as did Alga Shivers, who graduated from a school in Missouri, served in World War I, and then built round barns in Wisconsin. By the mid-1950s, he managed his family's 259-acre farm, milked a 20-cow dairy herd, raised oats and hay, and supplemented the dairy income by raising hogs. He also took an active role in local political discussions, which helped maintain his public presence. Lloyd Johnson and the Smith and Ward families operated in similar fashion and maintained strong ties with neighbors, political leaders, and agricultural experts to protect their rural livelihood. All of these farmers were overachievers; they worked hard, managed their finances, and expanded their operations.

They lacked the status of entrepreneurs like Coleman or Baker, but they helped implement the postwar production revolution.[24]

Black farm families in the Midwest operated without the support that their southern peers received from black agricultural or home demonstration agents employed in segregated agricultural extension services that were administered by 1890 land-grant colleges. Lincoln University, the historically black public university in Missouri, received funding for educating rural and farm youth, as outlined by the 1890 Morrill Land-Grant Act. Black and white Missourians attended short courses at the campus and at the university farm near Dalton, Missouri. They learned about a range of subjects from livestock care to pesticide and herbicide applications to installing electrical appliances in the home. Most black farm families throughout the Midwest, however, did not have access to training delivered by black experts and instead worked predominantly with white agricultural extension and home demonstration agents or country Farm Bureau employees.[25]

Education prepared African American youth for careers in the business of agriculture, not necessarily in farming. Small numbers had enrolled in midwestern land-grant universities before the war, but after World War II the education and employment opportunities in the North resulted in what some describe as a brain drain that robbed the South of potential agricultural leaders. Ironically, this out-migration of southern blacks coincided with the removal of legal restrictions on employment and accommodation that forced southern institutions to comply with the Civil Rights Act of 1964. Some of this legislation linked historically black land grants with programs for economically disadvantaged and ethnically diverse populations. The Agricultural Act of 1971 vested 1890 land-grant institutions with full authority over the "Small Farm Program" designed to serve such populations. Lincoln University qualified for this funding. The Cooperative Extension Service Act of 1977 directed more funding toward 1890 land grants to expand southern agricultural extension services. Neither piece of legislation affected agricultural services available to northern constituents. Ironically, while southern women discouraged their children from farming as a life's work in Mississippi, they did not stop their children from enrolling at northern land-grant colleges such as the University of Illinois, earning a degree in Agricultural Economics, and then becoming an employee of the U.S. Department of Agriculture in a midwestern county office. Such a career allowed them to be more than token employees in an Agricultural Extension Service office in the South and did not limit them to serving economically disadvantaged minority constituents if employed in an 1890 institution. It allowed them influence in agribusiness.[26]

Figure 8.3: Students at Lincoln University construct a grain storage bin, 1960s. Source: Image LUPC:30.0020, Lincoln University Picture Collection, Inman E. Page Library, Jefferson City, Missouri. Used with permission.

Figure 8.4: Jesse Gilmer spraying at Lampkin Farm across the Missouri River from Lincoln University, 1957–1958. Source: Image LUPC:30.0014A, Lincoln University Picture Collection, Inman E. Page Library, Jefferson City, Missouri. Used with permission.

The changes wrought by the Civil Rights Act of 1964 had little to no effect on midwestern rural routines, especially those of the numerically insignificant, socially separate, and economically solvent black farm families in the Midwest. The dairy farmers such as the Shivers or Haines families, truck farmers, market gardeners such as the Jordan family, wheat farmers and oil drillers in Nicodemus, Kansas, and ranchers in Nebraska or Missouri persevered as the vagaries of weather, markets, health, financial backing, and family allowed. But frustration over unequal implementation of national agricultural policy eventually prompted black farmers to organize a lawsuit, which the U.S. District Court of the District of Columbia certified as a class action in October 1998. The court approved the consent decree in April 1999. In *Pigford v. Glickman* and *Brewington v. Glickman*, plaintiffs claimed that the USDA had systematically discriminated against them between January 1983 and February 21, 1997, by denying them payments in the case of crop loss, denying them access to federally funded programs, and not including representative numbers of African Americans on country boards that implemented government programs at the local level. Midwestern farmers accounted for a disproportionate number of farmers seeking entry into the class, compared to their percentage of black farmers in the nation, and midwestern farmers realized a lower rate of success than the national average in gaining admission to the class or receiving settlement awards. Of the total of 22,181 farmers eligible for settlements, 749 farmed in the Midwest (3.4% of all farmers in the class). Of these, one half received awards and one half did not. Interest in *Pigford v. Glickman* confirmed that black farmers in the Midwest believed they had faced racial discrimination throughout the post–World War II period.[27] (See table 8.1.)

Public interest in black farmers increased during the late twentieth and early twenty-first century as legal issues and the media drew attention to the plight of those who had owned land but had lost it. Racism compromised some farming operations but others failed for other reasons. More must be done to document the challenges that small farmers, not just black farmers, faced in an era of production agriculture. Culture might account for black farmer distinctiveness, and preservation of that integrity might hold the secret to survival. But family farmers, white and black alike, face similar challenges as well, and diversifying production and prioritizing rural community over personal profit might sustain all farmers, not just black farmers.[28]

Back to the Country

After World War II, midwesterners enamored with rural life created new types of freedom villages or separatist utopias. They did not have to

TABLE 8.1 —Midwestern Farmers and *Pigford v. Glickman* 2004

State	Eligible Farmers	Receiving Award	Percent	Denied Award	Percent	Seeking Entry under Court-Mandated Extension	Granted	Rejected
Illinois	282	144	51%	138	49%	2,864	29	2,893
Indiana	39	13	33%	26	67%	350	1	351
Iowa	1	0	0%	1	100%	71	1	72
Kansas	48	24	50%	24	50%	125	1	126
Michigan	148	72	49%	76	51%	1,219	11	1,230
Minnesota	15	5	33%	10	67%	33	4	37
Missouri	147	80	54%	67	46%	299	2	301
Nebraska	2	2	100%	0	0%	33	0	33
North Dakota	0	0	0%	0	0%	3	0	3
Ohio	42	20	48%	22	52%	410	10	420
South Dakota	0	0	0%	0	0%	0	0	0
Wisconsin	25	13	52%	12	48%	280	2	282
Midwest (% of Total)	749 (3.4%)	373 (2.8%)	49.8%	376 (4.3%)	50.2%	5,687 (8.9%)	61 (2.9%)	5,748 (8.7%)
Nation (% of Total)	22,181 (100%)	13,411 (100%)	60.5%	8,770 (100%)	39.5%	63,816 (100%)	2,131 (100%)	65,947 (100%)

From: Arianne Callendar, "Obstruction of Justice: USDA Undermines Historic Civil Rights Settlement with Black Farmers" (2004), report prepared by the Environmental Working Group and the National Black Farmers' Association summarizing USDA compliance with the consent decree and subsequent court orders. See tables: "Nearly 9,000 Black Farmers Were Denied 'Automatic' Payments by USDA—All 50 States," and "Farmers Seeking Entry under Court-Mandated Extension—All 50 States," <http://www.ewg.org/reports/blackfarmers> (accessed June 2, 2010).

homestead the plains as the Exodusters had done during the 1870s to exercise their independence. Instead they organized semirural communities within commuting distance of urban centers. Thus urban dwellers could escape racial oppression, operate their own businesses, live in low-density communities, govern themselves, enjoy recreation, and even feed themselves from their gardens, chicken yards, and farm plots. Graft, corruption, and violence existed; these communities did not function as utopias, but they offered African Americans a semirural alternative to urban midwestern life.[29]

Black flight landed in all-black towns on the outskirts of midwestern cities during the postwar years. More needs to be done to document these communities, identify the forces behind their creation, and determine the goals their residents pursued, but evidence indicates that escape from urban life motivated many. Some residents from Robbins, an all-black community formed near downtown Chicago during the Great Migration of the 1910s, relocated to Pembroke Township in Kankakee County, Illinois. By1954, the all-black town of Leesville was incorporated into the township. Other black communities in the area included Hopkins Park and St. Anne's Woods. A mixed population participated in the development, including middle-aged and older families who maintained their rural homes but commuted to Chicago to work, market gardeners who catered to local or city markets, and youth seeking creative outlets. Residents of Pembroke Township supported a branch of the National Association for the Advancement of Colored People that drew Mahalia Jackson to sing at a civic center fundraiser during 1956. Fraud and corruption, however, soured race relations between town residents and white county officials. Many blacks experienced rural poverty, faced discriminatory hiring practices, and received inadequate education. Residents often built inexpensive impermanent buildings because they could afford nothing more substantial; newspaper reporters and social scientists described buildings as the equivalent of tarpaper shacks. Regardless, many remained committed to their piece of the countryside.[30]

The agricultural ghettos, as some social scientists called these rural enclaves, often failed to live up to expectations. Various factors may have accounted for this but overextension and undercapitalization likely undermined the viability of the investments. Urban dwellers unfamiliar with rural life may have been rudely awakened by the hard labor required to maintain expansive yards, let alone productive farms of even a few acres, and they may have determined that such a life was not for them. Furthermore, the isolation and quiet that defined rural life may have played on the nerves of urban dwellers and caused them to decide that the country was a nice place to visit, but they did not want to live there. Crime escalated as poverty bred desperation. Finally, all-black towns such as those in Kankakee County emerged at the same time that established rural communities faced serious challenges that undermined their stability. Few farmers could produce enough to cover their expenses, and youth left the farm to pursue their chosen profession, which often meant less physically taxing labor and more money. It proved difficult for those well versed in farm management, let alone those new to the business, to remain in agriculture after World War II.[31]

Tenacity was critical for those who entered or stayed in farming after World War II. During the late 1960s, farmers in Cass County, Michigan, established a cooperative to facilitate the processing and marketing of the fresh vegetables, fruit, and dairy products they produced. The cooperative employed local labor and invested in new infrastructure to support specialized agriculture. Members devoted countless hours to maintain their way of life and keep their chosen profession economically viable.[32]

Residents of Pembroke Township also specialized. Mike Latting operated the Pembroke Rodeo, a nationally sanctioned rodeo event held annually since 1976. He grew up with horses in Robbins, Illinois, before his grandfather purchased land in Pembroke Township. Latting bred horses on this land and raised bulls and calves needed for rodeo events. Others have turned to cooperative models to succeed. John Thurman remembered that his father came from Mississippi but did not want to raise his children in the city, so he settled on a farm in Kankakee County and raised hogs and a couple of cows and tended a garden while he made a living working for the Kankakee Water Company. John and his wife, Ida, farmed 29 acres in 2010, including five that he inherited from his father. Thurman and other small farmers in the area consulted with staff at the Kankakee County USDA-Farm Service Agency in 1999 to figure out ways to survive on their small cash-strapped operations. They created the only cooperative in the county, the Pembroke Farmers Cooperative, and its 20 members, mostly African American, decided that they could cater to those interested in the slow food movement by using chemical-free methods and selling processed range-fed chickens and other livestock to urban farmers' markets and restaurants. The cooperative, including 12 family farms, continues to support farmers in the area who want to make a living in agriculture, like Fred Jones, who worked in Chicago while strategizing about how to retire to a farm in Pembroke Township. Jones and other retirees diverge from the production agriculture model by practicing small-scale diversified agriculture. Residents of the rural township may lament the lack of amenities such as grocery stores, banks, and bookstores. Youth may still leave for college and not return. Those who dream of country life as they work in urban industry may still set aside their savings with the final goal of retiring to the area. Ervin Frazier accomplished his goal in 1987 when he invested in a small farm and began raising cattle, goats, pigs, chickens, and other poultry.[33]

Many goals other than farming motivated urban residents to relocate to the country. Some sought a more self-sufficient life, others sought an investment for retirement or a temporary or more permanent escape from the city, and proto-nationalists, particularly Black Muslims, wanted to be self-sufficient in food production so they could exercise their religious convictions. Developers facilitated the out-migration by creating real estate companies that sold lots and cottages through advertisements in urban newspapers. By 1912, developers envisioned a black resort in Lake County, Michigan, and by 1915, the Idlewild Resort Company purchased nearly 3,000 acres to resell to residents in midwestern cities, including Chicago residents from the West and South Sides. The 260-mile trip from Chicago along the Lake Michigan shore to Lake County, Michigan, did not deter those who vacationed at the resort, despite the discrimination that blacks faced at white-operated gas stations, hotels, and restaurants.[34] Other investors in Indiana created the Fox Lake Land Company in 1924 to settle black families on the lake just a mile from Angola, Indiana, in north central Indiana, 160 miles from Chicago's South Side. These investments, often financed with white capital, reinforced rural segregation even as they allowed urban blacks to escape other forms of racial inequity. So many residents of northern Indiana, Michigan, and Chicago invested in property sold by the Idlewild Resort Company that, by 1950, Lake County had the highest percentage of African Americans in residence of any county outside of the South. By its one hundredth anniversary in 2012, Idlewild's population had declined and so had its economic vitality, but enthusiasm for its history and enjoyment of its natural resources, particularly the lake, remained evident.[35]

The need for public accommodations for African Americans during an era of legalized racial segregation prompted development of private retreats as well as major resorts such as Idlewild. Mr. and Mrs. Robert Burns operated their fishing lodge and motel on the swampy banks of Lake Koshkonong in southern Wisconsin as a respite for vacationing African Americans. Travel writers such as the *Chicago Defender*'s Fred Avendorph actually warned readers away from such establishments, which were "nothing more than converted farm houses with no form of entertainment, plus the inconvenience of having to stumble and feel your way down a lonely lane in the moonlight in order to use the 'rest room.'"[36]

Fred Avendorph knew that there were resort areas that "roll out the red carpet...catering to Negro guests...[but] this policy is not generally adver-

Figure 8.5: Harry's Grocery and Meat Market, Baldwin, Michigan, catered to travelers on the road to Idlewild Resort. Source: Photograph by Stanley Kufta. Courtesy Archives of Michigan, Image C-3653. Used with permission.

tised on a nation-wide promotion." In other words, credible establishments did not always advertise in the *Green Book* or the *Travelguide*, publications created to make vacation travel more secure for African Americans.[37] Thus, Avendorph provided an important service to his readers when he recommended retreats in Michigan and Wisconsin that would "appeal to Chicagoans...because the trip can be made on a weekend and does not involve too much driving." The Calumet Toll Highway took vacationers directly to Angola, Indiana, where they could swim, boat, and fish in Fox Lake. Avendorph recommended the Mar-Fran Motel near there, operated by Frances Fleming. Its private sleeping units each had a bath and a radio, and Fleming made excellent meals. Some units even had television sets. Other vacationers seeking a retreat on Lake Michigan could drive or take the bus to Lake Shore Acres in Glenn, Michigan, 130 miles from Chicago. The owners, Mr. and Mrs. Carl McGuire, met guests who arrived by Greyhound bus and transported them to the resort, which offered cabins that accommodated as many as six people. Once there, guests could walk to Lake Michigan, fish, play golf, ride horses, or play a variety of games with their children.[38]

Some facilities apparently catered to clientele regardless of race or, in the post–Civil Rights Act era, could no longer legally discriminate against

Figure 8.6: Many found respite from urban life as they fished at rural retreats. Source: *Milwaukee Journal Sentinel*, July 27, 1941, Wisconsin Historical Society, WHS-11997. Used with permission.

African Americans. Leaders of urban Girl Scout and Boy Scout troops looked to rustic areas as camping trip destinations. The rural parks and camps gave them experiences otherwise unavailable to them.

Urban residents who wanted to flee inner city decay found that racially restrictive clauses blocked their entry into suburban developments, so they moved into the country, often choosing established settlements or "agricultural ghettos." This caused a rebirth of the freedom villages that had been home to extended kinship networks for generations, such as those in Cass County and Berrien County, Michigan, both close to South Bend, Indiana. Owners of property around Paradise Lake in northern Calvin Township put small lots on the market and advertised in urban markets. Chicagoans, already familiar with southwestern Michigan as a vacation destination and investment option, found the Paradise Lake resort development appealing. Many purchased land from white owners, which meant that more blacks owned land, and the geographic expanse of the "agricultural ghetto" of black property ownership increased.[39]

Hobby farming appealed to more affluent African Americans in the postwar period as they approached retirement. Those intent on farming purchased acreage adequate to operate a chicken or dairy farm or crop-and-stock operation. Their settlement tended to follow the dispersed model established in many antebellum northern black settlements. Others more interested in a five-acre plot to build a summer or retirement home found their needs met in platted communities.[40]

Joseph Walker Martin, who had grown up on his father's farm in Pike County, Mississippi, worked for the Illinois Central Railroad in Chicago in 1944 when he purchased nearly 80 acres near Allegan, Michigan. He planned to operate a chicken farm there, but a serious accident in the mid-1950s forced him to retire early. With his Illinois Central pension in hand, he retreated to his nest egg. While a tenant operated the farm, Martin lived on his investment property for three years before ill health forced him to return to Chicago. The family retained the property until 1990 when they sold the prime real estate to the State of Michigan and it became part of Allegan State Game Park, also known as Allegan Forest.[41]

Not all members of the urban black middle class, however, agreed with family members who participated in the postwar back-to-the-land movement. Valena [Velma] Martin, Joseph Martin's second wife, had experience with rural reform. Her brother worked at Prairie View A&M College, the traditionally black land-grant institution in Texas, but she planned to stay in her adopted home of Chicago rather than join her husband in rural Michigan. She told him that he could "come visit her any time he wanted."[42]

Figure 8.7: On May 7, 1955, Phyllis Sanders, a member of a Girl Scout troop in Madison, Wisconsin, gathered firewood prior to cooking lunch at the Roundup of the Girl Scouts, Brownies, and Intermediates of Districts II and IV of the Blackhawk Council of Girl Scouts. The Roundup occurred at the Henry Raemisch Hereford and Trout Farm near Dodgeville, Wisconsin. Source: Photograph by Arthur M. Vinje, published in the *Wisconsin State Journal* (May 15, 1955), Wisconsin Historical Society, WHS-36426. Used with permission.

Wealthy African Americans constructed country estates during the early twentieth century similar to those built by their white peers, and these became showplaces for vacationing blacks and those seeking a country experience. Wealthy Chicago mortician Mrs. Gertrude E. Cyrus lived at Brooks Castle Farm in Breedsville, Michigan, a 15-acre farm with a 22-room country house. City sojourners seeking "a day of rustic pleasure" could "enjoy basking in the shade of apple and pear trees, playing a variety

Figure 8.8: An African American Boy Scout troop camping near Cheney, Kansas, west of Wichita, Kansas. Lake Afton Park opened in 1942; Cheney State Park opened in 1964. Either could have been the destination for this troop. Source: DaRT ID: 213268, Kansas State Historical Society. Used with permission.

of games at umbrella covered tables dotting the lawn," playing badminton, volleyball, or croquet, and cooking out at the outdoor barbecue pit. Guests to the estate enjoyed "the most succulent of viands—golden brown fried chicken by the platters full, tender broiled steak, home grown green beans, macaroni and cheese, fried corn, tossed salad, hot rolls, coffee or tea and juicy peach cobbler."[43]

By the late 1960s, special interest groups facilitated out-migration from the cities. Black Muslims responded to members' interests in self-sufficiency and affiliated with the Progressive Land Development Company in Chicago to purchase farmland in Cass County in 1968. Leaders had experienced life in the country, but their choices furthered their religious conviction and political goals perhaps more than a quest for a more peaceful existence. Elijah Muhammad, the spiritual leader of the Nation of Islam and a native of Sandersville, Georgia, made his way to Detroit during the 1920s and worked in auto plants and in agricultural processing plants before converting to Islam.

He perceived landownership as a means to an end. Malcolm X considered the land critical to accomplishing the revolution that Black Muslims pursued. Muhammad's son-in-law Raymond Sharieff served as president of the Progressive Land Development Company, which facilitated the purchase of 1,000 acres near Cassopolis, Michigan, in early 1968. The Nation of Islam also purchased 1,400 acres near Albany, Georgia; nearly 1,000 acres near Pell City and Ashville, Alabama; and large tracts for farming in Bermuda, Jamaica, and British Honduras by 1972. They raised produce, dairy products, eggs, poultry, cattle, and sheep, which they marketed through their own stores and restaurants to meet their goal of self-reliance and self-respect. The property in Cass County, Michigan, already a destination spot for urban Chicago blacks, allowed the Black Muslims to pursue their goals outside the scrutiny of the white population.[44]

The appeal of southwestern Michigan continued into the late twentieth century for Black Muslims. Internationally renowned boxer and devout Muslim, Muhammad Ali purchased more than 80 acres near Berrien Springs, Michigan, during the mid-1970s. Ali claimed that the property had once belonged to Al Capone. The demise of gangsters likely opened the area for other investors, namely, urban African Americans who made the area a destination spot. The property also lay within 15 miles of the Black Muslim property in Cassopolis and 20 miles from Calvin Center, a place that fugitive slaves had called home since the antebellum era. Ali's purchase fit within two midwestern postwar traditions, the back-to-the-country movement and the Black Muslim rural retreat from white society.[45]

Reunions or homecomings allowed former residents to return briefly to rural communities that they remembered fondly. The events provided opportunities to visit with friends and family, nurture kinship connections, reminisce about old times, and monitor the conditions of the town's remains. They also provided opportunities for the elders who had experienced rural life to share the story with younger generations. For residents of Buxton, Iowa, a company mining town that operated between 1895 and 1923, the reunions began immediately after the Consolidated Coal Company closed the mine and the community in 1923. Former residents created Buxton Clubs in Iowa cities to convey information about reunions and support genealogy research by former residents. The annual gatherings at the abandoned town site drew large crowds. Thousands returned during the 1930s, and the reunions continued into the 1980s. Local residents often organized reunions, as did Mrs. Fannie Byrd, for those who lived in and near Beloit, Wisconsin, in 1996. "Back to Beloit: An African American Homecoming" has become an event the town recognizes as a valuable cultural resource.[46]

Conclusion

Understanding midwestern rural and farm life from a minority perspective confirms that African Americans sought the same sorts of rights and opportunities that other Americans sought. Their experiences could be described as quintessentially American, but such a conclusion does not recognize the issues that nonwhite Americans faced as they exercised their rights and pursued their personal and professional lives. At the core of rural American values lies the agrarian ideal that landownership brings independence. The midwestern story indicates that African Americans had access to land in the antebellum period when settlement took precedence over selectivity. Thereafter it became more difficult, though not impossible, to acquire land as values and competition to acquire it increased. Landownership allowed the small number of rural blacks to exert influence, albeit tempered by the majority opinion, over community development and production choices. Owning land made the farmers more secure and stable; some retained control of their farms through the transitions after World War II. The tenants who remained in agriculture became part owners and eventually owners; others left the business. Thus, ownership rates increased from 49.2 percent to 95.3 percent among black farmers in the Midwest between 1940 and 2007, even as the number of black farmers declined.[47]

By the first decade of the twentieth-first century, the choices made by some African Americans to invest in small acreages and diversify production for local markets had become fashionable and supported by agricultural experts, granting agencies, and urban consumers. This occurred even as other black farmers invested in fertilizers, pesticides, and machinery that sustained the production revolution. Black farmers, like their white peers, represented the range of possibilities open to those interested in farming and rural life. Many African Americans measured their success not by their individual wealth, size of machinery, or acreage in production but by their investment in a lifestyle that functioned within a close-knit community infrastructure, a novelty in the rural Midwest where others sought escapism and anonymity.

Appendices Tables follow

APPENDIX 8.1 — African American Farm Operators and Owners
REGIONAL COMPARISON, 1900–2007

	United States	United States Owners*	% BF	South	% BFSBF	South Owners	% BFOSBFO	% BFOSBFS	Midwest	% BFMBF	Midwest Owners
1900	746,715	187,797	25.1%	732,362	98.1%	179,418	95.5%	24.5%	12,255	1.6%	6,972
1910	893,370	218,972	24.5%	880,836	98.6%	211,087	96.4%	24.0%	10,432	1.2%	6,465
1920	925,708	218,612	23.6%	915,595	98.9%	212,365	97.1%	23.2%	7,911	0.9%	4,860
1930	882,850	181,016	20.5%	870,936	98.7%	176,130	97.3%	20.2%	10,083	1.1%	3,728
1940	681,790	174,010	25.5%	672,214	98.6%	168,751	97.0%	25.10%	7,466	1.1%	3,675
1950	559,980	NA		551,469	98.5%	NA			6,700	1.2%	NA
1954	467,656	NA		459,907	98.3%	NA			6,058	1.3%	NA
1959	272,541	NA		267,008	98.0%	NA			4,259	1.6%	NA
1964	184,004	NA		180,418	98.1%	NA			2,598	1.4%	NA
1969	87,393	69,854	79.9%	85,249	97.5%	67,967	97.3%	79.7%	1,534	1.8%	1,333
1974	45,594	39,890	87.5%	44,090	96.7%	38,567	96.7%	87.5%	1,109	2.4%	958
1978	37,351	32,444	86.9%	35,207	94.3%	30,581	94.3%	86.9%	1,451	3.9%	1,250
1982	33,250	29,483	88.7%	31,121	93.6%	27,617	93.7%	88.7%	1,344	4.0%	1,158
1987	22,954	20,648	90.0%	21,290	92.8%	19,167	92.8%	90.0%	1,038	4.5%	928
1992	18,816	16,762	89.1%	17,474	92.9%	15,541	92.7%	88.9%	807	4.3%	739
1997	18,451	16,560	89.8%	17,043	92.4%	15,270	92.2%	89.6%	822	4.5%	766
2002	29,090	26,488	91.1%	27,445	94.3%	24,928	94.1%	90.8%	879	3.0%	834
2007	30,599	28,037	91.6%	28,741	93.9%	26,280	93.7%	91.4%	1,019	3.3%	971

NOTE: Census of Agriculture returns did not consistently report tenure based on race in national or state summaries. See Chapter 10: Color, Race, and Tenure of Farm Operator, *U.S. Census of Agriculture 1959,* Vol. 2, General Report, Statistics by Subjects (1962), 1004–1005. See Table 34: Farms Operated by Negro and Races Other Than White: 1900 to 1969, *U.S. Census of Agriculture 1969,* Vol. 2, General Report, Chapter 1: General Information, Procedures for Collection, Processing, Classification (1973), 96–97.

Figures for 1900, 1910, 1920, 1930 United States are for continental U.S. only. "Black" was used in 1970 population census; "Two or More Races" was used for first time in 2000 census; 2002 and 2007 returns allowed operators to select more than one race, but national and state farm totals for Black operators include only principal operators who selected one race (black).

FOMBFO %	% BFOMBFM	North Atlantic	% BFNABF	North Atlantic Owners	% BFONABFO	% BFONABFNA	West	% BFWBF	West Owners	% BFOWBFO	% BFOWBFW
7%	56.9%	1,761	0.2%	1,150	0.6%	65.3%	337	0.0%	257	0.14%	76.3%
0%	62.0%	1,620	0.2%	1,033	0.5%	63.8%	482	0.1%	387	0.18%	80.3%
2%	61.4%	1,469	0.2%	889	0.4%	60.5%	733	0.1%	498	0.23%	67.9%
1%	37.0%	1,021	0.1%	696	0.4%	68.2%	810	0.1%	462	0.26%	57.0%
%	49.2%	1,432	0.2%	1,092	0.6%	76.3%	678	0.1%	492	0.3%	72.6%
		1,002	0.2%	NA			809	0.1%	NA		
		888	0.2%	NA			803	0.2%	NA		
		596	0.2%	NA			678	0.2%	NA		
		434	0.2%	NA			554	0.3%	NA		
9%	86.9%	254	0.3%	231	0.3%	90.9%	356	0.4%	314	0.4%	88.2%
4%	86.4%	125	0.3%	121	0.3%	96.8%	270	0.6%	244	0.6%	90.4%
9%	86.1%	229	0.6%	216	0.7%	94.3%	464	1.2%	397	1.2%	85.6%
9%	86.2%	231	0.7%	216	0.7%	93.5%	554	1.7%	492	1.7%	88.8%
5%	89.4%	181	0.8%	168	0.8%	92.8%	445	1.9%	385	1.9%	86.5%
4%	91.6%	142	0.8%	133	0.8%	93.7%	393	2.1%	349	2.1%	88.8%
6%	93.2%	150	0.8%	141	0.9%	94.0%	436	2.4%	383	2.3%	87.8%
1%	94.9%	230	0.8%	217	0.8%	94.3%	536	1.8%	509	1.9%	95.0%
5%	95.3%	261	0.9%	234	0.8%	89.7%	578	1.9%	552	2.0%	95.5%

1969 figures for Black farm operators adjusted up to 133,973 based on 1978 computations of under-reporting.

1978 figures for Black farm operators reported as 57,271: Table 42: Operators by Selected Racial Groups: 1978, *Census of Agriculture 1978*, vol. 1, Summary and State Data, Pt. 51, United States (1981), 209, but ownership was not linked to race; 1978 figures for Black farm operators reported as 37,351 in 1982: Table 34: Operators by Selected Racial Groups: 1982 and 1978, and tenure linked to Black race in Table 6: Selected Characteristics of Farms Operated by Females, Persons of Spanish Origin and Specified Racial Groups: 1982 to 1978, *Census of Agriculture 1982*, vol. 1, Geographic Area Series, Pt. 51, United States Summary and State Data (1984), 387; 4.

1997 figures for Black farm operators adjusted up to 26,785 (South: 24,950; Midwest: 1,016; North Atlantic: 193; West: 624) based on 2002 computations of underreporting. For explanation, see "Operators by Race," Special Report Part 1, AC-02-SR-1, *2002 Census of Agriculture* (revised April 2005).

Census compilations often reported totals for South, North, and West; the North Central census region encompassed the geographic Midwest. Regional totals result from adding state totals (see KEY for states included in each region).

KEY
* "Owners" includes full and part owners and owners who also farmed as tenants; after 1997 Total Black Farm Owners reports the number of principal operators who owned or partially owned the farm.
NA: Not Available. Census compilations for 1940 through 1964 reported tenure for "nonwhite," which included Blacks and other races. Most midwestern states had few nonwhite farmers. Percentages may not add to 100% due to rounding.
South includes South Atlantic (Delaware, District of Columbia, Florida, Georgia, Maryland, North Carolina, South Carolina, Virginia, West Virginia) and South Central (Alabama, Arkansas, Indian Territory, Kentucky, Louisiana, Mississippi, Oklahoma, Tennessee, Texas).
West includes Rocky Mountain (Colorado, Idaho, Montana, New Mexico, Wyoming), Basin and Plateau (Arizona, Nevada, Utah), and Pacific (Alaska, California, Hawaii, Oregon, Washington).
North Atlantic (Connecticut, Maine, Massachusetts, New Hampshire, New Jersey, New York, Pennsylvania, Rhode Island, Vermont).
Midwest includes Eastern North Central (Illinois, Indiana, Michigan, Ohio, Wisconsin) and Western North Central (Iowa, Kansas, Minnesota, Missouri, Nebraska, North Dakota, South Dakota). Totals for Kansas, Nebraska, North Dakota, and South Dakota are included even though only the eastern half of each state falls geographically within the Midwest.

% BF: Percent of Black Farm Owners of Black Farmers in United States
% BFSBF: Percent of Black Farmers in South of Black Farmers in United States
% BFOSBFO: Percent of Black Farm Owners in South of Black Farm Owners in United States
% BFOSBFS: Percent of Black Farm Owners in South of Black Farmers in South
% BFMBF: Percent of Black Farmers in Midwest of Black Farmers in United States
% BFOMBFO: Percent of Black Farm Owners in Midwest of Black Farm Owners in United States
% BFOMBFM: Percent of Black Farm Owners in Midwest of Black Farmers in Midwest
% BFNABF: Percent of Black Farmers in North Atlantic of Black Farmers in United States
% BFONABFO: Percent of Black Farm Owners in North Atlantic of Black Farm Owners in United States
% BFONABFNA: Percent of Black Farm Owners in North Atlantic of Black Farmers in North Atlantic
% BFWBF: Percent of Black Farmers in West of Black Farmers in United States
% BFOWBFO: Percent of Black Farm Owners in West of Black Farm Owners in United States
% BFOWBFW: Percent of Black Farm Owners in West of Black Farmers in West

Sources: Unless otherwise noted, figures were published in U.S. Population Census or U.S. Agricultural Census general reports and state summaries. 1900: W.E.B. DuBois, *The Negro Farmer*, U.S. Bureau of the Census, Bulletin 8 (Washington, DC: Government Printing Office, 1904), reissued with supplementary material in 1906 and reprinted in *Contributions by W.E.B. DuBois in Government Publications and Proceedings*, compiled and edited by Herbert Aptheker (Millwood, NY: Kraus-Thomson Organization Ltd., 1980), 296. 1910, 1920, 1930 from "Agriculture," Ch. 20, Negroes in the United States, 1920–1932 (1935); 1900–1950 "Negro" Operators, see Table 28: Number of Negro and Other Nonwhite Farm Operators, by Divisions and States: 1900 to 1954, *U.S. Census of Agriculture: 1954*, vol. 2, General Report: Statistics by Subject (1956), 948, 1057; 1940, 1950, 1959, see John P. Davis, ed., *The American Negro Reference Book* (Englewood Cliffs, NJ: Prentice-Hall, Inc., 1966), 171. For 1940, "Negro Farm Operators" with tenure classification, see Table 26: Farm Operators, By Race; with Nonwhite Races, By Tenure; By Divisions and States, 1940 and 1930, *Sixteenth Census of the United States: 1940, Agriculture,* vol. 3, General Report, Statistics by Subject (1943), 214. For 1969 BFO, see Table 15: Farms, Land in Farms by Race, Class, Tenure, Type of Organization, 1969, *Census of Agriculture: 1969,* General Information; Procedures for Collection, Processing, Classification, Ch. 1, Vol. 2: General Report (April 1973), 177; for 1978 BFO, see *The Decline of Black Farming in America: A Report of the U.S. Commission on Civil Rights* (1982), Appendix D (note figures for farm operators, not just black operators, for 1900 to 1940).

APPENDIX 8.2 —Midwestern Rural and Farm Population, 1900–2010

	TP	BP	% B of TP	RTP*	% RTP	RBP
United States						
1900	75,994,575	8,833,994	12%	45,997,336	61%	6,831,986
1910	91,972,266	9,827,763	11%	50,164,495	55%	7,142,966
1920	105,710,620	10,463,131	10%	51,768,255	49%	6,903,658
1930	122,775,046	11,891,143	10%	54,042,025	44%	6,697,230
1940	131,669,275	12,865,518	10%	57,459,231	44%	6,611,930
1950	150,697,361	15,042,286	10%	54,478,981	36%	5,649,678
1959 & 1960	178,464,236	18,871,831	11%	54,054,425	30%	5,064,191
1969 & 1970	204,053,325	22,578,273	11%	53,565,309	26%	4,212,971
1978 & 1980	226,545,805	26,495,025	12%	59,494,813	26%	3,901,009
1987 & 1990	248,709,873	29,980,996	12%	54,612,653	22%	3,832,616
1997 & 2000	281,421,906	34,658,190	12%	59,061,367	21%	3,556,401
2007 & 2010	308,745,538	38,929,319	13%	59,492,267	19%	NA
Midwest***						
1900	26,333,004	495,751	2%	16,167,692	61%	176,267
1910	29,888,542	618,233	2%	16,303,231	55%	148,655
1920	34,019,792	793,075	2%	16,326,304	48%	131,611
1930	38,594,100	1,262,234	3%	16,243,011	42%	154,412
1940	40,143,332	1,420,308	4%	16,705,849	42%	158,892
1950	44,460,762	2,227,876	5%	16,623,345	37%	138,396
1959 & 1960	51,619,139	3,446,037	7%	17,381,576	34%	148,778
1969 & 1970	56,590,294	4,566,259	8%	17,611,205	31%	124,209
1978 & 1980	58,866,998	5,337,095	9%	17,345,924	29%	117,027
1987 & 1990	59,668,632	5,715,940	10%	16,263,439	27%	137,036
1997 & 2000	64,392,776	6,499,733	10%	16,288,104	25%	112,414
2007 & 2010	66,927,001	6,950,869	10%	16,155,355	24%	NA
Illinois						
1900	4,821,550	85,078	2%	2,205,182	46%	24,085
1910	5,638,591	109,049	2%	2,158,656	38%	23,511
1920	6,485,280	182,274	3%	2,081,603	32%	20,546
1930	7,630,654	328,972	4%	1,994,927	26%	24,936
1940	7,897,241	387,446	5%	2,087,591	26%	30,326
1950	8,712,176	645,980	7%	2,089,204	24%	24,585
1959 & 1960	10,081,158	1,037,470	10%	2,185,710	22%	24,271
1969 & 1970	11,110,285	1,421,745	13%	1,862,046	17%	22,661
1978 & 1980	11,427,409	1,675,398	15%	1,908,479	17%	19,495
1987 & 1990	11,430,602	1,694,273	15%	1,658,015	15%	22,142

% RBP	% BRP	TF**	% FTP	BF	BFO	% BFTP	% BFTF	% BFRBP
77%	15%	5,737,372	7.5%	746,715	187,797	1.0%	13.0%	10.9%
73%	14%	6,361,502	6.9%	893,370	218,972	1.0%	14.0%	12.5%
66%	13%	6,448,343	6.1%	925,708	218,612	0.9%	14.4%	13.4%
56%	12%	6,288,648	5.1%	882,852	181,016	0.7%	14.0%	13.2%
51%	12%	6,096,799	4.6%	681,790	174,010	0.5%	11.2%	10.3%
38%	10%	5,382,162	3.6%	559,980	NA	0.4%	10.4%	9.9%
27%	9%	3,710,503	2.1%	272,541	NA	0.2%	7.3%	5.4%
19%	8%	2,730,250	1.3%	87,393	69,854	0.0%	3.2%	2.1%
15%	7%	2,257,775	1.0%	37,351	32,444	0.0%	1.7%	1.0%
13%	7%	2,087,759	0.8%	22,954	20,648	0.0%	1.1%	0.6%
10%	6%	1,911,859	0.7%	18,451	16,560	0.0%	1.0%	0.5%
		2,204,792	0.7%	30,599	28,037	0.0%	1.4%	
36%	1%	2,196,567	8.3%	12,255	6,972	0.0%	0.6%	7.0%
24%	1%	2,233,437	7.5%	10,432	6,465	0.0%	0.5%	7.0%
17%	1%	2,181,695	6.4%	7,911	4,860	0.0%	0.4%	6.0%
12%	1%	2,079,257	5.4%	10,083	3,728	0.0%	0.5%	6.5%
11%	1%	2,096,669	5.2%	7,466	3,675	0.0%	0.4%	4.7%
6%	1%	1,867,846	4.2%	6,700	NA	0.0%	0.4%	4.8%
4%	1%	1,460,707	2.8%	4,259	NA	0.0%	0.3%	2.9%
3%	1%	1,151,884	2.0%	1,534	1,333	0.0%	0.1%	1.2%
2%	1%	975,245	1.7%	1,451	1,250	0.0%	0.1%	1.2%
2%	1%	861,982	1.4%	1,038	928	0.0%	0.1%	0.8%
2%	1%	749,041	1.2%	822	766	0.0%	0.1%	0.7%
		806,191	1.2%	1,019	971	0.0%	0.1%	
28%	1%	264,151	5.5%	1,486	724	0.0%	0.6%	6.2%
22%	1%	251,872	4.5%	1,422	787	0.0%	0.6%	6.0%
11%	1%	237,181	3.7%	892	533	0.0%	0.4%	4.3%
8%	1%	214,497	2.8%	893	459	0.0%	0.4%	3.6%
8%	1%	213,439	2.7%	783	454	0.0%	0.4%	2.6%
4%	1%	195,212	2.2%	822	NA	0.0%	0.4%	3.3%
2%	1%	154,644	1.5%	439	NA	0.0%	0.3%	1.8%
2%	1%	123,565	1.1%	165	131	0.0%	0.1%	0.7%
1%	1%	104,690	0.9%	169	133	0.0%	0.2%	0.9%
1%	1%	88,786	0.8%	109	91	0.0%	0.1%	0.5%

	TP	BP	% B of TP	RTP*	% RTP	RBP
1997 & 2000	12,419,293	1,876,875	15%	1,509,773	12%	20,534
2007 & 2010	12,830,632	1,866,414	15%	1,477,079	12%	NA
Indiana						
1900	2,516,462	57,505	2%	1,653,773	66%	15,231
1910	2,700,876	60,320	2%	1,557,041	58%	11,895
1920	2,930,390	80,810	3%	1,447,535	49%	8,997
1930	3,238,503	111,982	3%	1,442,611	45%	8,940
1940	3,427,796	121,916	4%	1,540,084	45%	7,633
1950	3,934,224	174,168	4%	1,646,892	42%	7,803
1959 & 1960	4,662,498	269,275	6%	1,882,235	40%	8,411
1969 & 1970	5,193,669	356,261	7%	1,821,609	35%	8,036
1978 & 1980	5,490,224	414,785	8%	1,964,926	36%	7,532
1987 & 1990	5,544,159	432,092	8%	1,861,267	34%	9,130
1997 & 2000	6,080,485	510,034	8%	1,776,474	29%	8,216
2007 & 2010	6,483,802	591,397	9%	1,786,702	28%	NA
Iowa						
1900	2,231,853	12,693	1%	1,659,467	74%	4,596
1910	2,224,771	14,973	1%	1,544,717	69%	5,187
1920	2,404,021	19,005	1%	1,528,526	64%	3,660
1930	2,470,939	17,380	1%	1,491,647	60%	2,195
1940	2,538,268	16,694	1%	1,454,037	57%	1,351
1950	2,621,073	19,692	1%	1,380,888	53%	1,223
1959 & 1960	2,757,537	25,354	1%	1,306,519	47%	935
1969 & 1970	2,824,376	32,542	1%	1,207,971	43%	821
1978 & 1980	2,913,808	41,700	1%	1,205,576	41%	1,012
1987 & 1990	2,776,831	48,090	2%	1,110,186	40%	1,411
1997 & 2000	2,926,324	61,853	2%	1,138,892	39%	3,242
2007 & 2010	3,046,355	89,148	3%	1,096,099	36%	NA
Kansas						
1900	2,147,171	52,003	2%	1,140,799	53%	20,240
1910	1,690,499	54,030	3%	1,198,637	71%	17,834
1920	1,796,257	57,925	3%	1,152,772	64%	15,829
1930	1,880,999	66,344	4%	1,151,165	61%	15,063
1940	1,801,028	65,138	4%	1,047,087	58%	12,938
1950	1,905,299	73,158	4%	956,955	50%	9,065
1959 & 1960	2,178,611	91,445	4%	899,918	41%	9,085
1969 & 1970	2,246,578	106,977	5%	2,308,600	103%	5,826
1978 & 1980	2,363,679	126,127	5%	787,780	33%	5,334
1987 & 1990	2,477,574	143,076	6%	760,525	31%	5,801
1997 & 2000	2,688,418	154,198	6%	767,749	29%	5,252
2007 & 2010	2,853,118	167,864	6%	736,157	26%	NA

% RBP	% BRP	TF**	% FTP	BF	BFO	% BFTP	% BFTF	% BFRBP
1%	1%	73,051	0.6%	100	87	0.0%	0.1%	0.5%
		76,860	0.6%	98	89	0.0%	0.1%	
26%	1%	221,897	8.8%	1,043	587	0.0%	0.5%	6.8%
20%	1%	215,485	8.0%	785	456	0.0%	0.4%	6.6%
11%	1%	205,126	7.0%	570	305	0.0%	0.3%	6.3%
8%	1%	181,570	5.6%	461	275	0.0%	0.3%	5.2%
6%	0%	184,549	5.4%	373	261	0.0%	0.2%	4.9%
4%	0%	166,638	4.2%	310	NA	0.0%	0.2%	4.0%
3%	0%	128,160	2.7%	195	NA	0.0%	0.2%	2.3%
2%	0%	101,479	2.0%	113	106	0.0%	0.1%	1.4%
2%	0%	82,483	1.5%	107	101	0.0%	0.1%	1.4%
2%	0%	70,506	1.3%	85	81	0.0%	0.1%	0.9%
2%	0%	57,916	1.0%	50	49	0.0%	0.1%	0.6%
		60,938	0.9%	49	48	0.0%	0.1%	
36%	0%	228,622	10.2%	200	107	0.0%	0.1%	4.4%
35%	0%	217,044	9.8%	187	122	0.0%	0.1%	3.6%
19%	0%	213,439	8.9%	109	74	0.0%	0.1%	3.0%
13%	0%	214,928	8.7%	118	67	0.0%	0.1%	5.4%
8%	0%	213,318	8.4%	88	58	0.0%	0.0%	6.5%
6%	0%	203,159	7.8%	79	NA	0.0%	0.0%	6.5%
4%	0%	174,707	6.3%	66	NA	0.0%	0.0%	7.1%
3%	0%	140,354	5.0%	56	41	0.0%	0.0%	6.8%
2%	0%	121,339	4.2%	95	69	0.0%	0.1%	9.4%
3%	0%	105,180	3.8%	47	33	0.0%	0.0%	3.3%
5%	0%	90,792	3.1%	35	32	0.0%	0.0%	0.8%
		92,856	3.0%	31	26	0.0%	0.0%	
39%	2%	173,098	8.1%	1,782	1,053	0.1%	1.0%	8.8%
33%	1%	177,841	10.5%	1,532	978	0.1%	0.9%	8.6%
27%	1%	165,286	9.2%	1135	709	0.1%	0.7%	7.2%
23%	1%	166,042	8.8%	941	540	0.1%	0.6%	6.2%
20%	1%	156,327	8.7%	681	408	0.0%	0.4%	5.3%
12%	1%	131,372	6.9%	412	NA	0.0%	0.3%	4.5%
10%	1%	104,347	4.8%	310	NA	0.0%	0.3%	3.4%
5%	0%	86,057	3.8%	134	114	0.0%	0.2%	2.3%
4%	1%	74,171	3.1%	139	120	0.0%	0.2%	2.6%
4%	1%	68,579	2.8%	129	111	0.0%	0.2%	2.2%
3%	1%	61,593	2.3%	110	96	0.0%	0.2%	2.1%
		65,531	2.3%	147	145	0.0%	0.2%	

	TP	*BP*	*% B of TP*	*RTP**	*% RTP*	*RBP*
Michigan						
1900	2,420,982	15,816	1%	1,468,659	61%	5,807
1910	2,810,173	17,115	1%	1,483,129	53%	4,959
1920	3,668,412	60,082	2%	1,426,852	39%	5,076
1930	4,842,325	169,453	3%	1,540,250	32%	9,749
1940	5,256,106	208,345	4%	1,801,239	34%	13,881
1950	6,371,766	442,296	7%	2,037,142	32%	20,379
1959 & 1960	7,823,194	717,581	9%	2,410,687	31%	30,990
1969 & 1970	8,875,083	991,066	11%	2,321,310	26%	30,963
1978 & 1980	9,262,078	1,199,023	13%	2,710,527	29%	32,172
1987 & 1990	9,295,287	1,291,706	14%	2,524,411	27%	38,105
1997 & 2000	9,938,444	1,412,742	14%	2,518,987	25%	25,905
2007 & 2010	9,883,640	1,400,362	14%	2,513,683	25%	NA
Minnesota						
1900	1,751,394	4,959	0%	1,153,294	66%	464
1910	2,075,708	7,084	0%	1,225,414	59%	566
1920	2,387,125	8,809	0%	1,335,532	56%	559
1930	2,563,953	9,445	0%	1,306,337	51%	335
1940	2,792,300	9,928	0%	1,402,202	50%	397
1950	2,982,483	14,022	0%	1,366,303	46%	644
1959 & 1960	3,413,864	22,263	1%	1,312,011	38%	717
1969 & 1970	3,806,103	34,868	1%	1,273,170	33%	879
1978 & 1980	4,075,970	53,344	1%	1,350,768	33%	911
1987 & 1990	4,375,099	94,944	2%	1,337,347	31%	1,593
1997 & 2000	4,919,479	171,731	3%	1,429,420	29%	3,540
2007 & 2010	5,303,925	274,412	5%	1,417,614	27%	NA
Missouri						
1900	3,106,665	161,234	5%	1,978,561	64%	71,987
1910	3,293,335	157,452	5%	1,801,518	55%	52,990
1920	3,404,055	178,241	5%	1,899,630	56%	44,074
1930	3,629,367	223,840	6%	1,770,248	49%	53,886
1940	3,784,664	244,386	6%	1,823,968	48%	53,376
1950	3,954,653	297,088	8%	1,593,221	40%	36,834
1959 & 1960	4,319,813	390,853	9%	1,558,033	36%	36,564
1969 & 1970	4,676,501	480,172	10%	1,398,839	30%	23,079
1978 & 1980	4,916,686	514,276	10%	1,567,098	32%	20,131
1987 & 1990	5,117,073	548,208	11%	1,578,493	31%	20,715
1997 & 2000	5,595,211	629,391	11%	1,711,769	31%	16,810
2007 & 2010	5,988,927	693,391	12%	1,770,556	30%	NA
Nebraska						
1900	1,066,300	6,269	1%	813,598	76%	828
1910	1,192,214	7,689	1%	881,362	74%	1,068

% RBP	% BRP	TF**	% FTP	BF	BFO	% BFTP	% BFTF	% BFRBP
37%	0%	203,261	8.4%	626	472	0.0%	0.3%	10.8%
29%	0%	206,960	7.4%	640	502	0.0%	0.3%	12.9%
8%	0%	196,447	5.4%	549	403	0.0%	0.3%	10.8%
6%	1%	169,372	3.5%	427	337	0.0%	0.3%	4.4%
7%	1%	187,589	3.6%	634	490	0.0%	0.3%	4.6%
5%	1%	155,519	2.4%	745	NA	0.0%	0.5%	3.7%
4%	1%	111,817	1.4%	775	NA	0.0%	0.7%	2.5%
3%	1%	77,946	0.9%	198	191	0.0%	0.3%	0.6%
3%	1%	60,426	0.7%	188	173	0.0%	0.3%	0.6%
3%	2%	51,172	0.6%	171	168	0.0%	0.3%	0.4%
2%	1%	46,027	0.5%	110	108	0.0%	0.2%	0.4%
		56,014	0.6%	247	240	0.0%	0.4%	
9%	0%	154,659	8.8%	31	18	0.0%	0.0%	6.7%
8%	0%	156,137	7.5%	29	16	0.0%	0.0%	5.1%
6%	0%	178,478	7.5%	33	24	0.0%	0.0%	5.9%
4%	0%	185,255	7.2%	27	19	0.0%	0.0%	8.1%
4%	0%	197,351	7.1%	29	23	0.0%	0.0%	7.3%
5%	0%	179,119	6.0%	50	NA	0.0%	0.0%	7.8%
3%	0%	145,662	4.3%	55	NA	0.0%	0.0%	7.7%
3%	0%	110,747	2.9%	37	30	0.0%	0.0%	4.2%
2%	0%	98,671	2.4%	69	58	0.0%	0.1%	7.6%
2%	0%	85,079	1.9%	42	35	0.0%	0.0%	2.6%
2%	0%	73,367	1.5%	29	29	0.0%	0.0%	0.8%
		80,992	1.5%	22	19	0.0%	0.0%	
45%	4%	284,886	9.2%	4,950	2,657	0.2%	1.7%	6.9%
34%	3%	277,244	8.4%	3,656	2,104	0.1%	1.3%	6.9%
25%	2%	263,004	7.7%	2824	1,643	0.1%	1.1%	6.4%
24%	3%	255,940	7.1%	5,844	1,163	0.2%	2.3%	10.8%
22%	3%	256,100	6.8%	3,686	1,149	0.1%	1.4%	6.9%
12%	2%	229,958	5.8%	3,214	NA	0.1%	1.4%	8.7%
9%	2%	168,672	3.9%	1,684	NA	0.0%	1.0%	4.6%
5%	2%	137,067	2.9%	426	358	0.0%	0.3%	1.8%
4%	1%	114,963	2.3%	279	245	0.0%	0.2%	1.4%
4%	1%	106,105	2.1%	193	173	0.0%	0.2%	0.9%
3%	1%	98,860	1.8%	155	146	0.0%	0.2%	0.9%
		107,825	1.8%	179	172	0.0%	0.2%	
13%	0%	121,525	11.4%	78	45	0.0%	0.1%	9.4%
14%	0%	129,678	10.9%	96	75	0.0%	0.1%	9.0%

	TP	BP	% B of TP	RTP*	% RTP	RBP
1920	1,296,372	13,242	1%	891,079	69%	1,121
1930	1,377,963	13,752	1%	891,856	65%	640
1940	1,315,834	14,171	1%	801,686	61%	553
1950	1,325,510	19,234	1%	711,293	54%	781
1959 & 1960	1,411,330	29,262	2%	661,506	47%	1,154
1969 & 1970	1,485,333	39,911	3%	570,895	38%	683
1978 & 1980	1,569,825	48,390	3%	581,966	37%	672
1987 & 1990	1,578,385	57,404	4%	526,052	33%	1,008
1997 & 2000	1,711,263	68,541	4%	517,538	30%	920
2007 & 2010	1,826,341	82,885	5%	490,655	27%	NA
North Dakota						
1900	319,146	286	0%	295,733	93%	161
1910	577,056	617	0%	513,820	89%	311
1920	646,872	467	0%	558,633	86%	195
1930	680,845	377	0%	567,539	83%	161
1940	641,935	201	0%	510,012	79%	88
1950	619,636	257	0%	454,819	73%	152
1959 & 1960	632,446	777	0%	410,245	65%	452
1969 & 1970	617,761	2,519	0%	344,319	56%	293
1978 & 1980	652,717	2,568	0%	334,407	51%	158
1987 & 1990	638,800	3,524	1%	298,045	47%	308
1997 & 2000	642,200	3,916	1%	283,242	44%	373
2007 & 2010	672,591	7,960	1%	269,719	40%	NA
Ohio						
1900	4,157,545	96,901	2%	2,159,163	52%	31,915
1910	4,767,121	111,452	2%	2,101,978	44%	29,170
1920	5,759,394	186,187	3%	2,082,258	36%	30,212
1930	6,335,173	309,304	5%	2,139,326	34%	37,332
1940	6,907,612	339,451	5%	2,294,626	33%	37,374
1950	7,946,627	513,072	6%	2,484,322	31%	35,212
1959 & 1960	9,706,397	786,097	8%	2,875,914	30%	34,618
1969 & 1970	10,652,017	970,130	9%	2,626,254	25%	28,610
1978 & 1980	10,797,630	1,076,748	10%	2,879,371	27%	26,670
1987 & 1990	10,847,115	1,154,826	11%	2,621,836	24%	32,881
1997 & 2000	11,353,140	1,301,307	11%	2,570,811	23%	21,066
2007 & 2010	11,536,504	1,407,681	12%	2,546,810	22%	NA
South Dakota						
1900	401,570	465	0%	360,634	90%	270
1910	583,888	817	0%	507,419	87%	405
1920	636,547	832	0%	534,675	84%	492
1930	692,849	646	0%	561,942	81%	309
1940	642,961	474	0%	484,874	75%	163
1950	652,740	727	0%	436,307	67%	285

% RBP	% BRP	TF**	% FTP	BF	BFO	% BFTP	% BFTF	% BFRBP
8%	0%	124,417	9.6%	63	31	0.0%	0.1%	5.6%
5%	0%	129,458	9.4%	38	16	0.0%	0.0%	5.9%
4%	0%	121,062	9.2%	25	15	0.0%	0.0%	4.5%
4%	0%	107,174	8.1%	25	NA	0.0%	0.0%	3.2%
4%	0%	90,475	6.4%	17	NA	0.0%	0.0%	1.5%
2%	0%	72,257	4.9%	33	20	0.0%	0.0%	4.8%
1%	0%	63,768	4.1%	74	57	0.0%	0.1%	11.0%
2%	0%	60,502	3.8%	27	23	0.0%	0.0%	2.7%
1%	0%	51,454	3.0%	65	62	0.0%	0.1%	7.1%
		47,712	2.6%	9	6	0.0%	0.0%	
56%	0%	45,332	14.2%	18	13	0.0%	0.0%	11.2%
50%	0%	74,360	12.9%	22	18	0.0%	0.0%	7.1%
42%	0%	77,690	12.0%	26	11	0.0%	0.0%	13.3%
43%	0%	77,975	11.5%	10	5	0.0%	0.0%	6.2%
44%	0%	73,962	11.5%	4	1	0.0%	0.0%	4.5%
59%	0%	65,302	10.5%	26	NA	0.0%	0.0%	17.1%
58%	0%	54,928	8.7%	11	NA	0.0%	0.0%	2.4%
12%	0%	46,381	7.5%	22	19	0.0%	0.0%	7.5%
6%	0%	40,357	6.2%	19	17	0.0%	0.0%	12.0%
9%	0%	35,289	5.5%	10	10	0.0%	0.0%	3.2%
10%	0%	30,504	4.7%	5	5	0.0%	0.0%	1.3%
		31,970	4.8%	2	2	0.0%	0.0%	
33%	1%	276,719	6.7%	1,966	1,236	0.0%	0.7%	6.2%
26%	1%	272,045	5.7%	1,948	1,311	0.0%	0.7%	6.7%
16%	1%	256,695	4.5%	1,616	1,053	0.0%	0.6%	5.3%
12%	2%	219,296	3.5%	1,229	780	0.0%	0.6%	3.3%
11%	2%	233,783	3.4%	1,092	761	0.0%	0.5%	2.9%
7%	1%	199,359	2.5%	920	NA	0.0%	0.5%	2.6%
4%	1%	140,353	1.4%	636	NA	0.0%	0.5%	1.8%
3%	1%	111,332	1.0%	264	246	0.0%	0.2%	0.9%
2%	1%	89,131	0.8%	223	197	0.0%	0.3%	0.8%
3%	1%	79,277	0.7%	167	150	0.0%	0.2%	0.5%
2%	1%	68,591	0.6%	135	127	0.0%	0.2%	0.6%
		75,861	0.7%	181	173	0.0%	0.2%	
58%	0%	52,622	13.1%	17	15	0.0%	0.0%	6.3%
50%	0%	77,644	13.3%	67	57	0.0%	0.1%	16.5%
59%	0%	74,637	11.7%	47	33	0.0%	0.1%	9.6%
48%	0%	83,157	12.0%	40	26	0.0%	0.0%	12.9%
34%	0%	72,454	11.3%	27	17	0.0%	0.0%	16.6%
39%	0%	66,452	10.2%	31	NA	0.0%	0.0%	10.9%

	TP	BP	% B of TP	RTP*	% RTP	RBP
1959 & 1960	680,514	1,114	0%	414,260	61%	695
1969 & 1970	665,507	1,844	0%	368,879	55%	426
1978 & 1980	690,768	2,144	0%	369,991	54%	384
1987 & 1990	696,004	3,258	0%	346,868	50%	314
1997 & 2000	745,844	4,685	1%	363,417	49%	538
2007 & 2010	814,180	10,207	1%	352,933	43%	NA
Wisconsin						
1900	2,069,042	2,542	0%	1,278,829	62%	683
1910	2,333,860	2,900	0%	1,329,540	57%	759
1920	2,632,067	5,201	0%	1,387,209	53%	850
1930	2,939,006	10,739	0%	1,385,163	47%	866
1940	3,137,587	12,158	0%	1,458,443	46%	812
1950	3,434,575	28,182	1%	1,466,001	43%	1,433
1959 & 1960	3,951,777	74,546	2%	1,464,540	37%	886
1969 & 1970	4,417,731	128,224	3%	1,507,313	34%	1,932
1978 & 1980	4,705,767	182,592	4%	1,685,035	36%	2,556
1987 & 1990	4,891,769	244,539	5%	1,640,395	34%	3,628
1997 & 2000	5,363,675	304,460	6%	1,700,032	32%	6,018
2007 & 2010	5,686,986	359,148	6%	1,697,348	30%	NA

NOTE: This table follows the model established by Orville Vernon Burton, "Race Relations in the Rural South since 1945," *The Rural South since World War II*, ed. R. Douglas Hurt (Baton Rouge: Louisiana State University Press, 1998), table: "Southern Rural Population Change, 1940–1990," 56–58. Percentages may not add to 100% due to rounding.

* Changing definitions of "urban" affect the definition of rural. This makes comparison across years problematic. By 1950 the U.S. Census Bureau defined rural populations as "all persons living in incorporated places of 2,500 inhabitants or more and in areas (usually minor civil divisions) classified as urban under special rules relating to population size and density." In 1983 the Census Bureau defined "urban" and considered "rural" as everything not "urban." The 2000 census defined "urban" as all territory, population, and housing units in urbanized areas and urban clusters (2,500 to 49,999 residents) and "rural" as "all territory, population, and housing units located outside of urbanized areas and urban clusters." The Census Bureau considers "urban" and "rural" independent from any geographic entity except census block, so areas deemed "rural" or "urban" can incorporate metro and nonmetro areas. See "Decennial Management Division Glossary," U.S. Census Bureau, <http://www.census.gov/dmd/www/glossary.html> (accessed June 2, 2010). RTP for 1950 to 1980 reflect the 1950 urban definition; 1990 and 2000 reflect the 2000 urban definition.

** The definition of "farm" has changed numerous times. This makes comparison of farm numbers problematic. 1900: no acreage limitation; 1910, 1920, 1930, 1940: less than three acres required at least $250 in sales; 1950: less than three acres required at least $150 in sales; 1959, 1969: less than 10 acres required at least $250 in sales, and more than 10 acres required at least $50 in sales; 1974 to 1997: no acreage limitation but required at least $1,000 in sales in agricultural products. See Ranking of States and Counties, *1997 Census of Agriculture,* vol. 2 Subject Series, Part 2 (1999), vi. After

% RBP	% BRP	TF**	% FTP	BF	BFO	% BFTP	% BFTF	% BFRBP
62%	0%	55,727	8.2%	21	NA	0.0%	0.0%	3.0%
23%	0%	45,726	6.9%	23	14	0.0%	0.1%	5.4%
18%	0%	38,741	5.6%	30	23	0.0%	0.1%	7.8%
10%	0%	36,376	5.2%	12	11	0.0%	0.0%	3.8%
11%	0%	31,284	4.2%	7	4	0.0%	0.0%	1.3%
		31,169	3.8%	10	10	0.0%	0.0%	
27%	0%	169,795	8.2%	58	38	0.0%	0.0%	8.5%
26%	0%	177,127	7.6%	48	39	0.0%	0.0%	6.3%
16%	0%	189,295	7.2%	47	41	0.0%	0.0%	5.5%
8%	0%	181,767	6.2%	55	41	0.0%	0.0%	6.4%
7%	0%	186,735	6.0%	44	38	0.0%	0.0%	5.4%
5%	0%	168,582	4.9%	66	NA	0.0%	0.0%	4.6%
1%	0%	131,215	3.3%	50	NA	0.0%	0.0%	5.6%
2%	0%	98,973	2.2%	63	63	0.0%	0.1%	3.3%
1%	0%	86,505	1.8%	59	57	0.0%	0.1%	2.3%
1%	0%	75,131	1.5%	46	42	0.0%	0.1%	1.3%
2%	0%	65,602	1.2%	21	21	0.0%	0.0%	0.3%
		78,463	1.4%	44	41	0.0%	0.1%	

1950, the U.S. Bureau of Census no longer collected agricultural data; instead the U.S. Department of Agriculture (USDA) administered the Census of Agriculture each five years. Data for Total Farms (TF) and Black Farmers (BF), and Black Farm Owners (BFO), report Census of Agriculture returns for 1959, 1969, 1987, 1997, and 2007. Changing definitions accounted for undercounting of farmers in 1974, and census officials adjusted 1974 and 1978 data, which increased the number of total farms and number of black-operated farms for 1978. Officials also estimated undercounting in the 1969 returns (collected door-to-door) and 1974 returns (collected by self-enumeration by mail). For adjusted African American farm numbers, definitions, and undercounting explanations, see *The Decline of Black Farming in America: A Report of the U.S. Commission on Civil Rights* (1982), 3; Appendix A, B, and C.

*** Midwest compiled from "East North Central" and "West North Central" geographic divisions in census compilations or by adding totals reported for Midwest states.

Sources: Unless otherwise noted, totals were published in U.S. Population Census and U.S. Agricultural Census compilations. RTP (for nation), Table 18: "Population by Urban and Rural: Earliest Census to 2000," *United States Summary: 2000, Population and Housing Unit Counts, 2000 Population and Housing,* Part I, PHC-3-1 (April 2004); for individual states: U.S. Bureau of the Census, 2000 Census of Population and Housing, Vol. I (2004). BFO: "Table 112: Number of Farms Operated by Farmers of Specified Race Classified by Tenure, by Area, by Principal Source Income, and by Value of Products of 1899 Not Fed to Livestock: 1900," *Abstract of the Twelfth Census, 1900,* 3rd ed. (1904), 222. 1900: W.E.B. DuBois, *The Negro Farmer,* U.S. Bureau of the Census, Bulletin 8 (1904), reissued with supplementary material in 1906 and reprinted in *Contributions by W.E.B. DuBois in Government Publications and Proceedings,* compiled and edited by Herbert Aptheker (Millwood, NY:

Kraus-Thomson Organization Ltd., 1980), 296. 1900, 1920, 1930: *The Negro Farmer in the United States*, Census of Agriculture, *Fifteenth Census of the United States, 1930* (1933), 10, 30, 50. TF and BF, 1959/1960: U.S. Department of Agriculture, *1992 Census of Agriculture,* vol. 1 < http://www.ag-census.usda.gov/Publications/1992/index.asp> (accessed July 7, 2010). TF and BF, 1970/69, 1980/78, 1990/87, 2000/1997: U.S. Department of Agriculture, *1997 Census of Agriculture,* Complete Volume, <http://www.agcensus.usda.gov/Publications/1997/index.asp> (accessed July 7, 2010). 2010 statistics derived partially from Table 53: Black or African American Operators: 2007, United States, 2007 Census of Agriculture—State Data, 636. [Note: These figures do not include farmers who marked more than one race.] Table 56: Selected Principal Operator Characteristics: 2007 and 2002. 2010 data for resident population of states."

KEY

TP: total population
BP: black population
% B of TP: percent blacks of total population
RTP: rural total population
% RTP: percent of total population that is rural
RBP: rural black population
% RBP: percent of black population that is rural
% BRP: percent of rural population that is black
TF: total farmer population
% FTP: percent of total population that are farmers
BF: total black farmers
BFO: total black farm owners (including full and part owners)
% BFTP: percent of total population that are black farmers
% BFTF: percent of total farmers that are black
% BFRBP: percent of rural black population that are farmers

Notes

Acknowledgments: The author received a Council on Faculty Research grant (AY 2008–2009) from Eastern Illinois University (EIU) that funded research in Missouri. The staff at Booth Library, EIU, processed interlibrary loan requests and provided trial access to several digitized newspaper collections that gave this essay depth and breadth. Conversations with Martin J. Hardeman helped Reid structure the essay and enriched it with family stories. Charlotte M. Rayburn collected census data for the tables. Virgil Dean, Jean Van Delinder, and Letha Johnson suggested sources that helped put *Oliver L. Brown v. Board of Education, Topeka, Kansas,* in rural context. Clarence Lang's comments on this essay strengthened the final version. Brenda Smith offered support and encouragement.

1. Calvin L. Beale, "The Negro in American Agriculture," in *The American Negro Reference Book,* ed. John P. Davis (Englewood Cliffs, NJ: Prentice-Hall, Inc., 1966), 174, revised as "The Black American in Agriculture," in *The Black American Reference Book,* ed. Mabel M. Smythe (Englewood Cliffs, NJ: Prentice-Hall, 1976), 292. E. Franklin Frazier, an influential African American sociologist who earned his PhD at the University of Chicago in 1931, described rural black populations in 1944 as "widely scattered" in northern states. The same year, sociologist Gunnar Myrdal described blacks as "almost absent" from everywhere in the North but large cities. E. Franklin Frazier, *The Negro in the United States* (New York: Harper and Bros., 1944), 197; Gunnar Myrdal, *An American Dilemma: The Negro Problem and Modern Democracy* (New York: Harper and Bros., 1944), 386, both quoted in George K. Hesslink, *Black Neighbors: Negroes in a Northern Rural Community* (Indianapolis: Bobbs-Merrill Company, Inc., 1968), 4. W.E.B. Du Bois commented on mixed race residents in rural communities in Darke County, Ohio, in "Long in Darke," *Independent* 67 (October 1909): 917–18, and in *Colored American Magazine* 17 (November 1909): 553–55. Frazier believed that rural midwestern communities imbued former residents with traditions and values that ensured their success as urban professionals. He based this on interviews with Carl G. Roberts, a descendent of the Roberts Settlement in central Indiana, and incorporated it into *The Free Negro Family: A Study of Family Origins before the Civil War* (reprint edition) (New York: Arno Press, 1968 [1932]), 66–67; *The Negro Family in Chicago* (Chicago: University of Chicago Press, 1932), 131–32; and *The Negro Family in the United States* (Chicago: University of Chicago Press, 1940), 519–24; see also Stephen A. Vincent, *Southern Seed, Northern Soil: African American Farm Communities in the Midwest, 1765–1900* (Bloomington: Indiana University Press, 1999), 154. Mozell C. Hill, a sociologist trained at the University of Chicago, studied black towns in Oklahoma, "The All-Negro Society in Oklahoma" (PhD diss., University of Chicago, 1946). Robert L. Hall, "E. Franklin Frazier and the Chicago School of Sociology: A Study in the Sociology of Knowledge," in *E. Franklin Frazier and Black Bourgeoisie,* ed. James E. Teele (Columbia: University of Missouri Press, 2002), 47–67; Anthony Q. Cheeseboro, "Conflict and Continuity: E. Franklin Frazier, Oliver C. Cox and the Chicago School of Sociology," *Journal of the Illinois State Historical Society* 92 (2) (Summer 1999): 150–72; James E. DeVries, *Race and Kinship in a Midwestern Town: The Black Experience in Monroe, Michigan, 1900–1915* (Urbana: University of Illinois Press, 1984), quote on p. x.

2. "Your Negro Neighbor," *Wallaces' Farmer and Iowa Homestead*, May 5, 1958; Lewis Killian and Charles Grigg, *Racial Crisis in America: Leadership in Conflict* (Englewood Cliffs, NJ: Prentice-Hall, 1964), quoted in Hesslink, *Black Neighbors*, 25; James W. Loewen, *Sundown Towns: A Hidden Dimension of American Racism* (New York: New Press, 2005); Mark Schultz, *The Rural Face of White Supremacy: Beyond Jim Crow* (Urbana: University of Illinois Press, 2005); quotes on p. 7.

3. David Thelen, *Paths of Resistance: Tradition and Dignity in Industrializing Missouri* (New York: Oxford University Press, 1986), 92–99; Robert M. Crisler, "The Regional Status of Little Dixie in Missouri and Little Egypt in Illinois," *Journal of Geography* 49 (November 1950): 337–43; Louis Cantor, *A Prologue to the Protest Movement: The Missouri Sharecropper Roadside Demonstration of 1939* (Durham, NC: Duke University Press, 1969); Jarod Roll, "'Out Yonder on the Road': Working Class Self-Representation and the 1939 Roadside Demonstration in Southeast Missouri," *Southern Spaces* (March 16, 2010), <www.southernspaces.org/contents/2010/roll/1a.htm> (accessed June 8, 2010). French colonists brought slaves into the Illinois County as early as 1718, and their descendents remained in the area as lifetime indentured servants in St. Clair, Madison, and Randolph Counties in southwestern Illinois. Descendents worked as artisans or unskilled laborers in flour and feed mills and at other domestic and agricultural trades. Carl J. Ekberg, *French Roots in the Illinois Country: The Mississippi Frontier in Colonial Times* (Urbana: University of Illinois Press, 1998). The Database of Servitude and Emancipation Records (1722–1863), Illinois State Archives, includes 3,400 names drawn from records in nine counties, the U.S. Land Office in Kaskaskia, U.S. census returns, and Cahokia records, <www.cyberdriveillinois.com/departments/archives/servant.html> (accessed June 2, 2010). Shirley Jean Motley Carlson, "The Black Community in the Rural North: Pulaski County, Illinois, 1860–1900" (PhD diss., Washington University St, Louis, 1982); Shirley J. Portwood, "In Search of My Great, Great Grandparents: Mapping Seven Generations of Family History," *Journal of the Illinois State Historical Society* 92 (2) (Summer 1999): 95–118; Harold Preece, "The South Stirs, I. Brothers in the Union," *The Crisis* (October 1941): 317–18, 321; quote on p. 318.

4. Vincent, *Southern Seed, Northern Soil*, esp. xii–xviii, 132–46, 164–66. Some pioneers such as Free Frank McWorthy had pushed the limits of slavery since the late eighteenth century. Entrepreneurial business ventures allowed him to purchase property in western Illinois and freedom for 16 members of his family. See Juliet E.K. Walker, *Free Frank: A Black Pioneer on the Antebellum Frontier* (Lexington: University Press of Kentucky, 1983); Hesslink, *Black Neighbors*, 31–46; Everett Claspy, "The Negro in Southwestern Michigan" (Dowagiac, MI: privately published, 1967); Kenneth W. Goings, "Blacks in the Rural North: Paulding County, Ohio, 1860–1900" (PhD diss., Princeton University, 1977); Zachary Cooper, *Black Settlers in Rural Wisconsin* (Madison: State Historical Society of Wisconsin, 1994); Valerie Grim, "African Americans in Iowa Agriculture: A Portrait, 1830–2000," in *Outside In: African American History in Iowa, 1838–2000*, ed. Bill Silag (Des Moines: State Historical Society of Iowa, 2001): 166–85; Dorothy Schwieder, Joseph Hraba, and Elmer Schwieder, *Buxton: A Black Utopia in the Heartland* (expanded edition) (Iowa City: University of Iowa Press, 2003), 19–20.

5. Leslie A. Schwalm, "'Overrun with Free Negroes': Emancipation and Wartime Migration in the Upper Midwest," *Civil War History* 50 (2) (June 2004): 145–74; Hesslink, *Black Neighbors*, 169–70.

6. Travel times decreased even more after passage of the 1956 Federal Aid Highway Act and construction of Interstate 55 and Interstate 57; see Loewen, *Sundown Towns*. Fe-

lix L. Armfield, *Black Life in West Central Illinois* (Chicago: Arcadia Publishing, 2001), 6; Wesley C. Calef and Howard J. Nelson, "Distribution of Negro Population in the United States," *Geographical Review* 46 (1) (January 1956): 82–97; Beale, "The Negro in American Agriculture," 174.

7. James C. Warren, *The Tuskegee Airmen Mutiny at Freeman Field* (Vacaville, CA: Conyers Publishing Co., 2001), 29–44; Louis Osterman, *Freeman Field and Seymour: The Home Front in Indiana* (n.p., 1986), 5–24, 62–64.

8. August Meier and Elliott M. Rudwick, "Early Boycotts of Segregated Schools: The Alton, Illinois Case, 1897–1908," *Journal of Negro Education* 36 (4) (Autumn 1967): 394–402; Jean Van Delinder, *Struggles before* Brown: *Early Civil Rights Protests and Their Significance Today* (Boulder, CO: Paradigm Publishers, 2007). The 1868 Kansas statute regulated incorporation of cities of the first class (*General Statutes of Kansas 1868*, ch. 18, § 75); the 1879 amendment to § 75 read: "The board of education shall have power.... to organize and maintain separate schools for the education of white and colored children, except in the high school, where no discrimination shall be made on account of color" (*Laws of Kansas 1879*, ch. 81, § 1). At the time, only three cities in Kansas could legally segregate public schools (Leavenworth, Atchison, and Topeka). See Paul Wilson, *A Time to Lose: Representing Kansas in* Brown v. Board of Education (Lawrence: University Press of Kansas, 1995), 39. This and later amendments responded to court decisions (*Laws of Kansas 1905*, ch. 414, § 1, February 28; *Revised Statutes of Kansas 1923*, § 72–1724; *General Statutes of Kansas 1935*, § 72–1724; *General Statutes of Kansas 1949*, § 72–1724). Ulysses Graham's petition to attend an integrated junior high school prompted the 1949 decision *Oaland Graham v. The Board of Education of the City of Topeka, A.J. Stout, and Charles S. Todd* 153 Kan. 840 (1941), opinion available at Brown Foundation for Educational Equality, Excellence and Research, <brownvboard.org/content/opinion-graham> (accessed December 16, 2010). An oral history interview with Constance Sawyer whose father, Daniel Sawyer, helped organize local NAACP support for the Graham case indicated that Daniel descended from black homesteaders who settled near Topeka, and his father had helped start the Topeka NAACP branch in 1913. *Brown v. Topeka Board of Education* Oral History Collection: Finding Aid, Appendix A (Biographies of the Interviewees), Kansas State Historical Society, Topeka, Kansas, <www.kshs.org/p/brown-v-topeka-board-of-education-oral-history-collection-at-the-kansas-state-historical-society-fin/14000> (accessed December 16, 2010).

9. By 1952, after *Brown* litigation began, only six of the twelve listed cities in Kansas maintained segregated education (Coffeyville, Fort Scott, Kansas City, Leavenworth, Parsons, and Salina), but five others had either already ended segregation (Pittsburg and Wichita), had begun desegregation (Atchison and Topeka), or maintained only partial segregation (Lawrence). Only one of twelve had never segregated its schools (Hutchinson). See Wilson, *A Time to Lose*, 29–39. For background on local education, see Rachel Franklin Weekley, *"A Strong Pull, a Long Pull, and a Pull Altogether": Topeka's Contribution to the Campaign for School Desegregation*, Historic Resource Study commissioned by the *Brown v. Board of Education* National Historic Site (Omaha: Midwest Regional Office, National Park Service, U.S. Dept. of the Interior, 1999). NAACP branch president McKinley L. Burnett and petitioner Zelma Henderson's mother shared a birthplace (Oskaloosa, Jefferson County, Kansas); Zelma and Todd had both experienced integrated education in rural Kansas. Vivian Willhoite Scales and her sister Shirla Willhoite Fleming, both petitioners, grew up in Winfield, Kansas, but attended integrated schools because Kansas law did not

vest "second-class cities" with authority to separate white from black students in public education. Lucinda Wilson Todd, Topeka NAACP branch secretary, was raised in the small coal-mining community of Litchfield, Kansas, and experienced an integrated education. Lucinda's husband, Alvin Todd, was born in Oskaloosa, Kansas. See *Brown v. Topeka Board of Education* Oral History Collection: Finding Aid, Appendix A (Biographies of the Interviewees) for background on petitioners. Cheryl Brown Henderson, "Lucinda Todd and the Invisible Petitioners of *Brown v. Board of Education of Topeka, Kansas*," in *African American Women Confront the West, 1600-2000*, ed. Quintard Taylor and Shirley Ann Wilson Moore (Norman: University of Oklahoma Press, 2003).

10. Mark Stern, "Presidential Strategies and Civil Rights: Eisenhower, the Early Years, 1952-54," *Presidential Studies Quarterly* 19 (4) (Fall 1989): 769-95, quote on pp. 787-88, provides context, as does Stephen Ambrose, *Eisenhower: Soldier and President* (New York: Simon and Schuster, 1990), 367-68.

11. "Your Negro Neighbor," *Wallaces' Farmer and Iowa Homestead*, May 5, 1956; "Negroes Are Like Us," *Wallaces' Farmer and Iowa Homestead*, July 6, 1957, 6-7; "Farm Majority Favors Civil Rights Slowdown," *Wallaces Farmer*, January 16, 1965, 29; "Most Farmers Favor Civil Rights Law," *Wallaces Farmer*, February 6, 1965, 39; "Little Racial Bias among Iowa Farmers," *Wallaces Farmer*, September 4, 1965.

12. *Negro Families in Rural Wisconsin: A Study of Their Community Life* (Madison, WI: Governor's Commission on Human Rights, 1959). The Governor's Commission limited its study to communities of less than 5,000 residents, in keeping with the 1950 U.S. Census Bureau definition of "rural" (p. 5).

13. *Negro Families in Rural Wisconsin*, quotes on pp. 20, 29, 36, 43, 46.

14. "Horse Show: Illinois Farmer Holds Annual Event to Celebrate Birthday," *Ebony* 10 (2) (December 1954): 58-61, John Smith quote on p. 61; Anne Cook, "Black Farm Family's Area Roots Run Deep: Smiths Recall Labors of Love Growing Up near Broadlands," *Champaign (Illinois) News-Gazette*, clipping (n.d.), A-1, A-6, Brenda Smith quote on A-1.

15. Mark Schudel, "Demographer Looked past the Numbers to Discover the Heart of the Heartland," *Washington Post*, September 14, 2008. For comments on the crisis of black land loss and of the demise of black farmers, see Beale, "The Negro in American Agriculture," 161-204, quote on p. 161 revised as "The Black American in Agriculture," 284-315, quote on p. 284. [Robert S. Browne], *Only Six Million Acres: The Decline of Black Owned Land in the Rural South* (New York: Black Economic Research Center, 1973); Leo McGee and Robert Boone, eds., *Black Rural Landowner—Endangered Species: Social, Political and Economic Implications* (Westport, CT: Greenwood Press, 1979).

16. For Johnson's opinions about his inclusion in the Oral History of Illinois Agriculture project, see Chris Dettro, "New Web Site Covers Illinois' Ag History," *Springfield (Illinois) State Journal-Register*, November 4, 2009, <www.sj-r.com> (accessed December 29, 2009). For more on Johnson's experiences, see Greg Burns, "Farms Run by African Americans in Illinois Are 'Mighty Few' at 59," *Chicago Tribune*, June 12, 2005, 1. For Johnson's interview, see "Audio-Video Barn" at <avbarn.museum.state.il.us>.

17. John C. Hudson noted that "with a white population percentage of 97.5 in 1990, farming has become one of the whitest of occupations in the United States," quote from "The Other America: Changes in Rural America during the Twentieth Century," in *North America: The Historical Geography of a Changing Continent*, ed. Thomas F. McIlwraith and Edward K. Muller (2nd edition) (Lanham, MD: Rowman and Littlefield Publishers, Inc., 2001): 409-21, quote on p. 419. Greg Burns quotes Beale making the same statement in

"Farms Run by African Americans in Illinois Are 'Mighty Few' at 59," *Chicago Tribune,* June 12, 2005, 1. The 2007 U.S. Agriculture Census documented an increase in the number of farmers.

18. J.L. Anderson, *Industrializing the Corn Belt: Agriculture, Technology and Environment, 1945–1972* (DeKalb: Northern Illinois University Press, 2009); Manning Marable, "The Land Question in Historical Perspective: The Economics of Poverty in the Blackbelt South, 1865–1920," in *Black Rural Landowner—Endangered Species,* 19.

19. Walker, *Free Frank,* 170; Debra A. Reid, "Land Ownership and the Color Line: African American Farmers in the Heartland, 1870s–1920s," in *Beyond Forty Acres and a Mule: African American Landowning Families since Reconstruction,* ed. Debra A. Reid and Evan P. Bennett (Gainesville: University Press of Florida, 2012), 155–79.

20. "Berry Farmer [Matt Jordan]," *Negro Families in Rural Wisconsin: A Study of Their Community Life* (Madison, WI: Governor's Commission on Human Rights, 1959), 33–34. "Irrigation Farmer: North Dakota's Only Negro Farmer Runs New Test Farm," *Ebony* 12 (October 1957): 17–22.

21. W. Sherman Savage, *Blacks in the West* (Westport, CT.: Greenwood Press, 1976); Norman L. Crockett, *The Black Towns* (Lawrence: Regents Press of Kansas, 1979). Kenneth M. Hamilton discusses Nicodemus and other black towns in the West in *Black Towns and Profit: Promotion and Development in the Trans-Appalachian West, 1877–1915* (Urbana: University of Illinois Press, 1990). Robert Athearn, *In Search of Canaan: Black Migration to Kansas, 1879–1880* (Lawrence: Regents Press of Kansas, 1978); Nell Irvin Painter, *Exodusters: Black Migration to Kansas after Reconstruction* (New York: Alfred A. Knopf, 1977); Bryan M. Jack, *The St. Louis African American Community and the Exodusters* (Columbia: University of Missouri Press, 2007); "Wheat Town: Historic Nicodemus Is Center of Kansas Area Where Negro Farmers Grow Rich Grain Crop," *Ebony* 15 (12) (October 1950): 27–30, 32, 34.

22. "Chicago Firm, Farmer Partners in Cass County Farm Home Loan," *Chicago Defender,* February 19, 1949, 4; "Michigan Farmer Granted First U.S. Insured Negro Agency Loan," *Chicago Defender,* March 12, 1949, 4; Housing Act of 1949 Title V of P.L. 81–171, October 25, 1949; "First Housing Loan Presented Ark. Family," *Los Angeles Sentinel,* January 26, 1950, A6; "Forty Acres and a Flock of Turkeys," *Chicago Defender,* February 18, 1950, 6; "Insured Mortgage Loans," in *Negro Yearbook: A Review of the Events Affecting Negro Life, 1952,* ed. Jessie Parkhurst Guzman (New York: Wm. H. Wise & Co., 1952), 110.

23. "Push-Button Dairy Farm: Prosperous Farm of Ex-Detroit Bartender Is $100,000 Michigan Show Place," *Ebony* (November 1955): 105–6, 108, 110. The article indicates that Coleman worked with the University of Michigan's College of Agriculture, but the reporter likely misidentified Michigan State University, the land-grant institution. "$500,000 Cattle Auction: Negro Stock Broker Holds Largest Single Cattle Sale in Missouri Each Year," *Ebony* 7 (4) (February 1952): 15–18, 21.

24. *Negro Families in Rural Wisconsin,* 23–24, 30.

25. Doxey A. Wilkerson put programs in Missouri into a larger southern context in *Agricultural Extension Services among Negroes in the South* (n.p.: Conference of Presidents of Negro Land Grant Colleges, 1941). For photocopies of photographs depicting Missouri blacks participating in short courses and 4-H, see FF 17—Vol. 15: Events for Negro Members, RG 4 UW, RS-G 91, UM-System, President's Office, University Extension Division, 4-H Photographs (1914–1976), University Archives, University of Missouri–Columbia, Columbia, Missouri. For microfilm of the Annual Narrative and

Statistical Reports of Missouri extension agents documenting activities after 1940, see Collection 1042: University of Missouri, Agricultural Extension Service Records, 1912–1979, Western Historical Manuscript Collection–Columbia, University of Missouri, Columbia, Missouri. For photographs of extension work in Missouri, see Lincoln University Picture Collection, Archives, Lincoln University, Jefferson City, Missouri.

26. Donald E. Voth, Molly Killian, and Frank L. Farmer, "Selective Migration and the Educational 'Brain Drain' from the Lower Mississippi Delta Region in 1975–1980," *Southern Rural Sociology* 10 (1) (1994): 131–46.

27. The cases originated in the U.S. District Court for the District of Columbia (DDC) as *Timothy Pigford et al. v. Dan Glickman, Secretary, U.S. Department of Agriculture* and *Cecil Brewington et al. v. Dan Glickman, Secretary, U.S. Department of Agriculture*, 185 FRD 82; 1999 U.S. Dist. Lexis 5220, decided April 14, 1999; appealed three times to the U.S. District Court of Appeals, for the District of Columbia Circuit as *Pigford v. Glickman*, decided March 31, 2000; *Timothy C. Pigford et al. v. Ann M. Veneman, Secretary, U.S. Department of Agriculture*, decided June 21, 2002; and *Timothy C. Pigford et al. v. Mike Johanns, Secretary, U.S. Department of Agriculture*, decided July 15, 2005. For decisions, court orders, and arbiter and mediator statements, see the Office of the Monitor, <pigford-monitor.org> (accessed June 2, 2010). The Environmental Working Group (EWG) and the National Black Farmers' Association (NBFA) investigated USDA compliance with the consent decree and subsequent court orders. The report and tables based on 2004 data appear at <www.ewg.org/reports/blackfarmers> (accessed June 2, 2010).

28. For a call to create a more detailed context to understand black farmers, see Adrienne Petty, "The Jim Crow Section of Agricultural History," in *Beyond Forty Acres and a Mule: African American Landowning Families since Reconstruction*, ed. Debra A. Reid and Evan P. Bennett (Gainesville: University Press of Florida, 2012), 21–35. For a study of 24 black farmers in Ohio and the ways that kinship, community, and ecology motivated them, see Gail Patricia Myers, "Sustainable Communities: Traditions, Knowledge, and Adaptations among Black Farmers in Ohio" (PhD diss., Ohio State University, 2002).

29. William H. Pease and Jane H. Pease, *Black Utopia: Negro Communal Experiments in America* (Madison: State Historical Society of Wisconsin, 1963), 46–62; Harold Rose, "The All-Negro Town: Its Evolution and Function," *Geographical Review* 55 (3) (1965): 362–81; Morton Rubin, "Migration Patterns of Negroes from a Rural Northeastern Mississippi Community," *Social Forces* 39 (1) (October 1960–May 1961): 59–66; Valerie Grim, "From the Yazoo Mississippi Delta: Conversations with Rural African American Women concerning Their Experiences in Urban Communities of the Midwest, 1950–2000," *Frontier: Journal of Women's History* 2 (1) (Summer 2001): 126–44; Andrew Wiese, "Places of Our Own: Suburban Black Towns before 1960," *Journal of Urban History* 19 (May 1993): 30–54; Andrew Wiese, "The Other Suburbanites: African American Suburbanization in the North before 1950," *Journal of American History* 85 (March 1999): 1495–524. After 1950, the U.S. Census Bureau's definition of "rural" shifted to be anything not urban. Technically black towns could be classified as "nonurban," that is, smaller than 2,500 people and not densely built up or urbanized. Towns begun as separate communities caught between industrial employers and white suburbs could qualify as nonurban. Hudson, "The Other America," 409.

30. For discussion of northern community building prior to World War II, see Reid, "Land Ownership and the Color Line"; Hylan Lewis and Mozell Hill, "Desegregation, Integration, and the Negro Community," *Annals of the American Academy of Political and So-*

cial Science 304 (March 1956): 116–23; "Robbins, Illinois," in *Encyclopedia of Chicago*, <encyclopedia.chicagohistory.org> (accessed May 26, 2010); Beale, "The Negro in American Agriculture," 174; Lee Blackwell, "Mahalia Jackson…Off the Record," *Chicago Defender*, October 30, 1956, 8; Lloyd L. General, "Red Light District Splits Illinois Town," *Chicago Defender*, April 6, 1957, 5; Lloyd General, "Pledges Cleanup of Vice," *Chicago Defender*, April 13, 1957, 21; "Hopkins Park Center of School Board Fight," *Chicago Defender*, July 13, 1957, 5; Hillard J. McFall, "Charge 'Land Grab' in Hopkins Park; Negroes Lose," *Chicago Defender*, September 9, 1961, 1–2; "Officer's Arrest Stirs Old Controversy," *Chicago Defender*, October 13, 1962, 1–2; "Leesville in Drive to Lure Industry, Firms to Village," *Chicago Defender*, January 19, 1963, 7; Joyce E. Allen-Smith, "Blacks in Rural America: Socioeconomic Status and Policies to Enhance Economic Well-Being," *Review of Black Political Economy* 22 (1994): 7–24.

31. Wheeler and Stanley D. Brunn, "An Agricultural Ghetto: Negroes in Cass County, Michigan, 1845–1968," *Geographical Review* 59 (3) (July 1969): 317–29; Ted Watson, "Pembroke Official Dies of Wounds," *Chicago Defender*, December 14, 1974, 1; Earl Calloway, "Watching the Grass Grow," *Chicago Defender*, January 4, 1975, A3; Orville Vernon Burton, "Race Relations in the Rural South since 1945," in *The Rural South since World War II*, ed. R. Douglas Hurt (Baton Rouge: Louisiana State University Press, 1998): 28–58.

32. Wheeler and Brunn, "An Agricultural Ghetto," 328.

33. Mike Latting, St. Anne, Illinois, interviewed by Elizabeth Simmons (July 28, 2008), Oral History Archive, Illinois State Museum and Abraham Lincoln Presidential Library and Museum, Springfield, Illinois; John and Ida Thurman, St. Anne, Illinois, interviewed by Elizabeth Simmons (July 29, 2008), Oral History Archive, Illinois State Museum and Abraham Lincoln Presidential Library, Springfield, Illinois; see Michael Ableman, *Fields of Plenty: A Farmer's Journey in Search of Real Food and the People Who Grow It* (San Francisco: Chronicle Books, 2005), 146–54, for a feature on the Thurmans. Topher Gray, "From Farm to Food Desert: Black Farmers Need Customers, Black Chicagoans Need Healthy Food, Connecting Them Isn't as Easy as It Sounds," *Chicago Reader*, August 19, 2010, <www.chicagoreader.com> (accessed December 22, 2010). For a profile of Fred Jones and description of operations on Sunset Trail Ranch, see Graduate Profiles, Central Illinois Farm Beginnings, <illinoisfarmbeginnings.org/central> (accessed December 22, 2010). Don Terry, "Green Acres," *Chicago Tribune*, July 15, 2007, 12.

34. For an overview of Jim Crow and its effect on family vacations, see Susan Sessions Rugh, *Are We There Yet? The Golden Age of American Family Vacations* (Lawrence: University Press of Kansas, 2008), esp. 67–91; John Fraser Hart, "A Rural Retreat for Northern Negroes," *Geographical Review* 50 (2) (April 1960): 147–68; Lewis Walker and Ben C. Wilson, *Black Eden: The Idlewild Community* (East Lansing: Michigan State University Press, 2002).

35. Glory-June Greiff, *"Where the Neighbors Are a Little Friendlier": The Story of Fox Lake, Indiana: A Historic Community since 1927* (n.p.: Fox Lake Property Owners Association, 2003); Christopher Robert Reed, "Beyond Chicago's Black Metropolis: A History of the West Side's First Century, 1837–1940," *Journal of the Illinois State Historical Society* 92 (2) (Summer 1999): 138–39; Walker and Wilson, *Black Eden*, 169–237.

36. *Negro Families in Rural Wisconsin*, 35–36; Fred Avendorph, "Trips for Travelers," *Chicago Defender*, May 24, 1958, 12.

37. Rugh, *Are We There Yet?* 77.

38. Avendorph, "Trips for Travelers," 12; Greiff, *"Where the Neighbors Are a Little*

Friendlier."

39. Beale, "The Negro in American Agriculture," 174; James O. Wheeler and Stanley D. Brunn, "Negro Migration into Rural Southwestern Michigan," *Geographical Review* 58 (2) (April 1968): 221.

40. *Negro Families in Rural Wisconsin*, 23–24, 27–28; Wheeler and Brunn, "An Agricultural Ghetto: Negroes in Cass County, Michigan, 1845–1968"; Hesslink, *Black Neighbors*.

41. Interview of Martin Hardeman, grandson of the late Joseph Walker Martin, Charleston, Illinois, May 17, 2010, notes in author's possession; Albert E. Phillips and Hattie E. Phillips to Joseph W. Martin and Valena Martin, Warranty Deed, February 1, 1944; Joseph W. Martin to Edgar L. Martin (his son) and Julia M. Hardeman (his daughter), Warranty Deed, February 27, 1970; Edgar L. Martin to State of Michigan, Warranty Deed, January 16, 1990, Register of Deeds, Allegan County Court House, Allegan, Michigan.

42. Hardeman interview.

43. Marion B. Campfield, "'Brooks Castle Farm' in Michigan Delightful Spot for Park Manor Service Guild, CNDA Outing," *Chicago Defender* (July 21, 1962), 13.

44. Wheeler and Brunn, "An Agricultural Ghetto," 327–28; Donald Mosby, "Cops Have No Clue in Muslim Hike," *Chicago Defender*, February 6, 1969, 3–4; "Charlie Cherokee Says," *Chicago Defender*, December 12, 1972, 5; "Achievements Speak for Themselves," *Chicago Defender*, April 1, 1972, 3; "Races: Muslims in Alabama," *Time*, February 2, 1970; C. Erik Lincoln, *The Black Muslims in America* (3rd edition) (Trenton, NJ: Africa World Press, 1994), 175.

45. By June 1971, economists, lawyers, rural reformers, and individuals interested in black land loss met for two days in Atlanta, Georgia, to discuss the importance of land acquisition, retention, and development to reverse the decline of black-owned land and the demise of black communities. Attendees agreed that land formed the basis of black nation building; some believed that the federal legislation or government assistance should support such a cause. See [Browne], *Only Six Million Acres*, 7–9; Ethel L. Payne, "Parable of Omar (as Told by Muhammad Ali)," *Chicago Defender*, August 30, 1975, 6; "Oprah and Muhammad Ali Properties Up For Sale; Deloris Jordan Sells Arizona Home for $1.5 Mil," *Jet*, September 29, 2003; Wheeler and Brunn, "An Agricultural Ghetto," 318–20. For brief mention of white resistance to the Nation of Islam purchase of 3,600 acres in Greene County, Alabama, see William E. Nelson Jr., "Black Rural Land Decline and Political Power," in *Black Rural Landowner—Endangered Species*, 88–89.

46. Schwieder, Hraba, and Schwieder, *Buxton*, vii, 211, 221; Vincent, *Southern Seed, Northern Soil*, 152–56, 159–63; "The Roberts Settlement: Unique Community Dates Back 200 Years, Has Amazing Record of Family Achievement," *Ebony* 7 (1) (November 1951): 40–44, 46; Thad Sitton and James H. Conrad, *Freedom Colonies: Independent Black Texans in the Time of Jim Crow* (Austin: University of Texas Press, 2005), 182–83, 185–89.

47. African Americans own more rural land than U.S. Agricultural Census returns indicate, according to Jess Gilbert, Spencer D. Wood, and Gwen Sharp, "Who Owns the Land? Agricultural Land Ownership by Race/Ethnicity," *Rural America* 17 (4) (Winter 2002): 55–62. The coauthors reference results of the Agricultural Economics and Land Ownership Survey of 1999, a follow-up survey to the 1997 Agricultural Census that sampled tens of thousands of farmers and private landlords. The 1999 survey indicated that as many as 68,000 African Americans owned farmland. The 1997 Census of Agriculture, however, enumerated only 16,560 farms owned by African Americans.

NINE — HISPANICS IN THE MIDWEST SINCE WORLD WAR II

Jim Norris

In 1945, the 12 states that comprise the Midwest contained a very small percentage of the Hispanic people in the United States. In 2000, the region still was the home for the smallest total percentage of Hispanic residents in the nation. While those numbers suggest continuity, in this instance they mask the significant changes in how Hispanics live in the Midwest. In 1945, the majority of Hispanics who could be found in the rural Midwest worked there but did not live there. Most passed through the region as migrant farmworkers cultivating or harvesting commodities such as sugar beets, cucumbers, or cherries. They lived in Texas or Mexico, or if they resided in the Midwest they called a large metropolitan area home—Omaha, St. Paul, or Chicago. By 2000, however, Hispanics were less likely to be migratory farmworkers and represented a large percentage in some smaller Midwest communities, to the point that they were the majority population. Indeed, across the midwestern rural landscape, islands of Hispanics were conspicuous.

While the territorial boundaries of the Midwest were first penetrated during the 1500s by the expeditions led by Francisco Vásquez de Coronado and, two centuries later, by Pedro de Villasur, Hispanics did not make a permanent presence until the 1900s. The Mexican Revolution that erupted in 1910 and wreaked havoc on that country's economic infrastructure created the push necessary for over 500,000 Mexicans to migrate *al norte*. Between 1910 and 1930, some of these immigrants were pulled to the Midwest by a variety of factors. Most of these individuals were relatively young single males. Most did not plan to stay, but those who did soon arranged for wives, children, and other family members to join them.[1]

One pull factor during the early 1900s was created by American railroad corporations that employed thousands of Mexicans to construct and service rail lines throughout the Midwest and Southwest. Mexico had developed an extensive rail system during the last quarter of the nineteenth century, and many of these experienced workers were drawn to the United States during Mexico's revolutionary turmoil. Living and working in the often harsh isolated environment of the Midwest, Mexican communities began to take hold along rural tracks but also in the urban rail centers of Omaha, Kansas City, St. Paul, and Wichita. By the mid-1920s, around 90 percent of railroad maintenance workers in the Midwest, representing more than 10,000 individuals, were Mexicans.[2]

A second pull factor was the rapidly growing industrial employment in the Great Lakes states. With the onset of World War I, fewer Europeans could immigrate across the Atlantic. When the United States entered into that conflict in 1917, labor shortages developed. Manufacturers throughout the Midwest began to hire Mexican workers, especially as unskilled labor. By 1930, more than fifty thousand Mexicans had settled in such cities as Chicago, Detroit, St. Paul, and Gary and toiled in automobile factories, steel mills, and meatpacking facilities.[3]

The third draw was agricultural work, especially in the sugar beet fields that spread quickly across the Midwest throughout the early decades of the twentieth century. In the Great Lakes states of Michigan, Indiana, and Ohio and westward through Minnesota, North Dakota, then southward to Iowa and Nebraska, thousands of Mexicans performed stooped labor with short-handled hoes each spring and early summer in the sugar beet fields. In the fall, they harvested the beets, often under adverse weather conditions. By the end of the 1920s, more than forty thousand Mexican families came each year to work the sugar beets. Most of these Mexican migrants came north from the U.S.-Mexican border in train cars supplied by the sugar beet companies such as American Crystal Sugar Company or the Michigan Sugar Company. As some of the sugar beet companies experimented with settling Mexicans in the Midwest, *betabeleros* (as Spanish-speaking workers called themselves) began to take up residence in midwestern towns. By the 1920s, the vast majority lived in barrios in large cities, such as St. Paul and Chicago, but smaller enclaves could be found in smaller cities such as East Grand Forks, Minnesota, and Saginaw, Michigan.[4]

Hispanics in the Midwest through the 1920s failed to be assimilated as previous newcomers had for a variety of reasons. One important reason for this was that midwestern communities often exhibited prejudicial attitudes toward them. The fact that some Mexicans were in the country illegally further contributed to the slow pace of acculturation. But a key issue for many Mexicans was their anxiety that the United States' emphasis on individualism and acquisitive behavior would have a negative effect on their own culture and sense of morality. Thus, Mexicans in the Midwest attempted to protect their language and traditions through creating Spanish-language newspapers and other publications, mutual aid societies, and religious organizations, which sprang up quickly in the barrios of the Midwest.[5]

The Great Depression was a turning point for the approximately sixty thousand Mexicans who resided in the Midwest in 1930. One reason was that a large percentage of Mexican workers lost their jobs in the economic collapse. Unemployment rates for Mexicans were higher than those for Anglos in the region. Even in the sugar beet fields, sugar companies hired few betabeleros. The American Crystal Sugar Company reported between 1933 and 1935 that its workforce was virtually all Anglo. A second factor was that thousands of midwestern Mexicans were repatriated to Mexico, including many U.S. citizens. While no accurate figures were kept by officials for those who were repatriated, either voluntarily or under duress, during the 1930s the Mexican population in Chicago declined by about 50 percent; Detroit's Mexican population dropped about 70 percent.[6]

The third significant change of the 1930s was that more Mexican Americans from Texas began to appear in the Midwest. As New Deal programs began to take hold in the 1930s, many Anglos who had sought work in the sugar beet industry and other agricultural jobs during the first half of the decade abandoned that arduous labor for the government jobs. Sugar beet companies turned once more to betabeleros, and by the end of the 1930s, the vast majority of sugar beet workers in the Midwest were once again Hispanic people. By that time, fewer migrants arrived from Mexico. Many of those who had been repatriated were not interested in coming back. In addition, crossing the border had become more difficult, as the newly created border patrol in the United States better enforced immigration restrictions. Mexico's own economy was growing by the end of the 1930s, making staying there more attractive. Mexican Americans from Texas, however, were willing to toil in the sugar beet fields or canneries of the Midwest because agribusinesses began to recruit heavily in Texas and the wages they offered were better than those paid by growers in the Lone Star state. By the onset of World War II, the Hispanic population of the Midwest had been reduced somewhat and its composition based on nationality began to change slowly.[7]

World War II generated more alterations for the Hispanic population of the Midwest. First, the Hispanic population began to grow once again as some Mexican Americans from Texas dropped out of the migrant labor stream to take up permanent residence. A Puerto Rican population emerged in some industrial cities, lured to the region by wartime labor demands. Moreover, the Midwest witnessed large numbers of Hispanic seasonal workers brought in from Texas and outside the country. Mexican Americans from Texas were the primary contingent and worked mainly in sugar beets, asparagus, cucumbers, and other Midwest agricultural commodities, including wheat harvesting in the upper Midwest, an occupation previously mainly reserved for Anglos.[8]

Large numbers of Latino foreign workers also arrived in the Midwest. In 1942, the United States and Mexico signed agreements allowing temporary workers (*braceros*) to enter the United States to labor in agricultural enterprises and on U.S. railroads. These braceros were guaranteed minimum wages, housing, and health care and had their travel costs paid, among other benefits. Unfortunately, however, these guarantees were often not met, leading to disappointment and suffering for many braceros. The United States also forged similar agreements for Jamaican, Bahamian, Costa Rican, and other Caribbean workers, often lumped under the category of British West Indies, or BWI, workers. These laborers were also employed in Midwest agriculture, especially in the canneries. While the vast majority of braceros and BWI laborers returned to their own countries when their contracts expired, inevitably a few found ways to remain in the region. When World War II ended, the Hispanic presence in the Midwest remained small, usually concentrated in large cities, and most often employed in agriculture.[9]

An important development that began during World War II, which later had a significant impact on Hispanic settlement in the Midwest, was the first social service programs provided by religious groups for Mexican American migrant workers. The initial efforts came from Protestant organizations, such as Episcopalian, Methodist, and Presbyterian congregations, organized through the Home Missions Council of North America, based in Chicago. These groups supplied staff and money to operate health programs and to offer English language classes and summer schools for migrant children. One such operation begun in 1943 in Fisher, Minnesota, for migrant families drawn to the sugar beet fields of the Red River Valley provided health services for six hundred families and operated a summer school for about one hundred children by the time the war ended. Seeing the inroads made by the Protestants, the Catholic Church in the Midwest also began offering education opportunities to migrant children, day-care facilities, and other social services. Combined, these social services became an attractive draw for Mexican American migrants to the Midwest, both as seasonal workers and for those who later chose to settle in the region permanently.[10]

For the first two decades after World War II, the pattern of the Hispanic presence in the Midwest evolved slowly. To be sure, the majority of Hispanics continued to pass through the region as migrant workers, but the nature of that work underwent important change, especially as new crops, new processing methods, and mechanization altered the agricultural economic sector. Around the Great Lakes states, strawberry, tomato, and cucumber cultivation grew dramatically. These crops required extensive labor, and the number of Mexican American migrant workers increased substantially. Other commodities' production was being reshaped significantly by mechanization, new seed varieties, and more pesticides, which led to a reduction in the number of temporary workers required. This was especially true in beans, green peas, potatoes, and sugar beets.[11]

Sugar beet labor offers an excellent example of how migrant work could be affected by mechanization and other technologies. Prior to World War II, the sugar beet companies calculated that it required 78 hours of labor to cultivate a single acre of sugar beets; by the mid-1950s that had dropped to about 40 hours per acre. Better herbicides were important, but the most significant changes were from the segmented seed developed in the 1940s (which decreased the need for finger thinning and the short-handled hoe) and the mechanization of the harvest (which was accomplished during the decade after the war). Therefore, by the end of the 1950s, the number of betabeleros required by the sugar beet industry began to decline even while sugar beet acreage in the Midwest was rapidly expanding.[12]

Federal and state governments also began to focus more attention on Mexicans in the Midwest, especially migrant workers. The state governments sometimes took the lead in this matter. In Minnesota, Governor Luther W. Youngdahl created the Governor's Interracial Commission in 1946, which issued five reports on the conditions of Hispanics in the state between 1946 and 1949. The primary issue raised in these reports was living conditions: Hispanic migrant workers often lived in unhealthy crowded domiciles provided to them by growers. Moreover, the reports expressed concern regarding gaps in the migrants' labor season, that is, between sugar beet cultivation, which ended early in July, and other area work such as canneries, which did not hire until August. Other states such as Michigan, Wisconsin, and Ohio began to scrutinize migrant workers' conditions, too.[13]

At the federal level, President Harry Truman in 1950 created the

President's Commission on Migratory Labor to study the effect migratory workers had on the United States and the conditions under which migrants worked and lived. Part of the motivation for Truman's actions was organized labor's opposition to the bracero and H-2 (BWI workers) programs that had continued to bring temporary laborers into the United States after World War II concluded. U.S. labor unions argued that these programs depressed wages for all Americans and encouraged illegal immigration into the country, especially from Mexico.[14]

One aspect of the bracero agreement with Mexico allowed that country to bar workers from migrating to states that openly discriminated against Mexican people. Therefore, Mexico vetoed the use of braceros in Texas. That decision outraged the state's growers and politicians, and they put pressure on the U.S. border patrol to be lax in controlling the Rio Grande entry points. Consequently, a flood of Mexican workers crossed the border annually in the decade after World War II, leading to depressed farm wages in Texas that forced many Mexican Americans into the migrant stream. Mexican Americans living in southern Texas could make more money cultivating sugar beets in North Dakota than they could in the spinach fields around Crystal City, Texas. While Truman's commission focused considerable public attention on the plight of migrant workers, little substantial change in the migrants' condition occurred in the short run, and the bracero program with Mexico endured another decade.[15]

Scrutiny over illegal immigration into the United States did have one short-term outcome—the implementation of the ill-named Operation Wetback by the Immigration and Naturalization Service (INS). Beginning in June 1954 in California, INS agents, with cooperation from local law enforcement elements, began arresting in large numbers undocumented Mexican workers. Operation Wetback spread throughout the remainder of the Southwest and into the Midwest by 1955. In all, authorities apprehended and deported about 800,000 Mexicans by the time the round-up ended later that year. While the vast majority of these Hispanics were discovered in southwestern states, agents arrested some in the Midwest. For instance, in Chicago about 1,500 Hispanics were returned to Mexico.[16]

One result of the changes taking place in Midwest agriculture and the closer scrutiny of migrant working and living conditions was an attempt by agribusinesses and government to rationalize the deployment of migrant workers. Usually referred to as the "Annual Plan," this new system of the post–World War II decade was a collaboration of sugar beet companies, Midwest growers and canneries, and some state governments, such as Minnesota's. In essence, each spring these interest groups would meet with representatives from the United States Employment Service and the Farm Placement Service. They would determine the number of migrant workers needed for the Midwest, plus where and when these laborers would be required. Beginning first with the needs of the sugar beet companies, agribusinesses and government agencies developed a plan for the use of migrant workers over the course of the entire year. Hence, a betabelero working in Minnesota would be contracted for a later date to start work in a cannery, to pick cherries in Wisconsin, or to harvest cucumbers in Michigan. Before that temporary job ended, that same migrant might have a contract to harvest potatoes in North Dakota or cotton in Texas. While not always perfect in its implementation, the Annual Plan provided employers with a reliable workforce, addressed concerns of state governments regarding steady employment for migrants (without them becoming wards of the state), and provided some certainty of employment for the migrants.[17]

The result of more state oversight of the conditions for Mexican migrant workers and the steady expansion of social and education services provided to them led to slow growth in the permanent Hispanic population in the Midwest. In total numbers, Hispanics in the Midwest remained scarce—only about 300,000 by 1960. Some of this growth was fueled by Mexican immigration, but these Mexicans accounted for only than 20 percent of the Hispanics in the region. Mexico's economy was doing fairly well in the postwar era, diminishing the push factor from that country. While large numbers crossed the border annually, they were either braceros who would return at the end of their contracts or undocumented workers who toiled for brief periods in the Southwest before recrossing the border. Most of the growth in Hispanics living in the Midwest came from Mexican Americans moving in from Texas; Puerto Ricans migrating from that island to larger cities, especially Chicago; and from births, although overall the Hispanic birthrate declined slightly from the level of earlier generations.[18]

Most of the growth in the Midwest Hispanic population was in the established Hispanic enclaves of the larger cities, including Chicago, St. Paul, Detroit, Omaha, and Kansas City. Some used these cities as the new base for their migrant lifestyle, living there during the winter while they worked in the sugar beet or cucumber fields and canneries during the summer. More and more, though, they found permanent employment, especially in meatpacking plants, railroads, textiles, and other industries.[19]

Smaller midwestern cities also became places of residence for Hispanics. Saginaw, Michigan, had the largest number of Hispanics in that state, besides Detroit. Hispanics were drawn to Saginaw primarily for seasonal agricultural work but also found unskilled employment in manufacturing that supported the automobile industry. The Hispanic barrio in Davenport, Iowa, which initially grew from those pulled to the region for railroad maintenance, also increased in population from migrants who worked in the nearby sugar beet and onion fields and in mainly unskilled jobs for farm implement manufactures. Crookston and Moorhead, Minnesota, in the center of the Red River Valley sugar beet industry, became the permanent home for several hundred betabelero families in the two decades after World War II.[20]

The growing Hispanic population, however, did not assimilate to a greater extent than it had before the war. True, more Hispanic youth were receiving formal education. Mexican American organizations such as the League of United Latin American Citizens (LULAC) and the American G.I. Forum placed considerable emphasis on education, although the dropout rate remained high after middle school. In Milwaukee, Wisconsin, for example, the average grade attained by Hispanics in 1960 was the ninth, yet more Hispanics had English language skills. However, whether in large cities or smaller communities, Hispanics lived in rather segregated enclaves, usually called barrios or, sometimes, *colonias*. Anglo discrimination continued to manifest itself. Even in small towns, such as Lyman, Nebraska, Mexicans confronted signs in restaurants and stores warning "No Dogs, No Mexicans." In Minatare, Nebraska, the city council passed an ordinance limiting the area in town where Hispanics might purchase or rent housing. Hispanics also maintained a strong allegiance to their culture. Mexican Independence Day, *Cinco de Mayo*, and other important Hispanic cultural milestones continued to draw significant celebrations.[21]

As the Mexican population began to grow, especially in communities where heretofore their presence had been minimal, the Anglo population sometimes responded fearfully, viewing Hispanics as prone to criminal acts of violence. Local newspapers usually made any violent episode associated with Hispanics into front-page news. Sensational photographs accompanied many of the stories that named all the participants, including minors, a practice that was not followed when stories involved Anglo youths. In Clay County, Minnesota, for example, an eight-year-old Mexican American youth's name was revealed in newspaper stories regarding an accidental shooting. Communities' preoccupation with Hispanics as likely violators of the law led to local police harassment and civil liberties infringements. Again in Minnesota, a local sheriff made the rounds each spring during the 1950s to confiscate any weapons held by Mexican American sugar beet migrant workers without any legal charges ever being filed against the owners.[22]

Not everyone in these predominantly Anglo communities reacted fearfully to Hispanic migrant workers. Many smaller communities recognized their reliance on migrant workers and tried to make the environment more welcoming for them. Some local radio stations included Spanish-language programming and music when large numbers of migrants were present in their area. Grocery stores stocked tortillas and other food products preferred by Hispanic workers. Catholic churches offered Spanish-language masses, and church groups and local service organizations organized weekend dances and "fiestas" for Mexican migrant farmworkers. Often agribusinesses, especially sugar beet companies, took the lead in encouraging local community recreational services for migrant workers, acknowledging their importance for production. By the end of the 1950s, the Hispanic presence in the Midwest, especially in rural communities, had gained in visibility and importance.[23]

The 1960s represented a significant turning point for Hispanics throughout the United States, including those in the Midwest. A major change was the termination of the bracero program with Mexico in 1964 and the accompanying reform in the United States immigration policy. Hispanic voters organized into *Viva Kennedy* groups in Texas and California and in midwestern cities had played a key role in the Kennedy-Johnson electoral victory in 1960. The Kennedy administration, pressed by organized labor, LULAC, and the G.I. Forum, began to phase out the bracero program. These organizations argued that braceros reduced wages for Mexican American farmworkers. After Kennedy's assassination, the Johnson administration finally ended the bracero agreement with Mexico. In 1965 Congress enacted the Hart-Celler Immigration and Nationality Act. This was the first major change in U.S. immigration policy since 1924, and it signaled a new approach to Latino immigration. The 1924 act, which limited immigration into the U.S. from most of the world, exempted the Western Hemisphere. While Latinos, mainly Mexicans, did face legal restrictions on immigration such as health examinations and no permissible criminal record, there were no numerical limitations on how many Mexicans could enter the United States annually. Hart-Celler established a numerical ceiling on total annual immigration, and while it was not problematic at first, as more Latinos wanted to come into the United States, the limitations created controversy.[24]

The successful *Viva Kennedy* campaign was a harbinger of things to come in Hispanic political organizing. While some historians date the beginnings of the Hispanic civil rights movement to the school court cases of the 1940s or the Felix Longoria affair in 1947, which helped give birth to the American G.I. Forum, a civil rights movement emerged in the 1960s. In 1963, a slate of Mexican American candidates called *Los Cinco* captured control of the municipal government in Crystal City, Texas. Crystal City had for decades been a principal site for midwestern sugar beet companies to recruit migrant workers—perhaps 80 percent of the population migrated northward to the Midwest annually to work in various agricultural enterprises. Though Hispanics made up about 90 percent of the town's population, the Anglo minority had controlled city government and the school board. While Los Cinco was later co-opted by the local Anglo interests, the electoral victory promoted more political activism. Moreover, in 1965 César Chávez and his United Farm Workers (UFW) began their historic strike against grape growers in California. While initially unsuccessful, the strike and subsequent grape boycott campaign drew considerable national attention. By the early 1970s, the Chicano phenomenon—a social, cultural, and political movement driven mainly by younger Hispanics—was occurring throughout the nation, including the Midwest.[25]

While not the center of the Chicano movement, the Midwest followed the pattern emerging from the Southwest. The new G.I. Forum had spread into the region within the first year of its creation in Texas in 1948. By the end of the 1950s, Nebraska, Iowa, Illinois, Minnesota, Michigan, and Indiana had active growing chapters. In most of these same states, Hispanics created *Viva Kennedy* groups in 1960. Hispanics throughout the Midwest enthusiastically supported the UFW's grape boycott campaign. They also formed organizations to respond to local issues, such as the Latin American Union for Civil Rights in Milwaukee and the Latin American Council for Political Action in Detroit. While mainly in the larger cities, Hispanics in smaller midwest towns such as Scottsbluff, Nebraska, and Davenport, Iowa, followed this same pattern. The Hispanics in Davenport rallied to support the UFW grape boycott and then used the same organizing skills to seek political rights for Mexican American migrant workers in Iowa.[26]

Indeed, the Chicano movement particularly associated itself with the plight of Hispanic migrant farmworkers in the Midwest and was linked to farmworker unions in Texas and California. Beginning in 1966 in the lower Rio Grande valley, strikes by Mexican Americans broke out against growers. While unsuccessful, a strike among packing-shed workers occurred around Crystal City, and growers throughout the region complained of increasing worker militancy. Kinship ties among south Texas migrant Hispanics and those in Wisconsin soon led to the creation of *Obreros Unidos* (Workers United) in 1967. Obreros Unidos focused its efforts primarily on Hispanic cannery workers throughout that state. In another instance, the UFW helped with the formation in Ohio of the Farm Labor Organizing Committee (FLOC), also in 1967. FLOC was especially active with Hispanics working in the tomato fields. However, the large proportion of Mexican American migrants who worked in the sugar beet fields received little union attention. The sugar industry was the only agribusiness sector in which the federal government maintained set wages, and by the end of the 1960s an experienced betabelero could make more than the federally established minimum hourly wage. The relatively better pay had a negative influence on labor organizers' efforts to unionize betabeleros.[27]

Another major influence on the lives of Hispanics in the Midwest during the 1960s was the social programs associated with President Johnson's Great Society campaign. Inspired significantly by the various civil rights movements of the era, the documentary *Harvest of Shame* (1960), and Michael Harrington's best seller *The Other America* (1962), Johnson wanted the federal government to assume the lead in eradicating poverty in the United States. Such legislation as the Equal Opportunity Act (1964) and the Elementary and Secondary Education Act (1964) targeted the victims of poverty, among whom were large numbers of the Hispanic population. Much of the effort to eradicate poverty came through federal programs designed to improve the plight of Hispanics in the migrant stream. More health clinics appeared in rural areas to administer to migrant workers and their families. Under the Elementary and Secondary Education Act, schools for migrant children appeared throughout the Midwest. In the Red River Valley of North Dakota and Minnesota, five such schools taught migrant children during the summer months of 1967. Migrant schools also implemented Head Start programs and often served as day-care centers. In many instances, groups who had long worked with Hispanic migrants such as the Catholic Church and the Home Missions Council of North America directed these Great Society initiatives at the local level. New agencies staffed by Hispanics also appeared, such as Migrants, Inc., in North Dakota and Minnesota, to administer these "War on Poverty" efforts. By the early 1970s, most midwestern states had a coordinating state agency, such as the Office for Spanish Speaking People in Minnesota or the Nebraska Commission on Mexican Americans, which provided a vast array of social services to Hispanics, especially migrant families.[28]

The living conditions for Hispanic migrant workers were of keen interest for these organizations. In 1967, the U.S. Department of Labor mandated new standards for migrant housing and sanitary conditions. Michigan, Minnesota, North Dakota, and Wisconsin were four midwestern states that implemented programs to improve migrants' living situations. In 1969, Minnesota composed new regulations that, among other standards, stipulated how many square feet per resident migrant domiciles should provide, the number of electrical outlets per room, the number of windows (with screens) for each migrant house, and the square footage of food preparation areas. Each spring, state inspectors visited farms with migrant housing and goaded landowners to meet the federal and state migrant housing standards, albeit with mixed results. States allowed exceptions and grace periods for growers not meeting the requirements, and the results could vary enormously from state to state. In North Dakota, officials in 1967 found only 15 percent of migrant housing not in compliance with the minimum standards, which suggests that migrant housing was generally in good condition. Yet in Michigan that same year, inspectors tabulated a total of six thousand violations of migrant housing standards, suggesting that poor living conditions prevailed for migrant families. One problem was that the fines levied on growers who failed to meet the requirements were minuscule. Nonetheless, migrant housing in the states with established standards and some enforcement was having an effect; housing was improving. Some growers stopped providing it because of the maintenance costs, however, which meant, most often, that migrant workers were forced off the farm to find poor quality housing in nearby towns.[29]

The considerable number of Hispanic directors and staff members for these social service programs resulted from their rising attendance and graduation from colleges and universities throughout the nation, including the Midwest. Many of the teachers and medical staff in the migrant programs were recent Hispanic college graduates. Chicano students in the Midwest also pressured institutions of higher learning to actively enroll more Hispanics and to broaden the curriculum to include Hispanic/Chicano/Latino programs. While most large institutions in major metropolitan areas established such programs for Hispanics by the mid-1970s, this development also occurred in institutions of higher learning in smaller midwestern communities such as Moorhead, Minnesota, and Chadron, Nebraska, thus increasing the Hispanic presence there.[30]

The Chicano movement in the Midwest during the 1970s made common cause with other groups seeking civil rights. On college campuses, African American and Native American students often allied with Hispanic students to promote Chicano academic programs or to encourage higher education institutions to support Chicano cultural events at their campus. In Nebraska, an alliance between Chicano groups and members of the American Indian Movement (AIM) took place in smaller communities. The two sides found common cause over AIM demands that historic Fort Robinson and some other state land in western Nebraska be returned to Native American control, and complaints by Hispanics in Scottsbluff and Gering that local public schools were too Eurocentric in the history and social studies classes. In Scottsbluff, these issues created significant tension as some fights occurred and a school was firebombed before local school officials promised to reexamine the public school curriculum. While the Chicano movement waned somewhat near the end of the 1970s, other profound developments were gathering momentum that would reshape the Hispanic presence in the rural Midwest.[31]

Perhaps the most important development was a major restructuring of the meatpacking industry in the United States that began in the 1970s. Besides agricultural work in the Midwest, historically the highest concentration of Hispanic workers was found in the meatpacking facilities. The "big four" meatpacking corporations—Oscar Meyer, Swift, Armour, and Hormel—employed thousands of Hispanic workers in large midwestern cities. The work was difficult but steady, and as unions became established in meatpacking operations after World War II, wages and benefits increased. By 1970, an entry-level job in a meatpacking plant started at over ten dollars per hour with extensive health and retirement benefits included. Therefore, for many Hispanics in the large midwestern cities, employment in the meatpacking industry was a key toward moving into a lower middle-class income.[32]

Several developments came together in the 1970s that led to the restructuring of the meatpacking industry. With more American women entering the job market and having less time for household chores, families desired easier-to-prepare foods; therefore, demand rose for precut or preprocessed meats. In addition, neighbors of the large meatpacking facilities in the cities pressured the companies to reduce odors and eliminate other environmental hazards associated with meatpacking. Higher operating costs associated with government-mandated environmental and safety controls and the escalating wages and benefits achieved by the labor unions reduced the profitability once enjoyed by Swift, Armour, and the other industry giants.[33]

While the traditional leaders in the meatpacking industry struggled, new meatpacking companies—calling themselves meat processors—began to address some of these issues. Led by Iowa Beef Processors (IBP), Con Agra, and Cargill, major changes took place in the meatpacking and -processing industry during the 1970s and 1980s. For one thing, these companies set up operations in smaller midwestern communities. The rural Midwest suffered during this era from falling farm prices and subsequent population outmigration. IBP and the others often received significant financial incentives to operate in small communities where residents were also often willing to overlook odors and other environmental unpleasantness created by the meat processors in exchange for jobs. Moving into the countryside also meant being closer to livestock producers, thus cutting the meat processors' transportation costs. These new companies reduced operating expenses further by offering lower wages and benefits to a mainly nonunion workforce. Wages in some cases dropped from over ten dollars per hour to less than seven dollars; likewise, health benefits were slashed. And finally, these companies streamlined their operations and increased the pace of work. The processing line speeds increased in some instances threefold from what they were in the older meatpacking plants. These newer meat-processing firms prospered while the older companies declined. Therefore, in small midwestern communities such as Schuyler, Nebraska, Storm Lake, Iowa, and Garden City, Kansas, a new meat-processing industry emerged that was in need of workers.[34]

At the same time that the meatpacking industry was changing in the 1970s, more Hispanics, especially Mexicans, began coming into the United States, a trend that accelerated through the 1990s. Several factors contributed to this new push period in Hispanic immigration from the south. Mexico's economy, while continuing to grow rapidly through the 1970s, was not able to keep pace with its population growth. While speaking of the "Mexican Miracle" was common during that era, still the Mexican economy could not keep up with the country's population explosion. In 1960, Mexico had 35 million people; 30 years later it had nearly 90 million. That population was also becoming more concentrated along the border with the United States. The Border Industrialization Program (BIP), created in 1964, allowed for a ten-mile-wide duty-free zone along the boundary where assembly plants (called *maquilas*) could manufacture items solely for export, with the only tariff being on the value added. Maquilas became very popular with American and Asian firms. In 1965 there were 12 plants employing 3,000 workers; 30 years later there were over 2,000 assembly plants with a workforce of about 700,000. When Mexico's "miracle" economy collapsed in the 1980s, hundreds of thousands of Mexicans migrated to the border towns, such as Cuidad Juárez and Tijuana, in hopes of finding a job. Unfortunately for them, the maquilas could not absorb such numbers. The population of Mexico's six states that border the United States, where the BIP was established, was 5.5 million in 1960 but leaped to 13.2 million in 1990. In addition, where once several hundred thousand Mexicans could work each year in the bracero program, that door had closed in 1964. Simply put, a vast pool of unemployed or underemployed Mexicans had congregated on the border with little opportunity other than going further north. However, not all Hispanics crossing into the United States in greater numbers were Mexicans. Civil conflicts in Guatemala, El Salvador, and Nicaragua in the 1980s displaced thousands of people, many of whom chose to flee *al norte*. By the 1990s, more than 300,000 Hispanics were entering the U.S. annually—legally or without documents—looking for a job.[35]

While the largest share of the Hispanic population had been concentrated overwhelmingly in the southwestern states, it was rapidly growing and on the move inland, in many cases to the Midwest. Several factors accounted for this phenomenon. First, in 1986 Congress enacted the Immigration and Control Act that, among other things, provided amnesty for more than one million previously undocumented Hispanics, allowing them to apply for citizenship. Second, many of these now legal residents sought to distance themselves from the poor schools, drug use, and violence in many of the border region's barrios where they had been forced previously to live in order to avoid detection if they were undocumented. Third, anti-Hispanic sentiment among Anglos in some border states with their "English only" campaigns and California's Proposition 187 (restricting undocumented immigrants from receiving public education and other social services) created a climate of intolerance that many Hispanics wished to escape. And, of course, the newly restructured meat-processing industry in the Midwest was looking for workers.[36]

The local rural population in the communities of the Midwest where the new meat-processing facilities had established themselves was proving to be insufficient to meet the needs of these companies. As noted above, the wages offered by the companies were not very attractive and the line speeds were much faster than in the unionized plants. As most of the jobs were de-skilled, the work on the lines became ever more tedious and repetitive. Faster productive and repetitive motion led to more injuries and health problems. The U.S. Bureau of Labor Statistics by the 1990s characterized meat-processing work as a "hazardous occupation." Meat processing plants were "dark, wet, and noisy—conditions most workers [found] unpleasant." Local workers with nearby kin and high school diplomas often voted with their feet and left. Annual turnover rates ranged between 60 and 140 percent, a level much too high to be sustained by rural communities. Moreover, out-migration from many rural communities by Anglos continued in the late twentieth century. Consequently, the new meat-processing plants turned to outsiders, especially Hispanics, to fill their ranks.[37]

The method of recruitment of Hispanic workers varied. Many meat-processing companies advertised their positions in the national network used by state employment agencies. The companies also advertised jobs in local newspapers in areas where large numbers of Hispanics resided, such as Laredo, Texas. Applications provided to these prospective employees were in Spanish. However, once some Hispanics secured jobs at a particular meat-processing facility, chain migration became the norm as family and friends followed. Companies were often generous in allowing workers time off around holidays to return to southern Texas or Mexico, from which they sometimes returned with new recruits for the factories. In short order, Hispanics became the fastest-growing population to be hired by the meat-processing companies. In 1980, 74 percent of meat-processing industry employees in the Midwest were Anglos; by 2000 that number dropped to less than 50 percent. Conversely, Hispanic meat-processing workers leaped from about 10 percent to over 30 percent of the workforce during the same period. Indeed, in some meat-processing facilities in the region, Hispanics formed over 50 percent of the employees.[38]

A significant Hispanic population developed in the states where the new-style meat processers located. According to the 1970 U.S. census, Nebraska had 7,177 Hispanics, but by 1990 that figure jumped to 36,969, an increase of over 400 percent. In the 2000 census, that number had more than doubled again to over 77,000 Hispanics. Iowa, Kansas, and Minnesota also posted huge percentage gains in Hispanics during the last decade of the twentieth century. Iowa's Hispanic population increased from about 32,500 in 1990 to over 82,000 in 2000; Kansas climbed from over 93,000 to over 188,000; Minnesota leaped from about 54,000 to over 143,000 Hispanics. While the Midwest was still the home of the least number of Hispanics/Latinos on a percentage basis throughout the United States in 2000 (about 8 percent of the total population in the region), it was the second-fastest-growing region (the South was first) in the number of Hispanics. The population of Hispanics in the 12 midwestern states climbed almost 70 percent in the last decade of the twentieth century.[39]

The statistics testify further to their growing presence in rural Midwest communities. Between 1990 and 2000 Urbandale, Iowa, saw a jump of more than 156 percent in Hispanic residents; Overland Park, Kansas, the number of Hispanics grew by 155 percent; Grand Island, Nebraska, had an increase of 262 percent in the number of Hispanics. Sometimes the number of Hispanics was magnified further by the continued out-migration by Anglos from the region's rural areas. Emporia, Kansas, had an increase in Hispanics of 66 percent, but a decline in Anglos of 7.5 percent. Similar patterns occurred in Mason City, Iowa, Leavenworth, Kansas, and Grand Forks, North Dakota. The net result was growing islands, or enclaves, of Hispanic concentration in communities throughout the rural Midwest.[40]

Of course, not all of the growth in rural areas of the Midwest was brought about just by the meat-processing job opportunities. Hispanics found work in many other sectors, too, although most often these were low-paying jobs requiring little education. Education or the lack thereof remained a problem for the Hispanic population. According to U.S. Census Bureau statistics for 2000, in the rural Midwest 55 percent of the Latinos did not have a high school education. Therefore, in the other sectors where large numbers of Hispanics found employment in the rural Midwest—construction, light industry, service—they were most likely to be cleaners, helpers, and common laborers. The income of a Hispanic in the Midwest working a full-time job (at least 40 hours per week) averaged $19,650 a year in 2000. If both members of a couple worked, they would earn less than $40,000, so depending on the number of children present this might sustain a lower-middle-class status.[41]

Long-time Anglo residents in the rural communities of the Midwest did not readily accept the influx of Hispanics. Anglos often assumed that Hispanics were in the country illegally, prone to violence and domestic disorder, and most often receiving excessive social services. In some instances, there were justifications for Anglo angst. Local communities often did not plan well for the large number of newcomers, Hispanics or others, and hence local schools often became overcrowded and did not have enough teachers. In Lexington, Nebraska, public school enrollment rose from 1,670 students in 1988 to 2,166 five years later, an increase of more than 25 percent. Special programs in education were also swamped. In 1987, the Storm Lake, Iowa, public schools had 27 students with limited English proficiency (LEP). Within five years that number surged to 236 LEP students. School districts simply could not add classrooms and qualified teachers that rapidly. The same lack of planning negatively influenced social service agencies and medical facilities. Hospitals and clinics in particular were overextended because meat-processing facilities rarely offered much in the way of health insurance, and large numbers of workers with injuries and other health-related problems associated with that industry had nowhere else to turn.[42]

While evidence suggests that segregation of Hispanics in larger midwestern cities was declining, the new rural population continued to confront segregation. In Nebraska's largest cities—Omaha and Lincoln—there were clear signs that Hispanics were spreading out into various neighborhoods in these urban communities. Segregation occurred, especially among the poorest Hispanics, but Lincoln and Omaha were less segregated than before the 1980s. In one well-studied rural community—Lexington, Nebraska—the trend was not, however, so positive. In 1990, Lexington had a population of 6,600 of whom only 329 were identified as Latino (less than 5 percent). IBP opened a meat-processing facility shortly thereafter and, by 2000, over 50 percent of its workers were Hispanics. The U.S. census that year found that Lexington's population was over 10,000; incredibly, 5,100 were Latinos, representing the majority of the town's population.[43]

Obviously, rapid growth taxed the city's infrastructure, especially in housing. With rural property values relatively low and rentals scarce, Hispanics quickly purchased available houses. Most of them bought prefabricated and mobile dwellings. Thus, in 2000, over 50 percent of Lexington's Hispanics were classified as "homeowners." Considering the small size of the community, according to the 2000 census "tracts" in Lexington, the town was completely integrated. However, it was clear that numerous Anglo families had abandoned the town proper for rural developments or "acreages" nearby. One development on Johnson Lake, a few miles out of town, had about 70 new homes built late in the 1990s. These properties were more expensive, and therefore out of the price range for the Hispanics working at IBP. Of the 2,100 people residing at Johnson Lake in 2000, 98 percent were Anglos. What was beginning to occur in Lexington looked like the "white flight" phenomenon associated with large urban areas in the 1960s and 1970s. If so, Lexington will become an island of Hispanics in the middle of rural Nebraska. The evidence was inconclusive, however, as to whether white flight and de facto segregation might become more the norm in the rural Midwest.[44]

It was also unclear if the rural Hispanic population was becoming any more assimilated at the end of the twentieth century. The existence of white flight in the rural Midwest suggests the answer was negative. In addition, the inability to improve educational achievement significantly and move up in economic class retarded Hispanic assimilation. Catholic and Protestant Hispanics in rural communities overwhelmingly attended Spanish-speaking religious services, further promoting a segregated environment. That local Anglos questioned the presence of Hispanics in public areas and at traditional events such as county fairs or Fourth of July celebrations enhanced Hispanic isolation. On the other hand, more rural Hispanics spoke English and some Hispanic traditions, such as celebrating Mexican independence, appeared to wane in these small midwestern communities. Most likely, assimilation will only occur very slowly.[45]

The Hispanic population in the rural Midwest has changed enormously since World War II. When that conflict ended, concentrations of Hispanics resided in the region's metropolitan centers, but few were found in the smaller communities. Most often Hispanics in the rural areas came there only for short periods as migratory farmworkers. To be sure, they were crucial to the region's agricultural sector, but opportunities to leave the migrant stream were few. This trend continued through the 1950s, although a few more settled there permanently beginning in the 1960s, primarily because of Great Society program opportunities. The real change, however, occurred in the last decades of the twentieth century as the meat-processing industry pulled Hispanics into rural communities in vast numbers, while deteriorating economic and social conditions in Mexico and the U.S. Southwest pushed them to move to the Midwest. As of 2000, this process was still evolving. Since the start of the new century, however, the climate has changed somewhat with the virulent reaction to undocumented Hispanics by Anglos and the severe slump in the U.S. economy.

Notes

1. For an early Spanish appearance in the region, see John L. Kessell, *Spain in the Southwest* (Norman: University of Oklahoma Press, 2002), 41–47 and 310–14; the characterization of Mexican immigrants is from Juan R. García, *Mexicans in the Midwest, 1900–1932* (Tucson: University of Arizona Press, 1996), 5.

2. A thorough account of these railroad workers is García's *Mexicans in the Midwest*, 3–48. Also see Roger P. Davis, "Latinos along the Platte: The Hispanic Experience in Central Nebraska," *Great Plains Research* (Spring 2001): 31–32.

3. A comprehensive account of these industrial workers is Zaragosa Vargas, *Proletarians of the North: A History of Mexican Industrial Workers in Detroit and the Midwest, 1917–1933* (Berkeley and Los Angeles: University of California Press, 1993).

4. For Mexican migrant sugar beet workers in the early 1900s, see Kathleen Mapes, *Sweet Tyranny: Migrant Labor, Industrial Agriculture, and Imperial Politics* (Urbana: University of Illinois Press, 2009); Dennis Nodín Valdés, *Al Norte: Agricultural Workers in the Great Lakes Region, 1917–1970* (Austin: University of Texas Press, 1991).

5. García, *Mexicans in the Midwest*, 141–54.

6. Jim Norris, *North for the Harvest: Mexican Workers, Growers, and the Sugar Beet Industry* (St. Paul: Minnesota Historical Society Press, 2009), 39–45; Dennis Nodín Valdés, *Barrios Norteños: St. Paul and Midwestern Mexican Communities in the Twentieth Century* (Austin: University of Texas Press, 2000), 87–100. A comprehensive history of the Depression-era repatriation is Francisco E. Balderrama and Raymond Rodríguez, *Decade of Betrayal: Mexican Repatriation in the 1930s* (Albuquerque: University of New Mexico Press, 1995).

7. Valdés, *Al Norte*, 51–73; Norris, *North for the Harvest*, 48–51; Mae M. Ngai, *Impossible Subjects: Illegal Aliens and the Making of Modern America* (Princeton, NJ: Princeton University Press, 2004), 54–55.

8. Valdés, *Al Norte*, 97–99; Norris, *North for the Harvest*, 61–70.

9. Valdés, *Al Norte*, 93–95, 100–106; Valdés, *Barrios Norteños*, 131–47. For the braceros employed on railroads, see Barbara Driscoll de Alvarado, *The Tracks North: The Railroad Bracero Program of World War II* (Austin, TX: CMAS Books, 1999).

10. Valdés, *Al Norte*, 109–11; Norris, *North for the Harvest*, 65–68.

11. Valdés, *Al Norte*, 135–38.

12. Norris, *North for the Harvest*, 69–70 and 103–5; Terry L. Shoptaugh, *Roots of Success: History of the Red River Valley Sugarbeet Growers* (Fargo: North Dakota Institute for Regional Studies, 1997), 83–85 and 94–95.

13. Norris, *North for the Harvest*, 81–84; Valdés, *Al Norte*, 141–42.

14. Peter N. Kirstein, "Agribusiness, Labor, and the Wetbacks," *The Historian* (1978): 651–62.

15. Norris, *North for the Harvest*, 88–95; George O. Coalson, *The Development of the Migratory Farm Labor System in Texas, 1900-1954* (San Francisco: R and E Research Associates, 1977), 78–82.

16. Ngai, *Impossible Subjects*, 155–56; Valdés, *Barrios Norteños*, 162–63.

17. Norris, *North for the Harvest*, 122–23.

18. Rob Paral, "Mexican Immigration in the Midwest: Meaning and Implication," *Heartland Papers* (Chicago: Chicago Council on Global Affairs, 2009), 13–16; Valdés, *Barrios Norteños*, 130–42.

19. Valdés, *Barrios Norteños*, 134–41.

20. Valdés, *Barrios Norteños,*, 137–41; Janet Weaver, "From Barrio to 'ÂiBoicoteo!':The Emergence of Mexican American Activism in Davenport, 1917-1970," *Annals of Iowa* (Summer 2009): 224–29; Norris, *North for the Harvest*, 125–26.

21. Valdés, *Barrios Norteños*, 158–66; Mary Lyons-Barrett, "Chicanos in Nebraska, 1940s through the 1970s," *Journal of the West* (Spring 2004): 78–79.

22. Norris, *North for the Harvest*, 127–29; Valdés, *Al Norte*, 155.

23. Norris, *North for the Harvest*, 121–22; Valdés, *Al Norte*, 155–56.

24. Norris, *North for the Harvest*, 148–49, 153–54; Ngai, *Impossible Subjects*, 258–65.

25. John Staples Shockley, *Chicano Revolt in a Texas Town* (Notre Dame, IN: University of Notre Dame Press, 1974), 19–41; David Montejano, *Anglos and Mexicans in the Making of Texas, 1836-1986* (Austin: University of Texas Press, 1992 [1987]), 282–84.

26. Roger P. Davis, "Service Not Power: The Early Years of the Nebraska Commission on Mexican Americans, 1971-75," *Nebraska History* (Summer 2008): 68–69; Lyons-Barrett, "Chicanos in Nebraska," 79–80; Weaver, "From 'Barrio to ÂiBoicoteo!'" 239–49; Valdés, *Barrios Norteños*, 184–87.

27. Marc Simon Rodriguez, "A Movement Made of 'Young Mexican Americans Seeking Change': Critical Citizenship, Migration, and the Chicano Movement in Texas and Wisconsin, 1960-1975," *Western Historical Quarterly* (Autumn 2003): 275–90; W.K. Barger and Ernesto M. Reza, *The Farm Labor Movement in the Midwest: Social Change and Adaptation among Migrant Farmworkers* (Austin: University of Texas Press, 1994), 52–60; Norris, *North for the Harvest*, 156, 179.

28. Valdés, *Barrios Norteños*, 190–99; Norris, *North for the Harvest*, 157–59; Davis, "Service Not Power," 74–75.

29. Valdés, *Al Norte*, 174–75; Norris, *North for the Harvest*, 158, 174–75.

30. Valdés, *Barrios Norteños*, 199–210; Lyons-Barrett, "Chicanos in Nebraska," 82–83.

31. Valdés, *Barrios Norteños*, 202; Lyons-Barrett, "Chicanos in Nebraska," 83–84; Davis, "Service Not Power," 77–79.

32. For Hispanics in the meatpacking industry after WWII, see Valdés, *Barrios Norteños*, 142–50. For a good overview of the midwestern meatpacking industry itself after WWII, see Deborah Fink, *Cutting into the Meatpacking Line: Workers and Change in the Rural Midwest* (Chapel Hill: University of North Carolina Press, 1998), 40–62.

33. Several studies cover these developments for the meatpacking industry, includ-

ing Fink, *Cutting into the Meatpacking Line*, 56–71; William Kandell and Emilio A. Parreda, "Restructuring the US Meat Processing Industry and New Hispanic Migrant Destinations," *Population and Development Review* (September 2005): 452–55; Lourdes Gouveia, "Global Forces and Latino Population Growth in the Midwest," *Great Plains Research* (Fall 2000): 308–9.

34. Fink, *Cutting into the Meatpacking Line*, 56–71; Kandell and Parreda, "Restructuring of the US Meat Processing Industry," 452–60; Roger P. Davis, "Latinos along the Platte: The Hispanic Experience in Central Nebraska," *Great Plains Research* (Spring 2001): 41–42.

35. Michael C. Meyer, William L. Sherman, and Susan M. Deeds, *The Course of Mexican History* (9th edition) (New York: Oxford University Press, 2011), 498, 545–46; David E. Lorey, *The U.S.–Mexican Border in the Twentieth Century: A History of Economic and Social Transformation* (Wilmington, DE: Scholarly Resources Books, 1999), 93–137; Jorge I. Domínguez and Rafael Fernández de Castro, *The United States and Mexico: Between Partnership and Conflict* (2nd edition) (New York: Routledge, 2009), 148–54.

36. Davis, "Latinos along the Platte," 43; Gouveia, "Global Forces and Latino Population Growth," 312–13; Lionel Cantu, "The Peripheralization of Rural America: A Case Study of Latino Migrants in America's Heartland," *Sociological Perspectives* (Autumn 1995): 399, 405–7.

37. Kandell and Parreda, "Restructuring the US Meat Processing Industry," 457–58.

38. Cantu, "The Peripheralization of Rural America," 405–7; Kandell and Parreda, "Restructuring the US Meat Processing Industry," 458–60.

39. Davis, "Latinos along the Platte," 43; Gouveia, "Global Forces and Latino Population Growth," 313–14.

40. Evelyn Ravuri, "Changes in Asian and Hispanic Population in the Cities of the Great Plains, 1990–2000," *Great Plains Research* (Spring 2003): 75–92; Ann V. Millard and Jorge Chapa, *Apple Pie and Enchiladas: Latino Newcomers in the Rural Midwest* (Austin: University of Texas Press, 2004), 58–62.

41. Millard and Chapa, *Apple Pie and Enchiladas*, 70–72; Rosalie Torres Stone and Bandana Purkayastha, "Predictors of Earnings for Mexican Americans in the Midwest," *Great Plains Research* (Spring 2005): 101–13.

42. Valdés, *Barrios Norteños*, 261–63; Millard and Chapa, *Apple Pie and Enchiladas*, 104–22; Lourdes Gouveia and Donald D. Stull, "Dances with Cows: Beefpacking's Impact on Garden City, Kansas, and Lexington, Nebraska," in *Any Way You Cut It: Meat Processing and Small-Town America*, ed. Donald Stull, Michael Broadway, and David Griffith (Lawrence: University Press of Kansas, 1995), 96–97; Mark A. Grey, "Pork, Poultry, and Newcomers in Storm Lake, Iowa," in *Any Way You Cut It*, 118–19.

43. Ana-María Gonzalez-Wahl, Steven E. Gunkel, and Bennie Shobe Jr., "Becoming Neighbors or Remaining Strangers? Latinos and Residential Segregation in the Heartland," *Great Plains Research* (Fall 2005): 303–5, 308–16.

44. Gonzalez-Wahl et al., "Becoming Neighbors or Remaining Strangers?" 316–21.

45. Millard and Chapa, *Apple Pie and Enchiladas*, 177–85, 193–200; Valdés, *Barrios Norteños*, 265–70.

TEN — INTERNAL ALTERNATE

The Midwestern Amish since 1945

Steven D. Reschly

A handwritten sign in a shop window in downtown Chicago boasts "Amish Chickens," suggesting timeless family comfort amid the urban chaos. The explosion of Amish products such as Amish furniture, Amish cheese, Amish friendship bread, and Amish bacon creates the illusion of a brand identity in urban and suburban marketplaces. The descriptive term "Amish" conjures notions of authentic products and experiences. Far from this quaint presentation, however, the Old Order Amish are a highly successful collection of communities in the midwestern region of the United States. In contrast to the homegrown aura of quaint and simple lives, they demonstrate an alternative mode of rural life that makes selective use of technology while retaining small and intensive religious communities. They created this alternate culture in the Midwest during the second half of the twentieth century. In the early twenty-first century, they are visually, socially, and linguistically distinctive while also being fully integrated into the region and significant to the regional economy.[1]

Amish settlements have formed in almost every state and every Canadian province from the eighteenth century to the present. In 2013, settlements existed in 11 of the 12 states under study in this volume, the exception being North Dakota.[2] These 11 states hosted about 63 percent of the total Amish population in North America (see table 10.1). Amish migrants followed the movement of the frontier westward during the nineteenth century, albeit within a limited range of latitudes, from Pennsylvania into Ohio, Indiana, Illinois, Iowa, and Nebraska. The first Amish settlers entered Ohio in 1808; Holmes County in east central Ohio houses the oldest and largest Amish community in the Midwest.

Population growth, migration, and diversity are three central themes in Amish history. The growth rate of the Amish population is remarkable. In 1900, there were only about 5,000 Amish people in the United States and Canada. A century later, the estimated figure was 198,000, and in 2013, nearly 280,000.[3] The Amish birthrate is higher than the birthrate in the general population, although within the Amish, farm families tend to have more children than Amish families in which the household head works for wages. The birthrate is lower, as well, when Amish women operate businesses. Examples of Amish families who have lower birthrates include the Amish of eastern Illinois, many of whom work in woodworking and cabinet factories, and the Amish of northern Indiana, the "lunch pail Amish," who work in the mobile home and recreational vehicle manufacturing industries.[4] Amish population growth, land prices, and family migration all contribute to patterns of Amish settlement in the Midwest.

In 2013, there were 469 Amish communities located in 30 states and the Canadian province of Ontario, all resulting from a few individuals and families who decided to move and then invited others to join them. The pace of founding new settlements, with initial growth through chain migration as extended family members and acquaintances from home communities join new settlements, has increased dramatically, particularly in the upper Midwest, since 1990. The Amish do not colonize, as opposed to historic communitarian societies such as the Hutterites, but migrate in a trial-and-error fashion. Amish individuals and families have settled in almost every U.S. state and Canadian province as well as Honduras, Belize, and Paraguay. Traditionally, as reflected in collected Amish writings and oral tradition, Amish "scouts" have always sought suitable land for purchase and settlement. This is intentional exploration, not recreational travel. Every community has its own origin story. The first settlers in Indiana, for example, resulted from an 1840 scouting trip undertaken by four men from Somerset County, Pennsylvania. Preacher Joseph Miller, Daniel Miller, John Smyly, and John Shrock traveled the Ohio and Mississippi Rivers to explore land in Illinois and Iowa before deciding, instead, on Elkhart County, Indiana.[5]

The tradition of scouting for land continues. In summer 2010, a vanload of Amish land scouts from Prattsburg, New York, visited Alaska but failed to find suitable land. Another group, from communities in both Illinois and Missouri, traveled to Mexico on a similar mission.[6] Despite consisting

TABLE 10.1—Amish Population by State and Province, 2010

RANKED BY ESTIMATED POPULATION

State/Province	# of Settlements	# of Church Districts	Est. Population
Ohio	55	485	65,475
Pennsylvania	52	441	65,270
Indiana	23	348	49,070
Wisconsin	45	126	16,130
New York	49	118	15,930
Michigan	39	98	12,935
Missouri	41	92	10,765
Kentucky	35	75	9,375
Iowa	23	59	8,320
Illinois	18	50	7,000
Ontario	14	35	4,725
Minnesota	21	33	4,160
Tennessee	6	17	2,125
Kansas	7	13	1,755
Delaware	1	10	1,500
Maryland	3	11	1,485
Virginia	5	7	945
Nebraska	5	6	810
Oklahoma	3	6	810
Colorado	3	5	675
Maine	5	5	675
Montana	4	4	540
West Virginia	3	3	405
Arkansas	2	2	270
Florida	1	1	75
Idaho	1	1	75
Mississippi	1	1	75
North Carolina	1	1	75
South Dakota	1	1	75
Texas	1	1	75
Wyoming	1	1	75
Total:	469	2,056	281,675

Source: Young Center for Anabaptist and Pietist Studies, Elizabethtown College, Elizabethtown, Pennsylvania <http://www2.etown.edu/amishstudies/Population_by_State_2010.asp>.

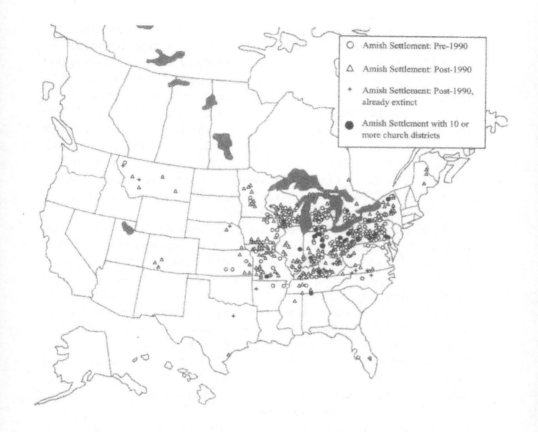

O	Amish Settlement: Pre-1990
△	Amish Settlement: Post-1990
+	Amish Settlement: Post-1990, already extinct
●	Amish Settlement with 10 or more church districts

Figure 10.1: Location of Amish settlements pre- and post-1990. The Amish have actively sought out new locations for settlements, most extensively in the Midwest. Source: Originally published in Joseph F. Donnermeyer and Elizabeth C. Cooksey, "On the Recent Growth in Amish Settlements," *Mennonite Quarterly Review* 84 (April 2010): 193. Used with permission.

of "scouts," these excursions are not secretive or covert. Historically and currently the main Amish newspapers, *The Budget* and *Die Botschaft*, are full of scouting reports and news about new settlements. Such reports indicate that Amish scouts find inexpensive land in rural areas experiencing depopulation under the onslaught of farm mechanization and the deindustrialization of small towns.[7] New settlements tend to cluster near established communities in states that already have Amish populations. This settlement wanderlust shows the Amish to be mobile and dynamic, in contrast to their static and timeless image in popular culture. Between 1990 and 2009, 171 new settlements were founded in midwestern states, while 17 settlements went extinct. Ohio (34), Wisconsin (33), and Missouri (29) saw the most new communities. Multiple new settlements appeared in southern Wisconsin, southern Iowa, and northern Missouri, and both sides of the Ohio River (see map). There are none in east central Illinois or north central Iowa, where the land is too flat for horse farming to compete with tractors. Eastern and northern Illinois are also too close to the urban sprawl of Chicago for land to be affordable and suitable. There are very few settlements west of the 98th meridian, the traditional eastern boundary of the Great Plains of North America. Similarly, there are few settlements in the South or the far West, or in New England. Midwestern states, along with Pennsylvania, New York, and Kentucky, thus host almost all the Amish population in North America.[8]

The Hutterites, also descended from the sixteenth-century Anabaptist movement, offer an illuminating contrast to Amish settlement models. Hutterite colonies are found almost exclusively in the Great Plains and intermountain regions of North America. In the American Midwest, Hutterites dwell in Minnesota, North Dakota, and South Dakota, overlapping with the northwestern extent of Amish settlement. Hutterites are communitarian and live in small villages or colonies of about 150 people, which is approximately the size of an Amish church district, but the two styles of social organization are quite different. Each Hutterite colony owns land and buildings in common, colony residents eat most meals together, and individuals own little private property. Farming and manufacturing operations are conducted with modern equipment and technology, although there are limits placed on media technology, with variations among the four Hutterite affiliations. Hutterites maintain a primary community by living in small villages while farming large tracts of land with large-scale technology, often specializing in one crop or one industry. By contrast, the Amish keep technology at a smaller scale in order to keep their separate family households closer together spatially and thus to preserve community. Amish farms tend to be more diversified with lower overhead costs, and Amish businesses are usually small and family-owned. Hutterite colonies are more self-sufficient, while Amish communities rely more on surrounding populations for markets and supplies. Hutterite colonies could not take advantage of the relative isolation of the Great Plains in the areas where the Amish population is concentrated, and Amish communities have not done well historically in regions where large farms, cash crops, extreme climates, and heavy machinery are the rule.[9]

In addition to being dynamic, not static, the Amish are quite diverse, not uniform, resulting from many schisms and a strictly congregational polity. Although Amish leaders consult one another with varying degrees of formality, each local church district sets its own *Ordnung* (lifestyle regulations) and ordains its own leaders. The extent of Amish diversity contrasts surprisingly with the outside observer's first visual impression of sameness, ranging from the very conservative lifestyle of the Swartzentruber and Nebraska Amish (the latter in Mifflin County, Pennsylvania) to "New Order" Amish, who are no longer considered part of the mainstream Old Order Amish. There are no fewer than 11 Amish "affiliations" (groups of church districts that recognize one another's Ordnung and ordained leaders) in Holmes County, Ohio, counting three "New Order" groups.[10] In fact, established Amish communities tend to develop several affiliations. There is also diversity among settlements, such as the Swiss Amish of eastern Indiana, around Fort Wayne, who speak a different German dialect and retain different cultural traditions in comparison to most other Amish communities.[11]

Another characteristic of established settlements, in contrast to newer settlements, is the presence of mediating offshoot groups who are more willing to explain themselves and their Amish neighbors to local media and government officials. Far from being insulated and isolated, Amish people form relationships with Old Order Mennonites and mainstream Mennonites, and there are often family ties with Beachy Amish, Conservative Mennonites, and other groups that originated in Amish settlements. Furthermore, while documentaries sensationalize the practice of *Rumspringa* by suggesting that Amish youth are abandoning their lifestyle in droves, the Amish retain a high percentage of their children. Recent estimates range from 85 percent to 94 percent. Even when a young adult leaves the group, he or she usually joins a similar group that is slightly higher on the Anabaptist ladder, to use Karl Baehr's 1942 terminology. This ladder, or escalator, includes more conservative choices as well. This range of identities stabilizes a core of Amish identity by clarifying limits that the mainstream Old Order Amish retain.[12]

The Swartzentruber Amish developed between 1913 and 1920 in Holmes County, Ohio, and now dwell in 15 states. The first breakaway bishop was Samuel E. Yoder, leading 107 families from two local church districts whose members desired a more conservative Ordnung. The long and painful process of an Amish church schism is poorly recorded (in contrast to the Protestant tradition of apology and explanation), reflecting a reluctance to admit and analyze conflict.[13] After Yoder died in 1932, he was succeeded by Samuel Swartzentruber. The bishop in the other district at the time was also named Swartzentruber, and the dissenting group eventually became known as Swartzentruber Amish. The visual manifestation of the Swartzentruber Amish is their typical use of reflective tape in place of government-mandated bright orange Slow Moving Vehicle triangles on the backs of their buggies. They avoid many small concessions to technological developments made by mainstream Old Order Amish groups, such as bicycles, indoor plumbing, Velcro, and manicured lawns. Swartzentruber men often wear one suspender to avoid the pride of two. In accord with older traditions, men are allowed to smoke cigars and pipes, and courting couples in some Swartzentruber districts practice "bundling" or bed courtship, the practice that has frequently captured and titillated the popular imagination.[14]

On the side of accepting more rapid change, the New Order Amish began in 1966 in Lancaster County, Pennsylvania. Almost every established Amish community has a New Order element composed of families who seek revitalization within Amish faith and tradition. New Order Amish do not allow cars, in accordance with Amish identity, but do allow telephones inside their homes and more colorful clothing, as seemingly minor concessions to the reality of change. They are more intentional and self-conscious about expressing faith and religious practice and are more comfortable with some Evangelical concepts, such as New Birth, revival meetings, and the vocalized assurance of salvation. New Order Amish make up about 3 percent of the total Amish population and are usually counted in Amish population figures, since they remain a horse-and-buggy group. Most live in Holmes County, Ohio, though there are New Order Amish communities in at least 12 states.[15]

Further up the ladder of Amish identity (the Amish themselves use "high" and "low" to describe the range of Ordnung distinctions), the Beachy Amish date to 1927 in Somerset County, Pennsylvania. In striving for a balance between the unquestionable tradition of the Old Order and conscious change, Beachy Amish leaders and members made collective decisions to permit limited change without going the way of individualized, unrestricted transformation.[16] Led by Bishop Moses M. Beachy, several families formed a new group in order to advocate a less strict form of church discipline, particularly ending the practice of shunning, or social avoidance, of former members who left the district to join a more liberal Amish or Mennonite group. Beachy Amish own cars, build meetinghouses, and conduct Sunday Schools. There are long-standing Beachy Amish communities in Indiana, Ohio, Pennsylvania, Illinois, Iowa, Missouri, Kansas, and due to missionary efforts, in several foreign countries. They sponsor Calvary Bible School for adults in Calico Rock, Arkansas, which is a clear departure from Old Order resistance to formal education past the eighth grade.[17]

Amish diversity makes it nearly impossible to generalize. "All Amish do/practice/believe..." seldom begins a viable assertion. Members of various

Amish affiliations in any given settlement appear to be comfortable with sorting out who belongs where. This is less true of government officials and policy makers, who seem perpetually puzzled when one church district disallows what another district permits. Amish members have run afoul of local, state, and national governments in education, conscription and warfare, Social Security, and a variety of local law enforcement matters.

The relationship of the church to civil society and civil government is one of the core issues for all groups descended from the sixteenth-century Anabaptist movement. The Amish are no exception despite their desire to live quietly and peaceably. The Amish, in general, cooperate willingly with civil law when it does not conflict with their faith and religious practices. When it does conflict, this cooperation can vanish, to the confusion of authorities.[18]

Public education has been a point of contention between governments and Amish communities. Amish parents sent their children to public schools when those schools were local and rural. Rural school consolidation and state legislatures' raising of the age of compulsory education in the early twentieth century led to Amish resistance. The most famous incident occurred in November 1965 in Buchanan County, Iowa, when Amish schoolboys ran into a cornfield to escape forced busing to a consolidated school. Amish parents had found themselves in conflict with local school officials for several years, and Amish schools with Amish teachers opened in 1962. The Amish children were considered truants, and their parents paid fines or refused to pay and spent three days in jail. Repeated attempts at compromise failed, as did requests for exemption from state teacher certification requirements. Following the dramatic culmination of the conflict in the forced busing attempt, Governor Harold Hughes intervened by issuing a moratorium on further actions against Amish children, and he ordered the state attorney general to seek a solution. Eventually, in 1967, the state legislature passed an exemption that allowed Amish schools to exist without further interference from public school officials. Similar compromises had been reached in Pennsylvania and Indiana, where Amish children attended Amish-run vocational schools between completing eighth grade and reaching age 16.[19]

Church-state conflicts seem monolithic on the surface, but Amish diversity means that individuals may respond differently to legal entanglements. Before the Iowa resolution occurred, Adin Yutzy sold his farm in Buchanan County, Iowa, early in 1966 and moved to Green County, Wisconsin, "to get away from all the trouble." Ironically, only two years later, in November 1968, Yutzy and two other Amish fathers near New Glarus, Jonas Yoder and Wallace Miller, were arrested for failing to enroll their three children in high school. They were tried and convicted in March 1969 in Green County

Court and fined five dollars each. By then, Yutzy had moved once again to seek relief from compulsory education laws, this time to southern Missouri. The Wisconsin circuit court also ruled against the parents, but the Wisconsin Supreme Court reversed and ruled in favor of the Amish on January 8, 1971 (*State v. Yoder*, 49 Wis. 2d 430). Chief Justice E. Harold Hallows wrote the majority opinion and argued that Amish children "would experience a useless anguish of living in two worlds." The state supreme court ruled that the First Amendment, made applicable to the states by the Fourteenth Amendment, prevented Wisconsin from compelling Amish parents to enroll their children in public high school.[20]

The state of Wisconsin decided to appeal its case to the U.S. Supreme Court. Funded by the National Committee for Amish Religious Freedom, which was organized by Lutheran pastor William C. Lindholm in Michigan in 1966, attorney William Ball of Harrisburg, Pennsylvania, represented the Amish from Green County to Washington, D.C. Oral argument in *Wisconsin v. Yoder*, 406 U.S. 205, took place on December 8, 1971, attended by bearded Amish leaders. Briefs of amici curiae urging affirmation of the Wisconsin Supreme Court opinion were submitted by such diverse groups as the Mennonite Central Committee, the Seventh-Day Adventists, the National Council of Churches, the National Jewish Commission on Law and Public Affairs, and the Synagogue Council of America. In a 7–0 vote, delivered by Chief Justice Warren Burger on May 15, 1972 (Justices Lewis Powell and William Rehnquist took no part in the case), the Supreme Court affirmed the Wisconsin decision that freed the Amish from compulsory high school attendance. Burger wrote, "There can be no assumption that today's majority is right and the Amish are wrong. A way of life that is odd or even erratic but interferes with no rights or interests of others is not to be condemned because it is different."[21]

Not until 1972 were Amish communities free to develop a comprehensive system of one-room schools, with parents serving on school boards. The first Amish parochial school, near Dover, Delaware, dates to 1925. The number of schools steadily expanded despite sporadic confrontations with local and state officials, and *Wisconsin v. Yoder* opened the school doors wide. Amish publishers in Pennsylvania, Ontario, Ohio, and Indiana printed increasing amounts of educational materials for use in the schools. Amish schools reflect and shape Old Order values, but each community seeks different ways to sustain and enhance its own distinctiveness. Driving through an Amish neighborhood in the Midwest without seeing a schoolhouse is unimaginable.[22]

The dramatic conflicts over education seem relatively benign compared to Amish problems with conscription. The Amish are conscientious objectors to military service. After intense pressure to join military forces during World War I and some incidents of violent punishment for refusing, Amish leaders joined other Historic Peace Churches representatives (Mennonite, Brethren, Quakers) to set up Civilian Public Service (CPS) programs in the 1930s as war appeared increasingly likely. They inserted language in the Selective Training and Service Act of 1940 to allow conscientious objectors to perform "work of national importance under civilian direction." For the most part, young Amish men of draft age served in rural areas, such as reforestation programs in Civilian Conservation Corps camps.[23]

During the Korean War, 1-W alternative service began in 1952, named for the classification used by Selective Service for conscientious objectors. Most 1-W work took place in urban hospitals, leading to wider experiences and acquaintances for Amish young men. Amish leaders worried about the impact of the urban environment on the decisions of 1-W men about becoming baptized members of the Amish faith. Vernon Bontrager worked at the general hospital in Indianapolis from 1963 to 1965. He lived in an apartment with five other Amish men and enjoyed working with dozens of co-religionists in maintenance and other duties, as well as sharing his peace convictions with hospital employees and patients.[24] This degree of self-consciousness concerning one's faith, along with attention to "witnessing" to non-Amish, is dangerous to Amish sensibilities. Only about half of those assigned to hospital work returned home. As a result, Amish leaders in 1966 met in Allen County, Indiana, and formed the Old Order Amish Steering Committee, the first permanent extra-congregational bureaucratic structure in Amish history. As the Vietnam War escalated, it seemed necessary to speak with a unified voice to the federal government, that is, to communicate in order to preserve a community that prized its sense of separation from the "English" outside world. The Steering Committee arranged for deferments to farms leased by the Committee, a suggestion made by Director of Selective Service General Lewis B. Hershey (who had Mennonite ancestors), to bypass the local denial of general farm deferments. A few Amish men refused to cooperate with these arrangements with the military and served prison terms, but in general, the Farm Plan worked well. The Amish successfully separated national citizenship from military service, as characterized by the modern nation-state since the eighteenth century.[25]

Andrew Kinsinger from Lancaster County, Pennsylvania, served as longtime chair of the Old Order Amish Steering Committee. The Committee was composed of nonordained Amish men, with state directors as communicators between the centralized Committee and local committees. Ordained leaders advised but generally stayed away from the minimalist bureaucracy. Kinsinger developed a congenial relationship with General Hershey. After Hershey was replaced as director of Selective Service by President Nixon in 1970, he continued to meet periodically with Kinsinger. After American involvement in the Vietnam War ended in 1973 and after Hershey retired that same year, he signed a certificate of appreciation to Kinsinger and arranged for it to be delivered personally by an envoy from Selective Service. For the first time since the Amish originated in the 1690s in Switzerland and Alsace, Amish representatives spoke to a government on behalf of almost all Amish members. The Committee gradually expanded its scope beyond military service to a variety of issues as the federal government continued to enlarge its bureaucratic and regulatory structures during the second half of the twentieth century.[26]

The Amish innovated to protect tradition; they engaged the federal government to protect their isolation; they created a central agency to preserve local autonomy. The danger of ethnic political activism to preserve tradition is that it usually results in assimilation. As anthropologist Marshall Sahlins observed in his study of Captain Cook's encounter with Hawaiians, every conscious attempt to prevent change or even to adapt to it brought other changes in its wake.[27] Indeed, the Steering Committee formalized its role in 1971 with standard procedures for choosing and replacing committee members and state directors and by claiming legitimate authority as "the voice of the Old Order Amish churches combined." The Committee arranged an exemption in 1972 from wearing hard hats or other safety headgear, which would replace traditional black felt hats and summer straw hats, after the Occupational Safety and Health Act (OSHA) passed a regulation requiring such gear in 1970. Also in 1972, the Committee instituted an agreement with the State Department to exempt Amish people from submitting photographic likenesses when emigrating from Canada to the United States. Other issues addressed by the Committee included milk cooling laws, education conflicts, Social Security (even though an exemption was granted in 1965 for self-employed Amish and strengthened in 1988, new Amish church members must submit Form 4029 to the Social Security Administration), Individual Retirement Accounts, Soil Conservation Service programs, Workers' Compensation, Federal Housing Administration loans, and many more. The paradox of acting to preserve detachment is playing out in Amish communities throughout the United States and Ontario.[28]

The diversity of the Amish meant that not all Amish communities recognized the Steering Committee's authority, and the concept of "speaking with one voice" did not always work out. The Swartzentruber Amish, for example, do not participate in or cooperate with the Steering Committee. Distinctions within and among Amish communities are even more difficult for government officials and courts to grasp when there is a committee claiming to speak for all Amish members. This problem played out in Minnesota in a case involving the Slow Moving Vehicle (SMV) sign and noncompliance by a Swartzentruber Amish group. Amish difficulties with brightly colored SMV signs began in Orange County, Indiana, in 1968. Additional court cases occurred in Ohio, New York, Kentucky, and Michigan. But the Minnesota case was the only one to reach the U.S. Supreme Court.[29]

Swartzentruber Amish families from Holmes and Wayne Counties, Ohio, settled in Fillmore County, Minnesota, in 1973–1974. At first, there were few problems with the Minnesota law requiring an orange-and-red triangular slow-moving vehicle sign to be displayed on buggies and wagons. Younger Amish, conscious of their position as newcomers and anxious to fit into their new community, tended to use the required sign. Some Amish preferred to display a black triangle outlined in white as a compromise. Others refused to use any sign. They believed the bright colors of the sign and the symbol itself would put their faith in "worldly symbols" rather than in God. Instead, they outlined their buggies with silver reflective tape. If stopped and ticketed, Amish drivers usually pled not guilty in court. Routinely, they were found guilty and then paid the fines. Concerns were raised by people living in the area. Occasional accidents involving slow-moving vehicles showed the need for such signs to protect public safety. In 1986, Minnesota law was changed to allow the black triangle with a white outline. Many Amish agreed to this compromise. But in 1987, when the law was changed again to require the orange triangle always to be carried in the buggy and used at night or in poor weather, the conflict grew. Amish buggy owners who refused to carry the sign began to be ticketed, fined, and sentenced to community service or jail time. Initial first-offense fines were $20 to $22, and first-time jail sentences were seven days. Jail sentences would be waived if there had been no additional violations within a six-month period prior to the current offense. Soon, however, repeat offenders began to appear back in court within the six-month period, refused to pay fines, and were required to serve time in jail.

In December 1988, Eli A. Hershberger and 13 others appeared before a judge for violation of the sign law. They asked the court to dismiss the traffic citations, explaining that their refusal to display the sign was based on their sincere religious beliefs and that the sign law punished them for their beliefs through fines and jail time. They wanted to practice their religion without interference from government as guaranteed in the First Amendment. They believed the law should allow an alternative that would not violate their religion—the use of silver reflective tape.

The judge refused to dismiss the citations, pointing out that even the Amish community itself was divided on whether their religion prohibited display of the sign. He therefore questioned whether the claim of religious belief was sincere. In fact, three different positions within the Amish community had emerged. The largest of the three used the black-and-gray SMV sign, while one smaller group used only reflective tape and the other accepted the red-and-orange triangle required by law. The judge also believed that highway safety was a determining consideration. However, the judge did ask the Minnesota Court of Appeals to consider the constitutional questions, which were then forwarded to the Minnesota Supreme Court. The Minnesota Supreme Court found that the law violated the Free Exercise Clause of the U.S. Constitution. As a result, the trial court's decision to refuse to dismiss the charges was set aside and all charges against the Amish were dismissed.

The state appealed to the U.S. Supreme Court and the court agreed to consider the case. At the same time, the court was considering a free exercise of religion case arising out of religious use of peyote. In this case, *Employment Division, Department of Human Resources of Oregon v. Smith*, 494 U.S. 872 (1990), the court significantly changed First Amendment free exercise analysis. The court held that a law of general application, which does not intend to regulate religious belief or conduct, is not invalid because the law incidentally infringes on religious practices.

The U.S. Supreme Court remanded the *State v. Hershberger* case to the Minnesota Supreme Court for reconsideration, applying the new standards decided under *Smith*. In addition to the *Smith* decision interpreting the First Amendment, the Minnesota Supreme Court also had to consider the protections offered by Article 1, Section 16, of the Minnesota Constitution.[30] The Minnesota Court determined that the language in the state constitution "is of a distinctively stronger character than the federal counterpart" in the First Amendment. On the basis of the state constitution, the state court decided a second time in favor of the Amish, ruling that the state failed to demonstrate that the alternative signs did not protect public safety, and therefore the application of the state SMV law to the Amish defendants violated their freedom of conscience rights protected by the Minnesota Constitution. The Minnesota decision does not apply to other states but will doubtless be cited in other SMV cases and, indeed, in other First Amendment proceedings.[31] The relationship of various Amish communities and affiliations to civil society is evolving as the modern and postmodern nation-state also evolves. It seems safe to predict more legal encounters and court cases in this complex interplay of church and state.

Precedent-setting court cases involving Amish litigants receive much attention in popular media, along with almost every aspect of Amish faith and life. While there is nothing in the Midwest region to compare with the impact of *Witness* (1985) or the Nickel Mines school shootings (October 2006) in Lancaster County, Pennsylvania, the Amish do make appearances in positive and negative ways in every kind of mass media. The Cinemax documentary *Devil's Playground* (2002) was filmed in Indiana, and a number of documentaries have been filmed in Holmes County, Ohio. The 1996 Hallmark Hall of Fame drama *Harvest of Fire*, with Patty Duke portraying an Amish woman, was filmed in Washington and Kalona, Iowa. In 1988, NBC presented a made-for-TV movie, *A Stoning in Fulham County*, depicting an incident of harassment in Adams County, Indiana, in which an Amish baby was accidentally killed by local teenagers throwing objects at Amish buggies. A very young Brad Pitt appeared as one of the rowdy boys. Episodes of *Bones, Murder, She Wrote, MacGyver, Picket Fences, As the World Turns, X-Files*, and many other TV series have portrayed Amish characters or themes, not to mention frequent appearances in David Letterman's Top Ten lists. Fourteen episodes of *Aaron's Way* ran on NBC in 1988, with football star Merlin Olsen as an Amish man who moves his family to California, with predictable urban-rural culture clashes. One website lists Amish references in science fiction novels. A reality TV show, *Amish in the City*, ran for nine episodes in 2004 on UPN. In 2010, four episodes of *Amish: World's Squarest Teenagers*, yet another choreographed Rumspringa among Amish teenagers, ran on Channel 4 in the UK. The National Geographic Channel screened *Amish: Out of Order* in 2012, with a protagonist living in Columbia, Missouri. Listing all the Amish appearances in mass media products would require a very large bibliography.[32]

A persistent and often sensationalized theme in TV shows, novels, movies, newspaper stories, YouTube parodies, and documentaries is Rumspringa, the institutionalized period of exploration allowed to Amish youth in some Amish groups. The tradition permits a taste of worldly culture so that an Amish young adult can make an informed decision on whether or not to be baptized and submit to the church's Ordnung.[33] After baptism, Amish members are subject to church discipline including banning and shunning. Stories of wild barn parties soaked in alcohol and illegal drugs, of fast cars, radio and television, tobacco, and sex, are staples of local media in northern Indiana. The producers of *The Devil's Playground* (2002) wanted to film in Lancaster County but were turned away and landed in Indiana instead. The film follows Faron, an Amish youth who turned to drug dealing to finance his own habit. He was arrested and helped authorities apprehend another drug dealer. The tale is doubtless breathtaking, but there is a danger of misrepresentation in taking a unique story as representative of the entire group at all places and all times.[34] Popular culture obsession and silly versions of Rumspringa in movies like *Sex Drive* (2008) have led many Amish communities to bring the more extreme tendencies of the tradition under control or to eliminate it altogether.

The Amish are not passive consumers or victims of mass media. They operate publishing businesses, communicate with one another in newspapers and magazines, and express concern about negative stories. *The Budget* and *Die Botschaft* are "collective diaries" of Amish daily life and are avidly read in many Amish households. *The Budget* was founded in 1890 and is published in Sugarcreek, Ohio. Amish "scribes" send local news, making *The Budget* a national small-town newspaper. It has a circulation of about 19,000 and publishes around 450 letters in each issue. *Die Botschaft* was founded in 1975 in Lancaster County, Pennsylvania, as an alternative to *The Budget*, as the latter published increasing numbers of letters from non-Amish writers. *Die Botschaft* has a circulation of about 11,000 and includes Old Order Mennonite scribes, the common denominator being horse-and-buggy transportation.[35] The letters create and sustain a community that has little to do with state or national borders, as Amish readers follow news from multiple locations as eagerly as if they were reading a nearby small-town newspaper.

Much of the news involves work on farms, in small businesses, and wage employment. One can follow, to some extent, the changing economic profile of Amish households. Fewer Amish families make their living from farming, and the trend toward non-agricultural professions is accelerating in many locales. Many Amish adults earn a living from tourism (directly or indirectly) by making and selling quilts, baking bread for local restaurants, or building furniture and other wood products. Amish women have created many successful small businesses, sometimes including the men of the household in their enterprises. Entrepreneurs mirror gendered life on the farm, with men working in building trades, factories, and agriculture-related businesses such as selling and servicing farm equipment while women produce food, create and sell fabrics and quilts, and pursue other home-based cottage industries.[36]

Amish tourism is itself a major industry that supports many cottage industries. Millions of tourists visit the three largest Amish communities every year (Lancaster County, Pennsylvania; Holmes County, Ohio; and Elkhart and Lagrange Counties, Indiana). All three locales have developed extensive and complex infrastructures of hotels, restaurants, and tourist shops. In fact, tourist businesses and information centers, such as Menno-Hof in Shipshewana, Indiana, help keep tourists from being overly intrusive in the daily life of Amish homes, resulting in little direct contact between outsiders and Amish individuals. As formulated by anthropologist Roy C. Buck, "staged Amish authenticity" and "pseudo participation" keep outsiders at bay and allow Amish communities to preserve a surprising degree of separation from the tourist hordes.[37]

The low-tech ad for "Amish Chickens" in Chicago—and any business anywhere that offers Amish-made goods and crafts—relies on the shorthand of "Amish" to mean homespun products of yesteryear's farm family. The simple life and, perhaps, a bargain lure the harried consumer more than his or her desire for chicken or cinnamon rolls. The advertising is not deceptive, even though the producers of these chickens may be well aware that their products function as edible souvenirs from a living museum. In a way, anyone purchasing eggs raised on Amish and Mennonite farms is a tourist, in the sense that he or she is experiencing vicariously the old-fashioned notion of raising one's own food and being self-sufficient.[38]

This tourist image of Amish uniformity and dormancy is contradicted by their recent history in the Midwest. Despite the mirage of stubborn sameness, they are actually a dynamic and varied ethno-religious group. They present the face of nostalgic Americana to many outsiders, but even as they draw on traditional American rural values the Amish are actually a set of innovative and expanding modern societies. They are doing well economically in many Rust Belt and Corn Belt states that find themselves in the throes of painful deindustrialization and depopulation. In keeping with their own historical tradition of flexibility, they incorporate constrained cultural change into their basic religious and social values. As midwesterners, their lifestyle is a productive and striking contrast to the stressed industrial political economy and infrastructure of the rest of the region. This success results from a model of life that is inconceivable to most midwesterners, who interact with the Amish seldom and superficially, happy to buy a dozen low-tech eggs to eat in the comfort of their own technology.

Notes

My thanks to the anonymous readers for their insightful comments and especially to my spouse, M. Lynn Rose, for her tireless multiple readings.

1. For overviews of Amish history and culture, see Donald M. Kraybill, Karen M. Johnson-Weiner, and Steven M. Nolt, *The Amish* (Baltimore: The Johns Hopkins University Press, 2013); and Steven M. Nolt, *A History of the Amish* (revised and updated edition) (Intercourse, PA: Good Books, 2003) For an Amish perspective with divergent interpretations of several key events, with a focus on Holmes County, Ohio, see LeRoy Beachy, *Unser Leit: The Story of the Amish* (Millersburg, OH: Goodly Heritage Books, 2011).

2. Amish communities have typically not survived west of tallgrass prairie zones in North America. Despite many attempts during the past two centuries, including very recent settlements in Idaho and Wyoming, only one Amish community in a shortgrass or high plains area survives as Old Order, and that particular community (near Yoder, Kansas) allows the use of steel-wheeled tractors. A similar concession was made by the Kalona, Iowa, group. See David Luthy, *The Amish in America: Settlements That Failed, 1840-1960* (Aylmer, ON, and Lagrange, IN: Pathway Publishers, 1986); David Luthy, *Why Some Amish Communities Fail: Extinct Settlements, 1961-1999* (Aylmer, ON, and Lagrange, IN: Pathway Publishers, 2000); John A. Hostetler, "The Old Order Amish on the Great Plains: A Study in Cultural Vulnerability," in *Ethnicity on the Great Plains*, ed. Frederick C. Luebke (Lincoln: University of Nebraska Press, 1980), 92-108.

3. The Amish do not count themselves as individuals but, rather, keep track of church districts and baptized members. Estimates of total Amish population are developed from calculating an average number of persons per church district (recently set at 136.6) and multiplying by the number of church districts. See estimates at Young Center for Anabaptist and Pietist Studies, Elizabethtown College, Elizabethtown, Pennsylvania, <www2.etown.edu/amishstudies/Population_by_State_2010.asp> (accessed July 2013). Amish church district figures and population estimates are often listed in *Raber's New American Almanac*, published in Baltic, Ohio.

4. The Amish may be experiencing a demographic transition similar to those recorded in societies going through a transition from a pre-industrial to an industrialized economy. In general, societies are theorized to change from conditions of high fertility/high mortality to low fertility/low mortality. The relevant aspect here is that the Amish birthrate tends to decline when children are no longer economic assets on farms because of parents moving into wage labor, cottage industry, or small business. For entry points into this economic and demographic literature, see John C. Caldwell, Bruce K. Caldwell, Pat Caldwell, Peter F. McDonald, and Thomas Schindlmayr, *Demographic Transition Theory* (Dordrecht, The Netherlands: Springer, 2006); Jean-Claude Chesnais, *The Demographic Transition: Stages, Patterns, and Economic Implications: A Longitudinal Study of Sixty-Seven Countries Covering the Period 1720-1984* (New York: Oxford University Press, 1993).

5. Dorothy O. Pratt, *Shipshewana: An Indiana Amish Community* (Bloomington: Quarry Books, 2004), 9-11.

6. Mark Scolforo, Associated Press story, July 28, 2010.

7. On the industrialization of agriculture in the Midwest and its impact on rural population, see David B. Danbom, *The Resisted Revolution: Urban America and the Industrialization of Agriculture, 1900-1930* (Ames: Iowa State University Press, 1979); Deborah Fitzgerald, *Every Farm a Factory: The Industrial Ideal in American Agriculture* (New Haven, CT: Yale University Press, 2003); J.L. Anderson, *Industrializing the Corn Belt: Agriculture, Technology, and Environment, 1945-1972* (DeKalb: Northern Illinois University Press, 2009); and Patrick J. Carr and Maria J. Kefalas, *Hollowing Out the Middle: The Rural Brain Drain and What It Means for America* (Boston: Beacon Press, 2009).

8. Walter Prescott Webb, *The Great Plains* (Boston: Ginn and Company, 1931); Joseph F. Donnermeyer and Elizabeth C. Cooksey, "On the Recent Growth of New Amish Settlements," *Mennonite Quarterly Review* 84 (April 2010): 181–206, map on p. 193.

9. Rod Janzen and Max Stanton, *The Hutterites in North America* (Baltimore: Johns Hopkins University Press, 2010).

10. See table 2.1, p. 36, in Charles E. Hurst and David L. McConnell, *An Amish Paradox: Diversity and Change in the World's Largest Amish Community* (Baltimore: Johns Hopkins University Press, 2010).

11. Steven M. Nolt and Thomas J. Meyers, *Plain Diversity: Amish Cultures and Identities* (Baltimore: Johns Hopkins University Press, 2007), chapter 6, 101–20.

12. Karl Baehr mentioned a "ladder of liberalism" in 1942, in his article "Secularization among the Mennonites of Elkhart County, Indiana," *Mennonite Quarterly Review* 16 (July 1942): 131–60. Leo Driedger described an "Anabaptist Ladder" of identity in "The Anabaptist Identification Ladder: Plain-Urbane Continuity in Diversity," *Mennonite Quarterly Review* 51 (October 1977): 278–91. "Anabaptist Escalator" comes from Hurst and McConnell, *An Amish Paradox*, 34–37. See also Cory Anderson, "Retracing the Blurred Boundaries of Twentieth-Century 'Amish Mennonite' Identity," *Mennonite Quarterly Review* 85 (July 2011): 261–411.

13. For a discussion of this phenomenon, see Steven D. Reschly, "From *Amisch* Mennoniten to Amish *Mennonites*: A Clarion Call in Wright County, Iowa, 1892–1910" (Master's thesis, University of Northern Iowa, 1987), 64–67.

14. Hurst and McConnell, *An Amish Paradox*, 37–43; Nolt and Meyers, *Plain Diversity*, 142–62. See also Joe Mackall, *Plain Secrets: An Outsider among the Amish* (Boston: Beacon Press, 2007). Mackall lived among Swartzentruber Amish in Ashland County, Ohio, for 16 years. The obsessions in popular culture with aspects of Amish culture have changed over time, from bundling to shunning, Rumspringa, and since the Nickel Mines school shooting in Lancaster County, Pennsylvania, in October 2006, the marketing of forgiveness.

15. Hurst and McConnell, *An Amish Paradox*, 48–52; G.C. Waldrep, "The New Order Amish and Para-Amish Groups: Spiritual Renewal within Tradition," *Mennonite Quarterly Review* 82 (July 2008): 395–426.

16. On the balance of limiting and allowing cultural change, see Gertrude Enders Huntington, "Dove at the Window: A Study of an Old Order Amish Community in Ohio [with] Appendixes" (PhD. diss., Yale University, 1956), ch. 3 and 8.

17. Elmer S. Yoder, *The Beachy Amish Mennonite Fellowship Churches* (Hartville, OH: Diakonia Ministries, 1987).

18. For an overview, see Paton Yoder, "The Amish View of the State," in *The Amish and the State* (2nd edition), ed. Donald B. Kraybill (Baltimore: Johns Hopkins University Press, 2003), 23–40.

19. Thomas J. Meyers, "Education and Schooling," in *The Amish and the State*, ed. Donald B. Kraybill, 87–106.

20. Albert N. Keim, ed., *Compulsory Education and the Amish: The Right Not to Be Modern* (Boston: Beacon Press, 1976); Shawn Francis Peters, *The Yoder Case: Religious Freedom, Education, and Parental Rights* (Lawrence: University Press of Kansas, 2003).

21. Steven D. Reschly, "Expanded Exercise: The Amish, Compulsory Education, and Religious Freedom," in *Encyclopedia of Historic U.S. Court Cases, 1690–1990* (2nd edition), ed. John W. Johnson (New York: Routledge, 2001), 978–82. Burger quote at 406 U.S. 223–24.

22. Karen M. Johnson-Weiner, *Train Up a Child: Old Order Amish and Mennonite Schools* (Baltimore: Johns Hopkins University Press, 2006); Mark W. DeWalt, *Amish Education in the United States and Canada* (Lanham, MD: Rowman and Littlefield Education, 2006).

23. Albert N. Keim, "Military Service and Conscription," in Kraybill, *The Amish and the State*, 43–64; Rachel Waltner Goossen, *Women against the Good War: Conscientious Objection and Gender on the American Home Front, 1941–1947* (Chapel Hill: University of North Carolina Press, 1997).

24. Keim, "Military Service and Conscription," 60.

25. Marc A. Olshan, "The National Amish Steering Committee," in Kraybill, *The Amish and the State*, 67–84.

26. Olshan, "The National Amish Steering Committee."

27. "The cultural order reproduces itself in and as change," quote from Marshall Sahlins, *Islands of History* (Chicago: University of Chicago Press, 1985), xii. See also Marshall Sahlins, *How "Natives" Think: About Captain Cook, for Example* (Chicago: University of Chicago Press, 1995); Werner Sollors, ed., *The Invention of Ethnicity* (New York: Oxford University Press, 1989); Kathleen Neils Conzen, "Making Their Own America: Assimilation Theory and the German Peasant Pioneer," German Historical Institute Lecture No. 3 (New York: Berg Publishers, 1990), 1–33.

28. Olshan, "The National Amish Steering Committee." See also Marc A. Olshan, "The Old Order Amish Steering Committee: A Case Study in Organizational Evolution," *Social Forces* 69 (December 1990): 603–16; Marc A. Olshan, "Homespun Bureaucracy: A Case Study in Organizational Evolution," in *The Amish Struggle with Modernity*, ed. Donald B. Kraybill and Marc A. Olshan (Hanover, NH: University Press of New England, 1994), 199–213.

29. *State v. Hershberger*, 444 N.W.2d 282 (Minn. 1989); vacated and remanded by the U.S. Supreme Court in *Minnesota v. Hershberger*, 495 U.S. 901 (1990); reaffirmed by *State v. Hershberger* (Hershberger II), 462 N.W.2d 393 (Minn. 1990). Information that follows comes from Lee J. Zook, "Slow-Moving Vehicles," in Kraybill, *The Amish and the State*, 145–60; Steven P. Aggergaard, "Religion, Speech, and the Minnesota Constitution: State-Based Protections amid First Amendment Instabilities," in *William Mitchell Law Review* 32 (January 2006): 719–67.

30. Article 1, Section 16, of the Minnesota State Constitution: "**Freedom of conscience; no preference to be given to any religious establishment or mode of worship.** The enumeration of rights in this constitution shall not deny or impair others retained by and inherent in the people. The right of every man to worship God according to the dictates of his own conscience shall never be infringed; nor shall any man be compelled to attend, erect or support any place of worship, or to maintain any religious or ecclesiastical ministry, against his consent; nor shall any control of or interference with the rights of conscience be permitted, or any preference be given by law to any religious establishment or mode of worship; but the liberty of conscience hereby secured shall not be so construed as to excuse acts of licentiousness or justify practices inconsistent with the peace or safety of the state, nor shall any money be drawn from the treasury for the benefit of any religious societies or religious or theological seminaries" (boldface type in original).

31. For a recent analysis of legal developments regarding the free exercise clause of the First Amendment and for the impact of *State v. Hershberger II*, see Kurt Van Sciver, "To Strict Scrutiny and Beyond! Interpreting California's Free Exercise Clause," *Southwestern Law Review* 38 (2009): 395–418.

32. For basic information, see David Weaver-Zercher, *The Amish in the American Imagination* (Baltimore: Johns Hopkins University Press, 2001), and David Weaver-Zercher and Diane Zimmerman Umble, eds., *The Amish and the Media* (Baltimore: Johns Hopkins University Press, 2008). There is a large and rapidly growing collection of Amish-themed literature, especially romance novels. Other genres include detective fiction, mysteries, memoirs, and even vampire and werewolf novels. See, for example, the analysis by Beth Graybill, "Chasing the Bonnet: The Premise and Popularity of Writing Amish Women," *Journal of the Center for Mennonite Writing* 2 (2010): http://www.mennonitewriting.org/journal/e/4/bonnet-fiction/ (accessed July 2013); and Valerie Weaver-Zercher, *Thrill of the Chaste: The Allure of Amish Romance Novels* (Baltimore: The Johns Hopkins University Press, 2013) .

33. Tom Schachtman, *Rumspringa: To Be or Not to Be Amish* (New York: North Point Press, 2006); Richard A. Stevick, *Growing Up Amish: The Teenage Years* (Baltimore: Johns Hopkins University Press, 2007).

34. Dirk Eitzen, "Reel Amish: The Amish in Documentaries," in *The Amish and the Media*, ed. Weaver-Zercher and Umble, 43–64. See also Lawrence P. Greksa and Jill E. Korbin, "Key Decisions in the Lives of the Old Order Amish: Joining the Church and Migrating to Another Settlement," *Mennonite Quarterly Review* 76 (October 2002): 373–98.

35. Steven M. Nolt, "Inscribing Community: *The Budget* and *Die Botschaft* in Amish Life," in Weaver-Zercher and Umble, *The Amish and the Media*, 180–98; "collective diaries" on p. 184. For a sampling of content, see Elmer S. Yoder, *I Saw It in* The Budget (Hartville, OH: Diakonia Ministries, 1990). One Amish publisher counted at least fifty Amish subscription publications in 2012 (cited in Kraybill, Johnson-Weiner, and Nolt, *The Amish*, 374–75).

36. Donald B. Kraybill and Steven M. Nolt, *Amish Enterprise: From Plows to Profits* (2nd edition) (Baltimore: Johns Hopkins University Press, 2004); William H. Martineau and Rhonda Sayres MacQueen, "Occupational Differentiation among the Old Order Amish," *Rural Sociology* 42 (Fall 1977): 383–97.

37. Roy C. Buck, "Boundary Maintenance Revisited: Tourist Experience in an Old Order Amish Community," *Rural Sociology* 43 (Summer 1978): 221–34. See also Roy C. Buck and Ted Alleman, "Tourist Enterprise Concentration and Old Order Amish Survival: Explorations in Productive Coexistence," *Journal of Travel Research* 18 (1) (1979): 15–20; Thomas J. Meyers, "Amish Tourism: 'Visiting Shipshewana Is Better Than Going to the Mall,'" *Mennonite Quarterly Review* 77 (January 2003): 109–26; David Luthy, "The Origin and Growth of Amish Tourism," in *The Amish Struggle with Modernity*, 113–129; David Walbert, *Garden Spot: Lancaster County, the Old Order Amish, and the Selling of Rural America* (New York: Oxford University Press, 2002); David Weaver-Zercher, *The Amish in the American Imagination.*

38. For a sophisticated analysis of tourism in Ohio's "Amish Country," see Susan L. Trollinger, *Selling the Amish: The Tourism of Nostalgia* (Baltimore: Johns Hopkins University Press, 2012). Trollinger shows how themed towns in Holmes County, such as Victorian nostalgia in Walnut Creek and frontier romanticism in Berlin, create a "nostalgia for the future" in which Amish residents both illustrate values from the past and generate hope for a better world in the future.

CONCLUSION — **THE INDISTINCT DISTINCTIVENESS OF RURAL MIDWESTERN CULTURE**

David Danbom

One of the great iconic films conveying a picture of contemporary midwestern culture is the Coen Brothers' black comedy *Fargo*. At its most positive, it portrays a Midwest—or at least an upper Midwest—of hockey, duck stamps, all-you-can-eat buffets, and guileless folks demonstrating "Minnesota Nice."

As a longtime resident of the real Fargo, I occasionally saw shades of the fictional one, as when my wife and I heard a diner at a nearby table answer the server's inquiry as to how she was by saying "Pretty darned OK!"

But mostly I didn't see much resemblance. The real Fargo is dependent on a service and high-tech economy. While there are still plenty of "sons" around, the growth segment of the population consists of non-whites and non-Anglos, including Hispanics, African Americans, and lots of "New Americans"—Somalis, Sudanese, Liberians, Bosnians, Kurds, and more. Fargoans mainly eat at franchise places and buy clothes at stores like American Eagle or Target. They watch *Celebrity Apprentice* and *America's Biggest Loser*. Among the city's biggest annual events are a film festival, a blues festival, a marathon, and a zombie pub crawl. Is there anything here that makes Fargo uniquely midwestern, or is it pretty much interchangeable with almost every other medium-sized city in the United States?

Now, I recognize that Fargo is a city, and that this collection deals with the "rural" Midwest of farms, villages, and small towns. Yet I contend that what is true of Fargo is true of the region generally: that an image of uniqueness that may be held elsewhere breaks down when one looks closely at the place in question; that whatever made the place unique or special at one time (and that has probably *always* been overemphasized) has been eroded by modern communications, population movements, and a market economy; and that what is most noteworthy about the region is its *Americanness*—its similarity to every other place. After all, when marketers try their products in Peoria, Illinois, or politicians and media moguls ask "how will it play in Peoria?" they do so not because Peoria or, by extension, the Midwest of which it is a part, is unique, but because it is so relentlessly the same as most other places.

Part of the problem with defining culture in the Midwest is that it is so difficult to define the Midwest itself—a protean region that bleeds off easily into the more distinctive East, South, and West that border it. As Andrew Cayton and Susan Gray wisely note in their introduction to their essay collection *The American Midwest,* "we were acutely aware that the Midwest lacks the kind of geographic coherence, historical issues, and cultural touchstones that have informed regional identity in the American South, West, and New England." They add that "historians writing about the Midwest carry a historiographical burden loaded with irony: rather than argue for the distinctiveness of the Midwest, they must always demonstrate the national, even universal, significance of what is generally considered both the most American and the most amorphous of regions." The burden on the contributors to this volume is rather different but no less onerous. We must try to find distinctiveness in a region that has always been amorphous and is increasingly so.[1]

A brief recapitulation of the settlement history of the Midwest illustrates why defining the rural culture of the region is so devilishly difficult. The Old Midwest, comprised of the states bordering the Ohio River, was settled in the early nineteenth century by two very dissimilar groups—Butternuts, from the Upper South, and Yankees, from New England and upstate New York. Oil and water mix more easily than those groups. The agricultural settlement history of much of the rest of the region was shaped largely by immigrants who poured out of western and northern Europe in the second half of the nineteenth century. They frequently settled in relatively homogenous communities, enabled by railroads and land companies eager to move large tracts quickly. Many of the celebrations that we consider markers of midwestern culture today—from hostfests to oktoberfests to fall suppers—are actually the descendants of ethnic celebrations, albeit sometimes polluted by such American abominations as tractor pulls and deep-fat-fried Snickers bars. These immigrants and natives developed agricultural systems that—if we are to accept Pete Daniel's notion that each crop has its own "culture"—contributed further to the cultural complexity of the region. Wheat farming, corn-hog farming, and dairy farming were only the most prominent of a number of agricultural regimes that dominated at various times in various places among various people. Add to the mix the industrial development of the region (Rust Belt as much as Corn Belt), which contributed further ethnic and racial diversity, imperiled rural isolation, and dramatically increased interaction between farm, town, and city. And keep in mind that all of this happened before World War I, when the real changes began. Whew.[2]

What was defined as midwestern rural culture by such diverse commentators as Frederick Jackson Turner, Lewis Atherton, Laura Ingalls Wilder, and James Whitcomb Riley, among others, achieved its apotheosis around the turn of the twentieth century. At its best, the rural Midwest seemed close to the realization of Thomas Jefferson's dream for the young nation. It was filled with sturdy, independent, patriotic yeomen, roughly equal in wealth and dedicated to democracy and liberty. Strong institutions—the family, church, and one-room school—bound rural midwesterners together. The values by which they lived were honesty, integrity, hard work, willingness to cooperate, and readiness to help a neighbor in need. As those in the early twentieth-century Country Life Movement who hoped to save them argued, they were the bedrock of American society and the repository of its finest values.[3]

This rosy and uplifting image of the Midwest was not universally accepted at the time, and even those such as Willa Cather and Hamlin Garland who contributed to the midwestern myth in some of their work recognized there were dark shadows on the land of contented farmers, barefoot boys, and apple-cheeked girls. Some went farther. In *The Story of a Country Town*, for example, Edgar Howe portrayed a region of intolerance, conformism, and cramped and judgmental moralism. With Howe raising the curtain, who could doubt that Sinclair Lewis, H.L. Mencken, and Sherwood Anderson were waiting eagerly in the wings? Viewing midwestern culture from a more modern perspective, scholars could see class bias, ethnic and religious bigotry, racism, and anti-Semitism.[4]

In recent years scholars have turned their attention especially to women and the role they played in the patriarchal world of the midwestern farm. Some scholars, such as Barbara Handy-Marchello, Joan Jensen, and Mary Neth, emphasized their role in propping up nature's noblemen who, when it came down to it, were not always all that noble after all. Others saw an even darker rural midwestern milieu for women. Deborah Fink, in her work on Boone County, Nebraska, exposed a family life of oppression, brutality, and sexual exploitation, while Jane Adams's Union County, Illinois, was a place where unfeeling patriarchs squeezed all the labor they could out of the wives and children whose lives they dominated. Perhaps Pa Ingalls was the midwestern exception, and Old Jules was the rule.[5]

However defined, midwestern rural culture—or cultures—faced wrenching changes and challenges during World War I and the interwar period. Relatively insular rural enclaves were impinged upon during the war by draft boards, bond salesmen, county agents, and other representatives of the federal government. In the case of some German American communities (always somewhat leery of the culture and government of the United States, as Jon Gjerde showed us), this outside attention was harsh and even brutal, but most ethnic communities were pressured to become 100 percent American, whatever that meant. The war also took young men and women away, to serve in the military or to pursue economic opportunities in war industries. Some never returned, and those who did had broadened horizons and altered expectations. As the popular song of the time put it, "How Ya Gonna Keep 'Em Down on the Farm (After They've Seen Paree)?" or for that matter, after they've seen Chicago or Toledo?[6]

Some of the changes that became apparent during the war continued and even accelerated afterward. Agricultural mechanization, encouraged by the wartime labor shortage, advanced smartly during the war and continued to expand in the difficult economic times that followed. One effect of this was to widen the gap between rural haves and have-nots. Another was to destroy some communal work patterns that bound communities together, as J. Sanford Rikoon demonstrated in his work on the demise of threshing rings, brought about by the increasing adoption of tractor-drawn combines. It is ironic that nearly every small-town midwestern museum today celebrates farm machinery, an innovation that contributed mightily to the demise of the traditional rural community. Another change with legs—or wheels— was the widespread adoption of the automobile. The automobile broke down the isolation that had nurtured cultural peculiarity, and young people especially clutched the opportunity to travel to town, or to roadhouses and dance halls, where they could meet rural youth from other—and frequently different—rural communities.[7]

Other changes seemed to burst on the scene. By the end of the 1920s such chain stores as Woolworth's and Piggly Wiggly had appeared even in relatively small towns, furthering the earlier efforts of Sears and Wards in standardizing consumption. Movies, and especially radio, exposed rural people to a wider culture, sometimes stimulating wonder, envy, or discontentment. In common with many other innovations, radio was a double-edged sword.

Rural people usually accepted it on their terms, using local programming to bind the community and reinforce local culture. But few stations were not part of national networks, and much of their programming was national in nature. Rural people were exposed to, and were often fascinated by, nationally produced soap operas, situation comedies, and adventure stories, and even to a centralized and homogenized rural culture in the form of the "National Barn Dance."

Then there was the agricultural economy, bad in the 1920s and worse in the 1930s. The economic travails of agriculture encouraged mechanization, rural depopulation, and the consolidation of such local rural institutions as schools and churches. Especially in the 1930s, federal agricultural and relief programs impinged on local communities in ways that may have been necessary but were not always welcomed. Neighborhood cohesion and cultural integrity were often casualties of these many and varied forces.

By 1940 it seemed time to declare the death of a distinctive rural culture in America. In his essay in the 1940 *Yearbook of Agriculture*, USDA historian Paul Johnstone contrasted the "old ideals" of rural America with the "new ideas" he believed had become predominant there. Johnstone proclaimed that farming had become a technologically sophisticated business, that farmers were increasingly embracing a modern, urban material culture, and that traditional "habits, customs, [and] institutions" were rapidly passing from the scene.[8]

Others were not so eager to let the old ideals go, especially when they had made a psychic investment in a particular vision of rural life. For many, rural America—and the rural Midwest was the most American part of rural America—represented what the country was about. For those sophisticated cynics whose spokesman was H.L. Mencken, rural America captured the worst of the nation—its intolerance, bigotry, narrow moralism, and anti-intellectualism. For New Dealers, the midwestern farmer was a common man, to be celebrated for his hard work, piety, decency, and patriotism. Too many had invested too much in these images to surrender them, tangible realities be damned. There was a reason why Grant Wood posed his *American Gothic* couple with a pitchfork rather than a radio. If Ma and Pa didn't fit the image outsiders had of rural midwestern life, would their portrait have become the most iconic in American history?

Rural midwesterners demonstrated little interest in shaping their lives to others' images, so they continued to pursue modernity. Because modern was increasingly equated with urban, this meant that their lives looked more and more similar to the lives of urban people. World War II played a big role in moving this process along. As Deborah Fink noted in her study of

"Open Country," a farm community in northwest Iowa, the war brought a dramatic increase in mobility as young people, especially, left for the service or for work in town. This exodus made it difficult to maintain the dense kinship groups that were the building blocks of local culture and society. Many of those who left did not return, and the ones who did return had altered expectations or brought spouses with different cultural backgrounds. Those who had lived in large cities or had been abroad were less likely to be contented with the cultural and recreational offerings of the rural neighborhood, just as they were less likely to be contented with outhouses and the lack of electricity.[9]

Technology continued to play a role in altering rural cultural patterns as well. World War II accelerated the production revolution in agriculture, which allowed fewer and fewer farmers to work more and more acres. Farm consolidation along with shrinking family size led to depopulation in most farming areas of the Midwest. In addition to initiating another round of school and church consolidations, depopulation meant that it was more difficult to maintain the local practices and institutions that had contributed to distinctive neighborhood cultures.

Electrification also played a critical role in altering midwestern culture. In 1935, Franklin Roosevelt's administration created the Rural Electrification Administration, which provided government loans to user-owned cooperatives wishing to generate, buy, and distribute electricity. In addition, the REA provided loans to customers who wished to wire their homes and buildings and purchase appliances. Rural electric cooperatives were formed all over the Midwest and began electrifying the countryside, a process that was interrupted by World War II but resumed afterward. As Ronald Kline has shown, early adopters were conservative, using electricity for lighting and little else, while holding on to their tried-and-true appliances. Spending the evening under a bare 40-watt bulb while waiting for dinner prepared on an oil, kerosene, propane (or worse, wood-burning) stove did not satisfy the expectations of the World War II generation, however. They wanted all-electric homes, and when television came along they wanted that too. Television, in addition to exposing rural people to a broader national cultural milieu, accelerated a process radio had initiated. Leisure was increasingly family-oriented and revolved around a box or a screen. In combination with depopulation, the privatization of leisure doomed many of the farmers' and homemakers' clubs, lodges, baseball leagues, and auxiliaries that had traditionally maintained a vigorous local culture.[10]

These ways in which technology—especially electrification—affected culture should be fairly clear and self-evident, but its impact was also more subtle, though hardly less significant. Electrification worked dramatic changes on the lives of women, in particular.

Electrification had a major impact on the work women did in the home. As Katherine Jellison showed in *Entitled to Power*, electricity obliterated many of the differences between farm women and their counterparts in towns and cities, fulfilling a longtime goal of country life reformers. Now they cooked and cleaned as urban women did. No longer did they smoke meat or can fruits and vegetables unless they wanted to. Convenience foods, vacuum cleaners, washers, and driers—advertised relentlessly on the ubiquitous television—were as available to them and as welcomed by them as these products were by urban women. Conveniences and appliances that could save time only saved time if their users aimed for that result, but they could save time. Sometimes the time saved could be devoted to field work, and Jellison speaks eloquently of the women who embraced this role. Time saved could also be devoted to the work women traditionally did to supplement and/or save family income. Women traditionally did dairy work, especially on farms with only a few cattle, raised chickens in order to market eggs and meat, and manufactured soap and other necessary items at home. But with a substantial assist from electricity, these traditional enterprises were doomed by the modern age. State governments began to require that milk be kept in refrigerated tanks—feasible now with electricity available, but cost-prohibitive for small-scale producers. Large-scale integrators such as Perdue, Townsend, and Tyson began raising the "Chicken of Tomorrow" in heated and lighted containment facilities and slaughtering them in centralized factories in such places as the Delmarva Peninsula or Arkansas. By 1960 the barnyard poultry flock was as rare on midwestern farms as a span of mules. And who would think of making her own soap when Tide and Cheer got clothes so bright?[11]

None of this meant that the average farmwife became June Cleaver with a mudroom, occupying her day with bridge parties and fancy dinners. No, farm women frequently took pride in their contributions to family income, but increasingly they earned that income off the farm. It was easier and easier to do. There were fewer young children at home to be looked after, more roads were hard-surfaced, and automobiles were more dependable. And while there were few jobs in the countryside, there were jobs in town, in retail, food processing, and light manufacturing for some, and in teaching, nursing, and other professions for the increasingly numerous farm women with college training. Far from being deprived or oppressed by their off-farm labor, many women took pride in making an economic contribution—and, significantly, providing health insurance—to their families. Work gave some a sense of pride and value and provided sociability too often lacking on farmsteads situated farther and farther from neighbors.[12]

By seeking paid employment, farm women were behaving as non-farm women were, and there was nothing ignoble about wanting to improve the financial security and living standards of one's family while simultaneously realizing personal goals. But the removal of increasing numbers of farm women from work at home further imperiled the maintenance of a traditional rural society and rural culture already under siege. One of the uncelebrated and frequently unnoticed contributions of farm women was the maintenance of neighborhood coffee circles, quilting and sewing clubs, homemakers' clubs, parent-teacher associations, and church and lodge auxiliaries. They were the people who planned the celebrations, cooked the fall dinners, and executed the bake sales. With fewer of them around, and far fewer of them available for extended work during the day, rural society's connective tissue weakened and sometimes snapped.

There were fewer people to maintain rural midwestern culture, and the economic basis for it was becoming relatively less vibrant as well.

At the end of World War II, agriculture was at the center of rural life in the country generally and in the Midwest particularly. Over half of rural Americans lived on farms, and most of the rest were directly or indirectly dependent on agriculture for their livelihoods. The annual rhythms of rural America were the unchanging rhythms of the agricultural year. Agriculture was central to the culture in most places, where parades, festivals, community dinners, and special church services celebrated the end of planting, the laying-by of crops, or the harvest. The central event in most rural communities, the county fair, though long polluted by extraneous and sometimes degrading additions, was still largely a celebration of agriculture.

Agriculture remained dominant in the sense that most rural land in the Midwest continued to be in farms, farmers continued to play a role in local political life disproportionate to their numbers, and farmers *represented* rural life to outsiders; but agriculture began a long economic, social, and demographic decline. In a sense, agriculture declined along with extractive industries and some manufacturing, eclipsed by a high-tech, service-oriented economy. But agriculture was also the victim of its own successes. Modern technology allowed fewer people to farm more acres, and narrow profit margins encouraged the inefficient to leave. As younger farmers left the enterprise and as older farmers retired, renting or selling their land to neighbors, farm consolidation and depopulation advanced. This was not a straight-line process. There were peaks and valleys along the way, as in the 1980s when the collapse of the commodities boom of the 1970s doomed thousands of midwestern farmers; exposed bitterness, resentments, and extremism in rural communities; and created what Osha Gray Davidson called the "rural ghetto." But the trend line was moving in one direction.[13]

By the early years of the twenty-first century the relative decline of agriculture was clear. Under 2 percent of Americans lived on farms, and only 7 percent of *rural* people lived on farms. Production agriculture contributed about 2 percent of the gross domestic product, meaning that its total disappearance would bring a mild recession for a quarter or two. There were over 2.1 million farms in the country, but over half were "weekend" or "hobby" farms marketing under $10,000 worth of produce per year. Only about 80,000 marketed crops valued in excess of $250,000 per year, thereby being considered commercially significant by the U.S. Department of Agriculture.[14]

Remarkably, even farmers were not very dependent on agriculture any more. On over half of farms both spouses had off-farm jobs, and on 80 percent at least one did. By 2007, over 90 percent of farm income was derived from off-farm sources. It all raises the question of whether it is even accurate to talk about farmers any more. Perhaps we should refer to them as nurses, teachers, clerks, factory workers, and truck drivers who farm.[15]

So, who are the other 93 percent of rural residents now, the ones who don't claim to farm? That depends a little bit on what part of the countryside you're talking about. Within commuting distance of major towns (much of the central and eastern Midwest, and less as you move west and north), the countryside is part of the "exurbs," filled with people who work in nearby towns and cities but who live in rural villages or the open country. In Cass County, North Dakota, where I lived for many years, most farmsteads are occupied, and the countryside is dotted by a number of exurban settlements of 10 to 20 homes each. The town of Casselton, about 20 miles west of Fargo, was once a farm-service center but is now a bedroom suburb. There are dozens—if not hundreds—of counties like Cass in the Midwest.

A number of factors make country living attractive to commuters. Housing is usually cheaper, as are property taxes and electric rates. In the countryside they have room for horses and can ride snowmobiles and ATVs close by. Some may desire to escape urban noise, urban schools, urban crime, and urban minorities. But whatever has drawn them to the countryside, exurbanites are part of a national, urban-based, and urban-defined culture. They are in the countryside physically, but culturally they are not.

The areas beyond the 30-to-40-mile commuting ring are where the rural Midwest is apparently "dying." These are the places visited by the *New York Times* or NBC News for their periodic "death of rural America" stories.

There are sometimes a few urban refugees in such places, but not many. The people who live there, however, are not predominantly farmers. They drive trucks, eke out a living in rural retail or call centers, or work in meatpacking or manufacturing plants that have located in areas where unions do not exist or are weak if they do. Do they embrace a culture that makes them distinctive? If they do, it is not apparent.[16]

So, where does that leave us in our search for a rural midwestern culture? If one ever existed, it is hard to see it now, but the absence of *culture* does not prove the absence of area-specific *cultures*. There may be some of those. In *Prairie Patrimony*, Sonya Salamon notes that ethnic German farm families in Illinois transmit "cultural beliefs" from generation to generation. Specifically, they convey how to "manage, handle, and pass on land, processes instrumental to the production and reproduction of...gender and social relations in...family and community." In his memoir of life on a South Dakota farm, Robert Amerson regrets the loss of the neighborhood closeness of yesteryear but believes that a "sense of community" still exists. Those who have been to a rural high school basketball game, visited a small-town diner in midmorning or a tavern in early evening, or witnessed neighbors coming together to bring in a local farmer's crop cannot deny that there is a sense of community in many rural places—albeit one modulated by race and class—that is less frequently found in cities. And there are still community celebrations, often ethnic in nature, county fairs, high school and all-school reunions, and town centennials, along with some traditional foodways and idiomatic expressions. But are these signs of vital and unique cultures, or as John Shover said of Scioto Township, Ohio, in his classic *First Majority, Last Minority*, "anachronistic institutions" in a modern age? Do they denote a living, distinctive midwestern culture, or are they straws we grasp in our effort to prevent the idea of midwestern culture from slipping away?[17]

Notes

1. Andrew R.L. Cayton and Susan E. Gray, "The Story of the Midwest: An Introduction," *The American Midwest: Essays on Regional History*, ed. Andrew R.L. Cayton and Susan E. Gray (Bloomington: Indiana University Press, 2001), 1.

2. Pete R. Daniel, *Breaking the Land: The Transformation of Cotton, Tobacco, and Rice Cultures since 1880* (Urbana: University of Illinois Press, 1986). For the evolution of the Corn Belt, see John C. Hudson, *Making the Corn Belt: A Geographical History of Midwestern Agriculture* (Bloomington: Indiana University Press, 1994).

3. For the Country Life Movement, see David B. Danbom, *The Resisted Revolution: Urban America and the Industrialization of Agriculture, 1900–1930* (Ames: Iowa State University Press, 1979).

4. Edgar Watson Howe, *The Story of a Country Town* (Atchison, KS: Howe and Company, 1883).

5. Barbara Handy-Marchello, *Women of the Northern Plains: Gender and Settlement on the Homestead Frontier, 1870–1930* (St. Paul: Minnesota Historical Society Press, 2005); Joan Jensen, *Calling This Place Home: Women on the Wisconsin Frontier, 1850–1925* (St. Paul: Minnesota Historical Society Press, 2006); Mary Neth, *Preserving the Family Farm: Women, Community, and the Foundations of Agribusiness in the Midwest, 1900–1940* (Baltimore: Johns Hopkins University Press, 1998); Deborah Fink, *Agrarian Women: Wives and Mothers in Rural Nebraska, 1880–1940* (Chapel Hill: University of North Carolina Press, 1992); Jane Adams, *The Transformation of Rural Life: Southern Illinois, 1890–1990* (Chapel Hill: University of North Carolina Press, 1994).

6. Jon Gjerde, *The Minds of the West: Ethnocultural Evolution in the Rural Middle West, 1830–1917* (Chapel Hill: University of North Carolina Press, 1999).

7. J. Sanford Rikoon, *Threshing in the Midwest, 1820–1940: A Study of Traditional Culture and Technological Change* (Bloomington: Indiana University Press, 1988).

8. Paul H. Johnstone, "Old Ideals versus New Ideas in Farm Life," *Farmers in a Changing World: The Yearbook of Agriculture 1940* (Washington, DC: GPO, 1940), 140.

9. Deborah Fink, *Open Country, Iowa: Rural Women, Tradition and Change* (Albany: State University of New York Press, 1986).

10. Ronald R. Kline, *Consumers in the Country: Technology and Social Change in Rural America* (Baltimore: Johns Hopkins University Press, 2002).

11. Katherine Jellison, *Entitled to Power: Farm Women and Technology, 1913–1963* (Chapel Hill: University of North Carolina Press, 1993). For the chicken of tomorrow, see Roger Horowitz, *Putting Meat on the American Table: Taste, Technology, Transformation* (Baltimore: Johns Hopkins University Press, 2006).

12. For women's off-farm employment, see Fink, *Open Country*; Adams, *Transformation of Rural Life*.

13. Osha Gray Davidson, *Broken Heartland: The Rise of America's Rural Ghetto* (Iowa City: University of Iowa Press, 1996). See also Kathryn Marie Dudley, *Debt and Dispossession: Farm Loss in America's Heartland* (Chicago: University of Chicago Press, 2000); and Catherine Stock, *Rural Radicals: Righteous Rage in the American Grain* (New York: Penguin Books, 1997).

14. "Agricultural Income and Finance Outlook," Economic Research Service, USDA, December 2009.

15. "Off-Farm Income, Technology Adoption, and Farm Economic Performance," Economic Research Service, USDA, February 2007.

16. For rural occupational transformations, see Deborah Fink, *Cutting Into the Meatpacking Line: Workers and Change in the Rural Midwest* (Chapel Hill: University of North Carolina Press, 1998); Shane Hamilton, *Trucking Country: The Road to America's Wal-Mart Economy* (Princeton, NJ: Princeton University Press, 2008).

17. Sonya Salamon, *Prairie Patrimony: Family, Farming, and Community in the Midwest* (Chapel Hill: University of North Carolina Press, 1992), 1; Robert Amerson, *From the Hidewood: Memories of a Dakota Neighborhood* (St. Paul: Minnesota Historical Society Press, 1996), 360; John L. Shover, *First Majority, Last Minority: The Transformation of Rural Life in America* (DeKalb: Northern Illinois University Press, 1976), 79.

CONTRIBUTORS

J.L. Anderson is Associate Professor of History at Mount Royal University. He is the author of *Industrializing the Corn Belt: Agriculture, Technology, and Environment, 1945–1972* (Northern Illinois University Press, 2009), as well as several articles and book chapters. His current project is a history of pigs in America.

Jenny Barker Devine is Assistant Professor of History at Illinois College and the author of *On Behalf of the Family Farm: Iowa Farm Women's Activism since 1945* (University of Iowa Press, 2013).

David Danbom is an independent scholar. He is the author of *Born in the Country: A History of Rural America* (1995; Johns Hopkins University Press, 2006) as well as numerous other books and articles on agriculture, rural life, and the Midwest.

Cornelia Butler Flora is Charles F. Curtiss Distinguished Professor of Sociology and Agriculture and Life Sciences at Iowa State University, fellow of the American Association for the Advancement of Science, and past president of the Rural Sociological Society, the Agriculture, Food and Human Values Society, and the International Community Development Society. She served as Program Officer for the Ford Foundation in Latin America and taught at Kansas State University, Virginia Polytechnic Institute and State University, Cordoba University in Spain, University of the Republic in Uruguay, and the Agricultural University La Molina in Peru. She is coauthor, with Jan L. Flora, of *Rural Communities: Legacy and Change* (4th edition) (Westview Press, 2013).

Jan L. Flora is Professor of Sociology and Extension Community Sociologist at Iowa State University. He is on the faculty of the inter-university, interdisciplinary Community Development Masters and of the interdisciplinary Graduate Program in Sustainable Agriculture. He is coauthor, with Cornelia Flora, of *Rural Communities: Legacy and Change* (4th edition) (Westview Press, 2012). His research and teaching center on social capital, sustainable communities, and the sociology of agriculture, specifically Immigration and Customs Enforcement raids and the contribution of Latino businesses to Iowa communities. In his Extension role, he works with Regional Food Groups in Iowa to assist them in incorporating immigrants and refugees into the local food chain.

R. Douglas Hurt is Head of the Department of History at Purdue University and a Fellow in the Agricultural History Society. He has served as the editor of *Agricultural History*, the *Missouri Historical Review*, and *Ohio History*. He is a past president of the Agricultural History Society.

Jim Norris is currently the chair of the Department of History at Rollins College. He received his PhD at Tulane University. His most recent book is *North for the Harvest: Mexican Workers, Growers, and the Sugar Beet Industry* (Minnesota Historical Society Press, 2009).

James A. Pritchard is associated with the Department of Natural Resource Ecology and Management and the Department of Landscape Architecture at Iowa State University. He is the author of *Preserving Yellowstone's Natural Conditions: Science and the Perception of Nature* (University of Nebraska Press, 1999) and coauthor, with Randal S. Beeman, of *A Green and Permanent Land: Ecology and Agriculture in the Twentieth Century* (University Press of Kansas, 2001).

Debra A. Reid is Professor of History at Eastern Illinois University and adjunct Professor in the College of Agricultural, Consumer, and Environmental Sciences at the University of Illinois-Champaign-Urbana. Her first book, *Reaping a Greater Harvest: African Americans, the Extension Service, and Rural Reform in Jim Crow Texas* (Texas A&M University Press, 2007) received the T.R. Fehrenbach Award from the Texas Historical Commission. She has edited *Seeking Inalienable Rights: Texans and Their Quests for Justice* (Texas A&M University Press, 2009) and coedited, with Evan P. Bennett, *Beyond Forty Acres and a Mule: African American Farm Owners since Reconstruction* (University Press of Florida, 2012).

Steven D. Reschly is Professor of History at Truman State University in Kirksville, Missouri. He earned his PhD from the University of Iowa in 1994 and also holds an MA from the University of Northern Iowa, an MDiv from Goshen Biblical Seminary, and a BA from Goshen College. His first book, *The Amish on the Iowa Prairie, 1840 to 1910* (Johns Hopkins University Press, 2000), was named the 2002 Book of the Year by the Communal Studies Association. His second book is a collection that he coedited with Kimberly D. Schmidt and Diane Zimmerman Umble, *Strangers at Home: Amish and Mennonite Women in History* (Johns Hopkins University Press, 2002). His current research examines rural consumer culture in Amish and related groups in 1930s Lancaster County, Pennsylvania.

Pamela Riney-Kehrberg is Professor of History at Iowa State University. She is the author of *Rooted in Dust: Surviving Drought and Depression in Southwestern Kansas* (University Press of Kansas, 1995), *Childhood on the Farm: Work, Play and Coming of Age in the Midwest* (University Press of Kansas, 2005), and *Always Plenty to Do: Growing Up on a Farm in the Long Ago* (Texas Tech University Press, 2011). She is the editor of *Waiting on the Bounty: The Dust Bowl Diary of Mary Knackstedt Dyck* (University of Iowa Press, 1999).

Kendra Smith-Howard is Assistant Professor of History at University at Albany (State University of New York). She is interested in the intersections of environmental, agricultural, and public health histories, and explores these themes in an environmental history of milk and dairy farming titled *Pure and Modern Milk: An Environmental History since 1900* (Oxford, 2013).

Wilson J. Warren is Professor of History at Western Michigan University in Kalamazoo. He is the author of *Struggling with "Iowa's Pride": Labor Relations, Unionism, and Politics in the Rural Midwest since 1877* (University of Iowa Press, 2000), and *Tied to the Great Packing Machine: The Midwest and Meatpacking* (University of Iowa Press, 2007). He is currently working on a global history of meat production and consumption.

INDEX

Lightning Source UK Ltd.
Milton Keynes UK
UKHW010853130123
415283UK00005B/431